RECOLLECTIONS OF LUCINA

THE BEST YEARS

Guild Craft of Indiana
6000 Sunset Lane
Indianapolis, IN 46208

© Copyright 1986 by Lucina Ball Moxley
Library of Congress Number 91-058-047
ISBN 1-878208-10-1
Second Printing 1991

My recollections form a continuation to the book Father wrote for me in 1940 entitled "Recollections of Lucina Ball." His expression of love moved me deeply.

I dedicate these "memory pictures" of my life to my dear parents, my daughters, Judy and Ann, and my grandchildren, Breck and Scott, Tracey and Bryan.

In recalling my childhood, I discovered how very different my life style was from that of my grandchildren's today. These recollections will give my family some insight into their heritage and to a way of life that exists no more.

Lucina

"An autobiography usually reveals nothing about its writer except his memory."

—*Franklin P. Jones*

COELUM TUERI

Ball.

BALL

The first of the ancient English family to reach America is believed to have been Col. William Ball. With his wife, Hannah Atherold, whom he married in 1638, and his family, he settled in Virginia about 1650. Anne, the second daughter of his younger son, Joseph (by Col. Ball's first wife) married Col. Edwin Conway, ancestor of James Madison, the fourth President of the United States.

In 1707 Joseph married Mary Johnson. To this union was born an only daughter, Mary, who in 1731 became the second wife of Capt. Augustine Washington.

Their first child, born Feb. 22, 1732, was George Washington, the first President of our country. From Col. William Ball was descended the Rev. John Arnold Ball who, with his son Caleb, fought in the Revolutionary War.

Caleb Ball also took part in the War of 1812, helping to build, at Erie, Pa., the ships which, commanded by Oliver Hazard Perry, decisively defeated the British fleet on Lake Erie in 1813.

The earliest record of the BALL family places it in Berkshire, England, where in 1480 William Ball held the Manor of Berkham.

Branches of the family were to be found in many parts of England, especially the southeast, and in Leinster, Ireland. In the latter country was born at Dublin, in 1840, the famous astronomer, Robert Stawell Ball.

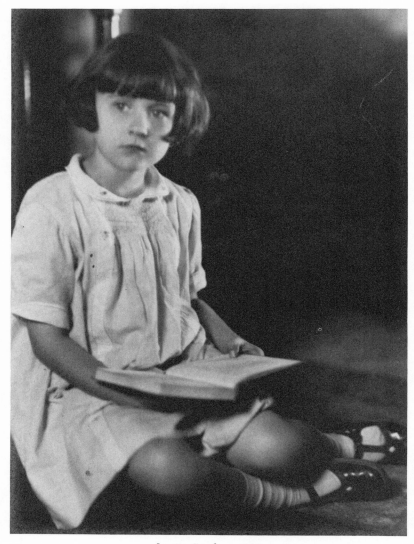

Lucina Reading, 1926

PART ONE
CHAPTER ONE

T HE Ball factory whistle blows at dawn. A distant train answers mournfully as it whines along the tracks. Every morning these sounds awaken me as I stretch in bed, loath to get up in the cold room. I snuggle down with my favorite pillow stuffed with pine needles, inhaling the wonderful scents of pine forests, and wait until my father comes in to light the fire in the grate.

When the firelight fills the dark room and Dad leaves after a morning kiss, I jump out of bed, dressing quickly close to the flames, warming each piece of clothing before putting it on. First, the garterbelt to fasten the long, ribbed cotton stockings, then the bulky bloomers over which hangs my straight wool challis dress, printed with dainty flowers and smocked around the neck. Finally, those high shoes laced around the ankles! I hate these clothes with a passion! Such outdated fashion puts me in a class by myself when all my schoolmates are wearing bobby socks and oxfords—and *belts* around their waists. The bloomers always hang below my dress to my infinite mortification.

These are early memories of my childhood growing up in the industrial town of Muncie, Indiana. The year is 1926—the first winter after we moved into our huge, stone house in Westwood on my eighth birthday, August twenty-first. That day my friends gathered on the grounds, still littered with piles of yellow stone, which later on would be used to build the porch. Nearby was a wonderful apple orchard with trees fit for climbing. We explored them all and chose our favorite "private seats," which we continued to claim throughout our tree-climbing years.

My favorite game was to climb to my special place in one of the trees with a book, reading and munching on apples—or to sit and dream fantastic dreams about the adventures I would have some day. My tree was a ship, and I was Captain Bloodybeard surveying the sea around me from the highest mast! I often dressed up in pirate clothes and carried a wicked, wooden sword which dripped with painted blood! I devoured as many pirate stories as I could find because they were full of high adventure and excitement. *Treasure Island* was my favorite of all, but I read all the Oz books and The Little Colonel series over and over until I almost could recite them from memory. I must have read *The Secret Garden* twenty times, even as it floated in the bathtub with me!

[1]

1926 was a memorable year. One day I found a book entitled *The Story of the Live Dolls*. In the first chapter the children were amazed to see live dolls acting as messengers, delivering circulars throughout the town with the announcement: "NOTICE! On the morning of June the fourth, all the dolls in Cloverdale Village will come alive!!" By a curious coincidence I read the book on June third. The next morning my father awakened me with the news that I had a baby brother. He became my "live doll."

William Hudson Ball Jr., named after our father, was called Hudson until he was fourteen. When he entered Culver Military Academy, he was required by Army regulations to use his first legal name. He chose to accept Bill as his name from then on, and our family adapted to the change with much effort. I will refer to him as Hudson in the following account during the period of his childhood.

The house in Westwood
House under construction

Lucina in pirate costume

Mother and Lucina, 1926
Lucina and Hudson, 1926

CHAPTER TWO

AFTER Hudson was born, I felt sure he would become a "sissy" from all the spoiling and baby talk from Mother and Dad. In order to "toughen him up" from such molly-coddling, I would talk roughly to him and give him a punch or two as he lay in his bassinette. I wanted him to be a brother who would climb trees with me and lead the rough and tumble life I thought a boy deserved. But Mother always dressed him in pretty, little clothes, clean as a whistle. She favored white and pastel colors, which were appropriate enough for a baby, — but as he grew older? He grew up hating to be dirty, and would run into the house to be washed if his hands were grimy.

He was not a sissy as I feared, but he certainly was spoiled. Everyone doted on him. He was a beautiful child and became very handsome — just like Dad. I was plain and ordinary by comparison. I truly loved Hudson, and all our lives we have remained friends, but we were never very close due to the vast difference in our ages. When I was a child, he was just a baby, and by the time we could converse and enjoy activities together, I was away at boarding school or college. We were never together for any length of time, even as adults. Each of us grew up, in effect, as an only child. We could have been from different parents, having opposite personalities and preferences.

His behavior was naughty, but he was never punished. His table manners were appalling, but thought "cute." When I did anything unlady-like at the dinner table, my father used to say, "If you were a boy, it would be wonderful, but you are a girl and it's terrible!" Hudson could never sit through a meal. Once, becoming restless, he marched around the table, using a silver teapot as a horn, blowing through the spout and "tooting" loudly. At each turn, Mother, as he passed, shoved a spoonful of peas (which he disliked) into his mouth. In this way his dinner was consumed, we thought. But some time later, when the maid was cleaning the silver, she discovered the teapot full of mouldy peas, which he had blown down the spout as he nonchalantly sang and marched around the table! He also disliked tomatoes and grudgingly said, "I'll eat those tomatoes, but I won't eat them dots!" He complained that steak "bent" his teeth.

There was a time when I began to wish for a pet rabbit. At every opportunity to make a wish, such as blowing out birthday candles, driving under a bridge or seeing a cat in a window (these were wish-making times), I would wish for a rabbit. It was unlucky to reveal a secret wish to anyone, so I never told a soul about these wishes, but suddenly I seemed to be buried in rabbits! They arrived as gifts at Easter, birthdays and even on no special days. They mated, and there were more and more bunnies until we had to build a large cage for them in the yard. I had only wanted one! I wondered, could my wishes have been heard this many times?

One rabbit became a very special pet for me. Beautiful, loving and very intelligent, he slept in my bed and acted more like a puppy than a rabbit. He followed me around, and I taught him tricks. I adored the rabbit. One day Hudson picked up my rabbit and threw him down the basement stairs. I will always remember the lifeless bundle of white fur on the basement floor. I hated my brother for this, even though he was only three years old at the time.

When Hudson was six, he started first grade at Burris School. Mother, apprehensive about this new experience for her son, need not have worried. The first day he came home bounding with enthusiasm. "Mother," he cried, "I'm in love! Her name is Donna and Vonna! She's twins, and she's beautiful!"

The same year Hudson started piano lessons, but did not take to it very well. So violin lessons were attempted. After a year of struggling with the instrument under his patient teacher, Mr. Trees, Mother and Dad felt Hudson's lagging interest might be stimulated with a little competition. I began to study the violin also, goading him into practising more diligently by telling him I would soon catch up to his level in no time. I quickly acquired facility on the violin, and the threat did inspire him to practise with renewed vigor. We studied together with Mr. Trees for two years, but then one day Hudson approached Mother and asked her, please, could he stop playing the violin? It sounded "just like street cars," he complained, and he couldn't stand it any longer. Without Hudson to keep the competition going, I was relieved to discontinue lessons also. I agreed the rasping strings sent goose bumps along my spine, and I still do not enjoy the sound of a violin. I became more convinced than ever the piano was my instrument.

Someone asked Hudson what he wanted to be when he grew up. Mother overheard his resigned reply, "Well, I'd like to be a 'saplorer,' but I guess I'll just have to be another Ball Brother." From then on Mother was determined he should go his own way and not work with the family firm unless he really wanted to. Hudson never became afflliated with Ball Brothers Company, but went into various businesses of his own. His desire for exploration came to fruition in 1983 when he climbed Mount Ararat in Turkey, searching for Noah's Ark. Unfortunately, it was buried twenty-five feet below the ice, and he and his party had to give up after digging down sixteen feet through the glacier when a storm drove them off the mountain.

Hudson, age 2

Hudson, age 10

Scarlet fever quarters

Hanover drive marker

Lucina at the keyboard

CHAPTER THREE

HUDSON was about seven months old when I contracted scarlet fever. It was a very dangerous disease in those days and required six weeks of quarantine. I was completely isolated in one wing of our house with a nurse. My parents were not allowed to come near me, nor another soul for the six weeks.

I became infected with the bacteria when Mother sent me to pick up a book she had loaned to a neighbor. The Turks were good friends, and I anticipated a visit with their sons, Tom and Fred. However, their mother, Elizabeth, met me at the door with the book, saying I couldn't come in as the boys, as well as Mr. Turk, were all "down with something." It was later discovered they all had scarlet fever, and the book I carried had been read by Mr. Turk. I was given an immunization shot, but had such a violent reaction that at first the doctor thought I had measles. It was the worst sickness I ever had. I became delirious and ran a dangerously high fever. The doctor finally realized I was much too ill for measles, in spite of the rash. The shot, in effect, had given me a small case of scarlet fever. The disease finally arrived after the normal incubation period, but I was not very ill. So perhaps the shot helped after all.

The quarantine period was not too bad. My closed-off section, the guest wing of the house, was quite luxurious. There was a large living room with a fireplace, a bathroom, dressing room and the sleeping porch. The porch was enclosed, but windows were the walls on two sides of the room. A small balcony off double doors was the third side. The beds, where the nurse and I slept, faced the doors, which gave us a lovely view of the treetops. I could have watched the birds build their nests, except it was winter time. In January the sleeping porch was very cold, but we had an electric heater which helped. It was fun to watch the snow all around us while buried snugly underneath the warm blankets and down comforters billowing up on top.

The nurse kept a fire going in the living room, which we sat near to keep warm. I played with paper dolls or read my treasured books. There was a telephone in the small entry to this part of the house and also a house phone. I could call my friends as well as anyone in the house. The house phone was connected to the kitchen, and I loved to talk to Celesta, our cook, and find out what "surprises" she was making for dinner.

I really was not lonely except for one day when I woke up and discovered I couldn't move. The nurse was on her day off so I was alone. I felt a heaviness in my chest. My breathing was labored. I panicked and began to yell as loud as possible. Mother heard me and came outdoors to the foot of the balcony and called up to ask what was the matter. I screamed back that I was paralyzed and could hardly breathe. In spite of the danger of infecting my infant brother, she rushed upstairs to my bedroom and began massaging my arms and legs. At last I was breathing easier and could move my legs a little, but it was a terrifying experience. Thankfully, Mother and everyone else in the family escaped the disease, but I feared for her, yet loved her so very much for endangering everyone else to "save my life."

When the isolation period was over, the nurse scrubbed me from head to toe in a Lysol bath. The odor disgusts me to this day. All my clothes, books, paper dolls and games, which the nurse and I had enjoyed together, were burned in the fireplace. Later, men arrived to fumigate the entire wing of the house where I had been.

The only after-effect I noticed which might have come from my illness, was the inability to see clearly when I returned to school. After missing six weeks of studies, catching up was difficult. So Mrs. Emerson moved me to the front row of the room. Even then I could decipher nothing on the blackboard. I was so fearful of the blurry vision that I kept it to myself, and my school work began to deteriorate. I didn't know what they would do to my eyes if they found out I couldn't see!

One day a doctor came to school to give us eye and hearing tests. We stood in long lines to get weighed by a nurse. I was afraid my secret would be discovered, and I trembled from head to toe. When my turn came, my throat was dry, and I pretended to read the chart that seemed miles away. The kind doctor, Howard Hill, said he would write to my parents, and I should have my eyes checked more thoroughly at his office. Fear rose in my throat and my imagination went wild. What would they do to me.?

The day of the office visit arrived. After the nurse administered the drops in my eyes, the doctor put me at ease as he skillfully tried various lenses to improve my vision. I finally realized he wasn't going to operate after all!

It was Christmas Eve when Dad and I drove to the optical shop to pick up my first pair of glasses. I put them on and was amazed to see a fairyland as Christmas decorations came into focus. As we drove home in the dusk, I marvelled that I could see each leaf on the trees, branches with clear sparkling lights, ornaments outlined and clearly distinguished. It was a wonderful Christmas being able to see again, and I pondered my earlier fears, telling myself how foolish I had been.

Hanover College in Madison, Indiana, always held a special interest for my father. He was on the Board of Directors and a Trustee until his death in 1980. A Presbyterian, coeducational college, it has maintained its high standards throughout the years.

In 1926 Dad made a large gift to Hanover, and in appreciation they reciprocated by naming their picturesque winding road through the campus, Lucina Ball Drive. Buildings at other institutions had been named in memory of my great aunt, Lucina, a sister of the Ball brothers. Lucina Hall at

[9]

Ball University was the resident dormitory for women there. "The Lucina" is the President's home at Keuka College, New York, where that college was founded for her about 1890. She was an educator and was to have been the administrator of Keuka but died before her home "The Lucina" was completed.

I felt proud to have the drive named for me and thrilled to be able to participate in the ceremony. I was to unveil the marker, which was covered by the American flag. I had no idea what was concealed beneath the flag and pictured a beautiful statue — maybe one of me underneath? At the appointed time an expectant hush fell over the crowd gathered there. I stepped forward, eager to see what I was to uncover, and carefully pulled the flag away. I nearly cried with disappointment! It was only a big boulder with a bronze plaque saying "Lucina Ball Drive."

The Drive is beautiful. It winds back and forth from the entrance gates of the campus, up the hill, skirting the river. The rock stands at the highest and most scenic spot overlooking the town of Madison as it curls into the river banks.

I didn't go to Hanover again until we drove our daughter Ann down to visit the school in 1960 as a possible college choice for her. We had an enjoyable day escorted around the campus by the Dean of Admissions and were impressed by the college and its beautiful surroundings. I had tried to find the plaque with my name on it, but it was not on the big boulder. I was secretly disappointed that it had been removed and questioned the Dean. He laughed, saying:

"Oh, is it gone again? Well, you must know the 'overlook' has been the trysting place for lovers on the campus as long as we can remember. When a couple becomes engaged there, they pry off the plaque and keep it as a souvenir. The plaques are removed almost as soon as they are put on. But this is a tradition at Hanover, even though it's a considerable expense to the College."

Somehow I felt better about my early feelings about the plain marker. It was memorable after all!

Ann's choice of college was not Hanover, but Centenary College in Hackettstown, New Jersey. But we were happy that Judy's daughter, Breck, chose to spend her college years at Hanover and was enthusiastic about every day of her studies and experiences there.

———◆———

Every child fantasizes and worries about his future. What will it bring by chance, or what could he make happen? Oddly enough, by the time I was eight I knew exactly what I wanted to do with my life. Although time and circumstances changed, my interests and pursuits remained the same. My first love was music, then horses, and I also loved to write stories. I wished to

[10]

make music my vocation, writing my avocation and horses my hobby.

As I grew older, music became more and more dominant in my life, and I practised very hard at the piano. My Mother had a beautiful, operatic voice and sang every day, often giving recitals. She wanted me to sing also, which I did, although it came too easily for me. I preferred the challenge of mastering the difficulties of the keyboard.

Not until I went to college did I realize my talents weren't strong enough to make writing my avocation. So this inward desire waned as I spent more time with my music.

The horses in my life deserve their own chapter.

CHAPTER FOUR

THE Christmas of 1926 was one of the most eventful in my memory. I slipped down the stairs in the darkness and hid behind the draperies drawn at the living room doorway, peeking though to see what delicious excitements lay ahead. The lights of the tree were on and piles of packages lay beneath, tantalizing with their ribbons and unusual sizes. It wouldn't be fair to go in without the family. So I bounded upstairs again to awaken them. Soon we were all ready, and together we proceeded to the magical room in great anticipation.

My eyes fell on a beautiful doll house complete with a family, standing on its own table, surrounded by a green felt lawn, with sponge bushes and trees. Atop the white frame was a gray, slate roof bedecked with a brick chimney, snowcapped to match the season. I played with this doll house with love and devotion until I was sixteen and went to boarding school. The day I came home on vacation from school in Indianapolis and saw an empty window niche where my house had stood made me weep with nostalgia for my childhood. Mother had carefully boxed all the furniture and bundled the house into the attic. When she saw me come in from a dance in evening clothes one night, turn on the lights of the house, and sit there "fixing" the furniture for awhile before going to bed, she decided I should make a definite transition from girl to woman.

That same Christmas day, after the packages were unwrapped and the excitement diminishing, my father called us to the back door where we stood in disbelief as a beautiful, brown pony drawing a shiny, red cart trotted up the driveway. It was Billy, a plump Welsh pony, five-gaited and able to draw us in a carriage as well. My love for Billy transcended all else. I prayed for his welfare every night even into my college days, until he died of old age at pasture.

I learned to ride Billy and was able to guide him into the slow gait and rack as well as the trot and canter. I also taught him to jump a little, although it

[11]

had to be done over a low hedge as he was heading for the barn! I still have a cinder embedded in an elbow from one of my many falls making this jump. He was also my circus pony, and I did tricks on his back as he cantered around the ring, patiently putting up with my whims and antics. I was jealous of anyone else who rode him, and so was he. As he was saddled, knowing someone else would mount him, he would gather in an immense amount of air in his stomach. Then when the unwelcome rider put a foot in the stirrup, he would let out all the air, and the loosened saddle and would-be rider would slip to the ground. On occasion, he also would kick. But he never pulled this trick with me.

We had good times together, sometimes heading across the fields to a creek where we would spend the morning exploring, enjoying the warm summer days. As he cropped grass, I would throw pebbles into the water or search for "treasure." I even taught Billy to respond to secret code words. When I would say "coca cola," for example, he would set off in a trot. "Whoop-ti-doo" brought on a full gallop. We understood each other, but Billy was stubborn as ponies are, and would not cooperate with anyone else.

I hated the day when I discovered I had outgrown Billy. But he also was getting old. We still met over the fence and communed as he enjoyed his pasture days.

By this time my parents had accumulated about seventy-five head of horses at Orchard Lawn Farm, including the brood mares and foals. Almost daily I rode and exercised horses for upcoming shows and trained the two-year-olds to tolerate me on their backs. I'd won a fine collection of ribbons and trophies, which were on display in the tack room. Mr. Morgan managed the stables for Mother and was a marvelous trainer. He was a lovable character who chewed tobacco until little trails of brown juice made a permanent stain at the corners of his mouth. I owe my riding skills to him. He told me, spitting out tobacco juice at every other word, "When you put your horse in a rack, hunch down in the saddle and rock with the horse like you're sitting in a rocking chair." When I put Major in a rack the "rocking chair" felt like a flying carpet as we flew down the straight-a-way. Major's rack was the fastest and most exciting of all our horses.

During the summer, in the gray light of dawn, I arose before anyone else, and set off for the farm, two miles away, on my bicycle. It seemed much farther because the long road to the farm was gravel, making it difficult to manage the bicycle, particularly as I peddled home at noon under the hot sun.

Arriving at the stable, I would exercise the horses, twenty minutes each, the stable boys preparing the horses for me to ride. A few hours later, Mother would come for me in the air-cooled Franklin, and we'd drive home and join the rest of the family for breakfast. Then she'd return me to the farm to continue riding until noon, when I bicycled home again, tired and ready for an afternoon in an apple tree with a good book.

[12]

Our horses were as fine as any in the Midwest, and we often made trips to Kentucky to the "blue grass" region to buy yet another stallion or brood mare to increase Orchard Lawn's stock. The line began with a wonderful old stallion named Cloud. We found him on a small farm near Harrodsburg, Kentucky. He was nineteen at the time but lived for eight more years, siring some beautiful foals. There was also King's Fancy, one of our own colts, who sired one of the best lines in our part of the country. His offspring still are making history in horse shows today.

Mother was an avid animal lover and was constantly in the business of breeding anything with four legs. She raised many breeds of dogs as well as horses. Why she had only two children of her own remains a mystery to me.

Unfortunately I am a victim of allergies, taking after Dad who always suffered from hay fever beginning without fail on August fourteenth and lasting until frost. My allergies began with "the green things growing" in May and increased with ferocity until the dead leaves were swept away in November. I also was violently allergic to cats, and woe is me! — HORSES! I couldn't enter the barns or the sneezing and tears would prevent me from riding at all. I always wore gloves and carried Dad's large handkerchiefs at the alert. During those summer days I spent many miserable hours "mopping up" after a horse show from exposure to the concentrated atmosphere of many horses, breathing in the dust kicked up by their hooves. Then there were no pills to ward off the worst effects, but I was given shots until I felt like a sieve. Nothing seemed to help, yet I loved the riding and suffered through it in spite of such discomfort. Finally, I gave up riding altogether after I went to college. Mother quietly sold off the horses, and when my favorite five-gaited mare, Marie Neal, was sent packing with the rest, my heart sank, as I abandoned this great love along with writing stories.

I turned to my music, my third love, which has been my constant joy.

The doll house

Mother with her favorite mare

William C. Ball

Emma and William with William Hudson

William C. Ball home, Minnetrista Blvd.

The Ball brothers: L. to R. George A., Lucius L., Frank C., Edmund B., William C.

CHAPTER FIVE

THE town of Muncie began as an Indian settlement where Chief Munsee's tribe tented around the White River. According to Indian lore, living on the horseshoe bend of a river brought good luck to the tribe. Pestilence would not afflict them, nor enemies conquer them. Around 1812 Muncie became a settlement when a trading post was built across the river from the Indians. As the white men gradually moved into the area, they forced the Indians to migrate further west. The Battle of Tippecanoe finally wiped out or drove the remaining tribes out of Indiana.

The five Ball brothers found their way to Muncie in 1887. Originally from Buffalo, N.Y., they had just incorporated their glass manufacturing business, making fruit jars for home canning. The big gas boom in Muncie brought them West. A report claimed: "The supply is inexhaustible. There are thirty-five mighty wells within two miles of Muncie's center, spewing a million cubic feet of gas per day, with only one-third being used." When Frank Ball arrived in Muncie to evaluate the location for their company, he found a small, country town with dirt streets and one hotel. The town was illuminated day and night by the ever-burning gas lights. Conservative estimates claimed the population would grow to fifty thousand within five years, bringing

[16]

many new industries to the "most important manufacturing city of the West." But the balloon burst as the wasted gas finally spent itself into the atmosphere within a few years, and the town had to rely on other energy sources to fuel their factories and homes.

In the meantime, the Ball family had built their factory and gradually settled in homes, which they built on that same horseshoe bend of the river where the Munsee tribe had lived. The Indian legend came true for them as fame and fortune followed quickly. They called the street running in front of their homes and beside the river, Minnetrista Boulevard, from the Indian words minne, meaning water, and trista — meeting place. The five homes, side by side, fill this beautiful curve. At one end is the small, unpretentious home of Lucius, his wife, Sarah, and their daughter, Helen. Lucius, the oldest brother, became a physician at the age of forty, fulfilling his lifelong ambition. He did not work actively in the firm, but served on the Board of Directors.

Next door is the dark, frame house where George, his wife Frances, and their daughter Elisabeth lived. George became president of the firm after Frank's death in 1944. Frank founded the company and remained president throughout his life.

In the center of the horseshoe is the Georgian-style home of my grandparents, William and Emma. Father was their only child, born when Emma was forty years old, and named William Hudson. Heinrich Hudson, the famous Dutch explorer of the Hudson River in New York, was an ancestor of my grandmother.

Grandfather Ball died of pneumonia in 1921 when I was only three years old. So I never knew his gentleness. But Grandma Ball, who died in 1942, lived to be ninety-six, and I remember her very well.

Although less than five-feet tall, her imperious demands and indomitable will belied her diminutive stature. She made Mother and Dad's married life miserable with her unreasonable demands and could be a holy terror when things didn't go her way. Although not fond of children, she always was very good to me. However, she was jealous of Hudson because of the attention he diverted away from her.

The nicest thing she ever did for me was to buy me a lovely Chickering grand piano, which she kept until I finally had a place of my own. Six-feet long, with a beautifully carved, dark mahogany case, it stood in her home, seldom played. It was equipped with a player attachment, called an Ampico, which played rolls of music. I did not like the Ampico as it damaged the pedal action and added a ton of weight to the instrument.

The piano was moved to my first apartment in Cincinnati in 1939, and three years and two moves later, I finally had the Ampico mecha-

[17]

nism removed and donated to the scrap drive in 1942. Esthetically, I was repelled by the "artificial piano player." At the time I was glad to rid the piano of its burden, but today if would be considered very valuable.

Continuing along the Boulevard, the great mansion of Edmund Ball was built between 1904-07 after his marriage to Bertha Crosley, of the Crosley Radio Corporation family in Cincinnati, Ohio. The house is made of gray stone and large enough to accommodate four children and many more. Bertha and Edmund's children were Edmund, Adelia, Janice and Crosley. Crosley died when he was a child after a tonsillectomy.

The largest and most impressive house of all belonged to Frank and Bessie Ball. They had a large family of five children — Margaret, Lucy, Arthur, Rosemary and Frank Elliott. Frank Elliott was killed in his plane while landing at Findley, Ohio in 1936. The plane caught fire after a wing suddenly fell off at the landing approach. He was just thirty-three. This tragedy touched all of us deeply, and Uncle Frank and Aunt Bessie never fully recovered from the shock.

I grew up feeling smothered by this large, aristocratic group of great uncles and aunts, and "cousins by the dozens." Of course I was proud to be a member of the family, but Uncle Frank and Aunt Bessie clearly dominated the life styles of all of us. We were expected to conduct ourselves in an exemplary manner. No scandal could ever touch us — no conduct unbecoming to any member of the *Ball* family! Their rules were stiff and unrelenting, and not all of us could live up to them. They lived in the prim, unreal world of the Victorian Age, not permitting any weakness of character to show. Consequently I had difficulty making friends with my classmates and lived a rather solitary life. The parties were always checked out carefully to be sure those attending were all right to associate with. I felt left out, put on a shelf, so to speak, and was embarrassed by others who made me feel different.

To counteract the surface of snobbery which I hated, I clowned and acted silly to become "one of the gang." I constantly dreamed of the day when I could leave Muncie and go somewhere else where I could be "Nobody." All I wanted was to be accepted for myself.

My family's influence even followed me to college in New York. The Lynds were on the Sarah Lawrence faculty and had just been made famous for their book *Middletown*, which was all about Muncie and the people living there — including our family. *Life Magazine*, looking for a story, sent Margaret Bourke-White, the famous reporter and photographer, to Muncie for pictures and an article that gave Muncie a certain notoriety which was not welcome. My Father in the barber's chair, his face covered with lather, was on the cover of the magazine. Our family group was shown sitting in our living room (with me at the piano — where else?) The other half-page showed a poor family sitting on the front steps of their shack surrounded by their chickens and pigs. The captions describing the two families were reversed by an unfortunate printer's error. The article about Muncie took up most of the issue of Life Magazine, and the townspeople rose in anger and wrote letters to the editor in protest, but the publicity and damage to the privacy of Muncie's individuals was already done. Everyone knew who I was when I arrived on campus, and my first assignment as a reporter for our Campus News was to interview the Lynds — the last people on earth I ever wanted to meet. I did the interview and wrote my article, but I was angry and insulted.

In all fairness to my imposing relatives, they were brought up by their mother, Maria Bingham Ball, to have high ideals and true Christian principles. Their sense of community spirit was strong, and to this day their descendants are committed to supporting the city's cultural and humanitarian goals. To Muncie, they brought prosperity and reknown from their efforts to build a fine community. Their generous contributions built Ball State University, Ball Hospital, the Y.M.C.A. and the Y.W.C.A., and the Masonic Temple, which contains a large auditorium for music and drama. Schools and churches also benefited from their support.

Uncle Frank was as high-principled a person as one could meet, and as the head of Ball Brothers Company, he also became the head of the family. Maria Bingham taught them as boys to band together if they were to be successful in life. Each one's strong points would combine to offset their individual weaknesses. Together, she believed, they could build a strong future. Not only were they in business together, but their lives and social structure also were interwoven with strong threads. When they bought land in Leland, Michigan, for their summer homes, they build the houses side-by-side around the lake, as in Muncie. There, every summer, the family would rejoin for a continuing "togetherness" in the Indiana Woods. My parents were the only "mavericks" who preferred to vacation in different locations every summer. Because of my father's hay fever, we would try to leave home, just before the onset of sneezing and red eyes, and return after Labor Day. Consequently, my late August birthdays were spent in different locations every year.

[19]

"Willie" Ball

Willie growing up

Sergeant William H. Ball, 1917

William in college

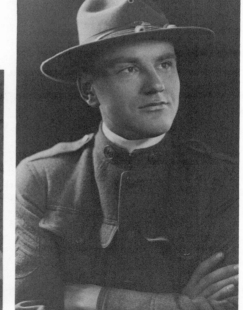

LIFE

Dad in the barber chair, Life Magazine

[21]

CHAPTER SIX

MOTHER, Agnes Medsker, was one of five children of Chauncey and Leora. My Grandmother hated her name. So she was known by all her friends as "Leo." As soon as I could talk, I began calling her Nana, and this is what nearly everyone called her from then on. The Medsker ancestors arrived on the Mayflower and scattered their roots along the eastern seaboard, into the South as far west as Missouri, and up into the midwest. Grandpa was very stern and somewhat Germanic, and all of us, including Nana, respected his desire for peace and quiet. For a long time he refused to have a telephone in the house, but when Nana pleaded for one, he finally agreed, adding he would never use it himself. He kept his promise. As long as he lived, he would not answer the phone, even if no one else was home. His library was his sanctuary. No one dared set foot in this room without his invitation. Nana called him "the old bear" with tenderness in her voice, but, inspite of his gruffness, he was kind and gentle. We all loved him.

The Medsker children were Mildred, Agnes, Chauncey, Margaret and Betty (or Jeanne as she preferred to be called.) Chauncey and Margaret had no children from their marriages, but the other three girls gave Nana seven grandchildren.

Mildred, the eldest, married Will Nottingham and lived in Eaton, Indiana, about nine miles north of Muncie. Their children were Corinne and Bill.

Bill was blinded at age six when a bread knife penetrated his eye. An infection caused the other eye to become blind as well. I always admired Bill for his courage, his intellect and his keen sense of humor. He also had the ability to play any musical instrument, having studied music in the Indianapolis School for the Blind where he graduated around 1928 with the highest honors of anyone up to that time. A very self-reliant person, he moved to New York where he lived alone and formed a dance orchestra composed of other blind musicians. He also had other positions, including a private secretarial job with an author. He married late in life, having met Nita in the Library for the Blind in New York where she worked as a librarian.

Corinne always lived in Eaton where she was born and married Lafayette Elliott from the same community.

Jeanne, the youngest daughter, married Eugene Wierbach. Her three children were David, Sandra and Lucina. My mother, Agnes, completed the roster of the seven grandchildren with her two, Hudson and me.

[22]

Margaret married Paul Fitzgibbon and moved away from Muncie, living in various cities as well as in Europe with her husband, who was in the advertising business. As I grew up, I usually visited them some time during the summers. I loved those special times with Margie and Paul and remember with fond thoughts the weeks spent in Cincinnati, Detroit or St. Louis. Having no children of their own, they treated me as if I belonged to them.

Chauncey married Ethel Hitchcock, a widow with two children, Helen and Jane. Jane became one of my closest friends.

Nana was the perfect grandmother. She was loving and devoted to us all.

My Mother and Dad who knew each other from their school days, became better acquainted when they were paired together in a local production of *Madame Butterfly*. Mother, of course, sang the title role, and my Dad who had a fine, tenor voice, sang the part of Pinkerton. Their romance blossomed, and they were married November fourteenth, 1917, at the time when all America was in a furor over the Great War and men were enlisting to go overseas. Chauncey was the first man in Muncie to enlist, and my father joined also, becoming a top sergeant in the Fifth Gas Division. He left for France in April, 1918 after receiving his training at Camp Logan in Texas. He also left Mother pregnant with me, and I was born the following August.

Three months later the Armistice was signed, but my father was then assigned to the Army of Occupation and could not return home until August 19, 1919 — two days before my first birthday. For a long time, due to inadequate communication from Muncie to the war zone, he thought he had sired a boy. I hope he was not too disappointed, but for eight years I tried hard to be a boy for him until my brother was born. My first birthday was spent in Niagara Falls with Mother and Dad, who, I suppose, felt they were taking their honeymoon after such a long separation.

<hr>

We lived downtown in a nice, square brick house at 222 N. Monroe Street. I remember especially the rather dark living room where my Mother practised her singing constantly. It wasn't long before I found my voice to protest against these endless scales, and at six months I was saying "Ma-ma — don't mi-mi!" It was useless, because she went right on singing in spite of my whining. Perhaps this is the reason I am not so fond of singing. According to the doctor's advice, she nursed me through "the second summer." This meant I was two years old before she realized the second summer was not the doctor's literal intention. I grew immensely fat, and sat in a high chair, unable to balance on my tiny feet. I was talking a blue streak before I finally walked at eighteen

[23]

months, my heavy jowls jouncing at every step.

One day Mother and I were driving somewhere, and I had a doll in my lap in the front seat. I remember the doll falling to the floor of the car and leaning over to retrieve it. Then my memory is gone. Mother had reached over to hold me back on the seat, lost control of the car, and ran into a tree. My head, cushioned by a silk cap, sank into the round ball on top of the gear shift. The cap really saved my life. I awoke to hear the doctor saying he had taken sixteen stitches in my head. I was two years old then, and to this day my head bears a three-quarter circle where the gear shift left its mark.

I used to run away from home — not because I wanted to leave home, but because nice neighbors lived around the block, and I loved to call on each one in turn. Invariably they would offer me freshly baked cookies. When Mother caught up with me, I would be rushed home and tied to the leg of the kitchen table, suffering silently and full of disgrace, until the next time that I longed for more of those good cookies! I still can't resist the temptation to eat cookies!

The Grays lived across the street, close friends of my parents, and their daughter, Derexa, became my constant playmate, although she was three years older than I. We were always good friends, even after we moved to the stone house in Westwood, which was far from Monroe Street. Mrs. Gray (Marie) had glossy thick, black hair. When long hair went out of style, she bobbed it and gave her hair to Mother to be made into a wig for a beautiful doll which I received one Christmas. I remember opening a closed door and seeing the doll sitting on a shelf. I knew it would be mine on Christmas, and I shut the door as quickly as I could to shut out the vision of a present meant to be a surprise. I never let anyone know I saw it before Santa brought it!

The doll had long curls and a sweet china face with blue eyes that closed when she was laid down. Her wardrobe was a collection of lovely clothes made for her by another friend, Mildred Hawke. The doll had many dresses and a coat and hat with real fur trimming. The clothes fit on small hangers in her very own trunk. She was the only large doll I ever played with because she was very special, with a wig made out of dear Marie Gray's hair and clothes lovingly made by another dear friend. Mildred played the harp beautifully. She played for Mother's wedding and at mine in 1940.

My parents always took me with them wherever they went. I was never left with a "sitter." At that time we did not have servants who lived in the house with us, as was customary. So if Mother and Dad longed to see a play, hear a concert, or just be with their friends, I went along. During the long concerts I learned to count — the people attending, the

[24]

number of light bulbs, the ornamental figures around the stage — whatever caught my eye. Dad always thought to bring a pencil along so I could draw on the program. In this way I learned not to squirm through the long evenings. But the music somehow penetrated, and after returning home, I would jump on the piano bench and pick out tunes I had heard at the concert. I was four years old when Mother decided I should take formal lessons, since I showed so much interest in the keyboard. I also was creating small pieces which Mother carefully wrote down and preserved as my first attempts at composition.

My early lessons were exciting, and I learned quickly from Mrs. Day, the wife of the Episcopalian minister in Muncie. After two years, however, her husband was transferred to Wisconsin, and from then on my teachers in Muncie were of a hit-or-miss variety. The teachers tried to stifle my love for music, it seemed. Although at the time I didn't know what was lacking in my instruction, I knew something was wrong. I began to wish for pupils of my own so I could teach them to love music as I did. From the time I was six, I began to show others the mysteries of the piano. I enjoyed teaching then — and still do.

When I was six years old we began construction of our new house. My parents sold their home on Monroe Street, and we moved into an apartment next door to my grandparents Medsker. Grandfather owned the building and often dealt in real estate, although he was a practicing lawyer until his death in 1939. He also built two savings and loan companies in Muncie.

We lived on the top floor of the rather antiquated construction, and I still remember the endless flight of steep stairs that had to be climbed in order to reach our front door. We lived there for two years, waiting for the new house to be finished, and I began school at Mrs. Emerson's Country Day, a one-room schoolhouse for children in the first six grades. We sat in our class groups and Mrs. Emerson taught us class by class during the day, while the rest of us studied until our turn arrived. I learned to read in a flash, and also began to study French.

Mrs. Emerson was a wonderful teacher. She was cross, however, and uncompromising, and all of us were intimidated by her old-maid personality. Those who misbehaved stood in a corner or were dismissed from the room in awful disgrace. The worst punishment of all was having to sit on her lap as she taught. We had a horror of having to submit to this punishment, as her chin bristled with whiskers, and we were fearful of having those whiskers tickle our faces. Poor Gilman Mason seemed to be a constant victim, being somewhat incorrigible in his behavior. Though some jeered at his predicament, I felt sorry for Gilman who always seemed to be the scapegoat in any situation.

[25]

We spent a great deal of time with my grandparents — more specifically with Nana, since Grandpa Medsker wasn't especially drawn to children. We usually had Sunday dinner with them and also special holidays, such as Thanksgiving and Christmas, when the entire family attended. Nana was a marvelous cook. The table groaned under the many dishes on those occasions. Her chicken and dumplings, or biscuits, were mouth watering. Grandfather always walked to town on Sunday mornings to bring back his favorite dessert — peach ice cream, which was wonderfully rich.

One morning before dawn I awoke in a half-dream about a book I had just read. I was determined I would join Peter Pan's band in "Never-Never Land." I dressed quietly, slipped down the stairs and began to walk along the deserted street. In front of Nana's house, I hesitated. I decided I couldn't leave her forever without saying goodby! I knocked on the door, and Chauncey, recuperating from pneumonia, answered and stared at me in amazement. I calmly announced that I was on my way to join Peter Pan but wanted to say goodby to Nana. He ushered me in with a straight face, and I climbed the stairs to Nana's bedroom, where, of course, she was still sleeping. She invited me to get into bed with her, and as I did so, I discovered to my great chagrin, that in dressing myself I had neglected to put on my bloomers! It would never do to go off to Never-Never Land in a state of undress! I was soon fast asleep with my adventure indefinitely postponed.

The Medsker house sat on a large corner lot near Muncie's town center. Nana's garden was the showpiece of the neighborhood. Her phlox and snapdragons grew high in neatly tended beds. Columbine and delphinium, not to mention large, lush roses, filled the back yard with a riot of color. In the middle of the garden a grape arbor sheltered a small path which led from the kitchen porch to the alley. Nana was the first person in Muncie to cultivate iris, and people would park their cars along the street to admire the garden and marvel at the iris. Nana spent many hours weeding and planting her garden, making it more beautiful every year.

As she worked in the garden, she made friends with her favorite birds, the cardinals. She fed them from her kitchen window, and one red bird became very tame. When she called to him "Peter, Peter, Peter" as she put out the seed or crumbs, he would fly to the back porch, perch on the rail and even enter her kitchen to receive his crumbs. He came every year, bringing his mate along, though she was never as brave as he and would not venture past the porch railing.

Washington Street was a residential street, a lovely avenue with trees lining the sidewalks and comfortable houses gracing both sides for the length of ten blocks or so. The cross streets ran into the business district — a modest collection of small stores, banks and two or three hotels.

It was fun to skate on the sidewalk in front of Nana's house. Madison Street, the wide cross street at the corner, was a main artery in and out of town, and since there was more traffic here, I was not allowed to cross this street by myself. The railroad track also ran along Madison, and every day long freight trains crept heavily along, bumping, stopping and screeching their steel wheels in protest at the snail's pace with which they were forced to proceed within the city limits. I loved to watch the trains and the workmen, who sometimes walked from car to car on top of the trains, or clung to the iron ladders running up the sides of the cars.

One day as I was jumping rope on the sidewalk, a train passed. One of the men threw something toward me from the train, waving and smiling. It landed on the grass near me, and I was amazed to see a huge piece of chalk. It was about three inches long and as fat as a broom handle! I had never seen such a grand piece of chalk before and ran into the house to show it to Nana. It was perfect for marking the sidewalk to play hopscotch! From then on, whenever the trains passed, I would call to the men above the rattle and din of the train, "Give me more chalk!" Sometimes I was lucky and was thrown a piece, but more often the men couldn't hear me, or perhaps, didn't have any to throw. In any case, the chalk provided fine marking for hopscotch, and my friends gathered to join me in the game, adding their pleas for chalk when the trains passed.

Fay Ogle was the nearest child neighbor to us, and we played together, roller skating on the sidewalk, or having tea parties on Nana's lawn, setting a small table with our doll dishes, and inviting our dolls to join us for tea and cookies. We also carried on a small business with a lemonade stand, selling Nana's good lemonade for a nickel a glass.

Every year the Hagenback Wallace Circus came to Muncie, arriving in its private train, beautifully painted and covered with signs advertising the glories of the circus. The unloading station was not far down the track from the Medsker house.

We would awake before dawn to walk the few blocks and watch the roustabouts unload the animals from the train, leading them to the circus grounds nearby. It was very exciting. Grandpa Medsker's horse, Old Stoner, was stabled in a barn on the grounds, and when the elephants, lions and tigers, and other strange smelling animals went by his stall, he would rear up on his hind legs, neighing in fear and excitement.

When the time came for the parade, the crowd would line the streets in anticipation, but our view from Nana's house was the best of all. The

[27]

fine array of performers and cages of animals would march slowly along to the accompaniment of the band's circus music. Horses and elephants were decorated in their finery, ridden by flashily dressed men and women. The tiger snarled and crouched in his wagon cage, its brightly painted wheels spinning like a kaleidoscope as it passed by.

The show lasted for several days, and we would sometimes see a night performance as well as a matinee. The side shows were in small tents leading to the "big top," and I remember the flea circus particularly.

Inside the tent was a display case covered by a magnifying glass through which one could see the fleas. Some were alive and did "tricks" by jumping through hoops or rolling tiny balls to each other. Others were dead and placed in match boxes, dressed up as clowns, brides and grooms, or ballet dancers. I marvelled that someone was able to dress such a tiny thing so perfectly.

⋯⟨◎⟩⋯

Mother had an Electric car, which she used while making her errands around town. It had a high carriage which was entered by stepping up on a running board. The inside was so roomy, one could stand erect. In front of the driver was a long, horizontal control bar, which was pushed forward for speed or backwards to slow and stop. The Electric was easy to manipulate and ran smoothly and quietly. I loved doing errands with Mother, and one day I went with her, carrying our precious little King Charles spaniel along. She stopped across the street from a grocery store and told me to wait in the machine as she would be right back. As she crossed the street, I decided impulsively to go with her. I opened the door and stood waiting for the cars to pass so I could join her. She turned, saw me at the curb and called, telling me to get back in the car and wait. The little dog heard her voice, jumped out of the cab and dashed across the street in response. Before our eyes, a car ran over her, and there she lay in the street — a little black lump. We loved the little dog. She was one of the most responsive and intelligent of pets, and this tragedy was impossible to forget. My eyes fill with tears as I write, nearly sixty years later. I cried myself to sleep night after night after saying my prayers, hoping God would forgive me for disobeying Mother. It was a hard way to learn a lesson about minding my elders, and I never forgot the consequence of disobedience.

One morning, about a week after that terrible day, I awoke, my pillow still wet with tears, to feel someting warm, soft and furry against my face. Mother had put another little spaniel puppy in bed with me. None of us felt for her as we did for our lost one. She did not train well and was always full of mischief, which plagued everyone. I noticed when she chewed on things, Mother would put a rubber band on her nose to punish her. One day she found my lovely doll with the beautiful long curls and chewed off her eyelashes. To punish her, with Mother

[28]

away, I did as I had seen Mother do. I put a rubber band around her nose
— but very tight! I was so angry I wound it around and around! The poor
little dog nearly suffocated before Mother fortunately returned in time
to save her.

The days of Monroe and Washington Street are behind me now. Only
snatches of events remain in my mind. The day I dashed across Monroe
Street to play with Derexa, a car barely missing me, brought punishment and a lesson not to dart into streets; the tiny midget-like black
maid who worked for us and taught me to be the superstitious person
that I am. Her name was Myrtie and her disposition was explosive. She
had no trouble sounding off at Mother when something displeased her.
From her I learned to respect black cats which crossed my path, not to
walk under ladders, never to leave a chair rocking empty or to put a hat
on a bed. She gave me lessons in dozens of superstitions that became
gospel to me. I have tried to shake these demons, but I can't forget the
early warnings she instilled so strongly in my mind.

Now let us return to Westwood where I began this story.

"Madame Butterfly" Agnes Medsker,
William Ball and Edmund Ball

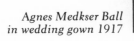

Agnes Medkser Ball
in wedding gown 1917

[29]

(Clockwise from top left): Dad meets Lucina on August 19, 1919; Mother and Lucina; The face in the mirror

222 N. Monroe Street, the Electric at the curb

Chauncey L. Medsker

CHAPTER SEVEN

AFTER I recovered from scarlet fever, my parents began discussing the possibility of having my tonsils removed. I always had many illnesses during the winters, and they thought I would be in better health and not miss so much school if I had the operation. I began to dream about it. I had terrible nightmares. I wanted my tonsils removed, but I dreamed my father would not allow the operation, and Mother secretly would take me to the doctor and the operation would take place. Dad would find out about it, become very angry and make the doctor put the tonsils back in again! This dream persisted night after night, until I found myself begging my parents to let me have the operation and get it over with.

At last, I was in the doctor's office, feeling calm and ready, anxious for it to be done. I was ushered in and made to lie on the operating table where a nurse and two doctors were waiting. I smiled to show them I was cooperating, but they said not a word to me. Instead the two doctors clamped me down with great force, holding my arms and legs while the nurse held my head down on the table. I began to fight back with indignation and alarm, trying to explain they needn't treat me so badly, but they gave me no opportunity to speak. One of them covered my face, and I couldn't utter a sound. Soon I was falling down a long black tunnel that had no end, but I could see an evil eye looking up at me from the bottom. I tumbled down faster and faster, and a roaring from the wind was in my ears — and then, almost as I reached that terrifying evil eye, I just as suddenly awoke, feeling sick and weak.

I was in a little, white room, on a hard, thin cot, but Mother was there quietly waiting, and I was not afraid any longer. When I stopped drifting in and out of sleep and nausea, Mother gave me a cube of ice to cool my burning throat, and began to read a new book to me, *Toby Tyler, or Ten Weeks With a Circus*. The book helped me forget the mean doctors who handled me so roughly, and who were not kind at all. I hated them for not trusting me.

The following summer our family planned a month's trip to Yellowstone Park. My brother was just one year old, and I would celebrate my ninth birthday in the Park. Hudson was too young to take along on an excursion such as this. So he was left behind with a nurse. Mother and I climbed into the bright yellow Franklin piled high with luggage, while Dad slipped behind the wheel, and we were off on our Great Adventure!

In 1927 there were no super-highways or even good roads of any kind. One never knew when one might encounter a filling station (or more aptly, "emptying" station, as Mother called them, since we would always take advantage of a stop to look for a bathroom of sorts.) We soon discovered the farther west we drove, the more primitive the conditions. Outhouses were the prevailing features near the longed-for gas stations, and these were pretty horrible. Water was scarce also, but usually there was a well handy with a tin cup hanging on the lip of the pump. Mother taught me to escape the deadly germs from who-knows-whose mouth by drinking with both lips inside the cup, — sort of like "Old Dobbin" at the trough.

Often, the sought-after station would not appear soon enough, and we would have to park on the side of the deserted road and take off into the bushes (if we were lucky enough to find any.) But this was far preferable to those dreaded outhouses! Dad would frighten us with tales of "suppose we run out of gas right here in these Badlands of South Dakota?" The visions of rattlers, parched throats and burning sun with no rescuers on the road to save us gave my imagination plenty of room to travel. I sat on the roomy back seat, gazing at the lonely landscape as it moved by in a slow panorama. What excitement when we finally saw the mountain shapes outlined in gray on the horizon far ahead! I played games as we drove along, pretending I could fly and would accompany the car outside, floating and keeping cool in the breeze as we winged along at the top speed of forty miles-an-hour.

One day, in the middle of nowhere, a hitchhiker appeared. She was thumbing her way, signaling frantically for us to stop. Hitchhikers were rare, and we had never heard of a woman doing such a risky thing. So of course we stopped to help her. The girl climbed in, and as we drove along, told us she was on her way to California.

We were passing through desert land when a huge bumble bee flew in the open window and immediately the girl began to thrash around, screaming in panic. She alone was afraid, and in the confusion, the bee flew against my ankle. Although it was not painful, I knew I had been stung. We stopped the car, freed the bee, and drove on again, but soon my ankle began to swell and throb, and by the time we reached a small town for the night I couldn't put my foot down to walk into the hotel.

My parents found a doctor who came to see my monstrous ankle and announced I was lucky to get some attention, as in an hour or more it would have had to be lanced. He gave us a solution and bandages to soak the leg, and by the next morning the swelling and redness had subsided a little. We stayed in the town the next day so the soaking could continue. The doctor explained the bee had been ingesting nectar from the poisonous plants in the desert, the reason for such a bad reaction to the sting. In the meantime the itching and pain were unbearable.

By the time we entered Yellowstone Park, my ankle was almost normal. We said goodby to the hitchhiker where we had left her in the little town.

[33]

As we climbed the mountains, awed by the gorgeous scenery, we were surprised to see almost every other car stalled beside the road, steaming and water boiling out of their radiators due to the high altitude and steep gravel roads. Even the big yellow park buses carrying tourists were in trouble. Our air-cooled engine never needed water. How fortunate we were to have such a clever car! It was also a very comfortable riding machine. We never had a problem of any kind except the inevitable flat tires one had every few hundred miles or so in those days. Dad was adept at changing tires and patching the inner tubes, so we never thought of it as a problem. It was just an inconvenience we accepted as normal procedure.

We were thrilled and amazed by the geysers which spewed boiling water to the heavens from time to time and the smelly sulphurous bowls of oozing, bubbling, gray clay that looked like something out of an Oz book. Some were quite beautiful, such as the Morning Glory Pool with its clear blue and serene, but quite deceptive depths. As the pool invited you to swim, it could incinerate anyone naive enough to attempt it.

We saw Indian dancing and stayed in lodges that looked like huge log cabins. Stuffed animal heads and skins decorated the walls, and beautiful Indian rugs brightened the floors and furniture. Carved pillars resembling totem poles held up the balcony around the great entrance hall of one hotel, I remember.

There were tourists, of course, but nothing equaling the disaster of today's influx of humanity. There were just enough people around to take the edge off the feeling of loneliness one feels in a wilderness. Guides were helpful, not harried. Yellowstone was clean, not littered with the trash left by campers and careless travelers. I was constantly impressed by the pristine, quiet beauty and the natural wonders within the Park. Deer, moose and elk grazed calmly, and rabbits and mountain squirrels abounded.

No one warned us the bears were dangerous. We were only told not to feed them. Dad was taking pictures of everything with his new Eastman movie camera, when we came upon a gentle, domestic scene of a mother bear with her two cubs. The sight was irresistible. Dad rolled down the window of the car and leaned far out to get the closest and best shot of this homey trio. Before we could bat an eye, or Dad a shutter, the mother bear reared up on her hind legs and strode towards the car uttering a ferocious roar. The movie camera recorded a huge, blurry head looming in the lens, tiny bright eyes and juicy, open chops in the last frame.

[34]

CHAPTER EIGHT

WHILE Mother was busy with her horse business, Dad acquired a hobby of his own. He started a dairy farm, designed to provide the newly-built Ball Memorial Hospital with fresh milk daily. The large farm consisted of nearly one-thousand acres of rolling land and woods in Eaton, where Aunt Mildred and Uncle Will Nottingham lived. Under the supervision of the superintendent of Ball Hospital, the latest equipment was installed and the utmost sanitary conditions maintained to keep the milk certified and ready for pasteurization at the hospital. The newest invention for milking was the DeLaval machinery, which milked the cows automatically and separated the cream at the same time. Dad was very proud of his herd of Guernseys and Jerseys, famous for their excellent quality of milk and rich cream.

On the property Dad bought were several houses which had been abandoned years before and were in a ramshackle condition. Dad decided to remodel them for tenants who would work on the farm and manage the dairy. One of these buildings was an old, square, brick house which once had been a school. During the renovation, several workmen were busy with their pickaxes hacking at the dirt floor to level and clean away the debris of the ages. Something glinted in the dirt and a workman put down his pickaxe to scrape the surface with his hand. He uncovered a large tin box filled with dynamite! One whack of the axe would have brought the house down with all the workers! More searching revealed a cache of nitro and ammunition in several boxes.

Could this have been where Gerald Chapman and his gang had hidden in the early 1920's? Chapman was Indiana's most wanted criminal, wanted for bank robbery and murder. He was a fugitive for several years before he was finally caught and hanged. Here was evidence that he had used this land as his hiding place.

Farther down the road in low-lying land beside a rushing creek was another farmhouse. The location was so attractive my parents decided to make it a lodge for guests and a summer retreat for parties and picnics. As workmen cleaned out the debris to remodel the house, they found two skeletons in the storm cellar beneath the house. Years before, the farmer and his wife who lived there had mysteriously disappeared. Circumstantial evidence now indicated the Chapman gang had murdered the couple in order to have a convenient location for their hideout. The house was far from the road, and the creek, winding in and out of the woods for miles, made an access to the house that was a perfect camouflage for the fugitives.

Money, bonds and jewelry stolen from banks was presumed burried by the gang in this area. After Gerald Chapman was hung for his

[35]

crimes, speculation arose that some members of his gang, still at large, knew of the hiding places. Posing as tramps (tramps were a common sight all over the country during the Great Depression) they may have wandered back via the creek and Mississinewa River to retrieve the loot. Nothing had ever been proved, and the mystery still existed.

There was the exciting prospect of finding buried treasure near the lodge. Jane Hitchcock and I spent many days around the banks of the creek, fruitlessly digging for the treasure in likely spots with large kitchen spoons!

Jane and I were lifetime friends. She became my cousin through the marriage of my Uncle Chauncey and her mother, Ethel. She was a bridesmaid in my first marriage and matron of honor in my second.

———◆◉◆———

Janice Ball and I were as close as sisters. She was the last child born in the second generation of the five Ball brothers, and I was the first born of the third generation. She is three years older than I, but we were inseparable. The playroom on the top floor of her home was enormous and contained all the playthings of the three children of Uncle Ed and Aunt Bertha. The center of the hardwood floor made a fine place for group games, bicycling or skating when the weather was inclement. Adelia (who was always called Diggy) had a marvelous doll house, as did Janice. These houses were larger and more elaborate than mine and were in the English Tudor style.

One corner of the room was used for a grocery store, child's size, into which one could walk to a counter and "purchase" cans of goods displayed on the shelf behind it. Many large, stuffed animals, such as bears and elephants, were mounted on wheels to be ridden. Dolls of all sizes filled a cabinet with glass doors to protect them from dust. It was a wonderful room, and Janice and I played there for years, mainly with the doll houses.

Outside in the yard was a playhouse with a railed porch running around three sides of it. There were two rooms downstairs, with a little curved staircase leading up to a tiny bedroom. The furnishings were quaint and complete. Janice and I often played "house" there. I also had a playhouse at home. It had a front porch, and the one room inside was decorated with Wizard of Oz wallpaper. This house became a "club house" later on for my friends and a retreat for reading during rainy weather. When I grew too large for it, the house was moved to the farm where it became the wellhouse. Years later the furniture stored in its attic was used by my own daughters in their playroom.

———◆◉◆———

Although ours was just the third house to be built in the new Westwood Addition, it wasn't long before houses began springing up in all directions. Streets were added to accommodate the residents, and soon there were quite a few children of my age to play with. The girls formed a separate group from the boys, but we were all good friends. When we played "war" or "pirates", we teamed up on our bicycles and rode around the neighborhood in pursuit of each other. Our weapons were large, ripe tomatoes, which we threw with deadly accuracy when an "enemy" was spotted.

My Uncle Chauncey worked for awhile at Muncie's Woolworth Ten Cent Store. Collecting the broken jewelry that otherwise would have been thrown away by the management, he gave me "diamond" necklaces, jeweled bracelets and earrings in a decorated tin box, which became our pirate treasure. The game was to hide it from the boys. They would search for it, and the girls would work hard to protect it. Once, when the boys found the treasured box hidden in the play house, the girls surrounded the house, and with the garden hose turned on full force, sprayed at the windows and door so the boys couldn't escape. The boys finally surrendered and gave us back our treasure. We won the fight, and I hid the box again in one of the stone pillars marking our driveway entrance. The pillars had lights inside to illuminate the driveway at night. I climbed to the top of one and placed the box securely inside the niche containing the light fixture. But someone found the hiding place, and to our dismay, the box disappeared forever.

The stone pillars stood at the four corners of our property, which was quite extensive. At the end of the road was a farm where my best friend, June Jack, lived. We were "chums" until I moved away from Muncie. June and I played together constantly. If Mother told me I couldn't go to her house, for some reason, I would run to the end of the apple orchard, climb the stone pillar and whistle loudly to attract June's attention. We set up a musical code of signals for each other. One tune asked if she could come and play at my house; her answer would whistle back, yes or no, as the case might be. In this manner, we would play together at each other's homes, almost daily. The Jacks didn't have a telephone, and I was fascinated by the outhouse which served as their bathroom. I was secretly disappointed when a real bathroom was installed in their home.

We often played with Marshall Hanley and Jimmy Hilty who also lived in Westwood. Frank and Emily Hanley, Marshall's parents, were good friends of my parents, and their home was the second one to be built in Westwood. One day the boys suggested we have a mock wedding and invite all the children of our neighborhood to the party at our house. Marshall and I would be the bride and groom, Jimmy, the preacher, and June, the maid of honor. We thought this was a fine idea and made all the arrangements.

[37]

The morning of the "wedding" June and I picked a large basket of wild violets, which grew in our yard. Alas, the fresh, purple faces so happy in the grass, became sad and wilted long before the event, but we made them into bouquets anyway. Marshall and I had fine outfits to wear. He had borrowed his father's top hat and wore a dark suit, gloves and even carried a cane to add to the general effect. Of course, I had a dainty white dress, long and filmy, topped by a lace veil of some sort, which June fastened to my head by weaving a coronet of the violets together on a ribbon. June, Marshall and I dressed in our finery in Dad's bedroom giggling and whispering all the while. Finally we marched together down the stairs and outdoors where Jimmy Hilty, in his long tails drooping to the ground, stood waiting holding the Bible. The ceremony was solemn with the onlookers duly impressed, and afterwards we all enjoyed lemonade and cookies served by Celesta, our beloved cook. At the end of the party, I threw my dead violet bouquet to June, and Marshall and I took off on our bicycles, pretending to leave for our honeymoon.

Years later, Marshall and I often laughed about that day, and referred to each other as our first wife or husband. He became a successful lawyer and won elections in local and state offices as a Democrat. Jimmy Hilty was the first of my friends to be killed in World War II.

Jane Hitchcock

Lucina, Janice Ball and June Jack

Orchard Lawn Dairy Farm, Eaton, Indiana

[39]

*June Jack and Lucina
in "Spirit of St. Louis"
made by June's brother Louis*

*Lucina and Hudson
on their bikes*

Playing pirates

Living Room in Westwood House [40]

CHAPTER NINE

M Y musical education was enriched in many ways, but largely by the Skinner organ installed in our house in Westwood. My parents had planned for the organ as they built the house by making a deep recess at the end of the living room, open to the ceiling from a half-wall, against which stood the organ. The sound from the pipes below in the basement was allowed to flow freely up and into the living room through this open space. The organ room in the basement contained a mysterious collection of stainless steel and wood pipes, which filled the room to overflowing. The pipes ranged in size from the huge pillars of steel to tiny cylinders, and the arrangement and quantity of them were fascinating. It was a forbidden area to enter, but when the technician arrived to tune or repair the organ, I loved to sneak in and watch quietly as he removed the pipes to clean or adjust them.

The organ itself had a beautiful tone and powerful volume. There was also a player mechanism as the Ampico players on many pianos, which were very popular in those days for those who loved music but were unable to play the instrument themselves. We had a large library of music rolls to choose from, which were stacked on top of the organ in alphabetical order so we could quickly choose our selections from symphonies or operatic arias to all kinds of classical compositions.

I took a few lessons on the organ and learned how to manipulate the foot pedals and the double manual, but I did not enjoy the feel of the keys and the automatic windy tones blown out at the touch. I preferred making my own tones with the gradations of color possible by just the finger's touch on the piano.

One of the most popular ways to entertain guests was to put on a roll. When my friends came to play I would ask what they would like to do. Almost invariably they would say, "Let's play the organ." The time was spent quickly as we sat two or three at a time on the long bench, choosing sides to select the stops to control or which roll to play next. I learned to sing every note of the many selections, but the composers meant very little to me then. When I went to college, I had a difficult time matching the correct composer to his work, though I knew the composition thoroughly. I baffled my teachers as they couldn't understand how I knew the themes so well, but couldn't tell the difference between a Brahms or Tchaikovsky symphony, for example.

Mother and Dad had many parties, and the house would ring with music. I often fell asleep to Mother singing operatic arias for the guests, such as "Un Bel Die" or the lovely Lieder of Grieg or Hugo Wolfe. Dad played the violin at such times and Mother accompanied him on the piano. Groups would form around the piano, and all would sing, but

Dad's tenor voice adding the harmony would rise above them all. It was a beautiful way to fall asleep, the laughter and gaiety downstairs making me feel secure and happy.

When artists came to Muncie on concert tours, we would often give parties after their performances. Sometimes the artists stayed with us instead of at the mediocre hotel downtown, and became good friends as a result. Lawrence Tibbett, Jeanette MacDonald, Arthur Rubenstein, Lauritz Melchior and his wife "Kleinchen," were a few of the celebrated people who became friends of the family.

One evening the Don Cossack Chorus from Russia gave a concert at the Ball Auditorium followed by a party at our house. I was sick with a cold at the time and was disappointed not to be able to hear them sing, but Mother promised to wake me when everyone arrived. The next morning I cried and accused Mother for not waking me and letting me miss the party. Mother said she did everything but hit me over the head, but I just wouldn't wake up. I understand the house rocked and reverberated with the noise the Russians made after a few vodkas (which they must have brought along with them since during Prohibition no liquor was served in our house.) They sang mightily, pulled up the rugs and did their famous Russian dances, entertaining everyone with their exuberance until four in the morning.

The Kitzelmans were a prominent family in Muncie, famous for their invention of the steel wire chain-link fences, which soon wrapped themselves around America. The three brothers lived in mansions surrounded by acres of woods and gardens. One of the homes, on University Avenue, had a swimming pool the size of an ordinary lake with a fountain that "played" in the changing colors at night. At that time fountains that changed motion and colors rhythmically were quite novel and must have cost a fortune to install. A.L. Kitzelman took such pleasure from his beautiful fountain that he would sit at the window with a remote control panel, changing the patterns as well as the color combinations. Everyone in Muncie enjoyed the rainbow of water, and many cars would line up along the avenue in the summer evenings to watch the show.

The Kitzelman homes were, of course, fenced in by Kitzelman fences. So there was no way to trespass and use the pool or other areas without an invitation. They lived rather secluded lives, not mixing too freely with the citizenry of the town.

Albo, the son of A.L. Kitzelman, had a brilliant and creative mind but a strange, introverted personality. Once he asked Mother if he could come to our house and use the organ for the compositions he was creating. He came day after day, barefooted and dressed in rag-tag

[42]

clothes, playing strange chords and melodies until the dissonance drove everyone mad. Mother finally had to ask him please, not to play any more.

In the turret of their home on University Avenue was an observatory which Albo had built himself so he could study the stars and the heavens at night. When "Bo" was in his twenties, he suddenly disappeared from Muncie. We heard he had gone west and joined The House of David, a bearded and barefoot cult. We never heard of him again.

"Bo's" brother, Donald, was another strange person. He thought up very unusual games to play when he was a child. One of his favorite occupations was to dress in ragged, dirty clothes and walk to one of the restaurants in the neighborhood. He would stand outside, pressing his rather wet nose against the window, looking with longing, hungry eyes at the food displayed there until the owner, unable to resist the sad urchin's face, would invite him in for a free meal in the kitchen. Donald did this every day for awhile, but one day a customer recognized him and told the owner who he was. The owner, outraged, phoned his mother, whereupon she sent her chauffeur to fetch him.

Marjorie, his sister, was also a character. She was very intelligent but lived a harem-scarem type of life. Her dare devil "living for kicks" attitude steered her into alcohol and drugs. Once she was flying an open cockpit, two-seated bi-plane when she discovered she couldn't pull the control stick back because a seat cushion was jammed between the seat and the stick in the front cockpit. She calmly unbuckled her seat belt, climbed onto the wing and walked on it to remove the cushion in the front cockpit. Throwing the cushion from the plane, she then climbed back to her rear seat and came down for the landing. Her husbands were colorful characters also. One of them was a rancher in Texas who herded sheep with his airplane — another, a muscle man. Marjorie's life ended prematurely in Mexico where she had lived in Taxco after her last divorce. She died in 1948.

Faye Kitzelman's daughter, Alice, looked like an angel with her creamy skin and long blond curls. She completed this angelic vision by learning to play the harp and was becoming quite accomplished when during her eighth year, she was stricken with polio and died. It was a terrible blow to her family, causing them to retreat even more to the seclusion of their homes. The tragedy brought out everyone's sympathies. Mother rushed to offer condolences and begged to do something to help. Surprisingly, Edna Kitzelman said Mother could help. The harp, standing forlorn and idle in the corner of the living room was a constant reminder of Alice, and the sight of it brought stabbing pains of grief to everyone in the family. She asked if Mother would please keep the harp until a time when the family could accept the sight of it again. The harp was moved to our house adding quite a nice tone to the decor.

[43]

Naturally, a windfall like this had to be taken advantage of. It was unthinkable for an instrument to remain unused in our household. As in the play "You Can't Take It With You" I began lessons on the harp. I was ten at the time, and Alice Singer was my teacher. I was very lucky to have such an accomplished and famous harpist living right there in Muncie. Alice was the first woman ever to win the coveted Grand Prix of Paris for her excellence on the harp. She also was very beautiful with a personality to match, and I loved her. Her father owned the Singer Bakery, which made wonderful bread and other delicious baked goods. For many years I thought all the bread in America was made by Singer.

I studied for two years, and then the fateful day arrived when Mrs. Kitzelman asked for her harp to be returned. I had to make a big decision then as Mother was willing to buy me a harp of my own. Although I loved playing the harp, I knew it would be a big investment for my parents and some sacrifice for me. Alice had frightened me by saying that, if I was serious about playing the instrument, I would have to be faithful to my practicing every day as the callouses on my fingers had to be developed, and even one day without practice could be a severe drawback. She also discouraged any kind of sports — golf, tennis and horseback riding — which could injure the hands or cause inflexibility of the fingers, as well as interfere with those precious callouses! I felt I could not maintain such a dedication for a lifetime. My preference was really the piano after all. So I said goodby to the harp, somewhat reluctantly, and it was returned to the Kitzelman's where it still stands unused in the corner of the living room. After the death of the Kitzelmans, the house was bequeathed to the Music Department of Ball State University. The furnishings have remained in the house, and the Music Department uses the facilities for recitals and workshops.

Brady, Dorothy Ann and Barbara Ball

Lucina and Hudson in Paris before flight to London, 1932

CHAPTER TEN

MY cousin Brady was the son of Arthur Ball and his wife, Frances. He was three years my junior. The family also lived in Westwood, and we attended the same school and often played together. We were driven to Mrs. Emerson's, usually by Arthur's chauffeur. Brady and I were good friends. He was a handsome, quiet boy with large, dreamy eyes, which expressed a sadness that seemed to reflect visions of a premonition of his future.

When Brady was three years old, he had a serious mastoid operation, and from then on his health was never robust. To give his family a healthier outdoor life, Arthur bought a ranch in Texas for winter vacations.

One winter, five years later, Brady again suffered a double mastoid, which developed into spinal meningitis. In a desperate attempt to save him, a double scalp operation was performed. The entire top of his head was removed in order to drain off the infection, but the effort failed and Brady died. His baby sister, Dorothy Anne, just two years old, was hospitalized at the same time with mastoiditis. She did not die, but after her operation, became totally deaf.

I will never forget the sadness of this double tragedy. When the family returned to Muncie, there was a funeral service for Brady in their home. The picture of this beautiful child, dressed in his sailor suit, knee socks and shiny black shoes, hands folded across his chest and head completely bandaged, turban style, is as vivid today as it was when I was eleven.

Dorothy Anne has lived her life in silence, but she learned to speak and lip read from an excellent tutor who lived with the family for many years. Dorothy Anne, naturally shy, has a brilliant mind. She graduated cum laude from Radcliffe College, married, and has two daughters. The family lives in Maryland where her husband works for the Government.

Thankfully, her sister Barbara, who was six-years-old at the time, escaped the illness that killed her brother and left Dorothy Anne deaf. Another son, George, was born about two years later.

———◄◉►———

On March 4, 1929, we went to Washington, D.C. to attend the Inauguration of President Hoover. I remember the excitement of the crowd lining the streets to watch the parade, the fascinating Smithsonian Institute and other historical sites. Before the election, we Republicans taunted the Democrats with nasty slogans, as they did to us. The children in Westwood rode around in groups on bicycles chanting, "Hoover, Hoover, he's the man! Put Al Smith in the garbage

[47]

can!" We really felt our slogan influenced his election!

In June, after his third birthday, Hudson became ill with a mastoid infection. It is understandable that Mother, Dad and I were paralyzed with fear for him, since it happened not long after Brady's death and he was the same age as Brady when Brady had his first operation.

Hudson also underwent a mastoidectomy and became thin and wan afterwards. The doctor advised my parents to "follow the sun" where Hudson could be out of doors and recuperate without the danger of reinfection from viruses, which invariably plagued us in the cold winter months.

To help Husdon regain his strength, we rented a cottage at Klinger Lake in Michigan for the month of August. The Crapo family, friends of my parents, suggested the idea, as they owned a cottage there and thought we would enjoy it. Mildred and Fred had three daughters, Betty, Janet, and Ann, about the ages of Hudson and myself. Everyone enjoyed the swimming, picnicking and partying except for Mother who found it an endless chore of "pick-up" and "clean-up." Never having learned to swim and terrified of water she was constantly alert for dangers to the rest of us when we put a foot into the lake. She decided summer cottage living was not her cup of tea.

The lake, however, was one of the loveliest that I remember, with a most unusual sandy bottom. There was not a single weed growing from its floor. The lake was also very shallow. I could walk far out into the water before it reached my waist. We had a canoe and a row boat, which I learned to manage. I did not learn to swim there, because the water was too shallow. My eleventh birthday was spent enjoying a big picnic with the Crapo and Hanley families.

———————◆◇◆———————

A new school had been built across the campus from Ball State Teachers College. It was to be an experimental school where the students of Ball College could train and learn from teaching in a real school as they earned their degrees. Named for the President of the College, Dr. Burris, it became my school as it was opened for classes, late in September, 1929.

The suburb of Westwood is located adjacent to the expanding campus from Ball State which meant Burris School was not too far from home. In nice weather I liked to walk home after school, although I was always driven to school in the morning. Our sixth grade class was the first to enter Burris.

School spirit ran high at Burris. There was plenty of pride in this institution, being the newest and most advanced in teaching techniques in town. The transition after five years of the small one-room school

[48]

houses at Mrs. Emerson's to the large new school building where our class had a room for itself, was an exciting experience.

I was sorry when our family had to leave for Florida right after Christmas to spend the rest of the winter there for Hudson's health, but the doctor had recommended a better climate for him.

We rented a Spanish style, stucco bungalow in St. Petersburg, Florida. Enrolled in the junior high school, I was bewildered by the huge four-story building and maze of rooms bustling with a thousand students. It was hard to find my way from class to class at first and everyone seemed too busy or unconcerned to help a newcomer. Because I was from the North, I was dubbed, "you Yankee." No one bothered to learn my name, and I was shunned by my classmates. Needless to say, I was not very happy in the unfriendly atmosphere. In addition, Janice, who had come down with us to be a companion for me didn't have to go to school! A tutor came along with her, and they sat under the palm trees leisurely doing lessons while I ran up and down stairs in the Florida heat, trying to get to my next class on time. The nicest thing about those days was the lunch hour where I could sit on the grass beside a lovely calm lake in front of the school and feed the swans with crumbs from my sandwiches. I remember nothing about the teachers, classmates or anything I learned there.

It rained a good deal. I remember we laughed about St. Petersburg being called "The Sunshine City" and wondered how it ever deserved the name. Our house was infested with spiders. Their bodies were the size of silver dollars, with legs so long and hairy the insects were at least six inches across. They perched on the ceiling, often above my bed, and dropped down on my sheet at night, crawling around and giving me nightmares.

Once I was about to run water in the tub for a bath and looked down to see one of the monsters in the bathtub. I shrieked and called Mother, who decided to drown it with the hot water from the tub. I perched safely on the wash basin and watched as she opened a floodgate of water to immerse the spider. At the first touch of water on its leg, the creature jumped with lighting speed out of the tub and landed beside me on the basin! I responded with lightning speed also — tearing out of the bathroom not to return for some time.

There was a patio outside the dining room of the house. It was enclosed by a high wall on top of which were embedded broken bits of colored glass to help deter possible intruders. Hudson played in the patio every day, stark naked, enjoying the sun when it shone, and began to take on a livelier, healthier aspect. Janice and I loved to dress him in all sorts of costumes, which we made out of anything we could find. We

[49]

turned him into a monk and tied a soap dish on his head. We dressed him as a little old lady with scraps of our clothes. A clown, a pirate, or any character we could think of, became his "outfit" for the day. We photographed him in each costume with our Brownie camera, and had quite a collection of quaint pictures by the end of the winter. He loved the attention and would stand quietly as we dressed and photographed him to our satisfaction.

Dad would fly down to be with us on weekends when he could get away from work at the office. When he arrived, our lives would accelerate with great speed. Not one to sit idle, he would have us up and going every minute, thinking of places to see and things to do faster than we could do them. In all his life, I never knew him to sit through a meal. He would jump up from the table to make a telephone call, run to get papers or letters to read to us, or just leave "to see about something." His witty remarks about everything created a hilarious party mood, and he often behaved outrageously "showing off" and sending us into gales of laughter.

Dad used language of his own invention, making up special words to stand for things only we understood. "Gietsadoot" or "Giebudge" meant wonderful. "Gieb" was good and "Heebeebah" was something deplorable. We spoke Pig Latin or "lecrect sanguage" (exchanging the first letters of words.) Dad pushed our energies to the limit. None of us could keep up with him, and we would beg for a moment to catch our breath before following him on yet another wild romp. Helen Hutzel once said of Dad, "When I go to heaven I want to go on Bill Ball's coattails to be sure I'll get in."

We explored the lovely beaches near the area. They were not heavily populated as they are now but rather deserted and very clean, with pure white sand. The city of St. Petersburg seemed to be a haven for very old people. Ancient forms sat side-by-side in wicker rocking chairs on the long verandas of the hotels, canes near at hand. Some of the more active ones bowled on the greens. There were many of these greens around the town, the game being very popular with the elderly. We scarcely saw young people or children, but there had to be some as my school, at least, was full of them.

We rented horses and rode through the woods and trails on the outskirts of St. Petersburg. They were such nice five-gaited horses that Mother and Dad bought two from the stable owner and had them sent back to Muncie when we left for home. These were our first horses, and for several years Mother, Dad and I made a trio on Golden Glow, Gay Defender and Billy.

At last the winter was over, and we were able to return home. Hudson's health had improved. It had been worth the effort to leave our friends and activities at home for the healing sunshine of Florida.

[50]

CHAPTER ELEVEN

ROBERTA Franklin and Mother were friends as they grew up in Muncie. They both married the same year, and Roberta's daughter, Betty Brown, was born a month before I was. After a year of married life, the Browns moved to Wakefield, Mass., seldom returning to Muncie. There were photographs of Betty and me lying side by side in our carriages, Mother and Roberta meeting to chat as they wheeled us on their morning walks. We looked like two peas in a pod, and I often asked Mother whatever became of that baby?

In the summer of 1930, Betty returned for a visit with her grandparents Franklin, the first time we had met since infancy. We discovered both of us had been curious about our baby pictures and became fast friends immediately. Betty was even shorter than I, a dainty, diminutive blond with sparkling eyes. We enjoyed each other's company so much she was invited to join us on an adventure in August when we took a freighter trip for two weeks on the Great Lakes. Hudson also was allowed to have a friend of his along — so Bud Brown (no relation to Betty Brown) completed our group.

We took a train to Toledo, Ohio and boarded the S.S. *James Davidson*, the largest of the Tomlinson Fleet, which plied cargoes of wheat and coal from Toledo or Cleveland to Port William and Port Arthur in Canada. The *James Davidson* could have made ocean voyages as it was constructed for the heaviest of seas. The fleet was owned by my Uncle George Ball as one of his private investments, and as family members, we were permitted to travel on the line, which ordinarily did not take passengers.

We boarded the ship in Toledo by climbing the ladder which hung over the side, dangling and jerking with every step on the rungs. It was a scary experience, but the crew helped to haul us over the side to the deck, and we were glad we had conducted ourselves as true seamen and didn't fall below into the oily waters of Lake Erie.

At the bow end of the ship was the super-structure containing three or four decks above the water line with very luxurious quarters for the captain and his guests. On the highest and smallest deck was the navigation room and the captain's private quarters. Below were the capacious staterooms and baths, where our family lived for the two-week voyage. The deck below us contained a long dining room and galley where great quantities of delicious, gourmet food were prepared. The officers had their cabins on this same main deck. At the stern of the ship was a smaller structure which housed the rest of the crew. The flat surface of the deck between the bow and the stern must have been a block long. Huge storage bins occupied all of the space, which opened up to the bottom of the ship and held the cargo. Coal had already been

[51]

loaded on, and the hatches were closed and bolted down when we boarded.

There was no protective railing around the deck, only a thick wire cable stretching along the open sides. I marveled the crew was not swept off the slippery deck in rough weather. We, of course, were not allowed to play near the open sides of the ship, but under supervision, could walk on the center hatches.

Betty and I shared one of the large staterooms, which doubled as a living room. The room was fitted with a couch, desk, a few comfortable chairs and twin beds on the far side of the cabin near the bathroom. Mother and Dad's stateroom was like ours on the port side, and between the rooms was a well equipped, nicely furnished library occupied by Bud and Hudson. Around the deck was a narrow, open passageway which we could use to pass around the entire superstructure outdoors, with ladders leading to the other decks. There was also an inside staircase.

We were joined at mealtime by the captain and his top officers. When a loud gong sounded in the galley, we descended to the dining room and sat at a long narrow table which could have accommodated twenty people easily, but there were usually only ten or twelve of us for the sumptuous meals.

We slipped along on the calm waters, slowly floating up Lake Erie, and on the first night, passed Detroit after dark. The lights of the city twinkled like millions of stars fallen to earth. As we continued north, land faded further from sight until we approached the passageway between Lakes Huron, Michigan and Superior. Here lies Sault St. Marie. It was a thrill to be aboard a ship passing through the great locks. We waited in one lock while the water rose and raised the ship to the level of the higher Lake Superior, permitting us to enter smoothly through the passageway. The operation took perhaps an hour, but it was absorbing to observe from the deck of the ship while interested tourists watched us from the high walls built up on either side of the locks.

For the first few days "at sea" the lake was a mill pond, hot and stuffy, and the trip became a little dull for us children, confined to quarters as we were. Once the Captain allowed us to watch the navigation of the ship, but we generally played cards or made up games in our large living-bedroom of the ship. Betty and I, just about twelve years old, were beginning to think about boys romantically. We goggled at the crewmen and began to imagine that one of them was responding to our giggles and leers. His cabin was directly below ours, and we hung over the rail of the passageway outside listening to his radio playing the latest dance music after he was off duty in the evening. He even turned it up a little louder for our benefit. We called him. D. and C. because his hair was dark and curly. We thought him quite handsome and very macho in his deck clothes, and we made up excuses to be on deck when he was working. Time passed more quickly when there was something to whisper about. But I wanted more excitement and began to wish for rough weather to liven things up. I wanted to feel motion on the ship. So far it was so calm we could have been sitting in port.

I only had wished for enough roughness to feel a nice rocking of the ship. What happened was far more violent. A storm came up on Lake Superior with wind and waves that battered us to and fro frantically. We could only lie in bed and hang on.

Lake Superior is enormous, and we were out of sight of land for several days, huge waves engulfing the flat mid-section of the ship. We rolled, pitched and agonized in the frenzy of the storm. We could have been on the ocean for the size of the angry waves and green-black, ugly color of the churning water. Lightning and thunder roared above the whistling wind, and frankly, we were more than a little nervous. But in two or three days, the storm went on its way, leaving us feeling frail and woozy. We were grateful for the steady return of the ship's motion under our feet, and I was careful not to make any more wishes.

At the end of the first week we arrived at Duluth, Minnesota, where we docked for half a day to unload our cargo of coal. We left the ship to see the city and have lunch with friends of my parents.

Late in the afternoon, we proceeded to Port William and Port Arthur with open hatches ready to receive grain for our return trip. It was interesting to watch the crew hosing and cleaning out the holds in preparation for the grain shipment. At the Ports, the grain was blown through the hatches from large machines on the docks. One after another hold was filled with the grain, and dust rose in clouds from the pressure.

When we were underway once more, and before the hatches were closed to keep the wheat dry and safe in the holds, Hudson and Bud began to play with the piles of grain heaped up like sand in the bins. It was a temptation Betty and I could not resist. So we joined the boys in their game of jumping into the bins and playing in the "sand piles." It was fun for awhile. The crew looked on, laughing as we jumped in and out, sinking down deep into the grain nicely warmed by the sun.

Dust was stirred up, and I began to feel the familiar heaviness in my chest after a few minutes. It didn't take long before I had a strong, allergic reaction to this caper. I was red-eyed and asthmatic, with red and swollen arms and legs where the grain had scratched my skin. I was glad when the hatches were closed, and I could no longer look at the tempting sea of wheat, but it took two or three days for my wheezing and sneezing to stop.

[53]

I will never forget the banquet served when I had my birthday on board. It came almost at the end of the trip and doubled as a farewell party. The food was even more elegant and special than usual. The surprise at dessert was a beautifully decorated cake and a carved ice block holding the ice cream. Serpentines and balloons decorated the ceiling. I couldn't believe such elegance could exist on a coal freighter!

We were sorry to arrive at the port of Cleveland. I have always wanted to return and do it again, but never have, although Dad took the same trip with a group of men the next summer and had a marvelous time.

CHAPTER TWELVE

BEFORE leaving on our freighter trip in the summer of 1930, I had my first camp experience at Camp Sing-a-Long near Cambridge City, Indiana. I had a happy two weeks and was sorry to leave the friendly group. It was a relaxed, unregimented atmosphere, and I also learned to swim there. The camp is under the aegis of the Y.W.C.A. and generously supported by the Ball Brothers Foundation.

Having had a taste of camp life, my parents thought I would like to go to a camp farther away from home. They chose the Joy Camp in Hazelhurst, Wisconsin. I spent a month there the following summer of 1931. Although the canoe trips were fun, and camping overnight in the woods was a new experience, I did not like it. I missed our own horses. I never liked hacking on trails on inferior horses or the regime of craft and sport classes. We were forced to swim in the icy lake every morning when the bell tolled to awaken us at six a.m. and to wear uniforms (white middy blouses and bloomers!) Frankly, I was a trifle homesick and couldn't wait to return home to my own horses and piano.

The campfires at night were fun. Once a week we had a picnic supper around the camp fire, singing songs, toasting marshmallows and listening to the counselor tell stories of Indian legends. Later, when the fire was down to embers and the stars were bright, we spread blankets on the grassy slope, lay on our backs and studied the constellations while the counselor told us how to find them. We learned the myths that grew up about the Big and Little Dippers, Cassiopeia, Orion and others as we gazed upward, awed by the immense heaven. We learned to tell the difference between the planets and the stars, and from this experience I have been fascinated by astronomy ever since.

I also loved walking through the dense woods with the heavy scent of pine from the tall trees, our feet crunching on the thick blanket of crushed brown needles. It was a gorgeous spot, and the lake was beautiful, but I never wanted to go back to any camp again.

[54]

CHAPTER THIRTEEN

AN experience which greatly influenced my future interests was our first trip to Europe in 1932. Dad had business in London, and wanting us all to be together, decided to allow Hudson and me to miss the first two months of the school year, two important grades for us, Hudson's first, and my eighth. We left home the last of August and returned on November sixth.

Dad had planned the itinerary to include an air flight over the English Channel. He thought one trip on the Channel's turbulent water sufficient, and booked us on British Airways for our return to London from Paris. British Airways was the first to initiate commercial flights over the Channel, beginning that summer of 1932. Dad always had to try anything new, and the upcoming flight intrigued him. The plane was advertised as the largest plane in the world. Mother was a little intimidated by our impending flight. None of us had ever flown in a plane. So she decided to try the experience at home first.

Muncie had a small field which was used primarily for mail flights and stunt shows. Signs were posted advertising short flights for courageous neophytes reading "Thrills in the air! Take a ride with us for only $3.00 a half hour!" Clyde Shockley was well known in Muncie as the best pilot. So Mother made an appointment for him to take us up without the thrills. His plane was an open cockpit, two-seater, and only one of us could go at a time. Fear was not in my vocabulary then. I hopped in the cockpit when my turn came, and off we went. I was given a helmet and goggles to offset the wild wind created aloft and wasn't nervous at all until Clyde began to tip the plane over so I could see the ground better. I was sure I would fall out, even though I was well secured with the safety belt.

I was never afraid to fly until after World War II, and then I developed "airphobia," my fear increasing with each flight. It would seem the first trip by air in that open plane with one sputtering engine should have been the most dangerous, but for me, the bigger the plane, the harder they fall!

I'd like to digress and relate an episode which happened one Fourth of July in Muncie. There was always a large picnic supper at the Delaware Country Club with fireworks after dark. We looked forward to the date as one of the best times of the year. The children with their sparklers made a show of their own, looking like a thousand fireflies darting over the grass in the darkness.

One year we had a special treat in addition to the regular fireworks display. Clyde Shockley did a stunt performance in his plane over the club with a finale of fireworks shot from the plane. Excitement mounted as we watched the lighted plane dipping low over the trees, looping and then shooting straight up in the air to begin a dive. In an explosive finale, roman candles burst from the tail of the plane, showering gold like a comet. Then a horrible thing happened. Without warning, flames enveloped the plane and it began to fall! Screams filled the air around us as we watched in horror. Men ran to their cars and rushed to the scene. Suddenly, in the midst of the cries and confusion, a small white object was seen drifting downward. The sky, illuminated by the burning plane revealed Clyde falling safely in his parachute. As he later explained, when he lit the first roman candle he saw a flame at the tail of the plane and knew it might explode. So he jumped a moment before the explosion.

———————<◦●◦>———————

All of the diaries except two which I had kept since I was eight or nine have been lost. The one relating to my first trip to Europe is still among the memorabilia of scrap books and photograph albums. My childish thoughts and experiences are now helping me recapture the memories of fifty years ago.

The trip made an enormous impact on me. I discovered the varied cultures of the Europeans and the fascinating background of their history. Everything I saw contrasted greatly with our country — homes, dress, terrain, climate and languages. It was an experience which made a lasting impression, and I have loved travel and study of history and cultures ever since.

———————<◦●◦>———————

After a day-and-a-half train ride to Montreal, Canada, Dad left us as he continued on to Quebec to conduct some business. The next day was spent in Montreal sightseeing and shopping, and the following day, on September second, Mother, Hudson and I boarded the British liner *Duchess of Bedford* for our ocean voyage to Europe. I remember our luggage consisted of two large trunks along with hand luggage. Who would ever travel with a steamer and a wardrobe trunk today? But at that time it was the custom to travel with trunks. Porters were available everywhere to cart them, and transportation facilities accommodated all types of baggage with ease.

The band played on deck, and serpentines were thrown from the ship to the pier as the passengers waved goodbye to friends ashore. We slowly pulled away from the pier and made our way down the St. Lawrence River, viewing the lovely countryside on both river banks until we entered the Atlantic at the mouth of the river. When we passed Quebec, we watched as a lighter approached our ship with Dad on board. We hung over the side, hearts in our mouths, watching while Dad boarded our ship from the bouncing lighter, a difficult task with both vehicles in motion. Dad, inexperienced, had some difficulty managing the transfer, but at last was safely aboard.

[56]

During the voyage, I met Basil Griffith, a young British boy who was mad about ping pong. We played constantly, and I found I played very well. In the evening we dressed in our nicest evening clothes for dinner and dancing. I had quite a few partners to dance with besides Basil, my ping pong adversary. Basil was handsome, but "veddy Briddish." He also was quite arrogant and opinionated. He did not like Americans and told me so explicitly. He resented the licking the British took in the Revolutionary War, and we had daily arguments about which of our countries was superior. Basil insisted all the best inventions were discovered by the British, and I countered by reminding him of Edison's phonograph and light bulb, or Bell's telephone. "Why, they were invented by the English long before!" he retorted. This kind of silly argument grew angry and heated between us, but he never gave in — and neither did I! Constant companions, we parted as friendly enemies at the end of the voyage.

When the sea became rough and seasickness overcame me for awhile, I continued to play ping pong, determined to win games over this arrogant boy, until the roughness made the game impossible. Then there was nothing to do but bury under many blankets on the promenade deck, breathe in the fresh air and roll with the ship. It was very cold and very foggy. The foghorn sounded mournfully every few minutes for most of the journey. I now know the northern route to Scotland from Canada is frought with icebergs, and that we were in peril during the heavy storm and fog. At that time there was no radar to help protect the ships from collision with floes or other vessels, but we made our way safely through the heavy weather and arrived in Greenock, Scotland, September ninth.

The excitement of approaching Scotland at dawn was overwhelming. After a week of isolation at sea, the sight of land on the horizon was beautiful indeed. Mist rose through the colors of the sunrise around incredibly green, lush hills, with uneven coastline ducking in and out of coves. We anchored in a peaceful bay, and after the immigration and health officers checked our passports, were allowed to disembark on a chugging lighter. The rest of the passengers continued on to Liverpool, England.

The lighter was a ferry, plying to and from small islands off the coast. It was rather dirty and filled to overflowing with Scots on their way to other parts to begin their work day. They were chatting together in loud voices, and I couldn't understand a single word of their conversation. Wasn't this supposed to be an English speaking country? I squeezed myself between two gritty individuals, smelling strongly of fish. The man was muscular, sucking on a steaming pipe, his cap pulled low, his clothes dingy down to his muddy boots. The ample woman on my other side carried a basket covered with a paisley shawl with another tied

[57]

around her head and knotted under her chin. Her cheeks were bright red from the small purplish veins over her face. In fact, I noticed all the faces of the Scots had permanently red, chapped noses and cheeks. I learned this characteristic is caused by the out door life the Scots lead in the severe winter climate. They all looked remarkably healthy, sturdy and had a no-nonsense air about them.

Everything in Scotland and England seemed to be doll house size. I was amused by the tiny trains and low thatched homes. Even the telephone poles were in miniature compared to ours in America. I wondered if this was because they had to make everything small to fit into such a tiny country, or was it because they didn't believe in wasting material as we do by making everything oversize?

The castles were huge, however, and sprawled over the hilltops, the ruins towering over the villages below. My fascination for castles began in Scotland. The first ruin we explored was the birthplace of Mary, Queen of Scots, Linlithgow Castle, built in 1542. I wanted to stay forever, finding secret passages and dungeons and unearthing past history about these people. When we drove to Edinburg Castle, and the guide led us to Mary's apartments where her son, James I, was born, I felt immersed in the past. Mary's bedroom was sparsely furnished, but her bed was there, along with a little desk and a few wall hangings. The room was in a tall tower. As I looked out of the window to the moat surrounding the castle far below, and to the green rolling hills beyond, the guide told us that from this castle window Mary had lowered the baby James in a basket to waiting horsemen below. He was carried to safety and hidden by Boswell's men, as Mary feared for his life — the future king of Scotland and England. Her many enemies were constantly plotting against her.

As I listened to the story I felt very strange as though it was I who was lowering the basket. I actually could see the men waiting below to rescue the baby, and I felt, as in a dream, that I was Mary. I turned to the guide and almost in a whisper, said, "Can we go down the secret passage now under that tapestry?" I pointed to a corner of the wall across the room. The guide stared at me and asked, "Have you been here before?" He led us across the room, lifted the tapestry, and there was an old door leading down a small, dark stone staircase.

I came back to reality, amazed by my intuition. Since that day I have felt sure I must have been Mary, Queen of Scots in a previous incarnation. I have such a strong affinity for her, as though I had suffered her same experiences. When we went to England and saw the pedestal on which she stood and the axe that took off her head, I physically felt her pain, and tears ran down my cheeks.

I always have had a lively imagination, but my feelings for Mary go deeper than just mental images. The empathy is unnaturally strong. Although I have always said, laughingly, that I must be reincarnated from Mary, Queen of Scots, down deep I don't feel that casual about it.

———◦◄❖►◦———

We continued on our trip, passing from Scotland into England, driving through the lovely region of the English lakes. Dad had left us again to attend to business in London, and Mother, Hudson and I were under the expert care of a chauffeur-guide. One entire day was spent in Wordsworth's territory, visiting his home, Dover Cottage, and the graveyard where he was buried. We explored more castles as we made our way south past Lake Derwentwater, Ripon, Harrogate and York. The cathedrals were breathtaking, and the countryside was spectacular. The pastureland where sheep grazed peacefully was measured out by low stone walls, hundreds of years old, punctuating the picturesque beauty of the landscape. Everywhere flowers adorned the homes of the villagers. Roses seemed to be the favorite. Most often they were pruned in a special way to resemble tall trees and lined the paths to the front doors of the thatched-roofed cottages. English gardens are of two types. The formal gardens are restrained by precisely trimmed hedges of boxwood, sometimes painstakingly shaped into animal or bird forms. The country gardens have no plan. Flowers in a riot of color crowd together leaving no room for paths or grass.

Our leisurely sightseeing was abruptly halted when we received a quick-scram telegram from Dad in London telling us to come there immediately. The urgent message, we learned upon arrival, was to bring us to the city in time to see a show! Dad had bought tickets for the musical *The Cat and the Fiddle*, and we barely had time to wash our faces before hurrying to the theater.

While Dad was conducting his affairs in London, he met the private secretary of Lloyd George, then Prime Minister of England. His name was David Jones, and he offered to take Hudson and me to the London Zoo for the day. He arrived wearing a bowler hat and carrying a black umbrella, the costume of all "important" Britishers. He reminded us of Charlie Chaplin. We laughed and laughed as this delightful, funny man regaled us with a constant stream of hilarious stories. We rode to the Zoo in the front seat on the top of a double-deck bus where we were frightened every second by the "wrong-way" traffic. We couldn't get used to driving on the left side of the road. Our hearts were in our mouths as oncoming cars seemed to plummet straight into us. At the end of the day, near our Hotel Metropole, Mr. Jones bought a bunch of violets from a lady on the street corner and presented them to me with a deep bow, doffing his bowler hat.

The last time I saw Mr. Jones was in 1934, two years later. He came to Indianapolis where I was attending Tudor Hall School, stopping be-

[59]

tween trains only long enough for tea and a visit with me. He was on his way to China on a diplomatic mission for Lloyd George. I met him at the station, embarrassed not to have time to entertain him properly and not to know a single place where afternoon tea would be served as an Englishman would expect it. I took him to Craig's Candy Shop, the nicest place I could think of that was open for snacks during the afternoon. He ordered his tea and frowned with distaste as it arrived in a paper bag to be dunked in hot water. We had a pleasant visit for as long as it took to drink a cup of tea. Then he was off by train to San Francisco, and on to China by ship.

Some time later we read in the paper that the first secretary of Lloyd George had been captured by Chinese bandits, tortured and killed. Our family wept for him, a most charming and intelligent man destroyed by senseless cruelty.

Our sightseeing in London continued, and one day we drove to Windsor Castle where I was enchanted by the Queen's doll house. I was amazed to see a tiny case of Ball fruit jars stored in its cellar beneath the kitchen. It was among the many miniature gifts which had been sent to Queen Mary from around the world.

From Windsor we drove on to Winchester for the night and the next day moved on to Southampton, viewing Stonehenge en route. At Southampton we crossed the Channel on the small ship Samaria landing at Le Havre, France, late in the afternoon.

We spent the night in Le Havre in a quaint, country inn, and the next day began our drive to Paris, stopping in Chinon to visit a family who had befriended Dad during the war. The Bertram family entertained us in their home at lunch, which included fifteen bottles of wine! There were a dozen of us around the table, and the noisy French conversation made our heads swim. I was shocked that even the smallest child was given wine to drink. We had been told not to drink the water in France, but there wouldn't have been an opportunity in any case as no water was in sight.

After lunch Mr. Bertram showed us his fabulous collections — playing cards, fans, coins, stamps, antiques, wine bottles and chests. Each collection was worth a fortune. Like many of the French, the Bertrams became poor because of the war, and Mr. Bertram wanted to sell his collections. Dad bought the playing cards — over seventy decks from every country in the world and had them shipped to Uncle George for safe keeping until we returned home. But we never saw the cards again.

We enjoyed the company of the Bertrams, who spoke no English, and were glad for the opportunity to speak French in our awkward way.

We toured several chateaux with them as hosts and then drove on to Paris.

I must mention we were not enamoured of the food served to us throughout France. The national dish was civet d'hare. We were served this entree with great fanfare by the waiters, but were appalled by its appearance. A dark brown gravy covered a mass of lumpy meat, which turned out to be rabbit. The taste was not helped a bit by the looks of it. I fished out bones and scraps of "inedible" pieces and even extracted a morsel from my mouth with rabbit fur attached!

Paris was beautiful, and we had a delightful time seeing the sights. We stayed at the Hotel Cecilia right off the Arc de Triomphe, on Avenue MacMahon. The small hotel is still doing a good business today, no doubt due to the personal attention and home-like atmosphere which we found so comforting in a foreign land. The front door was locked every evening at nine, and one would ring the bell for the concierge to open the door after that hour. An elevator in the corner of the lobby was triangular in shape and held only one person at a time. Being a temperamental gadget, it ran only when it was in the mood. I preferred using the staircase, even though our rooms were on the third floor.

The furnishings were fine antiques throughout the hotel, and I was delighted with the grand piano in the living room, which I played at every opportunity. I was told Paderewski had played it when he stayed at the Cecilia. Just touching the instrument gave me a thrill.

We stayed in Paris for ten days and saw everything from the Louvre to the Folies Bergere. I was shocked by all the nude women in the Folies, who were for the most part fat and old, and we all thought the show was tired and dingy. But other sights were exciting — especially the Eiffel Tower. I was frightened riding in the trams that loaded seventy-five people at a time in the open steel cages then went straight up on wheeled tracks. On top of the tower, the view of Paris was spectacular, but we were woozy from the height. I never had the courage to take the trip to the top of the tower again on later visits to Paris.

After our stay in Paris, we rented a car and drove through France, passing through the battlefields which Dad remembered during the war. We saw the trenches, foundations of houses that had been blown up and shell holes everywhere along the roads in the country. We passed through Soissons, where Dad and Chauncey had met briefly in 1917, and Epernay in sad ruins. Another village had been completely blown away. Not a thing was left standing. I believe the village was called Fimes. At Rheims we entered the magnificent cathedral with half of the roof gone. The cathedral was undergoing repairs, and we were told the Germans had deliberately dropped a shell on it. Dad was very moved throughout the trip, and when we came to the rivers, the Marne and

Vesle, Dad wept openly, remembering the dreadful fighting at this spot. We spent the night at a hotel in Rheims, which had been occupied by German generals. The Kaiser had stayed in a house next door, and at the end of the war escaped and fled to Holland.

I had been excited about going to France. Having studied the language since the first grade, I felt competent and eager to try my French, but for the most part, as hard as I tried, the people turned up their noses at my efforts, pretending not to understand. I was disappointed in the country and its people. They were dirty and urinated in the streets unless they happened on the "pisoirs" stationed on every corner. Within these circular booths one could see almost everything anyway. The "walls" only covered a man from neck to knees. Unless there was a proper drainage for the sewage, a bed of straw filled the base. They reminded me of a stable but much dirtier.

<hr/>

We drove through Belgium and Luxembourg and crossed the Rhine River over a temporary bridge of boats to enter Cologne, Germany. The old bridge had been blown up during the war, and this makeshift one was a little shaky. Boats, all of the same size, had been strung together to support the roadway. As we drove further away from France, the countries became noticeably cleaner, and in Germany everything was as neat as a pin. Even the manure from horse droppings along the road was quickly swept up by the farmers. Realistically, they collected the fertilizer for their crops, but the Germans were innately clean and orderly. The country looked pristine, and the people wore tidy, spotless clothing. It was a welcome change from the grubbiness of France.

Our hotel in Cologne was an attractive inn overlooking the Rhine. At dinner, couples danced to the music of a very good band. I couldn't have been more surprised when a boy about my age approached our table, clicked his heels together and indicated he wanted to dance with me. We had a good time, in spite of the language barrier, and danced several times.

The next morning before we left Cologne, Dad went to the barber shop. He told us five boys had followed him into the shop to ask about me, my age, and why we went to bed so early as they all had wanted to dance! I have never been so popular, before or since.

Reading the pages in my diary, I have remembered many more details about the trip. I recall the attitude of the people and how they reacted to us, as Americans. Some of our waiters were surly and insolent and gave us poor service. Others were curious to meet Americans, and if they could speak English, were quick to tell us of Germany's superiority. I quote from my diary one comment relevant to the situation in Germany at that time.

"October 10, 1932, One óf the men at our hotel last night said the world turned on Germany and mostly it was the Jews and Roman Catholics. He also said, 'The last war was for money, but it certainly would not be the last war. It would be another religious war like all the rest.' Times are terrible!"

We drove to Heidelburg, which I loved. The quaintness and the castle on top of the hill fascinated me as usual. But I will always remember the castle in Nürmburg. It was a museum filled with a gruesome collection of instruments of torture used in the Middle Ages. I was horrified to see the chairs full of nails, stretchers on which people were laid and pulled apart and instruments to extract tongues and finger nails. There were bone crushers and iron maidens, which looked like mummy cases, the insides filled with spikes in strategic places. When a person was placed inside and the door slammed shut, the spikes would run clear through the body.

I particularly remember one prison cell in the dungeon. With only a slit of a window near the ceiling, light scarcely penetrated. At the darkest corner, and only seen with the guide's torch, there was a stone, part of the wall, near the floor. It was worn shiny and smooth with a depression slightly larger than the shape of a human tongue. Apparently a trickle of water penetrated from some source, and the prisoners, desperate for water, found the dampness and licked the stone. How many tongues must have licked that place to cause such an indentation!

On another side of the cell was a stone ledge, less than a foot wide and a foot higher than the floor. Above the ledge, neck and wrist chains were fastened into the stone wall. Here several prisoners could be placed, standing precariously on the ledge, neck and wrists fastened into collars of iron. With no food or water, the unhappy victims would weaken. A foot would slip off the ledge, and they would hang to death.

Touring a castle in Munich, Mother admired the hardware fittings on the doors, which were beautifully wrought iron face plates, with handles shaped into levers. They had smooth double locks, and Mother thought they would be perfect for our house in Muncie. The guide told us the factory in Munich was still making the hardware. Mother did an incredible memory act by remembering every door, including the closets, on our second floor. She also had to remember the direction the doors opened and on which side the doorknobs were. She didn't make one mistake with her calculations, and the hardware, when it finally arrived in Muncie, fitted every door perfectly. When Mother and Dad moved to Indianapolis in 1960, the hardware moved with them. Today we are proud to have some of it in our house, reminding me of Muncie as well as our first trip to Germany.

[63]

From Munich we drove to Lucerne, Switzerland. In my diary I exclaimed, "I am glad we saved the best for the last." It was an immaculate country with gorgeous scenery, the Alps surrounding us in majestic grandeur. We saw the capital city of Zurich and then returned to Germany, driving through the Black Forest. The mountainous driving actually took us through the clouds which swept across the roads, giving us the feeling of an airplane ride. After passing through Freiburg and Basle, we arrived in Nancy, France. Dad put the three of us on a train back to Paris while he drove on alone to re-visit battlefields and cemeterys where friends of his were buried.

In Paris, Mother, Hudson and I returned to the Hotel Cecilia where we rested after the exertion of traveling and waited for Dad to return two days later. Our first commercial flight was near at hand, and we were excited and somewhat nervous, although the flight proved uneventful.

We spent another week in London, seeing more of that great city and going to the theater often. Mr. Griffith, Basil's father, escorted us through the House of Commons. It was interesting to have a glimpse of the workings of the English government.

Alex Scovell, our Australian friend, joined us several times in London. He and Dad had become good friends. Several times in later years, Mr. Scovell passed through Muncie to visit us on his return trip to Melbourne. He was kind and soft spoken with a lovely Aussie accent, his six-foot-five stature towering over us.

We had a chance to see a real London fog, which kept us indoors for a day. "Pea soup" is an apt description of the fogs which often cover the city like a blanket. I described it in my diary as "greenish-yellow-black clouds so thick you couldn't see the person standing next to you on the street."

We drove to Stratford upon Avon to see the environs of Shakespeare and finally, on October twenty-eight, Dad's birthday, went by train to Liverpool to board the sister ship of the Duchess of Bedford, the Duchess of Richmond. The two ships were almost identical, even to the furnishings. It felt like home because of the familiar surroundings. I climbed into the upper berth and snuggled down, ready for the voyage home.

There was a young bell hop who ran the elevator in the main foyer to whom I was very attracted. He was fifteen, red-headed and freckled, and I nicknamed him "Ginger" until I found that his real name was Jim Harrigan. He showed me all around the ship. There was a kennel where animals were kept during the voyage, and I was surprised to see a lioness, monkeys, dogs and even birds. I learned a great deal about the ship's operation on the tour.

[64]

I was in the foyer one day, talking to Jim and watching Hudson playing with two other boys. A woman, pearl necklaces drooping over her ample bosom, walked by. She turned to me, and waving an arm toward the three boys romping noisily around said, in a stilted Bostonian accent, "My dear, are these all yours?" I was so dumbfounded and taken aback by this remark I could only stutter, "No, just this one" — pointing to Hud. She breezed along the passageway, and I never saw her again to explain that I was only fourteen!

I was so stunned by her remark that I went back to the stateroom and looked at myself in the mirror. There I stood dressed in a heavy wool suit. The skirt came half-way to my ankles, and the jacket was tailored like a man's. I was overdeveloped everywhere! Hips, bust, football shoulders! I looked older than Mother, not only grown up, but grown *out*. No wonder the woman thought I could have three children!

The incident filled me with deep embarrassment. I realized I looked like a German haus frau, but in all fairness the fashion of the day did not help a bit. Clothes were made to look as unbecoming as possible, and uncomfortable as well. Girdles, stocking, gloves and hats were worn with every outfit. The hats were unmentionable things, shoved down on the head, mashing your hair and looking ridiculous. The skirts were tight and worn so long it caused you to walk with a mincing, hobbling kind of gait.

I changed my clothes on the spot, trying to find something more becoming, but it was not easy. I tried combing my hair a different way, but my permanent wave was too permanent. I had a matronly look about me, and that was that!

I returned to the salon and hid behind a book, thinking over the problem. I would not eat dinner and would be ten pounds lighter tomorrow! But I was starved, and when tea was passed, cookies came with it! I sighed and decided to make the best of my fate and cover up the plain facade with a good sense of humor.

That night I dressed in evening clothes and did my best to look nice. I must have improved a little because I danced quite a lot with several men. There was a passenger show and Mother sang. I also played the piano. After the show, people gathered around the piano, and we all sang. We went to bed late to make the most of our dwindling hours on shipboard.

The next morning fog rolled in on the St. Lawrence River, and we crept along, wondering if we would dock in time to catch our train for home. We decided not to take a chance. When the ship docked in Quebec, we debarked and took a train from there to Montreal.

Ginger and I had quite a case for each other, corresponding for over a year until we took a trip to Montreal again. The *Duchess* was in port, and Jim had leave for the evening. He came to our hotel, and we all went to dinner. Mother told me afterwards she and Dad laughed behind our backs. Jim's sea legs made him bow-legged, and I was slightly knock-kneed. Mother said we spelled OX as we walked down the street together. Finally our letters dwindled, and the romance died a natural death. He wasn't that attractive on shore!

We arrived in Muncie at midnight, November sixth, glad to be home again, but with the memories of a wonderful trip together.

The first thing I did the next morning was to go to the farm and greet the horses. I really had missed them.

CHAPTER FOURTEEN

WHEN I returned to Burris School In November, I didn't realize it was to be the last year with my class in Muncie. I was busy catching up with my studies after missing the first two months of school and was happy my classmates were as glad to see me again as I was to see them. My first "true love" was still the tallest boy in class, Paul Justice (Eagle Scout.) I was faithful to him in my thoughts from sixth grade through my sophomore year, but I don't know if he cared that much for me. We shied away from each other not knowing how to cope with such feelings, but other classmates seemed to be aware of our attraction and teased us incessantly. Without a word being said, Paul and I somehow communicated our feelings to each other.

As I write these "memory confessions" I recall a terrible thing I did while attending Burris School. There was a boy in our class who was always playing nasty tricks on the smaller children. His name was Vernon Arment. (We called him Vermin Ferment!)

One of his naughty tricks was to push children's faces down into the drinking fountain when they paused for a drink. I thought it was a very mean thing to do. One day I saw him at the fountain, and impulsively, to repay some of his unkindness to others, sneaked up behind him. As I pushed his head down into the fountain, I said, "This is what you get for being so mean!"

I was horror struck when he rose up. Blood was dripping from his mouth, and his front teeth were hanging on his lip. With tears of anger he cried, "I'll tell my Mother, and she'll fix you!"

As he ran down the hall and disappeared, I was shaking with fright. No one else was in the hall, and I hurried into my classroom pale and ashamed. I visualized Mrs. Arment calling my parents followed by a law suit involving much publicity and money, with me in disgrace. I also was sick at heart to have hurt Vernon. I looked for him every day at school to tell him how sorry I was to have hurt him so badly, but he never returned to school, and not a word was heard from him again.

—————◄◇►—————

In February our Eighth Grade Class had a roller skating party at the Naval Armory. The huge, hardwood floor made an excellent rink and the party had barely begun when I had an accident.

There were wooden, folding chairs lined up all around the big, square room to give the skaters a chance to sit and rest from time to time. I had just put on my skates and was beginning to get the feel of them, when two of my more exuberant friends — Mary Mix and Mary Ellen Covalt, skated up behind me and gave me a big shove. Caught off balance, I was propelled with great speed into the wall. The chairs collapsed, and fell beneath and on top of me as I sprawled painfully among them. When I was finally able to stand, I realized my wrist was throbbing and swelling. Mother was called to take me to the doctor.

Uncle Herman Bowles was our family doctor. He was Nana's brother, kind, gentle and as good a doctor as his father, my great-grandfather Bowles. Throughout my childhood, he was the one who looked after me in my illnesses, sewed up my head when I was two, and now examined my painful wrist. It was not broken, he told me, but badly sprained, and I must carry my arm in a sling for a few weeks.

I was angry and disgusted with the girls who had caused me to fall, even though they had always been good friends. But it was a mean thing to do. Instead of an apology they wrote a nasty poem to immortalize the event. I was so embarrassed by the poem I remember it to this day. The poem was circulated with great hilarity throughout the class before I finally saw it, and both Paul and I were deeply humiliated.

> *Oh, Paul and Lucina are deeply in love*
> *They go 'round together like two little doves.*
> *Together they fit like a hand in a glove*
> *But Lucina fell down when we gave her a shove.*
> *For she was skating without her dear Paul*
> *And the floor it did shake from the blow of her fall*
> *She sprained her poor wrist and how she did bawl*
> *But it's well now because it was kissed by her Paul.*

The incident nearly ended our case for each other, but he did invite me to our school dance in May, 1933, and we had a wonderful time. It was the first dance I ever attended, and it launched my social life.

I was in the ninth grade when I learned the meaning of my name. I was studying in the Burris Library and noticed a group of boys from my class whispering and giggling. From their covert glances at me, I knew I was the brunt of their joke. One by one they had gone to the big Webster dictionary in the corner of the room and returned laughing with the other boys in the group.

One of them came over and whispered, "We know what your name means. It's in the dictionary!" Of course I had to look it up. The definition read: "Lucina: In Roman mythology, the goddess presiding over childbirth. Also light and sunshine." I was mortified.

There were many social clubs in Muncie, and the highlight of the year was the Christmas dances. Each club tried to outdo the other with festive decorations and the best bands. Most of the dances were held in the Roberts Hotel Ballroom, which became transformed with sparkling, white Christmas trees, festoons of tinsel strung across the

[68]

ceiling, or balloons and serpentines. Sometimes a large crystal ball hung from the center of the darkened room, and the reflections of spotlights sent dots of reflected lights bouncing around the room and over the dancers as it slowly rotated. I thought this the most romantic of all decorations.

There was always a stag line of boys who had come without dates so they would be free to dance with as many girls as they chose. There was no drinking at these parties. Prohibition was in effect until 1933, and then only near beer was allowed to those over twenty-one.

I went to the dances and other parties with several boys but most often with Robert Wilson. We became friends because of our mutual love of horses and often rode together.

Robert had a little Redbug car. It was a small, two-seated vehicle which operated on one cylinder. The gasoline engine was mounted on a fifth wheel at the rear, and one sat close to the ground as in a racing car. Robert often drove to my house in his Redbug to pick me up and go to the farm for our horseback rides. We rode together so much, it was natural he would ask me to dances and other social functions. I found myself paired with him too often, however, and began to groan, saying, "I'll probably end up *marrying* him!

Paul Justice

I. Hilda Stewart

Bomar Cramer

Dorothy Merrill

Tudor Hall School

Pirates of Penzance — Lucina, Mary Ellen Buskirk and Patricia DePrez

CHAPTER FIFTEEN

I left Muncie in the Fall of 1933 as a sophomore to attend Tudor Hall School for Girls in Indianapolis.

My roommate, Betty Amos, a beautiful, petite brunette, was from Edinburg, Indiana, and we got along very well together. There were about twenty-five girls living in the Residence. I. Hilda Stewart was our authoritative principal, allowing only the upper school girls to live there. So we were all approximately the same age and became very close. A separate entity from the day students who attended Tudor Hall, we girls in the Residence developed lasting, lifetime friendships from our close proximity.

Betty and I shared a room fronting on Meridian Street at the end of one of the wings of the H-shaped building. Next door, Derexa Gray roomed with Maureen Potlitzer from St. Joseph, Missouri. My cousin, Janice, was also attending, as well as Rosemary White. Rosemary and I had been in the same class together ever since Mrs. Emerson's School in the first grade. It was comforting to have near me so many old friends in new surroundings. It didn't occur to me to feel homesick. Home was only an hour and a half away, and Mother and Dad usually came to Indianapolis on weekends. We would go downtown for lunch and a movie, or to a dreaded dental appointment with Dr. Mitchell, who was straightening my teeth!

In Indianapolis I studied piano with Bomar Cramer, the most outstanding teacher I ever had, and revolutionized the technique I had learned as a child. A student of the celebrated teacher and great artist, Josef Lhevinne, Bomar passed his artistry on to his pupils. I worked as hard as I could, restricted as I was by my heavy academic schedule at Tudor. I adored Bomar (who I thought looked like George Raft, a famous movie star). A nervous person, he was a chain smoker and strict in every sense of the word. Almost every lesson would find me in tears as I walked to the bus to take me back to Tudor. I had to re-learn ten years of badly taught habits. But I did learn. I gathered a great deal of good repertoire, and those are the pieces I still can play today with very little practice as the memory is still in my fingers. I studied with Bomar for many years off and on after my graduation from Tudor Hall, returning to his studio often for lessons and coaching.

—◆—

Tudor Hall was begun in 1902 by Fredonia Allen, and during World War I, the school was moved from central Meridian Street farther north to thirty-second and Meridian, where classes were conducted until 1961. The school then relocated to a new campus on Cold Spring Road. My daughter, Judy, was in the last class to graduate from its historical location on Meridian Street, and Ann, as a junior moved with her classmates to the beautiful site west of Indianapolis in the Fall of that year.

For those of us who attended the "old" school, it was painful to see the empty buildings where we had once studied go to wrack and ruin from vandalism and neglect. Finally, in 1980, the buildings were torn down and today a contemporary building stands on the site. I feel it is pertinent to record some details of the old school as it was an important institution in Indianapolis.

The Residence joined the school building by a covered passageway. The buildings of yellow brick were nearly covered with ivy, as the Class Night tradition each year was the planting of the ivy by the seniors before their graduation. The expansive lawn surrounded the buildings to include a tennis court and baseball diamond. There was a gymnasium on the top floor of the school building for basketball and other gym activities when the weather prevented outdoor games. There was also a swimming pool in the basement.

The auditorium was a combination theater, convocation hall and gymnasium for the lower school. It also was used for special occasions, such as the junior and senior proms. There was a small stage at one end of the room for student performances. High school classrooms were on the second floor, and the lower school was contained on the first floor. The basement housed the science department and laboratory as well as the art department.

Drama was an important focus at Tudor Hall with continual class plays, elocution and acting classes. The most important club at Tudor was the Masquers Club. All aspiring actresses tried to join this select group of thespians. A great deal of rehearsal time and extra hours after school were devoted to putting on a play, but the time was leniently allowed by the school's administration in short, Miss Stewart. I couldn't understand why music could not receive equal consideration. So I approached the choir instructor, Dorothy Merill, about setting up a music club. Two juniors, Barbara Hickam, Carolyn Stelk and I, with Dorothy's counsel, formed the Prelude Club to include membership not only for performers, but for those who appreciated music, even though they did not actively study it. The active members took turns performing each month at the meetings, and the associates were the listening audience. The associates enhanced the musical portions of the programs by presenting papers on the composers or music history, which related to the program given. At our first guest artist concert that year, I persuaded Bomar to play for us.

By the end of the first year, the Prelude Club had sponsored the first Gilbert and Sullivan operetta with the cooperation of the Masquers

[73]

Club and the Art Department. It was the biggest production the school had dared to attempt because of the expense and the involvement of so many people on the small stage. But the combined expertise of Miss Merrill and Miss Bucher, the drama teacher, resulted in a very successful production of *Patience*. Mary Lou Morris was the demure, petite Patience, and Pat DePrez and I were her "lovesick swains" vying for her attention.

Miss Stewart was so delighted with the success of *Patience*, she readily agreed to let us put on a Gilbert and Sullivan operetta every year, which we did, until World War II. In my junior and senior years at Tudor, I was the president of the Prelude Club, and we did *Pinafore* and *The Pirates of Penzance*. I was the heroine, and Pat DePrez was my "lover" in both operettas. Our voices blended well, and as we both lived in the Residence, we were able to rehearse together frequently.

<hr>

Alice and Mary Dickey were from Terre Haute and became my closest friends at Tudor. Twin sisters, they were also my classmates. I roomed with Alice when we were juniors, and Mary roomed with Mary Ellen Buskirk from Bloomington, Indiana. Mary Ellen (Bussy as we nicknamed her) was also a very close friend. She was a year ahead of us, and went to Vassar College after graduation. We have remained friends throughout our lives. On the other hand as close as the Dickeys and I were, we scarcely met again after graduation, and our correspondence dwindled to nothing. Alice worked for Scribner's in New York, and after her marriage, moved to Canada. Mary became a librarian and, after a brief marriage, lost her pilot husband on D-Day during the War. To my knowledge she did not remarry. I regret we lost contact with each other, but our lives took different directions.

My senior year roommate was Alice Crume from Peru, Indiana. We also lost touch with each other, but in 1976 I was asked to round up our classmates for our fortieth reunion on Alumni Day. Out of the class of twenty-four, only eight lived in Indianapolis, and Alice was the only one from out of town who came. She drove down from Fort Wayne and spent the night with us. We hadn't seen each other or corresponded all those years, but we rediscovered our friendship and have seen each other frequently since the reunion. Her husband, Francis Thompson, is as enjoyable a person as she is.

I could not discuss my years at Tudor Hall without commenting on our head mistress. I. Hilda Stewart was a principled woman and a strong director who ran a tight school administration. In close personal contact with each student, she knew not only their academic progress, but also intimate details of their personalities. She took particular interest in those girls whose parents might benefit the school financially, and in this way showed favoritism, which was blatantly unfair and lowered my estimation of her. However, in spite of this fault, one had to have the utmost respect for Miss Stewart. In every other way, she was a person to be admired. Her appearance was enough to subdue any girl's exuberance. Straight as a ramrod, her hair flattened to her head as though she had just stepped out of a shower, her eyes penetrated through you, seeming to read every thought you possessed. For some, she was terrifying — others called her their friend. I was not frightened of her, but I could not like her. I only felt the deepest respect for her competence in handling the girls and the administration.

She assembled a faculty of the highest caliber. The teachers were excellent, dedicated to us and the school. I worked harder and learned more at Tudor than at any other time in my life. Miss Stewart's description of me was apt, if not complimentary. She called me "a plodder." I think she was trying to tell me to have more fun out of life instead of being so serious. Little did she know what went on in the Residence "after lights"! Her flat hair would have curled like Topsy's, and we all would have been thrown out on Meridian Street if she had ever learned of our late night parties in each other's rooms.

There were strict rules, of course. Smoking resulted in immediate expulsion. Radios and phonographs were not allowed, but all through the years I kept a small radio at the bottom of my zippered dress bag. On Wednesday nights anyone able to sneak into our room after "lights" was invited to hear Henry Busse's orchestra and Benny Goodman's famous band. I plugged the radio in between our beds, and to hear the music, it was necessary to pile on the beds with ears close to the radio, as the volume had to be turned down very low. Sometimes six or seven of us gathered to hear the programs, and if we weren't too sleepy, the best of all began at midnight with the eerie sound of a creaking door announcing "Inner Sanctum", a horror show.

These radio parties were tame compared to some that went on. Once, Maureen and Derexa walked to the nearby Hooks Drug Store and bought a bottle of gin. On a Saturday night, before the bell rang for "lights out," about ten of us gathered in their room and began drinking. I sat and watched, not spiking my coke with any gin, but amused and shocked at the reactions that followed.

Mary Lou Allen, the Residence clown, put roller skates on her bare feet and skated breezily down the hall, long white nightgown flowing. Mrs. Ives, the house mother, Miss Kinnaird and Miss Wells, the other teachers who lived in the Residence, sat at their stations in the hall and smiled with indulgence as Mary Lou sailed by, all of them unaware of the cause of her actions.

Someone squashed the bananas and grapes in Maureen's lingerie drawer. The underwear was ruined with the mashed fruit stains. Our

[75]

strict housemothers never investigated the cause of the hilarious out-pouring from the back corridor. I couldn't believe we were not dis-covered! The girls opened the windows and smoked, hanging over the sills.

I never had the vaguest inclination to smoke, since my allergies and revulsion against the stench was enough to negate any interest in the habit, but most of the other girls did. A few were caught and even expelled when some of their antics compounded with smoking, such as leaving the Residence without permission or staying out after hours. Several times two girls came back to the Residence after their dates so drunk they were reeling. Their roommates quickly put them in the shower to sober them up before they were caught by Mrs. Ives. Both of these girls received a "T.H." award at Class Night. The Tudor Hall Award was one given to "the finest seniors representing the school."

Mrs. Ives looked like anyone's loving grandmother, but she could be cold as steel when aroused to irritation by any misconduct. In spite of this, I liked her very much. She played her part perfectly and ran a tight ship in the Residence. It was amazing any of our capers passed unnoticed, and that although I was in on most of the antics, I was never caught!

Mary Ellen Buskirk

Betty Amos

Pat DePrez

Alice Crume

Mary Dickey

Alice Dickey

Lucina with Marie Neal

Janice and Lucina on tandem bike in Bermuda

Dad, 1935

Lucina, age 16

CHAPTER SIXTEEN

W HEN school was out for the summer, I returned home to resume my avid interest — preparing for the up-coming horse shows. Truthfully, although I'm not prone to bragging, I was a good rider. Here is a scrap of newsprint from one of my scrap-books of the 1930's. I was surprised to find the clipping and cannot remember to what show it referred.

Muncie people should be very proud of their representatives in the show. Lucina Ball rode her good bay mare, Marie Neal, to the red ribbon in an open class of thirty-nine five-gaited horses in the morning, and in the afternoon repeated by riding Jean McDonald, the handy, black mare to second place in a class of forty-three horses. In both classes she gave her mount a better ride than the winning horse got. It gave this spectator a big thrill to see Lucina and her horse in the ring again. Both horse and rider seemed so completely happy in doing the right thing, that even those who had no interest in the outcome were heard exclaiming over the performance. Here are my ribbon-tied congratulations to Muncie for having such a fine rider and sportswoman as Lucina Ball in its city directory.

Later in the summer of 1935, my father prepared for another trip to England, where he was asked by Ball Brothers Company to set up a zinc rolling mill in Tottenham, a suburb of London. Dad invented a system of rolling zinc into thin sheets, calling the operation "The Bill Ball Transfer." The zinc was placed into a machine, rolled and passed down from one machine to the next, at each pass-through rolling the zinc thinner and thinner until it was the thickness desired for the product. Ball Brothers made other zinc items besides the liners for the jar lids. Battery cups (zinc sheaths which held batteries) were important items, as well as other small products made from zinc. Today Ball Corporation makes our copper coated zinc blanks that are sent to the U.S. mint to be stamped as pennies.

Mother told me recently Dad was paid $200,000 by Ball Brothers to set up this factory in England. He returned every dollar of it to the firm, never mentioning the fact to anyone.

Our family planned to travel to England in mid-summer, but on the verge of departure, packed and ready to leave, Hudson frightened us with another ear infection. It was necessary for Mother and Hudson to remain at home, but I was allowed to go with Dad. It was the only time I ever had my father all to myself for such a long period, and we had a wonderful trip together. As always, he was a perfect host and party partner.

We set off on the famous Southwestern Limited train to New York, which left Muncie every day about four in the afternoon, and arrived at Grand Central Station the next morning at eight. If people today think flying is more convenient than taking a train, it is because they never experienced the luxury and comfort of the railroad system at its best. Before World War II, the roadbeds and rails were smooth as silk. I could sleep like a top in the berths, rocking gently as in a cradle to the rhythmic clicking of the wheels over the rails. Riding a train anywhere became a magic journey for me. I always felt an undercurrent of excitement and anticipation. Besides enjoying the panoramic countryside through the big picture windows, it was a time of relaxation, reading or studying. The meals were excellent, expertly served by white-coated waiters in the dining car. Tables were set with white cloths and fresh flowers in silver vases, giving the atmosphere of a continental dining room. It was a time to meet strangers and make new friends. The lounge car also was a meeting place before and after dinner, where one could be served a drink and enjoy the company of others. Comfortable, upholstered couches and chairs with little cocktail tables set beside them, stimulated intimate, relaxed conversation.

My enjoyment of the ride peaked when I was finally enclosed in my private berth, the zippered green curtain swaying with the motion of the train. In the darkness, with the window curtain raised, I could watch the passing night until I fell asleep, the lights of the small towns flashing past, the stars and moon glittering in the sky.

It was convenient to arrive in mid-town New York directly beneath our hotel, The Biltmore. We'd be settled in our rooms early in the morning, rested, and have the entire day for business or pleasure. How different today when one arrives by plane, possibly delayed by weather or other circumstances. There's a wait while luggage is thrown down an escalator, bumping and breaking from the rough treatment and another wait for a taxi or bus, as competition for the vehicles runs high. The ride downtown, another hour in heavy traffic, costs a fortune. By the time you arrive at the hotel, you're exhausted and ready for bed. The sacrifice one has to pay for the questionable gain of a few hours time is not worth it to me. For me, travel is seeing the road as you go, feeling relaxation instead of nervous tension as you sit strapped and cramped in a seat with no elbow or leg room for hours with a roaring of motors in your ears.

CHAPTER SEVENTEEN

THE *Normandie* was the largest and fastest ship afloat, the French Line's newest and most extravagant. Dad and I boarded her on July tenth for her return maiden voyage to France, stopping at Southampton, England en route. The ship traveled at such a fast clip that everyone received a good massage from the vibration. One ship's joke was the formula for a whiskey sour. Combine lemon juice, bourbon, sugar and ice, then let stand one minute to mix.

Our table in the dining room was in one of the small, private alcoves on either side of the enormous main dining room. The entrance to this grand hall was down a flight of stairs, branching out on either side like a pair of butterfly wings. At the top of the staircase was a huge, gold statue of a woman, probably a mythological goddess of the sea. It dominated the room, even dwarfing the fountains and long buffet table, loaded with baskets of fruit, cheese and extravagantly decorated cold hams, turkeys, salads and cakes, looking too beautiful to eat.

Three other men shared the table with us. All of them worked for the French Line — Mr. Wells, John Saunders, the English representative and Enrico Squadra, the American representative. Enrico was the Italian husband of a very old friend of the family's from Muncie, Mary Ludington. Mary was an accomplished pianist who accompanied and coached opera singers in New York. Enrico was most attractive and witty. He made the trip a gala one with his gallant manner and charm. Mr. Wells was a quiet and unobtrusive gentleman, the main reason why I cannot remember him too well. It was John Saunders that captured my heart. I fell in love with him, my first agonizing love affair, doomed at the outset by two important facts. I was not yet seventeen, and he was twenty-five and engaged to be married! I knew he cared for me, but he was honest and told me of his "arranged by parents" betrothal of several years duration. He did not love her, he told me, and had constantly put off the date for marriage. However, he had every intention of going through with the marriage in the near future.

We had a Valentine sort of romance. He was a beautiful dancer and particularly loved to waltz. I couldn't hear "The Blue Danube" for years afterwards without tears in my eyes. We met for cocktails before dinner, which I was allowed, provided they were Orange Blossoms, of all things, because they were weak and innocuous. But I was intoxicated enough just being near him. He was tall, handsome, attentive, intelligent and serious with a fun-loving streak, and I was attracted to him like a magnet.

We danced, played ping pong (I still played a good game), cards and volley ring tennis, which I also mastered. We walked the deck together, lost in long conversations

By the time the ship reached London, we were both deeply entrenched in our romantic affair and made plans to meet daily for tea. He worked near Piccadilly Square at the French Line office. It was quite a walk from the Mayfair Hotel where Dad and I were staying, but every day, after Dad left on the train for Tottenham to supervise the factory operation, I met John for tea at a little tea house near his office. There we discussed our dilemma in desperation and with no solution. Once, Dad in his innocence, not realizing how heartsick I was, invited John and his fiance to go to dinner and the theater with us. I remember the show was *Anything Goes*, a lighthearted musical set on shipboard! I was deep in gloom while John sat between his fiance and me and held my hand throughout the performance. She sat unsuspecting, plain and mousey. Of course, I disliked her. I was so upset that evening I poured out my heart to Dad when we returned to the hotel, and he couldn't have been more sympathetic or helpful. He gave me courage to try and forget the lost cause, such as it was, and to look forward to later times when I would be old enough to consider a serious attachment to someone. He made me feel very young and silly about the whole thing.

I knew I would never see or hear from John Saunders again. Before we left, I gave him a very precious possession of mine which, looking back, seems foolish now, but at the time seemed appropriate. Mother had given me an exquisite, enameled and jeweled pendant of St. George astride his white steed, slaying the green, writhing dragon beneath him. Besides being useful as a pendant, it could also stand as a decorative piece on a table as it was three-dimensional. It was very valuable then and probably would be priceless now, but I wanted him to have it as a remembrance of me. It was many years before I gathered the courage to tell Mother about my gift to John.

It took a long while for me to forget him. Enrico Squadra told me years later John was one of the first to enlist when Britain declared war against Germany. He was a pilot and was killed early in the war.

Before Dad and I left for England, June Jack had asked me to try and meet her "pen pal" of several years, Bep Barkey of the Netherlands. They had become friends through their exchange of letters but never thought they would meet. June and I wrote Bep a letter together which introduced me to her and planned our meeting in The Hague. I was eager to meet her and looked forward to the weekend when Dad and I left for Holland on an overnight Channel ferry.

We arrived in The Hague and registered at the Hotel Des Indes. From there we taxied to Bep's apartment. She was very pretty, but her English was not as easy to understand as her letters. Her accent was thick and broken, but we smiled and she showed us her two tiny rooms where she lived with her mother. An avid movie fan, her bedroom wall was

[82]

literally wallpapered with photographs of Hollywood film stars.

She pointed out of the window to a tennis court across the street where two boys were playing a fierce game. She made me understand one of the boys was her fiance and the other would be my date for the evening. It sounded like fun, and soon after our visit, we returned to the hotel where I dressed for the evening.

Cars in Holland were at a premium. When the trio appeared to pick me up, they arrived by street car. Bep and I in long evening dresses and the boys in black tie were elegantly dressed for an evening of dancing. Dad stood at the doorway of the hotel to see us off, stifling laughter at the incongruity of the four of us, stylishly dressed, boarding a street car for our date! I was relieved they hadn't come on bicycles, as I had expected. Many more bicycles than cars were evident in Holland.

We had a wonderful evening. Bep, Laurens, Peter and I danced until after midnight at the famous Schevenigen dance hall, a great, barn-like, wooden building stretched out over the water on enormous pilings. The dance orchestra was big and loud — a good thing, since it was difficult to converse in English. We drank beer, laughed and enjoyed each other's company as we danced to good American jazz.

Bep and I not only corresponded from that time on, we have seen each other a number of times over the years. She married Laurens VanOosten about a year later. He became a doctor, and served in the Dutch East Indian and the Dutch Armies until his retirement. They had both been born in Indonesia, but didn't meet until their families returned to the Netherlands when Bep and Laurens were in their teens. World War II was severe for the Dutch people. The VanOosten's baby daughter, their first born, was killed in a bombing attack. Bep cannot talk of this even now. After the War they had two other children, Boudewin and Fanny. I will tell more of the VanOostens later.

Before Dad and I flew back to London, we did a little sightseeing. He was interested in visiting a dairy to compare its operation to his dairy in Eaton and arranged to be shown the largest and most prosperous dairy near The Hague. The plant was more rustic and not as sterile as ours, but the management was backed by centuries of experience. Dutch cheeses are famous the world over, and as we said goodbye to our host, he presented us with an enormous wheel of cheese. I am not exaggerating when I say the wheel was as large as a round sofa cushion and as deep. In fact, to find room for it in the taxi with us, I had to sit on it.

Back at the hotel, we lugged the cheese, which weighed twenty-five pounds easily, up to our room. We wondered how we'd ever get it back home — or even to England! The problem was soon solved for us.

Next morning we drove to Vollendam in time to watch the townspeople leaving the Sunday church service. They were in traditional Dutch clothes, making a quaint and colorful picture against the background of the old church and village square, with its cobbled streets and ancient buildings. The women were stunning in their peaked, lace headdresses and snow white aprons over colorful full skirts, their tight bodices laced over beautifully embroidered blouses. The men wore dark, sturdy wool suits, tight jackets and full, baggy trousers buttoned tightly at the ankles. The large wooden shoes dominated their costumes, making them walk in a strutting, lop-sided gait. A scarf around the neck, a jaunty cap and the outfit was complete. Most of the men added another picturesque touch by smoking heavy, curved pipes, or long clay ones.

We watched the parade of costumes as people left the church, the women held their prayer books, clustered together, gossiping and the men joined their friends to smoke and converse. The children ran about, free at last from the confines of the church pews, playing games of tag.

We left Vollendam and took a small, dirty ferry to the Isle of Markham not far from the coast, where life was poor indeed. The cleanliness of the Dutch people was not in evidence here. The homes were primitive, dark and filled to overflowing with large families. They were fishermen's homes, and for most of them, their lives began and ended here. We passed one home where several children were clustered at the doorway watching us. Their toothless grandmother beckoned to us, indicating she wanted us to enter their home. Curiosity overcame our hesitation, and we agreed to go in. The children and parents wore their everyday Dutch clothes, wooden shoes protecting their feet from the muddy street. Shoes were left at the doorstep, and we complied with this custom, leaving ours on the stoop. Most of the children were suffering from bad colds, or worse, and hadn't learned of the existence of handkerchiefs. Their clothes were soiled and grimy as well as their faces and hands. The mother opened a drawer in an old chest and brought forth one of the beautiful Sunday dresses, which she obviously wanted to sell to us. I was made to try it on, hating to touch anything from people who had never seen a bathtub. But Dad urged me on, and soon I was in full regalia, putting the clothes on over my own. After the little lace cap was in place, Dad took my picture with the movie camera, the family crowding around to get in the picture, too.

We apologized as best we could for not buying the costume and left with difficulty, with a sigh of relief and a good deal of depression, having seen the poorest of living conditions of the fishermen.

Back at the hotel after dinner that evening, we went to our rooms, tired and ready for bed. As we opened the door, an odor beyond belief drove us backwards. The cheese! We had left it, unthinking, on a table by the window where the sun had warmed it all day. The strong stench of a dairy at its worst filled the room with a smell you could almost see! Dad called room service, and when the waiter arrived, he presented him with the cheese with a great flourish. The waiter was ecstatic. He bowed and scraped, and thanked us profusely. We opened the windows wide and slept.

Another weekend was spent in Brussels visiting the World's Fair Exposition. I don't remember the Fair nearly as much as an incident that preceded our rush to the airport later to catch the plane for London.

We stopped for lunch at one of the many sidewalk cafes lining the streets of Brussels. I had been collecting souvenirs from everyplace on the trip, ash trays, napkins, stirrers, coasters, match boxes, tickets, notes and other small items to add to my over-stuffed scrap-books at home. I fancied the small silver cream pitcher on the table. Dad looked at his watch and stood up suddenly, saying, "We're late. Let's hurry and find a taxi." We were half-running along the street when I suddenly cried in dismay, "I forgot the cream pitcher!" We had not yet passed the cafe, and in an instant, Dad reached across the little hedge separating the tables from the sidewalk, seeing an identical one on an empty table. He scooped it up and dropped it into his pocket in one fluid motion, not stopping as we walked. "Oh, no," he moaned, "that pitcher was full of cream, — and it's running down my leg!" We doubled up with laughter as we ran toward a taxi, Dad awkwardly shaking his leg as he ran, trying to free the heavy cream from his trousers. All the way to London he groaned from the sticky feel of it. I refused to wash the pitcher for a long time because there was a drop of dried cream on the lip, making it a perfect souvenir of a funny afternoon! The pitcher still has a place in our bar as a jigger. The name of the cafe "Atlanta" is engraved across its side.

Mr. Scovell arrived in London, and we were glad to see him again. We spent a weekend together at Brighton Beach, one of England's most popular resorts. We walked the beach and watched as artists created incredible sand castles and statues. The beach was filled with many unusual creations, the artists sometimes receiving coins for their efforts as the crowd looked on. In the evening the stunning statuary was left to be swept out with the tide.

It was an unhappy hour for me when the time came to leave England. When we boarded our ferry to Dublin, a lovely bouquet full of Scotch heather was waiting for me in my cabin with a note from John Saunders. I preserved a bit of the heather in a tiny bottle of perfume, which I still have.

We had been invited to spend our last week abroad with our cousins, Lucy and Alvin Owsley in Ireland. Alvin, a charming gentlemen and diplomat, had served under Roosevelt in ministerial posts in Roumania and Denmark. Now he was our Minister to the Irish Free State.

Alvin met us at the dock with his limousine and chauffeur, and we were driven in style to their Embassy home, a veritable mansion set deeply in the woods of a great park in the city of Dublin. The approach to the mansion wandered over a long road through the park, shaded by enormous, old trees. Deer and rabbits grazed near the road, unfrightened by the motor car.

Lucy and their three children, Constance, Alvin Jr. and David met us at the door, and we had a happy reunion, since they had been living abroad for many years. Lucy is the daughter of Uncle Frank and Aunt Bessie Ball, and I was named for her. She, however, never cared for the name Lucina and preferred to be called Lucy. (I have never been called Lucy. My friends call me Cina.)

Lucy is a beautiful, statuesque lady with auburn hair, and she passed this attribute on to her children. All of them are red-headed and liberally sprinkled with freckles. A handsome family, they made a perfect representation for America. Lucy was a gracious hostess, and Alvin, a lawyer, was knowledgeable in his political role.

We were shown to our rooms by a pretty Irish maid, uniformed in black with a dainty white apron and tiny cap, setting off her dark hair. My room was spacious, sunny and beautifully furnished. I discovered the maid had been personally assigned to me. She unpacked my suitcase and hung up my clothes, taking my wrinkled things away to be pressed.

The week was an exciting one. We were shown the interesting sights of Dublin and were wined and dined in great style, but the highlight of the week was the International Royal Dublin Horse Show. We sat in a special box designated for "the Minister and his party," the center of all the activity. The box was draped in red, white and blue banners for the U.S. and was in the front row. I could almost reach over and touch the horses as they cantered by.

The best cavalry equestrian teams came from many countries to compete in the Hunter and Jumper classes. The hurdles were unbelievably high and difficult to maneuver — a rigorous competition for only the finest horses and riders. I cannot remember who the winning team was, overall, but I remember being very impressed by the teams from Italy, Germany and Russia. The riders had been trained to show the world they were superior. Their countries were preparing for war and world domination.

[86]

Finally, Dad and I were driven to Cobh by Alvin's chauffeur, where the S.S. Brittanic was docked, waiting to take on passengers for New York. We found ourselves heading home at last.

⎯⎯⎯⎯⎯⎯⎯◄◉►⎯⎯⎯⎯⎯⎯⎯

The meeting with Bep Barkey brought a new friend into my life. After we returned home from England, I received a letter postmarked from Java, in Indonesia. An exciting development! The letter was from Hans Flothuis, who wrote that his cousin Bep had told him all about our meeting in The Hague. He wondered if I would consider being his "pen pal."

Hans managed a tea plantation in Java, then a Netherlands colony. He lived on the plantation in a small, frame house deep in jungle territory. From time to time he sent me books and pictures so I could visualize his country more accurately. He was lonely, which he conveyed in every letter, but his letters were interesting, and judging from the snapshot of himself, he was most attractive. He seemed to be a gentleman and a gentle man. I tried to fill my letters with funny and interesting anecdotes to amuse him. He improved his English while I expanded my knowledge of life on the other side of the world.

The pictures of his living quarters looked comfortable enough, but the rooms were simply furnished and rather bare, something like a house in "Tobacco Road," the furniture typical of the 1920's. I did notice an old-fashioned, upright piano among the living room furnishings but couldn't imagine it would have much tone or action in the sultry, tropical climate. Nevertheless it was there — evidence of his interest in music.

In 1939 he sent me a delicately carved head of a Javanese woman made from teak for my graduation from College. I have treasured the beautiful carving, and though I have seen many like it since, I think mine is the most exquisitely done.

In 1940 Hans proposed. The letter arrived while I was living in Cincinnati and attending the Conservatory of Music. It was a pitiful letter, the outcries of a very lonely man needing companionship in a country far from modern civilization. He yearned for a more normal existence around friends his own age and race. Though desperately alone, Hans had no desire to cultivate relationship with the Javanese people. Moreover, as the head of a plantation, he could not afford to become socially or intimately involved with the people who worked under him. More importantly, he was not attracted to the native girls, even with their beauty and grace, because of the difference in their cultures, religion and level of education.

Hans wrote he had grown to love me through our exchange of letters and hoped I felt the same. He said he hesitated to ask me to sacrifice

[87]

everything I was used to and learn about a new way of life with him in Indonesia, but he felt compelled to try.

I could not bring myself to respond to his proposal at all, hoping he would think I had never received it. I felt very sorry for him in his loneliness, but I could not visualize myself living far off in Indonesia with a man I had never seen. Within a month of receiving his letter, I became engaged myself and wrote him the news. He then began to inquire for a bride by proxy in the Netherlands.

When the war began, letters were censored in the Netherlands and delivery was uncertain. Hans wrote me about his plans for a bride, and I forwarded his requests to his cousin, Bep. For a time we carried on a three-way correspondence, as America was not yet involved in the war. He finally found a girl in The Hague willing to move to Java and marry him. They actually were married by proxy, and she planned to proceed to Java as soon as the war ended and civilian travel was permitted. Hans was full of hope about the future in the last letter I received on March 1, 1942, dated February first. It took a month for letters to cross the seas at that time.

That same morning the *New York Herald Tribune* carried the blaring headline "Java Fallen to the Japanese."

Horrified, I read the article as it recounted the slaughter of helpless Indonesians, falling to the Japanese invaders. The invasion began the night of February twenty-eighth, and the country capitulated almost immediately, having no defenses. The article went on to say many Javanese attempted to escape by hiding in the jungles of the interior, but it didn't take long for all of them to be routed out and killed.

The mail arrived a little later in the morning. I trembled when I held Hans' letter, and then I wept. I knew he must certainly be dead even if he had been able to find refuge in the jungle. More likely he would have been one of the guerilla fighters trying to defend Java. No one, not even Bep, ever knew what really happened to him. Bep and I lost communication from then on, because Holland had fallen to Germany.

CHAPTER EIGHTEEN

MY senior year at Tudor Hall seemed endless. I was exhausted with the daily routine and constant studying. My long theme on Thomas Hardy required a great deal of reading and compositional skill. Our assignment was to read everything ever written by our chosen author, as well as everything written about him, including biographies and newspaper articles. The typewritten composition had to be at least fifty pages in length. I would have enjoyed doing this more if I hadn't had so much other school work to accomplish. I was also taking singing lessons with George Newton (to surprise my Mother) and Mr. Cramer was not letting up on his demands on the piano.

To compound the difficulties in allowing enough hours in the day for all my work, we were rehearsing for the operetta "Pinafore," which would be presented that spring. I studied hard on the leading role of Josephine. I also played an entire concert for the Prelude Club on last minute notice. In addition, I was in rehearsal for two concerts of one hundred and twenty-five pianos. All of these events took place in May.

Frank Wilking, the creative owner and manager of the Wilking Music Company, a Steinway franchise, thought up a good publicity stunt for selling a recently made, new model of piano — a tiny, baby grand Wurlitzer, only four feet in length. He conducted the concerts at the Butler Field House with two people at each of the one hundred twenty-five pianos, organizing a program for all stages of difficulty so even beginning students could participate. I was in the advanced group with adults and teachers. Our group of two hundred and fifty played "Pomp and Circumstance" with good precision.

A month later, on June fifth, I was marching down the aisle of the First Presbyterian Church to the stirring melody of that same piece by Elgar, in my graduation ceremony from Tudor Hall. By coincidence, this date later became my wedding date.

———————<◇>———————

Spring vacation was a welcome break. Aunt Bertha invited me to go with her and Janice to Bermuda, and we had a marvelous time! We sailed over and back on *The Queen of Bermuda*, leaving from New York. I only regretted it took such a short time to get to Bermuda, as I could endure ship life indefinitely.

Our hotel was the exclusive Waterloo House on a tiny beach close to the town of Hamilton. The nicest feature about the House was that it was run like a family residence with intimate, personal attention. The meals were delicious, gourmet feasts, served to everyone at a set hour, with an atmosphere of quiet dignity. We appreciated staying at such an extraordinary hotel, but Janice and I were looking for a little excitement, and there

[89]

were no young people of our ages there. However, the famous Princess Hotel just next door was a mecca for tourists. The vast neatly landscaped, flowery grounds also contained a private golf course and tennis courts. We often walked over to the hotel after dinner to listen to the dance music and perhaps find someone to dance with among the crowd.

The first thing we did after our arrival was to see about renting a bicycle. No automobiles were allowed on the island then. Horses and carriages, or bicycles, were the only forms of transportation other than one's own feet. Janice and I rented a tandem bicycle and had a great time riding through town and exploring the beaches. Coral Beach was almost an hour's pedal from Hamilton. Janice never learned to ride a bicycle. So it was up to me to do all the steering and balancing while Janice sat and hung on, a dead weight behind me. She learned how to pedal and apply the brakes a little later.

I thought I would be able to manage the unaccustomed burden of another person's weight along with the problem of balancing and handling the much larger and heavier bike. So we started off undaunted. Unfortunately for us the bike shop was situated at the top of a rather steep hill, and it was necessary to descend the hill to get to the main street, where the traffic flowed unabated. A Bobby stood in his safe box, squarely in the middle of the street, directing the traffic. Down we went, faster than we intended, avoiding with difficulty much foot traffic, horses and carriages and other bikers, but we couldn't stop in time to avoid a collision with "the cop in the box." The brakes, we discovered later, had to be controlled by both of us at once. We ended up in a heap, red in the face, and sure we would be spending our week's vacation in an airless cell. Fortunately, the Bobby was kind. He had seen us as we wobbled precariously down the crowded street and knew it was our first time out. With a gentle warning, he gave us some needed advice on operating the tandem, helped us with directions, and we were off, subdued but stable.

We found the lovely Coral Beach, and every day after that we pedaled there, taking care not to overdo the sun bathing. The last day, however, was too much of a temptation not to stay in the sun much longer. By that evening, when we boarded the *Queen* for our return to New York, I discovered how burned I was. I couldn't even bend my legs. The sea was rough the first night, and the combination of a very bad sunburn and heaving waves made me very ill. Poor Aunt Bertha and Janice were up with me the entire night sponging my back and legs with cold tea compresses and holding a basin for my sickness. Somehow Janice was not badly burned, but I will never forget how sick I was, and how embarrassed to cause such trouble for dear Aunt Bertha and Janice. I was in bed the entire trip to New York and arrived weak and shaky. Later, back at Tudor, I was the envy of all for my wonderful tan until it began to peel off in great sheets of dead skin!

CHAPTER NINETEEN

AFTER spring vacation in Bermuda, there were many luncheons and teas given by the girls in the senior class. Festivities and farewell get-togethers before graduation kept us busy socially, as well as studying constantly for final exams, college boards and scholastic aptitude tests. Because I had applied for admission to Sarah Lawrence, college boards were not required, but I did take the aptitude test, which was full of math problems (my biggest weakness.) I studied for the test with Miss Wells, an excellent math teacher at Tudor, who gave me a sample test to work from, and together we checked the answers.

When I finally took the test, I couldn't believe my eyes. The test was identical to the one I had studied the night before! I was so stunned at my good fortune I quickly set down the answers, knowing them to be correct and hardly took the time to read the problems. Finished in less than half the time, I sat in a daze wondering if I should admit my knowledge or not. I wrestled with my conscience and finally decided to say nothing. I didn't tell my secret to anyone for years, the only time I ever cheated on anything.

I was accepted at Sarah Lawrence, passing that examination as well as baring my soul on the psychological forms I had to fill out.

On May thirtieth Alex Scovell, the son of our dear Australian friend, arrived in Muncie. He was to visit us until mid-July. Mr. Scovell, nearing retirement, sent Alex on the business trip he had always taken. The Scovell Company exported the fine, woolen goods of Australia. Alex had already been to London and New York, and he had some free time coming, which he spent with us. Alex was twenty-six, charming, tall and handsome. I became enamoured of our interesting guest with the lovely Aussie accent.

June fifth was graduation day at last. I had invited Dick Dearborn to be my escort for the dance after commencement exercises. Dick lived in Muncie, and that evening, on his way to Indianapolis in a brand new car, he had two flat tires. It made no difference that I was without a date because Ed Cox, Olie Hedstrom and Alex were on hand. Janice and Jane Hitchcock, as well as Mother and Dad, made our group lively, and it was one of the best dances I can remember. In my diary I wrote, "I never had less than three cut-ins on any dance, and without a date!"

The graduation ceremony at the First Presbyterian Church at 16th and Delaware, was memorable. We wore white evening dresses, and each carried a dozen, long-stemmed red roses. I sang two solos in the musical portion of the program. Mother later had my dress cut up and the eyelet, embroidered organdy made into a set of place mats. I am still using them today.

The summer proceeded with a succession of dates and parties with friends, as well as preparation for riding in the upcoming horse shows. Alex left on short business trips, but while he was there, an interesting romantic affair developed. We were definitely attracted to each other, but again, the time was not ready for me to become too serious with anyone. It was easy for me to like anyone who showed an interest in me, and I always seemed to be more attracted to older men than to ones my own age.

I have mentioned Ed and Olie who came to my graduation. They were both from Hartford City, eighteen miles north of Muncie, and we became acquainted when they rode at Orchard Lawn. They were my dearest friends, along with Steve Trentman, also from Hartford City. I called the trio my Three Musketeers. We had wonderful times together. Steve was attending Princeton when I met him, but Ed Cox and Olaf Hedstrom had their businesses in Hartford City. Olie graduated from Dartmouth. He had a brilliant mind, keen as a razor, and quite a creative flair for art. Once, after a heavy snowfall, when Olie was home on vacation from college, he molded a strikingly good ice statue of a nude woman on his front lawn. Such statues are famous on the Dartmouth campus during the Ice Carnival. The local paper took up the story and reported Olie's artistic accomplishment, adding that "he did it all from memory."

Ed's wit and dry remarks kept us in stitches. His ambition was to become a playwright, and he read his situation comedies to me. I thought they were good, but when he sent them to Leland Hayward, the famous publisher and playwright, they were always rejected. Ed could not seem to transfer his spontaneous, witty remarks to paper.

Ed's father invented the Overhead Door. After his death, Ed ran the corporation in Hartford City, but he was not happy as a business man. He had too artistic a temperament for mundane office work. His disillusionment at his failure to write a publishable play made him bitter. He hated the business more and more but stuck to it until the war called him into the service.

On the Fourth of July our family left for Chicago where we joined Alex, who had been there for a few days on business. We boarded a train for Banff, Canada. Dad wanted to show Alex a little of our spectacular country before he left for Australia. Our trip west included the awesome grandeur of the great National Parks of Yellowstone and Glacier Parks in the U.S. and Canada.

The Banff Springs Hotel was an imposing structure amid gorgeous surroundings, reminding us of Switzerland. We enjoyed the swimming pool and danced to orchestral music after dinner. In this romantic setting it was natural for Alex and me to fall in love. Walking through the woods or sitting on a rustic bench watching the bobbing, reflected lights of the

[92]

moon play on the lake water, cast magical spells.

Lake Louise was a gem. Deep, cool blue, still water, reflecting the jagged, snow-peaked mountains ringing the lake, gave me a sense of being close to God.

We rode horseback through the sweet-smelling woods and absorbed the glory of Nature's gift to us. The scenery continued to be breathtaking as we drove on to Waterton Lake, over four hundred miles of dusty mountainous roads. The hairpin turns made us queasy. I remember our touring car was open on all sides, but there were isinglass side curtains that could be drawn along the top of the doors and snapped together if the elements were severe. Unfortunately, when the curtains were in place, you could not see through them. Most of the time we endured the cold wind billowing with dust, but there were blankets to wrap around us against the chill.

Eventually we arrived at Glacier Park, staying at the Prince of Wales Hotel. We visited both the Canadian and the American parks and from there dropped down to Yellowstone Park. Throughout the trip I was dizzy under Alex's spell. He very nearly proposed one night, but both of us realized we were only infatuated and not ready for any final commitments.

It was a strain when we finally separated at the Continental Divide. He continued west to Seattle and on to a ship for Australia, and we headed east on a train for Chicago. Alex insisted he would return the following year, giving us time to contemplate our feelings for each other, but he never returned. His father became ill, and he was needed at home. The war steadily approached, creating export and financial problems, and within three years it had changed our lives.

Alex always has remained dear to me. We continued to correspond, and from time to time Alex would send me gifts from Australia. During the war he was stationed in Lae, New Guinea, and once a box arrived containing interesting, crude articles made by the natives, such as a pair of carved wood idols, incised and painted with lime to offset the designs.

After Alex left, I spent most of the summer languishing over his absence, with many thoughts of "what if"? My romantic infatuation blossomed, and I waited eagerly for his letters with future promises which never materialized.

The Coxes, Hedstroms and Trentmans owned cottages at Lake James, a small lake near Angola, Indiana. Ed invited me for a weekend in August, and it turned into a memorable time.

Ed, Olie, Steve and I had great fun swimming, surfboarding and sailing. Olie's sailboat gave us a perfect sail, and I learned to manage the surfboard behind Ed's Chris-Craft.

Ed's mother was a lovable woman, but quite obese. Ed joked about her

[93]

appearance saying she bought her clothes at "The Tent and Awning Company." She had a sweet, little Pekinese dog, which seemed to spend its life in her lap. Ed loved to watch the dog's reaction when anyone spelled out the word C-A-N-D-Y. No matter how softly spoken or how inserted into a sentence, the dog would jump up in excitement when the word was spelled, begging for the treat.

Saturday evening we all crossed the lake in Ed's boat to Bledsoe's Beach where we danced and enjoyed the balmy, moonlit night. On Sunday, after another day on the lake, we went to Olie's cottage for a cocktail party, after which we played bridge until it was time for a midnight supper. The weekend was typical of the fun the four of us had together, some of the highlights of my life.

Olie married Carolyn Scofield on October 16, 1937, and we all went to their wedding in Cincinnati. Their marriage didn't hurt our friendship, for Carolyn was a welcome addition to our close group.

Two weeks after the weekend with Ed at Lake James, our family left on another trip, and this time we took Ed Cox along with us to liven up the party. We took the train to Boston and from there drove to Maine in a borrowed car.

On the way, we paused at the Essex Country Club near Marblehead to watch the great tennis player, Helen Jacobs, defeat the top players of the year and then pressed on to Portland, Maine.

One of the most embarrassing moments of my life occurred during the ride. Dad was driving with Hudson on the front seat, and Mother, Ed and I were in the back. Hudson, squirming about as usual, turned around to face us. Suddenly he blurted out, "Look at Cina's hairy legs!" I nearly died of humiliation. Conversation stopped dead, and my face bloomed with hot, red blushes. I never forgot the dreadful remark, but I certainly began to shave my legs from then on. Mother had not permitted me to do it, but even she agreed the time had come! I was ready to murder my brother!

I could hardly face Ed the rest of the day, though soon everyone but I forgot the incident. Ed with his great, good humor, passed it off as nothing. By the time we reached Darkharbor, an island off the coast of Maine, it was my birthday and a celebration was in order. I remember how very cold and dismal it was in Maine.

The hotel in Darkharbor was filled with the snobbery of high society and the nouveau-riche. The cream of society came here for their summer vacations. The evening we arrived, there was a fancy dress ball. Ed thought of borrowing the uniforms of a bell hop and maid for our costumes, as we had nothing with us to wear for such an occasion.

We had fun posing as the hired help, delivering drinks and doing other services for the guests. We played the game to the hilt in our disguise.

[94]

Finally, Ed decided it was time for us to dance. When we began to dance, the haughty stares of the costumed people followed us everywhere, not believing we were also guests of the hotel.

We laughed, mimicking the stilted accent of the Bostonians. All the Drexels and "Pretzels," the Biddles, the Dibbles and the "Dribbles" were there enjoying the expensive, cold, wet, summer in their ultra-posh vacation homes.

While dabbing for flounder off the pier in Bar Harbor, Hudson caught a large live starfish. He was ecstatic and begged for permission to take it home with us. Driving back to New York, the water in the bucket holding the starfish sloshed over our feet. At night in the hotels, the bathtub was reserved for the animal. By the time we finally arrived in New York, we were all in urgent need of a good bath, because for four days the starfish had held the bathtub rights.

After a busy day of shopping in New York, we returned to our room at the Biltmore. As we opened the door, a decayed odor filled the room, and we knew at once the starfish had met its Maker. Mother fished the limp creature from the tub, opened the window on our twenty-first floor and threw him out! Before he had fallen two floors, a great cloud of pigeons and gulls appeared from nowhere with a great shrieking outcry. They converged on the falling starfish, and in one swoop, the victor carried off his prize pursued by a swarm of the birds fighting over the remains. Hudson sat down and cried over his loss, but the rest of us were relieved to be rid of the foul-smelling creature.

After leaving New York and the excitement of the city, the theater and famous restaurants, we boarded a train for Utica, New York, where we were met by Verne Gransdon, a classmate of Dad's at Cornell University. We spent three days with him and his wife at their lodge at Lake Hamilton, one of the most beautiful spots I can remember. The Gransdons owned the entire lake and one thousand acres of land. It was peaceful and yet wild with game roaming through the woods. The lodge was almost a mansion and furnished as one might expect, with heavy rustic furniture and colorful rugs. It was a place I would have loved for myself — completely isolated, surrounded by nature. We played tennis on the well-kept courts, canoed on the lake and hiked through the deep, wild woods.

We returned home on August thirtieth. It had been fun having Ed Cox with us, and I began to turn my attention his way, though I was still very much in love with Alex.

1936 was a year of romances. I fell in and out of love with Alex Scovell, discovered I loved Ed Cox, but also dated many other boys. There were movies, dances, or "coke dates" at the North Pole or Pig Stand. It was a year of concentrated work at school, piano lessons and long hours of practice. I rode in many horse shows. There were the trips to Bermuda,

[95]

Glacier Park and Maine.

It was the year I entered the adult world of society, going to luncheons, teas, lectures, symphony concerts and the theater with my parents, as well as with my own group of friends.

It was the year my father became the first President of the Board of the newly-formed Indianapolis Symphony Orchestra. He was instrumental in hiring Fabien Sevitsky as the conductor, after the founder, Ferdinand Schaeffer, retired.

Mother and Dad were members of the Traders Point Hunt Club in Indianapolis, and for a long time my friends had urged me to ride in the Hunt with them. I had no interest in hunting or jumping, but at last I agreed to give it a try.

I was given a horse who knew a great deal more than I about the rules of the game. I said a little prayer, "Oh, God, let me make it," gave the horse free rein, clung tight with my knees, and we were off.

I can't describe the panic I felt as we tore over the countryside jumping over logs, gullies, rocks and other impediments. I was fearful the mare might stumble over the rough terrain and fall, but she was sure-footed and knew her territory. I had always ridden within a fenced, tanbark ring, or on neat, cinder bridle paths. I had never jumped, except for my games with Billy. I was, quite frankly, terrified. Once we tore through a grove of trees, and I was almost swept off the horse's back by a low-hanging limb. I flattened myself to her neck at the last moment and escaped with inches to spare.

I talked to my horse and let her have her head, knowing she would pull me through with her expertise, if I could only keep from interfering. Trying to hold her back would only have made her frantic and insecure. I hated the day and the wild gallops across the fields and told myself I would never do it again.

I was a nervous wreck when the Hunt finally ended. Sweating and visibly shaken, I could hardly walk to the car where Mother and Dad waited. We did not stay for the cocktail party, as I was too exhausted, but headed for school where I went to bed at once, in tears from the shock but mostly relieved I had not fallen and disgraced myself.

I was encouraged to try again by the Master and Mistress of the Hounds, Marge and George Bailey. Mrs. Bailey was a beautiful woman who rode sidesaddle and looked elegant on her horse. The Baileys were good friends of my parents. She convinced me I would enjoy the Hunt if I wore the proper clothes — boots, bowler and all the trappings to insure more safety on the rides. I agreed the bowler hat might save me from a concussion, and the boots would protect my legs, but the expense of the outfit seemed ridiculous when I had no intention of ever adopting this style of riding.

However, I was challenged. My Indianapolis riding friends were making snide remarks about my "sissy" kind of riding. I needed to prove I was as good a rider as any fool on a jumper. Marge Bailey took me to Ayres and helped me choose the correct clothes for the Hunt. I had always worn soft jodhpurs and jackets, comfortable low boots and a soft hat for show riding. The new clothes were heavy, tough, scratchy wools. I was required to buy an expensive stock to wear with my shirt, and the bowler hat looked very snappy, but it weighed heavily on my head, reinforced with steel bracings.

The boots were miserable to pull on and off. I had to use boot hooks to pull them on, and a helpful friend to yank them off. Once on, they were not too uncomfortable. I was outfitted, and with these clothes I would be transformed into a bonafide rider of the Hunt.

So I rode again, and this time, knowing what to expect, it went a little better. I even had the same nice mare to ride. Wearing the proper clothes, I found, was helpful, giving more protection against injuries that could occur during the ride.

I still did not like cross-country racing. My feeling for riding centered on my ability to make the horse perform as perfectly as possible. My joy came from feeling the horse respond to my signals, not just giving me the excitement of a fast ride.

The third and last time I rode with the Traders Point Hunt was the time my parents hosted the Club at the dairy farm in Eaton. A fox scent was dragged over the country, marking the course. The group arrived in trucks with their horses and stable boys, and, after the running, a festive picnic was held at the Lodge, where Jane and I had once dug for treasure.

The event was enhanced by the appearance of Margaret Bourke-White, who took pictures of the Hunt for the *Life Magazine* issue of May, 1937.

CHAPTER TWENTY

B EFORE graduating from Tudor Hall, I had decided I wanted to take a year off to study or relax as I pleased. I had never worked harder at school than at Tudor, and I was tired. I wanted more time at home with the horses. I planned to enter college the fall of '37.

I chose Sarah Lawrence for a number of reasons. Constance Warren, the College President, came to Tudor to speak, and I liked her immediately. The curriculum was such that the student could concentrate in the field of her choice. There were no compulsory courses. It was a two-year college, as well as four, if one desired a degree. There were no exams — no grades at all — just periodical statements from the teachers evaluating academic progress. It sounded very attractive.

The College is in Bronxville, New York, only a half-hour train ride to New York, where I could attend concerts and the theater. The biggest attraction the school had for me was that Lee Pattison was on the faculty. He was famous for his two-piano artistry with Guy Maier. Together Pattison and Maier toured extensively, playing all over the country. I was anxious to study with him, but I felt I needed more time to be ready and planned months of practice to meet his standards.

I continued to board at the Tudor Residence for one semester so I could continue my piano lessons with Bomar Cramer. I also attended French classes and wrote another long theme, this time on Joseph Conrad. I even took an art course on scale drawing, my first experience of this kind. Miss Stewart allowed me a private room at the farthest corner of the Residence, where I needn't be subject to house rules, such as lights out or rest periods. I was free to go and come as I wished, and though I didn't receive credit for the extra work, I didn't care. I was doing what I enjoyed, and it was a great feeling to be under no pressure.

After the semester was over, our family took an adventurous trip to Guatemala and Mexico. We left on February 7, 1937, by train to New Orleans. Ours was the first train allowed to pass through Louisville, Kentucky after a disastrous flood swamped the city. Devastation was the word to describe the view as the train inched slowly through the still flooded area. But the danger had passed, and the Ohio River was subsiding.

It was Mardi Gras time in New Orleans, and the city was abuzz with revelers. We saw the parade from our Roosevelt Hotel windows and attended the Proteus Ball that evening. The costumes were spectacular and the men unrecognizable in their masks. We were seated in the balcony overlooking the dance floor and could only watch the festivities. I thought it very dull not to be able to dance.

We spent a day sightseeing and haunting the antique shops on Royale Street, Mother's favorite pursuit in her favorite city. We even visited the old French cemetery and were amused to see that most of the flower vases holding bouquets on the graves were Ball jars!

After dinner at the famous Antoine's Restaurant, relishing their original and incomparable oysters Rockefeller, we boarded the S.S. *Santa Marta*, a United Fruit Line ship.

There were quite a few unattached young men on board, which made the voyage fun for me. We danced until late every evening, and, before giving up the night reluctantly, strolled the decks in the balmy, tropical air.

At first, the waters were very rough, and we experienced one violent storm. The best place for me, I found, was bundled up in a deck chair to watch the wind and waves fight their battle. There I kept my nausea under control fairly well until a thoughtless man sat down beside me. His cigar, blowing downwind into my face, did the trick. I was back in our cabin in no time.

Enroute to Puerto Barrios we stopped briefly in Belize to load on a cargo of bananas. There was a revolution going on. Men with guns swaggered along the roadside, and trucks passed, loaded with soldiers and ammunition. The confusion plus the torrid heat kept Dad exclaiming, "Pl-ease, get me out of Belize!"

But we didn't leave until the bananas were loaded on the ship. I was fascinated by the operation. Workers carried enormous stalks of green bananas on their backs to the cargo nets, which, when full, were hoisted and swung over the deck and lowered down into the holds. It took half a day to load them. By the time the ship returned to New Orleans and the bananas were unloaded and shipped, they would be ripened and ready for retailing.

When we arrived at Puerto Barrios, a dance was held for the passengers in the central square. It was a small park strung with Christmas lights, and a bandstand held a few musicians. Dad commented, "They can't play good, but they can play loud!" It was a rather pathetic effort to entertain us, but the tropical night with the full moon out-shining the Christmas lights, made up for the poor music.

The village was a small community of unpainted, sagging buildings and poor, ragged people. The boy children were naked from the waist down, but the little girls wore shifts to cover their bare behinds. All were barefoot with runny noses and tangled hair. They crowded around begging for coins, and we could scarcely move or breathe from the pressure of their bodies. It was very dirty and unbearably hot.

The only form of transportation from the coast to Guatemala City was by train. No roads had yet been built in or out of the country. The train was an antique model, open along the sides to permit as much air as possible to enter the coaches. So we hurried to find seats close to the open section. The benches were made of woven straw. Many years of sitting on them had caused tears and rips in the basketry that scratched and stuck to our backsides all during the long, hot ride. It took twelve hours to cover the one-hundred-and-fifty-mile journey, which began at 6:30 in the morning. We chugged laboriously up the mountain from sea level to the five-thousand-foot altitude of the city. We felt we were on the little train that kept saying, "I think I can, I think I can," but the coach filled with jabbering Guatemalans seemed unconcerned as they cooled themselves with large palmetto fans.

As we inched upward, villagers all along the way thrust large platters of tropical fruit through the windows, hoping for a sale. Other food was offered too, but it was hard to define, hidden so thoroughly beneath the top layer of flies. There were crudely made wooden toys and other crafts, such as baskets the people were desperate to sell. But everything was so dirty, we resisted it all. It was hard enough keeping the merchandise out of our faces. If we backed away from the windows, we suffocated in the stifling air inside the train.

The lavatory was almost impossible to use. Once, the train stopped mid-way on its journey for lunch to give the passengers a rest. There was a large barn sitting in the middle of the jungle. Inside were long tables covered with oilcloth and benches lining either side. We were served something to eat, but somehow no one was very hungry and we sort of picked around the plate of dark brown food. We did enjoy the wonderful fruit, however, once we had peeled it and shooed off the flies.

I can't forget how hot, slow, dirty and long that train trip was, but it was a beautiful, scenic journey through the jungled mountains and an interesting insight into the lives of the poorest of people. We arrived exhausted in Guatemala City, sober and full of painful thoughts about our Central American neighbors.

Once in the capital city, we were amazed by the change. The city was modern, clean and sparkling, with wide, immaculate streets and large white buildings. The shops offered well-made crafts and beautiful textiles. In this more prosperous setting, the people were clean and well-groomed, wearing the gorgeous costumes of their native villages. All were barefoot, but healthy and rugged, clear-eyed and happy. They carried everything on their backs, and sometimes the loads looked impossibly heavy, such as pieces of furniture. But to them it seemed all in a day's work.

Guatemala City was buzzing with festivity, decorated with banners, flags and huge posters for the inauguration of the President, Jorge Ubico. He had been elected in 1931 for a term of six years, but the government gradually became a dictatorship under his power, and the inauguration was merely a symbol of re-election. Ubico was dictator until 1944, when at last he was forced to resign, as the country embraced the communistic ideologies.

In 1937, a military parade passed by our hotel window, where we watched for two hours, impressed by the show of manpower and military strength displayed in the parade. That night the streets were alive with celebration, and fireworks showered sparks of color over the city. We remained in the hotel, afraid to be on the streets, had a good dinner and listened to the unfamiliar sound of a delightful marimba band.

We made the drive most popular with tourists — a circuit from Guatemala City to Antigua, Chichicastenango, and back to the capital. The roads have been much improved since 1937. My husband, Sam, and I were there in 1959, and the roads had been paved, straightened and widened into good highways. Our 1937 tour in a vintage auto, however, was hair raising with many twists and turns around the precipitous mountains. There were no guardrails or safe shoulders, and the graveled roads made the car skid around turns. Our driver, well acquainted with the road, whipped along, creating a dust bowl behind us. I felt sorry for the stream of villagers walking along with their impossible burdens, breathing in the grit of the road as they trudged. Straps around their foreheads held great bags of fruit or firewood, and they walked bent nearly double from the strain. The climb uphill in the altitude must have been a labor indeed. I marveled their bare feet could stand the graveled roads, but always shoeless, they developed callouses as thick as stone and feet wide and flat to support the great weights they had to carry. Their clothes were colorful and made of intricately woven wool material, resistant to the cold mountain air and tropical rains.

Animals on the road were additional hazards. Cows, goats and burros wandered aimlessly about, sometimes looming in front of the car at the most dangerous hairpin turn.

At last we came to Antigua and registered in a lovely inn surrounded by flamboyant gardens filled with bougainvillia, orchids and birds of paradise. Tropical birds in cages hanging from the trees sang in a foreign language. A little girl on her bicycle rode around the paths with a pet parrot on her shoulder. We discovered she was the daughter of the innkeeper. Neither she nor the parrot could speak English, but I learned the song the parrot kept singing every time the bicycle started wheeling along the paths. "Vamos a la mar!" sang the parrot over and over. It was more than ten years later before I finally knew what the bird sang. "Let's go to the sea!" I still remember the tune and the parrot's perfect pitch.

Guatemala is a country full of active volcanoes, and near Antigua there is a cavernous lake of unknown depths, caused by an ancient volcanic eruption. Lake Atitlan, treacherous for boating or swiming, is the subject of many mysterious legends. The high hills rising above the vast body of clear, blue water are covered with lush jungle growth, and, at the low side of the lake, nestles the village of Antigua. Antigua was the capital of Guatemala until it was destroyed by an earthquake in 1776.

The next day we drove on to Chichicastenango, one of the most inaccessible and remote villages in the high altitude of the mountainous country. We discovered a picturesque village swarming with activity. Of Mayan descent, the men were dressed in black wool knee pants and short bolero jackets, bright sashes around their waists, and turban style wool caps. They walked from their farms on the outskirts of the village, carrying produce to sell at the marketplace in the zocolo (city center.) Their women crouched over the goods spread on the cobbled street. Wearing long skirts of brightly patterned wool and white blouses covered with beaded necklaces. With long earrings and colorful ribbons tied into their hair, they were even more striking than the men. A rebozo around their shoulders warmed them or helped to carry their babies, tied behind securely in the strong shawls.

The people worshipped in the white church, Santo Tomas, standing high above the village square and dominating the view. It was built at the top of a pyramid of steep stone steps, which we, as foreigners, were not allowed to climb. The natives sat on the steps, selling firewood, or burning candles as they prayed, climbed the steps on their knees, sometimes taking hours to reach the church door.

We were allowed access to the church by a side door, which led up a staircase to the sanctuary, but, none the less, the Mayan people resented our presence, defiling their holy place of worship. The services, we were told, are a mixture of the ancient Indian rites and Catholicism. We were deathly quiet and respectful as we stood with heads covered, awed by the golden altar, swinging lanterns and flickering candles below the image of the Virgin. The aroma of incense lay heavy in the air.

Although the days were warm and bright with sun, the nights in the extreme altitude were very cold. In the pre-dawn, our room boy would slip in noiselessly on his bare feet, carrying a load of firewood. Quietly he laid a fire in the fireplace, and, a little later, as the room warmed, our maid would enter with trays of steaming hot chocolate and bizocochos (rolls). She placed them on a low table beside the fire and retired with a "buenos dias," leaving us to enjoy our breakfast by the fireside.

The famous Mayan Inn earned its reputation from excellent service, wonderful food and beautiful decor. I decided it was the place I wanted to return to on my honeymoon, a paradise of beauty, serenity and historical fascination.

———————◆———————

The flight in a Pan-American plane from Guatemala City to Mexico City was exciting. We flew over active volcanos and could look down into the fiery craters. The mountains and jungles made for an awesome, scenic journey. There was an altimeter in the cabin of the plane and we watched it rise to sixteen-thousand feet as we soared over the tallest mountains. There was no oxygen for the passengers and in those days no pressurized cabins. Our family plus two other men were the only passengers on the plane, which could accommodate perhaps twenty people. Dad was rushing up and down the aisle of the plane, excitedly taking pictures of the smoking, burning volcanos below us, when suddenly he sagged down into a seat across the aisle from me, looking very green. He could not get his breath in the rarefied atmosphere, and, for once, was subdued enough to sit still until the plane reached Mexico City.

Mexico City was the first place I had ever been that I never wanted to see again. We spent five days there, but compared to Guatemala it was a shock. Poor people, ragged and diseased, ate horrible looking food from newspapers as they sat in the gutters of the filthy streets. Men and children urinated and defecated in public. In Guatemala we had seen healthy people, clean and strong. The Mexicans walked the streets, begging, with terrible eye infections and amputated limbs. They appeared distressed, sinister, angry and hopeless. They whined and held out thin, little arms, caked with grime and sores and slept in the streets or in public buildings wrapped in ragged, dirty serapes.

On Sunday afternoon we had an excellent dinner at the home of the Aguierre's, who handled our tours in Mexico. The mid-day meal was quite sumptuous, and, after this, we were taken to the bullfight. We sat on the sunny side (the less desirable side, but much cheaper seats).

I was excited by the fanfare and the noisy crowd. The pageantry of the parade was stirring as the band played paso dobles, and the participants marched into the arena with great ceremony. The toreros in their gorgeous trajes de lux, (suits of light) led, followed by the picadors on their decorated horses, with the senoritas bringing up the rear, exquisitely dressed in Spanish garb. Their lace mantillas were draped over high combs, and they fanned themselves seductively with large painted fans. The panorama of the parade created an exotic, hypnotic atmosphere.

All around the dusty arena, the crowd was screaming in one voice with excitement and anticipation. We were packed together like a can of sardines. My knees poked into the back of the person in front, and someone's knees behind me became my back rest.

All eyes were on the arena as the brave bull charged in, looking from side to side at his new surroundings. I was interested in the ballet-like cape movements the torero made with the bull, but I did not like to watch the horses tortured by the bull's horns when they rammed their sides. With each impact they were literally lifted off their feet, even though a heavy pad covering the horses somewhat protected them. Occasionally a bull is able to gore the horse from beneath the mattress-like pad, disemboweling the animal on the spot, but fortunately this did not happen that day. The poor horses were nothing but skinny nags, ready for the glue factory, but my heart bled for them.

At the moment of impact, as the bull charged, the picador thrust the "pic", his long lance, into the fatty muscle at the base of the bull's head, weakening the muscle until the bull was unable to hold up his head. Then the torero began his ballet by tossing a pair of bandarillas into the same muscle, as the bull lowered his head and charged. Gay, little ribbons

[103]

fluttered at the handles of the darts as the bull whirled away, startled by the sting. The game was played three times until six bandarillas were imbedded into the bull's neck. Now he looked neither bold nor proud. The torero would be able to shove his sword into that muscle later on, when the bull, exhausted, confused, tongue hanging limp from his throat, tried one final time to stagger a charge at his adversary.

We watched until this final moment. The torero missed his mark. It was not a clean kill to the heart, but a butchered thrust. The bull staggered on. Boos roared from the crowd and pillows were tossed into the arena to show disfavor. Finally, at the third attempt, the bull finally dropped, giving up the battle. The torero left the ring in disgrace.

I was not moved by the scene until a pair of mules were led in hauling a litter and the bull was placed on it and dragged unceremoniously away

At this moment, I was suddenly and violently sick, overcome by the tragedy of the bull's demise. I was wearing a new, attractive, white straw hat with a very wide brim, perfect for a sun shade. Desperately I whipped it off, turned it upsidedown on my lap, and it became a perfect basin. The act was so swift, silent and complete that not even Mother sitting next to me was aware of what had happened. All eyes were on the bull ring. The crowd was anxiously awaiting the next fresh bull to enter.

I continued to watch the subsequent bull fights with detachment, no longer excited but disgusted by the dangerous game that is almost always lost by the unsuspecting bull. The odds against the bull are more than ninety-nine percent.

Even though I had many opportunities to see more bull fights, I never went to another. I would have liked to have seen Cantinflas when we lived in Mexico, but tickets for his appearance were always sold out months in advance. He was a great actor, clown, singer and entertainer and was also adept at the art of bullfighting. He never killed the bull, and his antics were skillful and hilariously funny.

We were staying at the new Reforma Hotel, the ultimate in hotel luxury at that time. Coincidentally, the J . K . Lillys from Indianapolis were honeymooning in Mexico, and we met them in the lobby of the hotel, where they also were staying. They invited us to join them for dinner in their suite, and, afterwards we all attended a Jai Alai game.

We enjoyed the game so much we returned the following night for another exciting evening. The only thing I did not like was the pall of cigar and cigarette smoke, which hung in the air so thick, everything looked gray. I had an asthmatic reaction, and my eyes became so red and swollen I could scarcely open them to see the game.

Jai Alai is a difficult game of great skill and requires strength, agility, quick reflexes and accuracy. The ball travels almost two-hundred miles an hour as it is flung from the cesta to the walls. There is danger to the players as death could result from being struck by the hard ball traveling at such speed. The game is very exciting with constant fevered betting. As the odds keep changing, the betting becomes louder and more frantic.

I noticed a weird little man eyeing me on both nights, and when we left for our hotel on the second night, I was aware he was following us. I was very nervous, having seen his leers and winks at the games. He had the nerve to enter the Reforma Hotel behind us, and, as we walked into the elevator, the door closed on him just in time, leaving him looking disconcerted but still with a smiling "come-on" look. I was frightened and was careful to stay close to my parents after that.

We toured Mexico City, its museums and the great pyramids outside the city. We also rode in barges on the canals of Xochomilco to see the floating gardens and were serenaded by mariachis on nearby boats. I remember Mayor Jimmy Walker of New York on the barge ahead of us, entertaining a noisy group of friends. Their boat was connected to another one, which held a large mariachi band and a bar. Singing and drunken laughter from their boat rang through the canals above the cacophony of the many separate bands serenading the tourists for pesos.

The following day Hudson was unable to get out of bed. Mother, in alarm, hovered around, asking questions. The only answer from Hud was, "My legs hurt." Mother was wild. Could he be coming down with polio? He did not seem to have a fever. Finally, the realization dawned. He had climbed to the very top of the giant pyramid the day before and now was muscle-sore. He crept out of bed and limped painfully for a couple of days.

Our Mexican trip concluded with a flight to Brownsville, Texas, and were met by Madeline and Ken Frazier. They drove us to Corpus Christi, where we fished for two days, Mother and Hud the only successful fishermen. Dad never caught anything on fishing trips but odd things, such as an old shoe. Once he hooked a pelican!

The Fraziers were attractive friends of my parents. Madeline was French and had a charming accent. Her English was still quite broken after living in the States for two years. She told us a funny story about herself. The morning after her marriage to Ken in Paris, they called his parents in Texas to announce the news. Madeline had not met Ken's parents but wished to greet them, somehow, in the best English she could muster. All she managed to say was, "What a man — Ken — he is!"

We finally reached home after devious peregrinations through Texas and Louisiana, changing trains several times. A frustrating interurban ride, as well as a crowded bus trip from Louisville to Indianapolis brought us home in total exhaustion.

CHAPTER TWENTY-ONE

IN the summer of 1937, Dad gave me a used, Pontiac convertible with a rumble seat, and I learned how to drive. Though the car was something of a rattletrap, I thought it was "snazzy."

Guy Dickerson, the head garage mechanic at Ball Brothers taught me to drive at the farm on the winding bridle path through the hickory grove. I got the feel of the car before taking it on the trafficked roads — an excellent idea. I only had a few mishaps in the process and soon was driving everywhere, after I applied for my license.

It often happened when I was driving that a program called "Death Rides the Highway" was on the car radio. The theme song was the lugubrious, slow movement from Beethoven's Seventh Symphony — a veritable funeral march. The highway police sponsored the program, which related stories of accidents and deaths due to careless driving. As a neophyte driver, I identified with the program and I, as well as my passengers, listened and applied the situations to ourselves. We laughed and joked and soon the theme became my personal dirge.

The summer also found me riding in horse shows and enjoying them immensely. The Dayton Horse Show in Ohio one June weekend was particularly exciting. It was a dressy show. I wore my tuxedo and top hat for the three-gaited stake and changed to the less formal black outfit and bowler for the five-gaited stake. After the shows, we celebrated our winnings at the Kittyhawk Room in the hotel, dancing with our newly acquired friends from the show. I wrote in my diary, "I placed in all but two classes, altogether winning $250.00."

The Arlington Show in Indianapolis was always a good one. It was a social event as well as a collection of top horses in the area, and it was fun to meet many old friends there. The biggest show of the summer, however, was the week-long event at the Indiana State Fair, the first week of September. The State Fair Show culminated the summer's competition, and winning the stakes was a very prestigious honor for both horse and rider. The horse show at the Kentucky State Fair was even more important, and we usually drove to Louisville for this event, staying at the famous Brown Hotel and meeting old friends for dinner at the Pendennis Club, the hub of society gatherings in Louisville. Riding in the State Fair shows was pure excitement. It was thrilling to be awarded a ribbon because I was competing with the cream of horseflesh from the top stables around the Midwest. ——————◆——————

An important social event dominated the scene in Indianapolis that June. Evie Lilly, the daughter of Eli Lilly, made her debut into Indianapolis society. It was a tremendous splash of a party, never to be forgotten by anyone who was fortunate enough to be invited. The star of the evening was really not Evie, but Benny Goodman's band, especially hired for the occasion.

It so happened a young English earl was visiting us in Muncie at the time of the debut, having business at Ball Brothers, and I took him to the party as my date. He was good looking, but rather stiff, and I was self-conscious entertaining The Earl of Shrewsbury. But we had a good time, even though it was hard to find a meeting ground for conversation. We sat and listened to the marvelous music belted out by Benny Goodman. No one danced. The music was too good. We were glued to our seats watching Gene Krupa flash his drumsticks and Benny Goodman direct the music, playing his clarinet as only a master can.

Because of the hundreds of guests, the party was held outdoors on the neatly landscaped lawn of the Lilly estate. We entered the front door of their home, greeted the hosts and Evie in the receiving line and then proceeded through the house to the porch and on to the gardens beyond. Tables were set up around a dance floor constructed for the night's event, and lights were strung in lanterns from the trees, illuminating the festive setting.

We found a table close to the orchestra and never left our seats, or we would have lost our vantage point to others hoping for a closer view of Benny Goodman. Bob Eaglesfield found us there and livened up the evening for me by just being with us. I had met him that summer. We'd had a few dates, and he was good company, fun to be with. He joked and broke down the little ice barrier the Earl somehow created.

The party lasted well into the next morning. Everyone hated to leave, but finally the last guests straggled out, and the three of us went to the Waffle House for a four a.m. breakfast.

The summer passed quickly. I had dates with many friends and enjoyed the flirtations. One boy I dated was Harter Urban, the brother of Isabel Ball, Edmund's wife. Harter was 6' 7" tall and thin as a pair of scissors. He had a wry sense of humor. One evening we were dancing, and suddenly he looked down at the top of my head, saying, "Lucina, please stop chewing on my belt buckle." I couldn't dance any more as I laughed so hard at his remark. It was true, though. I barely reached to the top of his trousers.

I was also falling in love with Ed Cox. Being nine years older than I, he felt I had some growing up to do, and he was right. But he waited too long. My love wore thin from waiting almost three years for his declaration, and finally, I realized what I thought was love was just the tenderest admiration for a very dear friend.

That summer I began teaching piano to a few students. I didn't charge them for lessons because I enjoyed it so very much, and it was good experience for me also. Mother had raised me to feel I should never work.

[107]

In the depths of the Depression when jobs were scarce, she felt it would be wrong for anyone to have a job if they could afford not to work. Ball Brothers Company thrived in depression years, as these were the times when people raised their own vegetables and canned food to save money at the groceries. The sale of fruit jars hit an all-time-high between 1929 and 1935. During these years, I heard much discussion in the family about the Depression and the economic and political conditions in the country. Mother impressed on me the fact that I would never have to work, and, in fact, should not take a position for pay, as it would put someone in need out of a job.

I always had a great desire to teach but never thought I would do it professionally. The pupils I had throughout the years up to 1951 benefited without paying me, but they were all friends of mine. I didn't care about the money. I wanted to teach them to love making music as I did.

One child, the daughter of Dr. and Mrs. Will C. Moore (Dr. Moore was the top surgeon in Muncie) came to me every day for a lesson. Nancy was very spoiled. She had temper tantrums if things didn't go her way, but I liked her and assumed we got along well during the lessons. One day I was at their farm in Yorktown, just outside of Muncie. Nancy was an excellent rider, and most of her energies were spent on this skill. Her favorite pet, a cat, had just given birth to a litter of kittens, and she was proudly showing them off to me. I told her I loved seeing them but couldn't hold one as I was quite allergic to cats. With that, she picked up the feisty mother cat and threw her squarely into my face with great force, causing the cat to rake her claws down my arms and legs. At the same time, I was amazed to hear her spit out, *"That's what you get for giving me piano lessons!"* Within minutes she watched the scratches swell, redden and bleed, while my nose and eyes turned into a river. I was overcome with asthma, but she never said a word of apology. I suppose she was relieved when the lessons stopped.

———————◈———————

I spent several summers in Leland, Michigan visiting Janice. The summer I spent the month of August with her, Ed Cox and Steve Trentman came up for a weekend and also A.C. Bernstein, another boy I had a great many dates with. Lake Michigan was a good lake for swimming but often cold and forbidding in poor weather. Lake Leelanau nearby was where the Balls kept their boats, and we would drive there for motor boat rides or fishing.

The village of Leland boasted a post office and a general store, which sold everything from household goods, drugs, groceries, and gifts to clothes and furniture. The short main street was mostly filled with the unpretentious homes of the townsfolk, who lived there year round. There was also a country pub and restaurant, where we went in the evenings for a little diversion. The juke box provided out-of-date music, but it was peppy,

[108]

and we danced to it. Only beer was served here, so we drank cokes, not liking beer too well.

One night Janice and I dreamed up an activity that ended in disaster. We decided it was time to find out how much we were able to drink so we would never disgrace ourselves on a date. Janice and I had the cottage to ourselves, as Aunt Bertha was away for a short time. We drove to Traverse City and bought a bottle of dark rum. After dinner, in front of a roaring fire in the great living room fireplace, we sat and methodically spiked our cokes with the heavy Myers rum. The experiment proved too silly for words, as we soon became drunk and could hardly talk to each other. Janice had sense enough to stop when we ran out of coke, but I was determined to finish the bottle of rum and continued to drink mine straight with ice.

At last the experiment was over, and so was I. Janice helped me upstairs to bed where I promptly became sick. I never felt so terrible in all my life. The room swam in circles, and the bed felt worse than a ship in a storm. I was unable to get to the bathroom, but Janice took care of me all night at my bedside. Fortunately she was not as drunk as I.

I was even sicker all the next day. I couldn't hold up my head for the pain. I vowed it was the last experiment of this type I would ever attempt, and I was always careful from that day on not to overdo my drinking. I was appalled to see the empty bottle of rum the next day. We (or I) had finished the entire fifth. I never have been able to drink dark rum in any form since then, but I also never disgraced myself on a date!

CHAPTER TWENTY-TWO

T HAT fall it was time to pack and leave for college. I had farewell dates with all my special friends, and on September fifteenth, Mother, Dad and I were on the Southwestern Limited bound for New York.

In Bronxville, I found my tiny room in Dudley Lawrence dormitory, unpacked, and then we went into New York City to find an easy chair, ottoman and appropriate curtains for the windows in my room.

Mother and Dad left for home after two days of shopping and theaters, and I returned to Sarah Lawrence for the weekend to orient myself to the campus before the rest of the students arrived.

Helen and Leland Robinson (Cousin Helen Ball, the daughter of Uncle Lucius) lived in Bronxville, and it was comforting to have family there to help me get my "sea legs." They were always wonderful to me, hospitable and helpful during the two years I was in school. I spent my first Sunday with them at dinner after church and became better acquainted with Leland, whom I had never known too well. Leland was a brilliant philosopher, who taught at Columbia University until his retirement. His conversation was erudite and informative. Helen was soft spoken and a little shy, but, typical of our family, very intelligent and attractive. I loved them both and will always remember their kindness toward me.

The girls were arriving in great numbers when I returned to campus later that afternoon, and I entered my room hearing loud conversation and laughter coming from the room adjoining mine through the connecting bath. My suitemate had arrived, and the room was full of her friends. As I walked through the bathroom to meet the girls and introduce myself, conversation stopped dead. All the girls were having such a pleasant reunion I felt I had intruded, so, after a few words of greeting, I left the room to be out of their way. Lucretia Houghteling was the plump, pretty blonde I had drawn as a suitemate. As I walked through the door, I heard her exclaim to the others, quite loud enough for me to hear, "So *that's* what I have to room with!" Loud laughter followed.

It was a painful introduction to my new life at Sarah Lawrence. I left my room and walked out of the building to get over the hurt, tears in my eyes, bewildered and angry. That I was not as attractive as she had hoped had to be the reason for her comment, since we had not spoken two words together for her to form an opinion of me. But in that instant I knew what kind of person she was.

There was a six-week period of orientation with one's roommate. After that time, anyone wishing to change partners could do so. I was not surprised when Lucretia explained that her friends, all from California, wanted to be together in the same dorm, and she would like to move in with them. It was all right with me. We had nothing in common. She spent her free time with the other girls, and we didn't even share classes. I scarcely knew her and was relieved when she departed and the tension left our suite.

A new girl moved in with me. Doris Rosenbaum, an attractive, Jewish girl from New York, and we became friends. Dee-Dee was very cordial and did many nice things for me. Because she lived in New York, she went home nearly every weekend and sometimes she invited me to accompany her for a visit with her family. Once, at Sunday dinner, a tasty casserole was served, which I thought was chicken. After we had finished, they told me it was eel! I had to admit the eel had been good, but, somehow, I could never knowingly order such a dish, anymore than I could order frog legs, though I have eaten them, too, and liked them.

Dee introduced me to her friends, and to one boy in particular, who grew so attached to me it became a problem. He monopolized all the free time I had for dating, and I never had an opportunity to meet anyone else. His name was Bob Jacobson, and he would come to school and interrupt my studies to ask me out. He often appeared at the window of my practice room as I pounded away, rapping on the pane to attract my attention. I became weary of too much attention. Though I liked Bob as a person, I did not want to get too involved with him.

Coming from a small, midwest town, I was unprepared for the snobbery of the east, and the prejudice against the Jews. One of the boys I dated most often at home was A.C. Bernstein, a Jewish boy. To me a person was judged for himself, not for his religion. In any case, before the year was over I realized I was shunned by nearly everyone at school because I happened to have a Jewish roommate! I refused at first to believe this, preferring to think it was something about myself, until a group of girls, who were always together, invited me to join them for a movie one weekend. We splurged and went to dinner off campus. It was such fun to be included with these girls, whom I had liked very much from the beginning of school. I told them during the evening I was seriously considering not returning to Sarah Lawrence the next year. I confessed I had not made any friends and was also disappointed in the music department. To my chagrin, Lee Pattison had resigned from the faculty and was teaching privately in New York. His replacement on the faculty was far below his caliber. So I had chosen to study with Mr. Grenell, another faculty member in the music department. He had not turned out to be a very good teacher for me.

I confided my problems to the girls, who had offered their friendship, and told them the snobbery of Sarah Lawrence was offensive to me. They told me, frankly, I would make other friends if I changed roommates, as they knew the reason for the social ostracism was my Jewish roommate. I couldn't believe it. Doris was the only person on campus who had

[111]

befriended me, but I finally understood I was hearing the truth.

Doris and I remained good friends and suitemates for the rest of the year, but, as she was away from school over the weekends, I spent most of my free time with the other girls.

Sarah Lawrence was a new college, only ten years old when I entered. It was an experimental school with new concepts of teaching, and we were the "279 guinea pigs" in the avant-garde establishment. The girls were mostly from wealthy families, who could afford to send their daughters to the most expensive college in the country. Tuition then was $2000, an unprecedented amount, but the college was new and unendowed, which necessitated a high tuition. Bennington College in Vermont was the only other institution like Sarah Lawrence, in that they both embraced liberal education concepts.

The girls, with few exceptions, were spoiled snobs, setting up little cliques among themselves and ostracizing all others. One group of students were hot-headed liberals who tried to influence students to join the American Student Union. I thought them a Fascist group of rabble-rousers. The American Student Union was bent on revolution, and members were sympathizers of the Spanish Revolution in 1938-39. The A.S.U. created an unhealthy atmosphere on campus and enhanced the unfavorable aspects of Sarah Lawrence's reputation. In my opinion, they were the ones to shun at all costs.

The same sextet of girls who were nice to me, became my special friends. They all lived on the same floor of the Dudley Lawrence dorm. Anne Lewis was my best friend in the group, a pretty blond from Dallas, Texas, with a seductive southern drawl. Two of the girls were from Winnetka, Illinois. They were Dorothy (Dore) Warner, who was a clown, keeping us in stitches of laughter, and Georgette Hill, another gorgeous blonde with a peaches and cream complexion. Jean Fuller from San Francisco was a flashy blonde, who looked like a Radio City Rockette. She tripped along the campus paths in the highest possible heels, but she was soft, kind and affectionate, belying her rather "floozy" looks. Midge Rile from New Jersey and Sue Wendt from Buffalo, New York, completed the sextet.

Later on Valerie Becton joined our group and became my roommate the following year. She was from Rutherford, New Jersey, the daughter of Becton of the pharmaceutical company of Becton and Dickenson.

I was much happier having these girls as companions. They all shared classes with me, bringing us closer together than Doris and I.

———————◆———————

A funny thing happened as I browsed through the Sarah Lawrence library. Libraries have always fascinated me. At Tudor Hall I tried to read every book in the library in alphabetical order, but somewhere in the C's I gave up. I still thirst for books in my drought of time for reading.

Far back in the stacks in a remote corner I spotted D.H. Lawrence's *Lady Chatterley's Lover*, a book I had heard of that was spoken about in shocked whispers. I wondered how it happened to be in our school's library if it was all *that* bad. Sneaking it off the shelf, I peered around to be sure no one saw me, sat down on the floor against the wall and began to read.

The high, wide window behind me supplied plenty of light, and I became absorbed in the book. I read on, trying to discover what gave the book its shocking reputation. As I was finishing the last chapter, the pages became very dim, and I had trouble reading. Concentration broken, I looked up, astonished to find the only light was coming from the darkening window at my back. I was suddenly aware of dead silence in the room. The low buzz of voices was gone. I peeked around the stacks, down the center of the room to the main desk, and all was darkness. I was locked in!

Panic gripped me when the heavy door wouldn't budge, and I returned to my corner by the window wondering how I would fare all night sleeping on the floor. I was fearful at the prospect, but more afraid of being discovered in a stupid situation. Desperately I tried several windows, finally finding one I was able to open wide enough to crawl through.

The library was on the ground floor of a building built about six-feet below ground level and surrounded by a dry moat. It was easy enough to climb through the window and not drop too far to the ground, but considerably more difficult to scale the slippery six-foot grassy hill to reach the level of the walkways. I breathed a sigh of relief when I emerged on top successfully without being seen. I reflected guiltily on my lust for sex education. After having ploughed through the book, I came to the conclusion it wasn't that bad after all — but I wondered if I had completely understood it. . . . .

Maria and Fabien Sevitsky often came to New York, where Fabien would engage new artists or audition prospective new members for the Indianapolis Symphony. While he was busy, Maria would call me to meet her at our favorite rendezvous, The Russian Tea Room. Carnegie Hall was next door, and, before or after concerts, it was the most convenient place for good food with a Bohemian atmosphere. Maria seemed to be interested in my progress at school, and I confided my problems to her over borscht and piroshkas.

She suggested I write Madame Isabella Vengerova at the Curtis Institute in Philadelphia for an audition and study with her. Madame Vengerova was one of the most prestigious piano teachers in the country and a friend of the Sevitskys, who had known her in Russia. Maria also encouraged me to study voice. She herself had been an opera singer in Europe and now was retired from her professional career, giving a few voice lessons in Indianapolis. She urged me to audition for Queena Mario, a noted, retired Metropolitan Opera singer and teacher, living in New York. I pondered her suggestions and finally wrote to Madame Vengerova requesting an audition.

Three courses were recommended for entering freshmen at Sarah Lawrence. I had chosen Literature, German and Dramatics as well as Music History and Analysis. Of course the applied piano with Mr. Grenell constituted another course, which involved several hours of practice every day. I did not get along very well with Mr. Grenell, mainly because I was disappointed that he was not Mr. Pattison. But also, Mr. Grenell was very different from the exacting Mr. Cramer, and I did not respect him as a teacher.

My first progress evaluation came at the end of the first quarter. Mr. Grenell wrote, "I don't know why she is studying music. She doesn't even like it." Little did he realize the "not liking" was more personal.

The day I received a letter from Madame Vengerova confirming a date and time for the audition in Philadelphia, I was called into the office of President Constance Warren, a lady whom I admired deeply. She discussed my school report, with reference to Mr. Grenell, saying she was well aware I had been disappointed when Mr. Pattison was no longer on the Sarah Lawrence faculty. She knew he had been a big drawing card for me when I applied for admission. Miss Warren told me she had called Mr. Pattison to inquire if he would be able to accept me as a student, if I passed the necessary audition. I was thunderstruck. Of course I would audition for him as soon as I could get to New York! Miss Warren said the college would pay for my lessons for the balance of the year. I felt this a more than fair offer from the administration.

I was excited to meet Mr. Pattison when I went to his apartment on East 79th. St. We got along very well, and he was sympathetic when he heard about my experience with Mr. Grenell, but mostly disturbed to learn that his replacement on the faculty was unsuitable. Mr. Pattison was a distinguished, handsome man, very much an English gentleman type. His wife was an invalid in a wheel chair, the result of having polio at the time their daughter was born. She was one of the reasons, in addition to a heart problem, that he had curtailed his teaching load and resigned from the faculty at Sarah Lawrence.

I studied with Mr. Pattison for the remainder of the year and continued my lessons the following year when I returned to Sarah Lawrence.

More to please my Mother than myself, I finally auditioned for Queena

[114]

Mario, and soon I was going to the city twice a week for piano and voice lessons. Miss Mario had an opera class on Saturdays in conjunction with the lessons, and she urged attendance to teach us the dramatic actions of the operatic roles. The finale Saturday mornings would be a small recital of an opera excerpt in costume by the more advanced students. Attending the opera class gave me an opportunity to meet other students of Miss Mario, and I formed lifetime friendships with two of them.

Miss Mario and I had great empathy for each other, perhaps because we had the same August twenty-first birthday. We were the same in stature (5'2") and also shared a very similar temperament and philosophy of life. I adored her. She was a great voice teacher, dedicated, warm and understanding toward her students. For the first time, I felt singing to be an exciting pursuit.

In school, I added a class in Italian to learn the correct pronunciation of the Italian songs. I also joined a diction class in the Drama Department. Now I was carrying ten subjects instead of the normal three required by the school. I was busy, involved with all my interests, and, finally, happy. I felt independent and secure and had a few good friends.

Every student had her special counselor, or don, whom she visited on a weekly basis. My don was Mrs. Wing, who was also my German teacher. I was devoted to her and admired her intensely as a teacher. She was so remarkable I was able to learn the German language in two years with greater ability than I had learned French in thirteen. I could converse smoothly and also read a great deal of literature (all in the old-fashioned German script.) We read and memorized poetry and acted out German plays when our German Club had meetings. The club had many activities. We went to New York as a group to attend German plays, movies or the opera. We learned German songs and gathered around the piano as Mrs. Wing played the accompaniments and sang along with her lovely voice. She broadened and enriched our lives in many ways. As my don, she gave me sensible advice on my problems, particularly at the beginning of school when I was unhappy and she was instrumental in pulling me through the first difficult year.

Another teacher who influenced me a great deal was my drama teacher, Miss Heinlein. She was truly marvelous and taught a professional approach to acting. I had loved acting ever since I took part in the operettas at Tudor, and I dreamed that in the future I might be in a company which performed operettas or musicals and have a leading role. I preferred the Gilbert and Sullivan operettas, but I knew that was an impossible dream as the D'Oyly Carte Company in England was the only troupe performing them regularly. I had no ambition to be an opera star but often wished I could be in the Metropolitan Opera Chorus. I also loved singing in groups. I joined the Sarah Lawrence Chorus, and for many years after graduation, sang in my church choir, and much later on, in the Indianapolis

Symphonic Choir for twenty-five years.

Christmas vacation, home again in Muncie, was a whirl of dates, dances and days rich with old friends. We went to Indianapolis often to tea dances, performances of the Princeton-Triangle show, Cornell Glee Club and the Mask and Wig, all followed by gala balls at the Athletic Club.

That Christmas I had a tea dance for my friends in Muncie, and I remember dancing The Big Apple, a dance craze that lasted about as long as our Christmas vacation.

Ed Cox's birthday was January fourth, and the snow was deep that year. By Western Union I sent him an ice cream cone every hour during the day at his office, the messenger singing, "Happy Birthday," with each delivery. He laughed for years over the joke I played on him.

When I returned to school, the days were full to overflowing with more time spent in New York for music lessons, concerts and plays, than devoted to studies at school. After arriving in Grand Central Station on the commuter train from Bronxville, I would walk throught he tunnel to the subway, which carried me to West 72nd Street. Then I would see daylight for the first time after being in the city for an hour.

After my lessons with Miss Mario, I would walk to 79th Street to catch the crosstown bus east to Mr. Pattison's for a piano lesson. The balance of the day might be spent with friends from school, meeting them "under the clock" at the Biltmore. We would have lunch in intimate restaurants, attend a concert or movie, and occasionally, do a little shopping. Often after dinner I would go to another concert at Town Hall — mostly by myself — recitals of Brailowsky, Iturbi or Rubenstein. I never missed hearing any pianist, if I could help it.

Sometimes I would return to school on the last train possible before the gates were locked for the night. The only rule at Sarah Lawrence was the strict one for signing out before leaving campus and signing in again upon return. After the main gate was closed for the night, woe be it to anyone having to ring the bell for admittance.

Don Brewington, a friend from Muncie, was attending Annapolis Naval Academy, and he invited me to come down for a football weekend and hop. It was a big weekend, featuring the Army-Navy game, and the train was full of girls heading toward Annapolis. Several friends from other colleges were on board, among them Pat DePrez, and we had quite a reunion.

Don was a tall, attractive, rather shy boy, and I liked him very much. He was one of the first boys in Muncie to be killed in World War II. I was heartbroken to learn of the Japanese attack on his ship. Don was on the bridge and caught direct fire from the diving plane.

[116]

Another exciting weekend was the spring concert at Williams College. The Sarah Lawrence Chorus combined with the Williams Glee Club for a concert, followed by a dance. The boys drew lots for their dates with us, and I was the luckiest of all. His name was George Hayward Reed, and "Hay" was not only the most attractive boy in the Glee Club, but a perfect host with a delightful personality. Our Schools' combined choruses sang the Polevetzian Dances by Borodin, the feature selection on the program. I sang the solo, and Hay, who had a good tenor voice, had a solo part in the men's section. After rehearsal we had supper together as a group, then all dispersed to dress for the concert, which was a big success.

I recounted the evening in my diary: "My date was an ace. After the concert he gave me one perfect time. (It was) a grand bunch of boys. After (the) dance we really had fun in the Rec. Room — played piano, danced wildly and drank foul things. It was hilarious. Two other boys threw themselves at my feet. We all took off our shoes and danced a minuet. Finally left (to say goodnight) but Hay and I were waylaid by an invitation to some guy's room. Stayed there talking to these boys (who were in p. j.'s) till 5:00. Honestly, Hay went to sleep so soundly another boy brought me home. I came off with one of their prize possessions — a picture of a communist! They gave it to me. What a night! I've never had so much honest-to-goodness fun. I hope I'll never forget all the marvelous incidents."

The next morning Hay arrived about noon to pick me up for Sunday dinner, after which the Sarah Lawrence girls left on the bus for Bronxville. The boys who had entertained us in their room came to see me off. We all hated to leave after such a good time, but I saw Hay again when I invited him to a Western Barn Dance at Sarah Lawrence the following weekend.

[117]

Anne Lewis and Sue Wendt

Helen and Leland Robinson, Sally and Lucius

Doris Rosenbaum

Valerie Becton

Jean Fuller

The Barn Studio,
Bethel, Conn.

Queena Mario

An opera set
in preparation

CHAPTER TWENTY-THREE

QUEENA Mario planned a summer of concentrated opera study for her students at her farm in Bethel, Connecticut. Ten of us gathered there in July and August of 1938.

The physical lay-out of the farm was perfect for a camp as well as a school. The land was lovely with rolling fields and even boasted a small lake with a row boat. Miss Mario urged us to swim every day, as she did, after our early morning exercise class on the lawn. The main house was her residence. Her sister and brother-in-law, the Harold Van Rensselaers, lived with her, supervising the maintenance of the farm and planning the meals. It was an old, Victorian home, large and rambling, charmingly furnished with antiques. We had our meals on the long, narrow porch and every day were required to speak a different language at the table. Two days were designated for French, two for German and two for Italian. On Sundays we were free to speak English. I didn't get much to eat on the Italian days, as we had to ask for everything in Italian before we got our food! Italian was not my forte.

The girls lived in two small houses near the main house. The little farm house where I lived had a living room with a piano, where we took turns practicing. I roomed with a tiny Italian girl, Marie Marlo. She had a powerful coloratura voice with an unusual, beautiful quality. A friend of Miss Mario's discovered her singing in a cheap smokey night club and sponsored her from then on. She was only sixteen, but her natural voice was unusually mature and her talent and stage presence impressive. Maria was temperamental and her fiery disposition kept us on edge a good part of the time, but I was so interested in this tiny ball of fire, I tried to help her as much as I could to fit in with the others. I have often wondered what ever became of her after she left Miss Mario's studio for a career.

Our voice lessons and opera classes were in the big barn on the rise of the hill, which made an excellent studio with a stage at the far end. Miss Mario did all the directing, staging and casting for our productions, and the girls took turns singing the leading roles and chorus parts. We also worked with the sets and lights backstage.

Each of us had a specific job to do at the farm. Mine was driving the station wagon on various errands, giving me the opportunity to see much of the Connecticut territory and familiarize myself with the little towns nearby. Bethel was so small it was practically a crossroad, but Danbury was a more significant community, and we often drove there to place posters in the store windows, advertising our opera evenings. People came from as far away as New York and Boston to see our productions, and our notices in the papers even drew talent scouts.

My biggest part that summer was the role of Gretel in *Hansel and Gretel*. Two girls who became my lifelong friends were in the opera also.

[121]

Carol Rubin sang the part of Hansel, and Veola Nelson made a sinister witch. We learned the entire opera, singing it in German. (Miss Mario was credited for making the role of Gretel famous at the Met.)

Our first production at the end of July included one act from Romeo and Juliet, an act from *Faust* and one from *Aida* (I was a black slave.) On September second, the last night before we left the farm, the productions were Manon, with Miss Mario singing the title role, *La Traviata* (I was Anina), and *The Secret of Suzanne*, a one-act opera in which Dorothy Sarnoff sang the lead. Dorothy later had a career on Broadway, including a leading role as the mother of the King's children in *The King and I* with Yul Bruner and Gertrude Lawrence. She was also in the premier performance of *Peter Grimes*, an opera by Benjamin Brittain.

For Miss Mario's birthday, we planned a surprise party. Carol Rubin and I scouted antique shops in the area and found an old weathervane. All the girls chipped in, and after the party Miss Mario had the brass eagle proudly placed atop the barn. The party turned out to be a surprise for me as well as Miss Mario, as we shared our August twenty-first birthdays.

Mother and Dad, as well as Mrs. Wing and Mr. Pattison arrived the last weekend to see our final performance. There was a gala celebration afterwards, and all of us were sorry to see the wonderful summer come to an end and the close proximity of our lives severed. Mother, Dad and I drove home, taking Carol Rubin and Dorothea Pope along with us as my house guests for a week.

CHAPTER TWENTY-FOUR

I made the most of my scrap of September in Muncie before I boarded the train to return to Sarah Lawrence. I planned parties for Carol and Dorothea and trips to the Indiana State Fair. Martin Warren, a newcomer to Muncie, became very attentive. He was most attractive with dark hair and snappy black eyes. He also had two brothers who squired my guests. Though Ed Cox was still the most important man in my life, Martin was quite a flirt, and we played the game of dalliance lightheartedly without serious intent. However, before I left for school, both Martin and Ed declared their love for me. I was flattered but a little confused about how to deal with both of them. Although I could never take Martin seriously, I could not hurt his feelings by rejecting him for Ed. Besides, I loved being with him because he was so much fun. I felt my attitude toward them both should be light, uncomplicated and happy, as good friends and companions should be. They knew I cared for both of them but was not committed to date steadily with either.

On the train to New York, I met Anne Lewis, coming from Dallas. We had a great reunion, talking late into the night about our exciting summers. Back at school, our group convened in our new dorm, Titsworth. My new roommate was Valerie Becton. I was glad I had finally decided to return to Sarah Lawrence, as events evolved that year which changed my life.

Reading my diary, recounting the years from 1936-40, I can't believe how busy I was, particularly during the two years at Sarah Lawrence. I was back and forth to New York almost daily. Classes and studies continued, but most of my activities were concentrated in the city. At school I spent most evenings with friends — dinners off campus, movies or just gab sessions and bridge games in each other's rooms. I also found time to study and practice. Eventually, the Administration decided I was carrying too many courses, as I was taking seven more than were required. In March I reluctantly relinquished my voice lessons with Miss Mario and dropped Italian. All of a sudden I felt I had nothing to do!

Every weekend found me off campus. One weekend I went to Smith College in Northampton, Mass. visiting Betty Brown, whom I hadn't seen in a long time. Several girls from Tudor days were attending Smith, and we had a joyful reunion, catching up on our activities since graduation.

Another weekend I went to Poughkeepsie, New York to visit Alice Crume at Vassar College. It was fun to get together with her. Bussy was also at Vassar. We saw each other there and also met in New York occasionally.

I met Carol and Veola frequently on my trips to the city and spent the weekends with them in their apartments. I always kept in touch with my friends, girls and boys, seeing them as often as possible or writing them long letters. Bob Jacobson was something of a problem, however, as he was too persistent, but my nature kept me from being rude to anyone, and I continued to see him.

There was a Halloween party at Miss Mario's farm in Bethel — a gorgeous, crisp weekend and a happy gathering with our friends of the past summer. Bill Pitts drove a full carload of us to the farm where we went for a long afternoon walk in the brisk air admiring the trees in their autumn dress ablaze with color. That night there was a costume party in the barn, which Miss Mario had decorated with hay and Indian corn and spooky lanterns. She really knew how to throw a party. I don't know when I had a better time.

Later that semester, I had a part in the play *Madchen in Uniform*, and it was the night of full dress rehearsal. My role was small but important as I was first on stage and set the general tone and pace of the play.

I had felt tired all week, dragging from class to class, and that morning I

[123]

had painful, swollen glands, which I reported to the nurse in the infirmary. The doctor examined me and sent me on my way, passing my condition off as unimportant.

That night at a break during rehearsal some of the girls went to the cafeteria. I ordered an egg salad sandwich and a coke, but found the food tasteless. Jean Fuller, always ravenous, devoured them.

At midnight I dragged myself to bed, slept like a stone and was awakened late in the morning by the maid who came in to clean my room. She took one look at me and exclaimed, "Lordy, Miss Lucina, but you do look a sight! What's happened to your face?"

The mirror revealed a bloated, red face and neck that looked ready to pop. I knew I had to have mumps and went again to the infirmary. This time the doctor admitted the swollen glands were out of control and slapped me into bed and quarantine in the infirmary.

Another girl learned my part in the play in record time, and I was told she did an excellent job. I was miserable, low in spirit, anticipating the entire Christmas vacation spent in Bronxville isolated in the school infirmary! I couldn't believe my bad luck.

There was a phone beside my bed, and I called home to Mother, who told me Hudson had a light case of mumps over the Thanksgiving weekend when we were all together. My case came just three weeks later, the exact incubation time, just one week before school was out for Christmas vacation. The doctor said I would be quarantined for two weeks!

The mumps were painful for three days, then the swelling began to subside, and I felt fairly normal. On the fifth day, I had no swelling or temperature, but the doctor would not let me get up. I knew I was well and was frantic and miserable over missing my vacation. I longed to see Ed and Martin. There were parties planned for every day and night, which I couldn't bear to miss.

I began to fight back at the doctor. I hated her to begin with. What did she know? She hadn't even recognized the disease when I first went to see her. It was her fault I'd probably spread the virus throughout the school! Now that I knew I was well, I felt she was keeping me confined for nothing! I gave her a good case of tantrum — my first and last attack. When I screamed at her in my frustration, it only made her more adamant to keep me in the infirmary against my will.

Helen Robinson came to visit, and I cried my troubles to her. She sent her family doctor to see me, and he agreed it would be all right for me to leave school. I was ever grateful for his kindness and understanding. I tore from the infirmary bed in a whirl, packed my clothes and was on the train for Muncie that same afternoon, two days into Christmas vacation.

[124]

Those who caught the mumps from me thanked me when I returned to school. They came down with the disease at the end of vacation and were able to spend two more weeks at home! Jean Fuller was particularly grateful. She didn't get home as frequently, living in San Francisco. She told me my sandwich and coke was the best meal she ever had!

Mother, age 35

Lucina's graduation picture, age 21

Playing for children at Day School, Sarah Lawrence College

Lucina as jester in Twelfth Night

CHAPTER TWENTY-FIVE

A UNT Bertha had told me if Mrs. Harris Childs, her good friend, ever called me, to be sure to meet her, as she was a very interesting person and also a music lover. While I was in the infirmary with the mumps, Mrs. Childs did call, inviting me to join her for lunch and a New York Philharmonic concert.

After vacation, I returned her call, and she invited me to spend a weekend with her and attend a dinner party honoring the Sevitskys. She told me, "You will represent your father, and I have arranged an escort for you." (Dad was still the President of the Indianapolis Symphony.)

On January twenty-sixth I appeared at her apartment, and a maid showed me to my room, passing through the gloomy, overly-furnished living room. I was aware, through the dim light, of an elderly lady engrossed in conversation with a young man. The fading daylight through the window was the only illumination in the darkening room, but I saw the young man embracing a cello with one arm as he conversed with Mrs. Childs.

I quietly unpacked and finally, Mrs. Childs ushered the musician to the door, and came to my room to greet me. I was soon infatuated with this fascinating lady. Less than five-feet tall, a white haired little butterball, she was definitely a dowager in manner. Her main interest in life was music. Although she did not have unlimited funds to help aspiring young artists financially, she knew everyone worth knowing and would arrange auditions for them which could mean more to a career-bent musician than money in the long run.

That evening we attended a dinner party preceding a thrilling Philharmonic concert, featuring George Enesco, conductor, and Yehudi Menuhin, renowned concert violinist. The next day I went with Mrs. Childs to a rehearsal of the Philharmonic conducted by John Barbirolli and heard Rudolf Serkin play. I cannot forget the vision of Mrs. Childs as we left Carnegie Hall. In the midst of the heavy traffic crossing 57th Street, she walked into the middle of it all, held up an arm imperiously, stopping traffic to permit us to parade across the street and enter a taxi. The lady was courageous!

The Frohnknects' dinner party honoring the Fabien Sevitskys was that Saturday evening. I had bought a beautiful, burgundy velvet evening dress at Henri Bendel's especially for the party. It was the most luxurious and extravagant gown I had ever owned. The skirt was lined with horsehair, which made it look a little like a crinoline. Around the skirt was a wide eighteen-inch border of pink changeable taffeta. The bodice was tight, with wide straps over the shoulders. It was simple but elegant. The dress meant very much to me, and I still have it. My daughter Ann remade the dress into a skirt, removing the bodice after it wore out.

[127]

Our escort was very handsome and stood ramrod straight, looking much taller than his six feet. Edwin Breck Eckerson, a surgeon, was a close friend of Mrs. Child's son, Edward (Eppie) Childs, who was also a doctor. He and Eddie had gone to medical school at Columbia University's College of Physicians and Surgeons and had graduated in the same class sharing top honors.

The party was formal and elegant. It was good to see the Sevitskys, but I knew no one else at the dinner for twelve. I sat beside Eddie. He talked to the lady on his right, and I talked to the gentleman on my left. We didn't share much conversation. When he took us back to Mrs. Child's apartment, clicked his heels together and bowed formally as he said goodnight to us at the door, I thought I hadn't made much of an impression on him.

I was surprised when he called me at school two weeks later and asked me to meet him in New York for lunch at Le Coq Rouge. He drove me back to Bronxville, and after dinner we went to a movie in Mt. Vernon, where he lived.

We had another movie date in New York in March, after dinner at Le Coq Rouge, and later that month he asked me to drive with him to Darien, Connecticut to see a patient.

It was Sunday, a lovely spring day for a ride in the country. As we drove, we somehow communicated without conversation, enjoying each other's company, relaxed and contented. We arrived at the Dunn's home, and Eddie disappeared into Roswell's bedroom with Emily Read while I sat in the living room and entertained their three young children. Ros had broken his back falling off a ladder. It was a serious injury, and Ed was concerned about his friend's recovery. He and Ros had graduated from Princeton University in the class of 1927.

It seemed a long time before Ed reappeared, and we were driving back to New York again. We went into the city and had dinner once more at his favorite spot, Le Coq Rouge. After I returned to school that night I wrote in my diary: "It was a gorgeous, perfect day and I feel wonderful at one a.m. (not tired) for the first time!"

Eddie was a very busy surgeon. He lived in Mt. Vernon with his mother and father and had an office in their home on Cottage Avenue. His father, also a doctor, was now terminally ill, and Ed was caring for his father's patients as well as his own. He also had afternoon office hours in New York on Park Avenue, sharing the office with another prominent surgeon, E.J. Donovan. Ed was on the staffs of four hospitals, making rounds and operating at each one daily. He did not have much time for socializing as his practice took up most of the day and night. Ed had been a doctor for eight years when I met him, and Mrs. Childs told me he had been written up in a medical journal as "the coming surgeon of New York."

[128]

Ed was thirteen years older than I. I was a little in awe of this mature, serious man but admired him tremendously. His rather stiff, professional manner disappeared when we were together, and I began to see his soft, gentle qualities.

———·——◆——·———

Friends of Mother and Dad, Lauritz and "Kleinchen" Melchior, invited me to lunch at their apartment in the Ansonia Hotel. Lauritz was one of the most famous opera singers of all time, and I was thrilled to meet him. He was enormous, barrel-chested and beer-bellied, but handsome, with twinkling light blue eyes and a baby's complexion. Kleinchen, his second wife, suited her nickname as she was a tiny person but very vivacious — a fashion plate with a dashing personality. Lauritz had met her in Denmark when she was a stunt performer in movies. Lauritz's son, Ib, whom I met a little later, was dark and attractive. The Melchiors wanted to get Ib out of New York and thought if he could work in Muncie at Ball Brothers he would forget his dream of an acting and singing career. Dad was arranging a position for Ib, but he was disturbed to hear Lauritz wanted Ib to begin his business career with the most menial job in the factory.

The truth was, Lauritz was intensely jealous of Ib. He did not want any competition, recognizing Ib's beautiful voice and great flair for acting. Melchior's daughter was confined in a convent in Denmark, but Ib had left school and was in New York looking for a career.

Ib lived at our house in Muncie for a year, working at the Ball factory as a laborer and then went to California to pursue a career in the theater, in spite of his family's opposition. He formed a company with friends to produce films and was somewhat successful in his venture. During the war he worked in cryptology for the Government and became an expert. He was so fascinated with decoding he continued to pursue it after the war, becoming interested particularly in the age-old subject of the authenticity of Shakespeare's writing. He was positive the cryptic epitaph which Shakespeare wrote for his own grave held the answer and proof that he, and not Francis Bacon had written the plays. He tried to prove that the original manuscript of Hamlet was hidden somewhere in the dungeon recesses of Elsinore Castle in Denmark and received permission to explore there with a group of archaeologists. Life Magazine accompanied them to take pictures and cover the story, if, indeed, he found the lost manuscript. It was an unsuccessful venture, but Ib never lost his conviction that the writings were there. Life Magazine printed the story during the 1950's.

———·——◆——·———

Mother and Dad were in New York when we went to Toscanini's last broadcast of the N.B.C Symphony. It was a beautiful concert, and I was excited to be seated near the great Kirsten Flagstadt and Katherine Cornell, where I could see them at close range. Flagstadt was the fabulous, dramatic soprano, who was paired with Melchior in the Wagnerian operas. To hear them sing together raised a mountain of goose bumps. Katherine Cornell was a great actress, very stylish and beautiful. The evening climaxed at the Melchiors' apartment with a midnight supper. I played the piano and sang and was thrilled when Lauritz offered to give me voice lessons. Usually he did not teach, so I felt particularly honored by his offer. It made me feel disloyal to Miss Mario even to consider the idea, but I was complimented that Lauritz thought enough of my voice to suggest it.

The Melchiors gave me a pass to the Press Box at the Met for a very special performance of *Die Gotterdammerung*. For the first time in America it would be the original, uncut version. This last great opera, which closes the story of The Ring of the Niebelung, began at four in the afternoon and concluded at midnight, with an hour's break for dinner.

When I arrived for the performance, the seats in the box were already occupied by the Press. I was the only female but no one offered his seat to me, and I stood for four hours until the dinner break. I hurried to a nearby snack bar and grabbed something to eat as quickly as possible, returning early to the box, hoping to find an empty seat. But I was out of luck again and stood until the curtain fell at midnight. By then I could hardly walk to Grand Central Station for my train to Bronxville. During the opera I became so entranced by the singing of Flagstadt and Melchior and the splendid production, I was scarcely aware that I stood for eight hours.

Another time I was invited to the Melchiors' elegant party for the Crown Prince of Denmark. The dinner was at the Gripsolm Restaurant and included many celebrated guests as well as my family. It was preceded by a performance of Lohengrin at the Met — very spectacular, with Melchior and Flagstadt singing gorgeously. Ib sat next to me at the opera, and I finally had a chance to get acquainted with him and was glad he was to be in Muncie with us.

———————◄◉►———————

Mother and Dad had come to New York to see me perform in Shakespeare's *Twelfth Night*. I missed the important dress rehearsal to join them at the Melchiors' dinner and the production of Lohengrin but made up for my absence by playing the part of the king's jester very well. I learned to play the mandolin in order to accompany myself singing two songs in the play. I unearthed the Renaissance music to the words in the script at the New York Public Library, excited to learn of the existence of the music. I worked very hard learning to accompany myself on the mandolin as I sang them, and my fingers became sore and raw from the effort. Our rehearsals were long and tiresome, lasting until after midnight every night, but the result was worth it. Quite a contingent of friends came on opening night, including Mother and Dad, Margie and Paul Fitzgibbon, Mrs. Childs, Eddie Eckerson and Ib Melchior. I was embarrassed to

[130]

have anyone see me in my awful costume. It was the most unbecoming outfit — a tight-fitting leotard complete with hood that fitted tightly around my head. All my bulges, fat legs and hips were now more pronounced than ever. But I played my part, sang the songs and played the mandolin as if I were an expert.

I was amazed to learn from Dad that he had played the same part in *Twelfth Night* when he attended Cornell University. Our pictures in costume looked so similar we could have been twins, and we laughed at the coincidence in our lives.

--------◄◉►--------

The Melchiors had another large party, and this time invited me to bring two of my friends from school to be dates for three brothers who were also invited. I asked Anne Lewis and Sue Wendt, and the three of us checked into The Biltmore Hotel, where we waited for the boys to call.

The three Plants brothers were Harvey, Jack and Bill. We discovered they had drawn lots to see who would squire whom, and Jack had drawn my name. He was very tall, six-foot-five, and the best looking of the three, I thought. We got along famously! We stopped at the Monkey Bar for a get-acquainted drink, then proceded to the Danish Restaurant, which was reserved that night for the Danish Guard Ball. The Melchior party had a table reserved for at least twenty guests.

The boys showed us a marvelous time, and it was a fabulous evening! The dinner-dance was elegant, and a great deal of aquavit was served, followed by beer chasers. Aquavit is a fiery liquid that tastes like caraway seeds going down, and, once down, kindles a fire! Each dram of the "fast water" must be swallowed in one gulp. There were many toasts, champagne flowed freely, and the party was exuberant.

The six of us became very tipsy, but we were not aware we had a problem until we decided to go downtown to end the evening. The Plants were now well potted. We drove to a German Rathskeller for beer, before heading to The Biltmore, not willing for the evening to end.

The Rathskeller was a popular, college hang-out in New York. Jack was attending Princeton, his brother Bill finishing at Lawrence and Harvey had graduated from Princeton the past year. The six of us shared a one-gallon stein — the biggest "brandy snifter" I ever laid my four eyes on!

The boys returned us reluctantly to The Biltmore at five a.m., promising to call "first thing in the morning," and we weaved our way up to our room. I'll always remember dainty Anne Lewis, floating around the room as she undressed slowly, singing softly over and over to no one in particular, "I'm naked as a jay bird!"

From then on, Jack and I dated constantly. He was so much fun to be with, but I knew at heart that he was a perennial playboy. He became my

[131]

"potted Plant." Every time we were together there were always too many drinks and too many late hours. After a few dates, he proposed, but I refused to take him seriously. He peppered the phone line with calls and sent letters and telegrams asking me to marry him.

The week before graduation I was very busy seeing my friends in New York for the last time, including Eddie and the "Potted Plants." The tenth of June finally arrived. Sarah Lawrence was buzzing with activity, and we were dressed in our white robes and mortarboards. The graduation exercises were held on the lawn in front of Westlands on a beautiful warm day. I left with no regrets, looking forward to going home at last and ready for a future with new experiences.

CHAPTER TWENTY-SIX

ANNE Lewis went home with me for a visit before returning to Dallas. I had made many plans for entertaining her in Muncie. The first night I had a dinner party for twelve including Ib Melchior and Martin Warren. The Arlington Horse Show was in Indianapolis, and we planned to go, but suddenly, only two days after our arrival, Grandpa Medsker had a stroke and died late that afternoon.

With a death in the family, Ed, Steve, Olie and Carolyn entertained Anne while I was in mourning with my family. It was a sad time for Nana and for all of us. I was shattered. After Grandpa's funeral on June fifteenth, I left with Anne for Dallas, Texas.

She showed me a wonderful time, and the ache over Grandpa's death eased a little. I enjoyed her friends and her mother, who was very cordial and nice to me. We shopped, had beauty treatments and even had our eyelashes dyed! The Nieman-Marcus Department Store was stunning, and we browsed, admiring the fabulous displays. Anne and I dated two of the Marcus brothers, very enterprising and interesting young men.

I left the end of June for Muncie with the summer full of promises and exciting developments. I dated Ed Cox and Martin Warren as well as other boys and suddenly realized I was no longer in love with Ed. It made me sad because he obviously felt the same toward me as always, but I was having far too much fun enjoying the company of many boys to settle on just one.

In late July Jack Plants arrived for a visit. We played golf, rode horseback and went to horse shows, where I rode and collected some ribbons. The evenings were devoted to aquavit!

One night, for a lark, Ed, Ray Warren, (Martin's brother,) Ib, Jack and I drove to Chesterfield, Indiana, a town near Muncie, where there was a reknowned spiritualist camp. We had an entertaining evening at a seance. I heard Grandfather Medsker's voice, miraculously sending greetings and advice. Frank Elliott spoke through the "trumpet" and also Brady Ball. Ed "spoke" to his father, and Ib, trying to trick the medium, asked for a Danish relative who had never learned English. Amazingly, the relative spoke to Ib without a trace of accent and in perfect English. Ib shook his head in disbelief.

Later, we drove back to Muncie to the Roberts Hotel, and Jack ordered French 75s! After two of these, we weren't worth much of anything. Back home later that evening, Jack and I walked out to the swing in the yard, and again he proposed. Weakened by the effects of the French 75s, I agreed to marry him.

When we told my parents, they were dead set against the marriage, with good reason. I knew in my heart Jack was not right for me but I still was infatuated. We made plans, agreeing to wait until Jack had graduated from Princeton. He was a year younger than I and had one more year of college.

When I told Ed about my engagement to Jack, I felt miserable about hurting him. But Ed didn't give up easily. I am sure he thought that Jack was a passing thrill which would soon die a natural death. He told me he still loved me and would always be around in case I changed my mind.

After spending a week in Leland, Michigan with Janice, I returned home, and Jack arrived at the end of August to spend a week. I was ecstatic, but disturbed about my family's attitude toward him. I was torn with emotions, and on three separate occasions over the next few months, nearly eloped with Jack. He was quite persuasive, but I am glad my common sense saved me in the end.

On September first, the Indiana State Fair began, and Orchard Lawn entered horses in many classes. I always enjoyed seeing old friends again in the stables, where they rented space for their horses and tack. Colored banners, ribbons and trophies of the individual farms decorated the stalls. I found our section draped in green and white, the colors of Orchard Lawn Farms and sat to chat with the stable boys and Jack Rogers, our trainer since Mr. Morgan had retired. They were busy currying the horses to a high gloss and braiding their forelocks with green and white ribbons.

Lupton and Veazy Rainwater walked by, greeted me warmly, and asked if I would ride one of their mares entered in the ladies' five-gaited stake. The Rainwaters had a nice stable of horses in North Carolina and were old friends. I agreed to give it a try, provided I could exercise the horse first.

I rode the mare twice, and she was responsive and easy to handle. We did very well in the stake, extracting a red ribbon from the judge in a large class. Lupton and Veazy thanked me by taking me to the Wharf House to dance and celebrate. Little did I know it was the last ride I would ever have on a show horse. Mother began to sell off our horses soon after I moved away from Muncie, and my opportunities to ride disappeared.

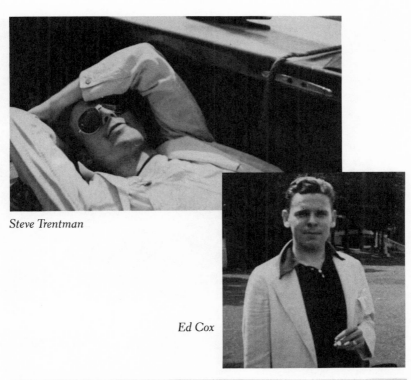

Steve Trentman

Ed Cox

A. C. Bernstein and Janice at Leland, Mich.

Cincinnati Conservatory

Severin Eisenberger

Leone Kruse

[136]

CHAPTER TWENTY-SEVEN

I had hoped to return to New York in the fall and resume lessons with Mr. Pattison and Miss Mario. Everything about the city stimulated me. I was in love with the tall buildings, the feeling of privacy in a crowd, the advantage of every possible form of entertainment, the cosmopolitan atmosphere and the friends I had made. New York was a place where I felt I belonged. It was home to me.

But Mother and Dad would not give me permission to have an apartment in New York. As it happened, I would not have been able to continue lessons with Mr. "Pat" anyway, as he had accepted a position as head of the music department at Scripps College in Pomona, California.

The Cincinnati Conservatory of Music had an excellent reputation, and I elected to continue my studies there as a graduate student, provided I could have a place of my own. Dormitory living did not appeal to me any more.

The George Baileys, our friends from the Traders Point Hunt, had moved back to Cincinnati, where they had lived originally. George had retired from his business in Indianapolis, and the family had returned to manage their rental properties in Cincinnati. One of the apartments was at 33 E. Macmillan, where the Baileys lived, quite close to the Conservatory. They offered to rent it to me, completely furnished.

I was pleased with the apartment. The living room and small parlor faced onto Macmillan, where street cars ratcheted back and forth every few minutes, but down the long hall to the rear of the apartment were three, quiet bedrooms and a large, bright kitchen overlooking the garages. Dad gave me a snappy, red Buick coupe for my birthday, and I later housed it in one of the garage stalls.

It was decided Nana would keep house for me. She was lonely without Grandpa, and we felt it would be a good change for her. I hoped Nana was as happy as I about the arrangement. I knew nothing about house cleaning or cooking and thought I would have little time for it, anticipating many classes and much practicing.

On September eighth I moved into the comfortable, old-fashioned apartment, transferring the Chickering piano from Grandma Ball's, where it was placed in the little parlor. This became my music room. I was very excited about my new independence and eager to begin a new regime.

The next day I registered at the Conservatory, a sprawling Victorian mansion on top of a hill, and selected my classes — not for credit, but for fun; Modern Harmony, French, German, Drama, voice with Leone Kruse and piano with Severin Eisenberger.

Mother felt I progressed more with Miss Kruse than with Miss Mario as the year went on, but my allegiance with Miss Mario was stronger, though I liked Miss Kruse very much.

At first I was disappointed with Mr. Eisenberger. I thought I needed a firmer hand, and he seemed too soft and permissive. Renowned in Europe as a teacher and concert artist, he was not too well known in America. I grew to appreciate him as I learned that underneath his softness was an iron will. He really knew how to get the best effort from me.

The Drama department was elementary compared to Sarah Lawrence's professional approach. I was given the part of Yum-Yum in the *Mikado*, which I enjoyed, particularly since Nanki-Poo was quite handsome and had an excellent tenor voice.

Nana and I went to movies in the evenings, enjoying each other's company. After awhile I began to meet people, and our social life became busy. Letters from Jack arrived every day, and I was thinking of him constantly but also dated boys from the Conservatory.

Elwood Emerich (Woody) was in my Modern Harmony class. We became friends when I tutored him in German. He invited me to a class party at the Conservatory, and we had a grand time dancing and playing ping pong. We dated often after that. Our favorite pastime was roller skating at the rink not far from my apartment. After skating, Woody always stopped for ice cream and oatmeal cookies to take back to the apartment to share with Nana. He was wonderful to Nana, and she liked him too, inviting him over for dinner now and then. He appreciated the attention, as he was not too flush with funds.

Woody didn't have an overcoat, and when the weather was bitter, snowy and cold he wore a muffler, wool gloves and turned his suit collar up around his neck, claiming he was not cold. But I worried about him and picked him up in my car whenever I could.

Jack had given me a red, cocker spaniel puppy to keep me company. I promptly named him Struwwelpeter, (Pater for short,) because he had a tuft of wild hair standing on top of his head that wouldn't brush down. I grew up with the Goop books, and Struwwelpeter was a similar book for German children. Struwwelpeter was a little boy who never combed or cut his hair and always looked disheveled. Pater was good company for us and behaved very well in the apartment.

In October Mother and I went to New York to see Jack and meet his parents, who had driven to the city from Hornell, New York. The brothers gave a party for us at Harvey's apartment, but at the end of the five-day visit, Mother was more determined than ever to break up our romance. Her attitude nearly precipitated an elopement.

After I returned to Cincinnati, Martin Warren arrived with Ed Hall, a numerologist friend of the Warren family. Martin introduced him to my

[138]

parents, who became hooked on his "clairvoyance." That night, Mr. Hall kept me up until 3:30 a.m. explaining why Jack was not good for me. I didn't believe him when he swore my parents had not discussed my relationship with him, but in spite of myself, I felt Mr. Hall's hypnotic influence.

The next day amidst copious tears, I wrote Jack a long letter saying we should cancel our plans for an early marriage, and sent back his ring. I was miserable but knew I had done the right thing. It was important for me to keep peace in the family, even though I did not want to give up Jack.

Ed Hall influenced me more than I wished. Later he sent me my horoscope for the years 1939 to 2000. Strangely, most of the events he predicted have come true.

My life in Cincinnati became a kaleidoscope of activities, emotions and new friends. People came and went in great numbers. My car attracted many boys who had no transportation, and I think they cultivated my friendship for my "wheels." But Woody was not like some of the others. He was sincerely fond of both Nana and me.

I really loved Cincinnati, my studies and my new life of partial independence. I gave a few parties, but the biggest splash was the one for Mother's birthday on December third. Mother and Dad arrived with friends from Richmond, Indiana, the Harry Bockoffs, and also brought Janice. I invited Perrin March, the first boy I had dated in Cincinnati, and Harry Meuser, the son of Hans Meuser, principal bassoonist of the Cincinnati Symphony. I served sherry and a surprise birthday cake for Mother in the apartment, and then we all went to the Snow Follies, a beautiful ice show. Afterwards, we attended an extravaganza — a Charity Ball at the new Netherland Plaza Hotel. The ball was "done" by Elsa Maxwell, the most famous party hostess of all time. We arrived wearing our most glamorous evening clothes, but Elsa met everyone at the door and handed out crazy costumes to wear.

When the symphony season began in October, I bought subscriptions for Nana and myself. Eventually, I met several members of the orchestra through the conductor, Eugene Goosens. I met the Goosens through Dad and the Sevitskys, and they invited me to several post-concert parties. Mrs. Goosens was rather attractive with beautiful, auburn hair, but her complexion was dead white. She looked as though she had arisen from the catacombs. Large eyes surrounded by gray shadows accented her ghostly skin.

Hans Meuser, the principal bassoonist, renowned for his artistry, asked me to perform with his woodwind ensemble in December. I felt honored to be asked and thrilled to have a new type of literature to study, and I

[139]

worked hard to meet their standards. The men, all first chairs in the Cincinnati Symphony, came to my apartment once a week for rehearsals. They were patient and understanding while I learned how to balance my piano with their instruments. Besides Hans, Marcel Dandois was the oboist, Clarence Elliot, the clarinetist, Joseph Fenboque, the flutist, and Weldon Wilber played the French horn.

We performed at Ball State University on December seventeenth. I accompanied Mr. Meuser in the first movement of the bassoon concerto by Mozart and played with the ensemble in several numbers. The program was varied and unusual. I loved the texture the woodwinds brought to the music.

It was exciting for me to play with such prestigious men before so many friends in Muncie. I soon forgot my nervousness and became involved in participating with the ensemble. Dad recorded the program backstage on his new reel-to-reel tape machine.

After the concert, Mother and Dad had a large party for us. The house was alive with cordial, happy people. The Eisenbergers were there and were very complimentary about my "professional" performance. Other friends from Cincinnati, Indianapolis and nearby towns added to the lively group from Muncie. Dad recorded their voices, adding Christmas greetings and congratulations for the artistic performance. I still have the tape of that special evening.

As it happened, each of the men had a problem that night, but professionals overcome physical discomfort and perform without a murmur. Mr. Fenboque had a painful fever blister on his lip. Mr. Meuser was miserable, due to enter the hospital the next day for a hemmorhoidectomy. Mr. Dandois and Mr. Wilber both had nasty colds. Mr. Elliot was the only one who appeared well. A large, dignified man of eighty, he was loved for his great artistry and his lovable disposition. That night, unexpectedly, he died in his sleep at the Roberts Hotel. It was a terrible shock, particularly to the men in the ensemble, who had been such close friends for many years. Clarence Elliot was one of the finest clarinetists in the country, and Koussevitsky had tried several times to hire him away from Cincinnati to play with his orchestra in Boston. But Mr. Elliot refused to leave his friends, in spite of the temptation of a much larger salary. The men were heartsick over his death and disbanded their ensemble. I was sorry I couldn't continue working with them as it had been a wonderful experience.

Yum-Yum and Nanki-Poo in The Mikado

Cincinnati Woodwind Ensemble: L. to R. Hans Meuser, Clarence Elliot, Lucina, Joseph Fenboque, Marcel Dandois, and Weldon Wilber

[141]

My Valentine hat, Feb 14, 1940

Grandma Ball at our wedding, age 94

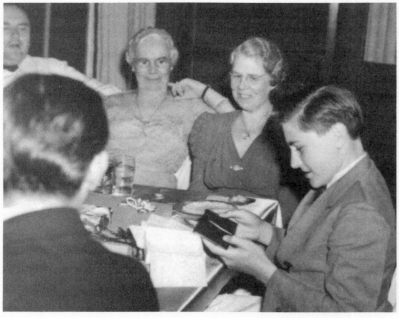

Bill celebrates his fourteenth birthday: L. to R. Dad, Aunt Bertha Ball, Elizabeth Eckerson, Bill Ball

CHAPTER TWENTY-EIGHT

THAT Christmas I presented my parents with a pastel portrait of myself done in Cincinnati by Ed Firn. He did a rather good likeness of me in a bright, red shirt with Struwwelpeter in my lap.

The holiday was festive as usual, and I returned to the Conservatory, ready to tackle the Grieg Concerto with a vengeance and settle down to a winter of concentrated work. Nana was busy working on another quilt. Her work was meticulous and creative, and I loved to watch her sewing the tiny stitches around the little leaves of bright colors. Nana saved the scraps from old dresses to make her quilts, and I searched for familiar patterns, recognizing something of Mother's or mine in the material.

When Nana hooked rugs, she dyed old silk stockings in vegetable juices, such as beet or spinach to make the colors. Her designs were original and beautifully done. The rugs and quilts are lovingly stored in my cedar closet to keep them from wearing out. Years from now I hope my great grandchildren will treasure them as relics of a generation that worked with love and dedication to create things of enduring beauty.

That winter Nana confessed she had felt a lump in her breast for some time. I was horrified she had not seen a doctor in Muncie when she discovered the lump almost a year before. She explained she knew all the doctors at home too well and was embarrassed to be examined *there* by anyone. I begged her to let me find a doctor in Cincinnati, but she refused.

About the middle of January I received a letter from Eddie Eckerson saying he would like to visit me in Cincinnati, if it would be convenient. I couldn't imagine why he would want to come to a prosaic spot like Cincinnati when he had always gone to Miami, Florida for excitement and glamour on his vacations. I looked forward to seeing him again but wondered how I could entertain this New Yorker in Cincinnati. I turned to Mother for some suggestions. Mother's answer was a normal response for her, as she was always looking for an excuse to go to her favorite New Orleans. She made plans for all of us to fly down there for a few days. Ed had never been west. Except for his internship at the Leahy Clinic in Boston and vacations in Florida, he had never been outside of the New York environs. We planned to show him a very different section of the country.

I talked to Nana again, telling her Ed was an excellent surgeon and to please consider having him examine her when he came. She was noncommittal, murmuring only, "Maybe, if I like him."

When Ed arrived, on February ninth, just at my semester break, I told him about Nana at once, and, later that evening, she allowed him to examine her. At last Nana agreed to get the medical attention she needed. Ed scheduled surgery to remove the tumor after our return from New Orleans.

My parents, Ed and I flew to New Orleans in Ed Ball's plane, a twin-engine Cessna. It was good to be in warm weather again after the cold, below zero temperatures and piles of snow at home. We showed Eddie our favorite spots in the city, and that night, after a gourmet dinner at Antoine's, went to a revue at the Roosevelt Hotel, where we were staying. Eddie and I danced for awhile in the hotel ballroom and finally went up to our suite to talk before going to bed. A living room was between the two bedrooms, Dad and Eddie sharing one and Mother and I the other.

As I climbed into bed, Mother drowsily asked if we had a nice evening. I told her I had a strange feeling that Ed was going to ask me to marry him. Mother, almost asleep, asked me what I would say. I replied softly, "I think I'll say 'Yes'!"

Although Ed had given me no indication he was seriously interested, an intuition began to stir and grow within me. I considered what I might do in the event he proposed and excitement built with anticipation as I realized I was in love with him.

It was Valentine's Day, and *Life Magazine's* cover had a picture of a girl wearing a heartshaped hat decorated with an orchid. Ribbons holding the flat, little heart to her head came down and tied under her chin. It was a fetching picture, and we saw it all over town in the news stalls on the street corners. Later that morning a florist box arrived for me with a card that read, "Be my Valentine — Ed." There in the box was an exact duplicate of the flowered hat — a bright, red, silk heart with a large, purple orchid lying on top. It was whimsical and very becoming. I wore it all day, receiving many glances of admiration — the living model of *Life Magazine*!

That night Ed treated us to dinner at the Roosevelt, and ordered champagne, which he loved. His gesture gave me more tingles of excitement than the bubbly champagne ever could. After dinner and dancing, Mother and Dad excused themselves and went to bed, but Ed and I stayed on listening to the music, outwardly calm, but inside I felt intense excitement — so strong I could scarcely breathe.

Suddenly Ed asked me, quietly and seriously, "I love you, Lucina. Will you marry me?" For a moment my heart stopped, and I could say nothing at all. After a long silence, feeling my throat closing and tears near the surface, I managed a soft yes. Ed exploded with animation, saying, "You will? You WILL? — Let's get out of here!" When we got to our suite, he took me in his arms and kissed me for the first time. Then we talked and that very night made plans for a June fifth wedding.

———◄◉►———

I had no doubt this was right for us. Mother and Dad were both agreeable and genuinely seemed to like Eddie, though they felt he was too old for me. Thirteen years seemed a big difference to them but the age difference was insignificant to me.

[144]

We drove to Pass Christian for lunch and sat on the warm, sandy beach, basking in the sun. But our time together in New Orleans was at an end, and Nana was already in the hospital in Muncie being prepared for her operation.

PART TWO
CHAPTER TWENTY-NINE

T HE day of Nana's operation I was very upset. I loved her so much and was sick with worry. I drove my car out of Muncie and down unfamiliar country roads to get my mind off the fearful thing that was happening to her. Crying, I wrestled with the thoughts of Ed operating on my grandmother! How could I marry a man whose business it was to cut into people? How could I ever understand that part of him? Was I making a mistake after all? What kind of life would I have, married to a dedicated surgeon? What if Nana died during the operation? I was in agony as these questions tortured me. I prayed for Nana and finally turned the car around and began to find my way back. I had no idea where I was, but eventually found a familiar road home.

All of a sudden my prayers and answers to the many questions spinning in my head were resolved, and I found myself calm and steady, knowing everything would work out happily. I returned to Ball Hospital and joined the family in the solarium to await the outcome of the operation.

Soon Ed appeared, still in his operating gown, to reassure us that Nana had come through the operation well. But the cancer had spread to her lymph nodes. He had performed as radical an operation as he dared and felt she would be all right, but he could give us no assurance the cancer would not return.

Ed asked me to wait for him until he was dressed, and when he returned announced, "I'm starved! Where can we go for lunch?" Was this the man I was going to marry? I wondered how could he eat at a time like this? But we went to a restaurant, where I watched him put away a huge meal with relish.

———————◄◉►———————

Ed wanted to give me an engagement ring. So we drove to Indianapolis to select the ring at Petri's fabulous jewelry store. Two days later the lovely solitaire was ready for my finger, and the same day, Ed left for New York after assuring us Nana was on the road to recovery.

My life became very busy with the wedding plans, selecting furniture for our future apartment in New York and buying clothes for my trousseau.

I returned to Cincinnati to ship my belongings back to Muncie and say goodbye to my friends and teachers at the Conservatory. I really hated leaving before the year was over, but there was so much to do. I sent Struwwelpeter back to Jack with my compliments and a final word of parting.

[146]

Mother and I went to New York in March, where I selected my wedding dress, a beautiful, ivory, Valencon lace with a scalloped mantilla, which would be covered with yards of tulle veiling. Elbow, lace mitts completed the ensemble. I still think of it as one of the most beautiful and timeless wedding dresses I have ever seen. Twenty-three years later, my daughter Ann wore my dress at her wedding.

While in New York, I went apartment hunting and finally found a tiny, four-room apartment at 192 East 75th Street, practically on the corner of Third Avenue, where the noisy elevated trains clattered along day and night. It was fun to plan the decor with the help of Francis Macomber, the decorator at Charles Mayer's outstanding department store. Eddie liked the location of our apartment as it was near his new private office at 862 Park Avenue.

Eddie took me to Mount Vernon to meet his family. Elizabeth, his mother, was gracious and friendly, and we became very close through the years. Margaret and Libby, Ed's younger sisters, were both married. Peg's husband was Henry Schiebel and their daughter Patricia, was Hudson's age. Libby's husband was Carl (Cal) Giegerich, and their daughter, Gail was about two years old. Albert, Ed's brother, was just my age. I also met Mrs. Eckerson's mother, Grandma Breck, who was as dear a person as my own Nana.

The family home in Mount Vernon was a large, gray house on the corner of Cottage Avenue, where Mrs. Eckerson lived alone, but Eddie had an office in a section of the house and every morning saw patients there. Sometimes he stayed in Mount Vernon, but he also had a small apartment at the Volney Hotel in the city at 23 East 74th Street. It was convenient for him in the event he was delayed at one hospital or another late at night. He was on the staffs of Post-Graduate, St. Lukes and Babies Hospital in the city, as well as the Mount Vernon Hospital. After our wedding we would be living at the Volney Hotel until our furniture arrived.

The time crept and flew. Many parties and showers were given for me, and the gifts rolled in, one exciting package after another. The wedding in Muncie was to be outdoors in the garden, near the old apple orchard at home. Tables were set up on the front lawn, with a large tent covering the area as a precaution against rain. But the day turned out to be extraordinarily beautiful.

Ed arrived a week before our marriage to attend the 500 Mile Race at the Indianapolis Speedway on Memorial Day. I had never been before and was unimpressed. The day seemed endless, noisy, and fumes of burned castor oil, which lubricated the cars, gave off a sickening odor that permeated the air over the grandstands. In later years, I learned to enjoy the races, but that first time my mind was occupied with more important things.

Our bridal dinner was at the Delaware Country Club in Muncie, culminating a week of parties honoring us. Hudson celebrated his fourteenth birthday during the bridal dinner. He unwrapped his gifts, and toasts were drunk to him as well as to us. He was surprised, because with all the excitement over our wedding, he thought he had been forgotten. Ed's family had arrived, and also Ed's good friend, John Melvin, the manager of the Volney. He was an usher along with Cal Giegerich, Henry Schiebel, Ed Ball and John Fisher (who would marry Janice in August.)

Our wedding was talked about for years as one of the most beautiful and enjoyable by the many guests who attended. For us, it was a blur of excitement, an unforgettable day. Eight of my best friends were bridesmaids, who held ribbons lining a path for Dad and me to walk from the house to the end of the garden. There, the minister, Reverend MacDavitt, Eddie and Albert were waiting. The bridesmaids were Betty Brown, Peg Schiebel, Libby Giegerich, Lucile Nichols Clark, Joan Parry, Jane Hitchcock Green and Carolyn Hedstrom. They, and all the women guests, wore long tea gowns with hats and gloves, as was the style in 1940.

Diggy's daughter, three-year-old Barbara Morris, looked adorable as she walked ahead of us swinging a little parasol. She was supposed to scatter rose petals as she went along, but they didn't appear.

I saw Barbara again for the first time forty-four years later, at the wedding of our cousin, Jerrold Fisher, Janice and John's youngest son. Barbara confided with some excitement she had just found the dusty parasol in her attic. It was carefully tied up, and as she untied and opened it, discovered it to be full of paper rose petals. She had no idea they were hidden inside.

———◄◉►———

Ed and I went to Sea Island, Georgia, for our honeymoon, stopping in Washington, D. C. for two days. There were no planes flying to Sea Island then, and the train trip was long and tiring. Breaking the trip in Washington was a good idea.

We spent ten days in Sea Island at the Cloisters, a dreamy, lovely resort with miles of hard, white sandy beaches. We bicycled on the beach and down roads shaded by old trees, dripping gray moss. Taking picnic lunches along, we sat in remote places on the beach searching for shells and swam in the warm Atlantic. At night, after wonderful meals, we danced under the stars. "Tuxedo Junction" was the orchestra's favorite piece and became ours too. It was a very romantic spot and has always been my favorite resort.

Two weeks after our wedding, we were back in New York, living at the Volney and waiting for the van of furniture to arrive. The apartment looked handsome, and we were happy and comfortable there after the furnishings were in place.

[148]

A Jamaican girl, Estelle Leed, had kept house for Ed and three other medical students at Columbia P. and S. Essie worshiped Eddie, and he suggested she might work for us, if I wished. I was delighted with her. She had a wonderful sense of humor, knew how to do house work in the most polished manner and taught me everything I know today about cooking, sewing and cleaning house. Essie was good company also. Whenever we talked about anything funny, she would laugh so hard she'd fall on the floor and roll in convulsions. Ed enjoyed her cooking so much he preferred her gourmet dishes over the finest restaurant food. Her lobster thermidor, one of Ed's favorites, was the best I have ever tasted. Essie never used recipes. All I had to do was describe something Ed liked, and she made it better than the original.

It wasn't long before I discovered I was pregnant. Both of our mothers were irate, and blamed Ed for causing such a "disaster" so soon in our married life. Ed's mother shook her finger under his nose and said, as a doctor, he should have known better! I tried to explain my condition away to my Mother, saying we had done everything possible to prevent it. Her caustic answer was, "It seems to me you forgot one thing."

I realized Mother was upset because she remembered the difficult time when she was carrying me with Daddy away in France. Times seemed to be repeating themselves as war had already begun in Europe with ominous rumors of a possible World War II. But our happiness covered everything like a blanket, and we ignored the political unrest.

Ed had made it clear to me the most important thing in his life was his profession, and I appreciated his dedication. He was called nearly every night on a hospital emergency. It actually depressed him to sleep through an entire night without being called. I was filled with love, pride and respect for him, and though I was alone a good deal, I had many things to do to pass the time. Unfortunately, my pregnancy made practicing the piano uncomfortable. My back ached, and I was constantly nauseated. So I visited with my friends during the day, began to do needlepoint and read a great deal.

The New York Philharmonic Orchestra gave Friday afternoon concerts, and Ruth Melvin and I went together, sitting in the topmost balcony of Carnegie Hall. It was so far from the stage the musicians looked like a group of busy ants, but the sound was glorious. Ruth and I became close friends as we were interested in the same things — art, music and the theater. We attended matinees and museums, shopped and enjoyed each other's company. Ruth and John had a baby girl, almost two years old when Ed and I were married. Later on, when our Judy was born, we strolled in Central Park together with the girls.

Ed saw to it I had the best obstetrician in New York, Kyle B. Steele. It was fortunate he was my doctor as with anyone else I would certainly have had a Caesarian section. I wasn't aware any problem existed until Dr. Steele left on his vacation, and I saw his assistant at my regular visit. He asked if I had made my reservation for a hospital bed yet, which would be necessary for the Caesarian section. I nearly fainted with shock but managed to keep a straight face. That evening I told Ed what the doctor had said, and he was very upset.

Dr. Steele was angry when he returned from vacation and learned his assistant had "spilled the beans." He told us there should be no problem at all, but he planned to take X-rays at the eighth month to be sure there was enough room for the baby to be born.

A few nights before I was due, Mother and Dad arrived to be on hand for the event, and we went to see the new Broadway show *Arsenic and Old Lace*. In the middle of the second act, I developed pains and left the theater expecting to deliver that night. But it was a false alarm, and I regretted missing the end of the suspenseful mystery. A few nights later, I did begin labor, and Ed took me to the Women's Lying-In, a section of New York Hospital. It was a long and arduous labor, but eventually our daughter was born, weighing in at eight pounds on March twenty-six, 1941.

She was beautiful, but it took me a few days to find the courage to peek under the blanket that wrapped her so tightly. I was afraid the nurses would chastise me if I disturbed her blanket. I finally found her little hands and discovered she really had two feet with five toes each. When I turned back the blanket covering her head, I discovered she had red hair, a beautiful shade of strawberry blonde! How exciting! Ed and I had not been able to come to an agreement about her name, but now she had to be Judith! It seemed to fit her. When Ed came that evening to visit, he also couldn't believe she had red hair, saying, "But I don't like red-headed women!"

I had cried when our baby was not a boy because I was sure Ed wanted a boy to carry on the Eckerson name but discovered he was delighted to have a little girl, and now, after getting over the shock of "a woman with red hair," he couldn't have been happier. There wasn't anything he adored more than little Judy.

After ten days in the hospital, we went home with a nurse to care for Judy for two weeks while I continued to recuperate. The pediatrician, Herbert Jackson, was most particular about Judy's welfare and would not permit her to leave the apartment until she was six weeks old. After this, she had to be out for airings twice a day. Grandma Breck gave us an elegant English carriage, and Judy was perambulated among the hundreds of children paraded in this manner around Central Park. Mothers and nursemaids would meet and chat for the required "airings," and Judy and I both developed rosy cheeks from the exercise. On Sundays Ed would join us on our walks as we proudly showed off our daughter, often meeting the Melvins with Andrea, or the Conklins with Elizabeth.

Reginald Conklin was in internist at St. Luke's Hospital and a good friend of Ed's. He and Laura lived nearby, and we became good friends. Their daughter was about six years older than Judy. We played bridge often, and once a week went to the ice and roller rink near LaGuardia Airport. After dinner, Ed and Laura would ice skate while Reg and I roller skated.

The year was full of new experiences for me. I met many new friends, the doctor husbands and wives Ed had known for years. Ed met and liked the friends I had made while in college also. Carol had married Seymour Meyer, and they lived not too far from us. Veola was married to Ludwig Lederer who owned and operated a smart women's accessory shop on Fifth Avenue. We gave dinner parties often and had many social activities during our brief two years in New York.

———⋅————◆————⋅———

War was spreading and poisoning the world. We were peacefully listening to the New York Philharmonic's Sunday broadcast on the radio December seventh, 1941, when the music was suddenly interrupted with the news of the Japanese bombing Pearl Harbor. We could no longer hide our heads in the sand and pretend the war couldn't touch us. We were involved.

Ed was determined to enlist before the hospitals froze him on the staffs and he would be unable to do his part in the service. He applied for the Navy, but was told he would have to wait for a commission. So he enlisted in the Army and received a Captain's commission right away.

Our world turned black with news and ominous threats from across both oceans. One day from our apartment, I saw a truly, black sky filled with roiling smoke from the harbor. The great ship *Normandie* was burning at the pier, where it had been brought for safekeeping during France's occupation by the Nazis. Tears burned my eyes as we listened to the radio report. The ship was completely destroyed. It was never proved whether it was an accident or sabotage.

Air raid shelters were created all over the city in preparation for possible bombing attacks from Germany. President Roosevelt and Congress had declared war on both Japan and Germany, and a full fledged war was in progress.

[151]

Dad and I have matching profiles   *Cutting the cake*

Mother, Ed, Lucina, Elizabeth Eckerson, and Dad

The Bridal party: L. to R. Carolyn Hedstrom, Henry Schiebel, Peg Schiebel, Joan Parry, Carl Giegerich, Elizabeth (Libby) Giegerich, Albert Eckerson, Lucina, Edwin Eckerson, Janice Ball (married to John Fisher in August) John Fisher, Betty Brown, Edmund Ball, Lucile Nichols Clark, John Melvin

Four Generations, June 1941

Judy at one month

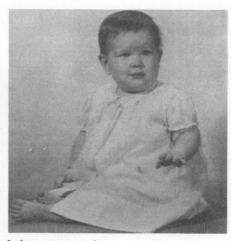

Judy at nine months

Captain Edwin Breck Eckerson

Lucina and Ed at the Persian Room, Drake Hotel, San Francisco, California

CHAPTER THIRTY

I N April, Ed was called into service and was given one month to terminate his affairs in New York. He was to report for duty in Wichita Falls, Texas, on May fifteenth. Ed thought I should go home to Muncie as he felt New York would be vulnerable to attack, but I was determined to be with him as long as possible. We packed and shipped everything to Texas. We wanted Essie to go with us, but she couldn't bear to leave her friends and her beloved New York.

My parents were delighted to keep Judy for us until we could find a place to live in Wichita Falls, and we drove tearfully away from New York on May fifth, 1942. Three years later on this date Ed was buried.

We planned a little extra time to stop at the Cloisters for a couple of days to rest and break the long drive to Texas. We were excited over the new venture of Army life, but, at the same time, sad at the turn of events which had disrupted our life in New York.

Ed was disappointed to leave his practice, of course. He had started a sympathectomy clinic at St. Luke's, which he told me was "going great guns" and had also devised a method of wiring aortic aneurisms at Post-Graduate Hospital. While he wired the fine filaments into the aneurism of the patient, another doctor ran the machine, spinning out the wire. He had done many successful operations of this type, but there would be no one to do it after he left. His specialty was the thyroid, though he practiced general surgery, and he was known all over the East Coast for his successful thyroidectomies.

After two blissful days at the Cloisters, we began the long drive to Texas, choosing the highways along the Gulf in order to revisit New Orleans, where we were engaged. We stopped at Pass Christian again and had lunch at the same picturesque hotel on the beach, pausing for awhile to sit in the same spot as before and contemplate our good fortune to have each other. It all seemed so long ago.

In New Orleans, Ed put on his uniform for the first time in spite of the suffocating heat of the city. He was uncomfortable and self-conscious but looked extremely handsome.

At last we arrived in Wichita Falls, a town reminding me of Muncie, about the same population and size. We found a nice, frame house at 1704 Pearl Street with a large, shady back yard full of pretty trees yielding delicious pecans. There was also a small guest house in the yard, for maids who came and went in rapid succession later on.

The house needed a face lifting inside. I had fresh wallpaper and painting done almost before the furniture arrived. As soon as we were settled, Mother and Dad brought Judy down and visited awhile before going home. Judy, now walking and talking a blue streak, was a joy for us every day.

We were getting used to Army life, and though Ed was restless, I loved the set hours, knowing he would be home from the base every afternoon at 5:30 with no interruptions until time to go back to Sheppard Field the next morning. He was rested, but hated the inactivity. He felt nothing was being accomplished and he was wasting precious time.

There were a great many social gatherings at the officers' homes and dances at the Officers Club. Ed never drank at all in New York as he was always on call at one hospital or another, and he never risked even one drink when he was working. But being in the service made a difference. It didn't matter if he drank or not. There was no business and scarcely any surgery for him. He was bored, and so he drank with the rest. All the doctors were bored with the inactivity in their profession, and it was sad to see. Many were not even able to practice their specialty, assigned by the Army to a branch of medicine foreign to them.

We lived in a comfortable, congenial neighborhood. Across the street lived a recently married couple who became good friends of ours, Jim and Claire Carter. Jim was a young doctor, a Lieutenant, stationed at Sheppard Field also. Another couple, friends of ours in New York, were Dodie and Herbert Lloyd. Herb was not a doctor but had been a patient of Ed's. Now he was stationed at Sheppard Field.

One day, while Dodie was visiting me, we heard a scream from my next door neighbor. Rushing out to see what the trouble was, we found Mrs. Renfro about to faint, holding her arm, and dripping with blood. She had run it through the wringer of her washing machine, and it was badly mangled. I drove while Dodie sat with her in the back seat, applying a tourniquet. It seemed forever before we reached the hospital. Due to our quick actions, Mrs. Renfro recovered and was more than grateful to us. I remember tutoring her son in geometry, as he had a terrible time getting the "hang" of it.

In August I was pregnant again, and, as before, I felt ill constantly. Mrs. Eckerson came to visit us for Thanksgiving, and my parents were planning to join us too, but Grandma Ball died, and they were unable to leave Muncie.

———————————◄◉►————————————

One night Ed was called about three a.m. The Military Police had found a soldier on the railroad tracks, both legs mangled from a train running over them. He was drunk and had passed out on the tracks. There was no time to take him to the hospital on the base. So they had rushed him to a Catholic hospital in town. Ed was out of the house in a flash. When he returned a few hours later, he told me he had had to amputate the man's legs. When the M.P.s carried the wounded soldier into the operating room, he needed them to hold the man down. They were strong and muscular, but when Ed began to operate, they both fainted dead away. Ed said he had great respect for the two Sisters attending. They calmly moved the M.P.s out of the way, stepped in and held the man's legs throughout the amputation, never flinching. He felt their patient stoicism and inner strength was remarkable. In general, he had little respect for most nurses. He couldn't tolerate any inefficiency in his profession.

Bill Forrest and Ed,
San Fernando, California

1704 Pearl St., Wichita Falls, Texas

Captain Charles Clark and Ed

The Pines, Muncie, Indiana

Judy and Ann

CHAPTER THIRTY-ONE

E D's orders arrived in early December. After only seven months, we had to leave our little house and friends in Wichita Falls. He was to proceed to Keesler Field in Biloxi, Mississippi. We knew I would have to return to Muncie in January as Ed would not permit me to go to a post hospital and have our baby possibly delivered by an "E.N.T. man!" (ear, nose and throat doctor.)

We packed our possessions, shipped everything to Muncie for the duration of the war, and Judy and I accompanied Ed to Biloxi. I planned to stay with Ed through the Christmas holidays.

The Edgewater Gulf Hotel in Biloxi had been converted into temporary housing for the military. We rented a room there for one month. The hotel was an enormous building situated on the Gulf, intended to accommodate wealthy tourists seeking sun and pleasure. I made friends with other Army wives, and Judy played with the many children living there.

Judy loved to play around the great, circular fireplace in the center of the huge, lobby-living room. A fire burned there constantly during the winter months. It was beautiful to watch and comfortable to sit near on chilly days. There were three steps stacked with fresh logs going up to the hearth, where Judy would continuously walk up and down.

One evening I was undressing her for bed and saw an ugly tick buried in her stomach, kicking its nasty little legs to burrow further in. Fortunately Ed was there, and in a matter of moments had cut the tick out, head and all, before it could bury itself completely into her body. There was no blood, and Judy was not even aware of the incision, it was done so smoothly. Ed was concerned, as Rocky Mountain Spotted Fever was prevalent in the area.

Another time, even though I tried to keep Judy away from the fireplace thereafter, she fell on one of the steps, breaking a corner off a front tooth.

The accident turned out to be a fortunate one. I had X-rays taken later in Indianapolis to be sure there was no injury to a permanent tooth, and it was discovered she had too little space in her jaw for the permanent teeth to grow. If the teeth had been allowed to come in normally, her face would have been deformed. Braces were put on her baby teeth when she was four years old to realign her jaw. When the permanent teeth erupted, they lined up in perfect position. The dentist thought she would have to have braces later after her permanent teeth were in, but it was never necessary.

In January, Mother and Dad came down to Biloxi to drive Judy and me back to Muncie with them. Ed and I took sorrowful leave of each other, but I needed to spend the last four months of pregnancy near the doctor who would deliver the baby. Ed selected Gerald Gustafson in Indianapolis to be my obstetrician.

Grandma Ball had owned a small, furnished country home just outside of Muncie, adjacent to Orchard Lawn Farms, where Mother still kept a few brood mares and foals. She called it "The Pines," as beautiful, tall pine trees grew in the front yard. It was a perfect place to sit out the war. I was among old friends again and being near my family was comforting.

Gas rationing, along with all kinds of food and clothes rationing, curtailed much of our lives during the war. The last month I stayed in Indianapolis at the Columbia Club on Monument Circle to be ready for a quick dash to Methodist Hospital. Judy moved in with Mother and Dad, and I lived in "solitary confinement" in Indianapolis. I was at the awful stage of hugeness and didn't want anyone to see me. When I took my daily walks, I hoped I wouldn't encounter a soul I knew. I could hear passersby murmur, "poor thing," as I lumbered along.

The only amusement I could think up was to wander through the lovely L. S. Ayres Department Store, one floor at a time, seeing all the "goodies" displayed and longing to wear a pretty dress again. I was enormous! At one point the doctor even suspected twins.

On May fifteenth, thinking the time had come, Ed arranged for leave to be with me when the baby was born. It was wonderful to have him there, but Ann wasn't ready to greet the world yet, and all our hopes for her to cooperate were dashed. I even tried a dose of castor oil, an old remedy that can sometimes induce labor.

At breakfast, Ed brought the six-ounce bottle of castor oil into the dining room of the Columbia Club and poured it into a large glass of orange juice. I couldn't believe it all had to go down and knew I couldn't make a display of myself in a room full of diners. So Mother, Dad, Ed and I paraded out of the dining room and into the elevator to my room, while I carried the big glass of orange juice. My face was red, feeling all eyes were on me. In the privacy of the bathroom, gagging, I downed the nasty, slick liquid with determination.

Nothing happened. It could have been plain water for all the effect it had on me. Ann remained in her cocoon, and Ed left for Keesler Field, leaving us all disappointed.

Mother stayed with me from then on, but it wasn't until dawn, May twenty-ninth, that I was awakened by a funny feeling inside like a chicken pecking at its shell. Suddenly my water broke, and Mother and I made haste for the hospital, after stuffing bath towels between my legs. But labor pains had not begun.

The birth was easy compared to the difficult time I had had with Judy.

Ann was another large baby, weighing over nine pounds.

During the war, the maternity time spent in hospitals was cut to five days, but Dr. Gustafson, mercifully, gave orders that I was to remain in the hospital for ten days because of the long drive to Muncie and the post natal care for Ann. She was a "blue" baby, needing oxygen after the dry birth but soon picked up color and stamina.

Ann was just one week old when Ed called from Biloxi to say he had been given orders to report to the air base in Pittsburg, California in preparation for overseas duty.

The emotional jolt was terrible. I cried ceaselessly. Ed planned to fly to Indianapolis to see us before reporting to Pittsburg. Dr. Gustafson released me from the hospital a day early to spend the night at the Columbia Club with Ed. Mother and Dad brought Judy to Indianapolis, and we were all together for the brief visit. Ann remained in the hospital, but Ed was able to see her before she left.

The next day Ed flew to California, and I drove home with Ann and a nurse. Mother and Dad were wonderful throughout the ordeal. They helped so much, giving me the support I desperately needed.

The practical nurse had planned to stay with Ann for the usual two weeks, but toward the end of this time, I heard from Ed that he might not be leaving for Pacific duty as soon as he had thought. He was to be assigned to a new hospital ship under construction, the U.S.S. Comfort, as chief of surgery, but it was indefinite when the ship would be ready for action.

I made up my mind to join Ed for as long as possible and persuaded the nurse to stay on with the children indefinitely. I was packed and on a train for San Francisco almost immediately. Mother and Dad were not happy with my decision. They thought I should stay with the children, but I knew I should go while I was assured of competent care for our new baby.

On the long train ride, I had three more days to regain my strength, and by the time I reached Oakland, felt well and bursting with excitement. Ed met me at the station, and we ferried across to San Francisco for a celebration — together once again!

He had rented a room in a widow's home in Pittsburg, where we stayed during the week while he was on duty. To while away the hours when he was on the base, I bought a large rug to needlepoint. Pittsburg was a small town known for its oil refinery. The smell of oil hung heavily in the air. We could not open our windows at night for fear of being overcome by the thick stench. Black smoke rolled over the town, and it was hard to tell if it was the day or night.

We looked forward to the weekends when we headed for San Francisco and good times. The California Hotel was particularly accommodating to

[163]

service men, and they gave us a suite, which we shared with Agnes and Charles Clark. Charlie was an orthopedic surgeon who would be on Ed's operating team on the *Comfort*, Agnes had come west to stay with Charles for as long as possible, and the four of us became fast friends. We had a wonderful time playing in San Francisco and found special places to which we returned over and over again.

One of our favorite restaurants was Julius's Castle, situated on a rocky point overlooking the harbor of San Francisco Bay. We loved to arrive before sunset in order to watch the gorgeous color spread through the sky. As the sky darkened, the lights came on the ships and Golden Gate Bridge, transforming the city into a fairyland of twinkling lights.

The most exotic place of all was Trader Vic's in Oakland. The tropical island decor, oriental food and fancy drinks were irresistible. The Tonga became my favorite. It tasted inoccuous, a delicious fruit mixture, but rum lurked in the background and once caught up with me in no uncertain terms. There was reason for over-celebrating that evening as Ed had just received his promotion to Major. After that evening Ed declared Trader Vic's "off limits" for me.

———————◁◉▷——————

After three wonderful months, Ed finally had orders to report to San Pedro, California, where the *Comfort* was berthed. I followed him there. As delays were the theme of the day, no one knew how long the men would be standing by.

Ed was assigned to a barracks in Torrence near the San Pedro harbor. It was about the ugliest place we had ever seen. The only vegetation, outside of a few scraggly palm trees, were the thousands of oil derricks sprinkled over the flat, dismal land. Agnes found a beach house, where she intended to live as long as the men remained in port. It was attractive and suitable for them and being on the beach made up for the poor territory surrounding it.

Ed and I stayed in Los Angeles at the large Ambassador Hotel, but after a few days, the men were required to stay on the base. Before I left for home, Ed took me aboard the *Comfort* and gave me a tour of the ship.

The *Comfort* would be staffed by a Navy compliment of four hundred men, and the hospital was manned by Army personnel of the same number. It was the first hospital ship with a divided compliment of both Army and Navy. Two sister ships were to follow, the *Hope* and the *Mercy*.

The operating rooms were centered below deck on the ship, where motion would be the steadiest, and the wards at the stern would accommodate seven hundred wounded. The ship was equipped with the best facilities possible, and Ed was very proud of his operating rooms.

I saw Ed's tiny cabin and the mess where the officers would have their meals. Now I had a clear picture of the ship in my mind to take home with me, and I could visualize his life aboard through his letters.

As much as I hated to leave Ed, I was very anxious to see my babies. Three months had passed, and Ann had grown into a very pretty, blond baby. Judy's red hair still shone like burnished gold. The nurse had looked after them competently, but now I didn't need her anymore as I was home for good.

Still the *Comfort* did not sail. Finally, the ship was commissioned, and on May 5th, 1943, a trial run was made. Delays continued until November after which the men were given leave to go home for Christmas. The ship was due to enter active duty in the Pacific in January, 1944.

It was wonderful to have Ed home, and he was delighted to see the children, amazed at how much they had grown in the past six months. We treasured every moment we had together, and Christmas with the family was a beautiful, but bittersweet time.

This time, when Ed left, we knew it would be a long time before we could be together again. The time dragged on from month to month. I was now living for his letters and hung on the radio for every scrap of news that came from the Pacific.

The *Comfort's* base was Hollandia, New Guinea, where she waited until the Battle of Leyte Gulf and then proceeded to pick up the wounded and return with them to Hollandia. Ed was unable to give me any details of the action because of Army censorship, but he was given official permission to have the only camera on board. Later on, I had the movie films developed and was able to distinguish some of the places Ed had described. He'd filmed part of the Battle of Leyte, but most of the pictures were of the men on shore at Hollandia with the natives. The Comfort returned to San Pedro in March to bring back the wounded, but no leave was granted except a three-day shore leave, as the ship returned immediately to New Guinea.

Agnes Clark had remained in hopes the ship would return and she could see Charlie. All their married life they had longed for children and had almost given up hope. Now she discovered she was pregnant, and they were both thrilled. She returned to La Grange, Illinois to live with her sister and brother-in-law after she saw Charlie in March.

[165]

Bill's graduation picture, Culver Military Academy

CHAPTER THIRTY-TWO

L ife at The Pines continued. The routine of the days caring for Judy
and Ann kept me busy enough, but the nights were lonely, dreary
times.

Mother gave me a darling, wire-haired puppy, and Judy named her
Penny. She was good company for us. Ann slept in a corner of my large
bedroom in her crib, and Judy had a room of her own. Because we were in
the country, many mice found their way into the house. I was terrified of
them. At night they were so brave they climbed up on Ann's bath table. I
watched them from my bed afraid they would crawl over the children as
they slept. I hoped Penny would be a "mouser," but she was as afraid of
them as I was.

Ot Cushing, my knight in armor, came to the rescue time after time.
He managed the Orchard Lawn Farm next door. He set and emptied
mouse traps and saw to furnace problems or anything else that went
wrong.

I started to practice again while the children were napping in the
afternoons. I hadn't played the piano for almost three years, and now
music was a godsend. I lost myself drilling on technical exercises to regain
agility in my fingers. I took out the Grieg Concerto and started work on it
again, as well as the Chopin Etudes and other favorite compositions I had
learned. When I felt I was playing reasonably well, I resumed lessons with
Bomar, taking the train to Indianapolis once a week instead of driving,
because of the gas rationing.

Early in June, 1944, after Ann's first birthday, we were enjoying a pretty
day outside. Ann was manuevering her walker around the driveway, and
Judy was exploring a part of the yard near the rail fence. We burned trash
right behind the fence where she was playing, but I wasn't concerned
because I had told the help who came occasionally never to throw bottles
on the trash pile because they could explode with the heat and scatter glass
around. I heard Judy call me, saying, "Look, Mommie, I'm playing
horsie." I looked up in time to see Judy straddling the rail fence, and a
second later she slipped off and fell into the pile of ashes on the far side.

She began to cry, and I rushed over, lifting her up and out of the dirty
pile. As I brought her over the fence rail, I saw a great, jagged gash on her
ankle, welling with blood. I called out to the maid, telling her to watch
Ann, and rushed Judy to the hospital.

I broke all the speed records and had Judy at the emergency door in ten
minutes. She looked as if she might go into shock. Her face was ashy and
blood was gushing over the towel we had put under her. I was shaking and
numb with fright.

[167]

It was fortunate Anson Hurley was on duty. He was an excellent surgeon, and we couldn't have had better luck. Anson told me Judy's leg had been cut to the bone, severing a tendon. Because I had been so quick to get her to the hospital, he had been able to find the receding tendon and sew it together. But the wound was so dirty and filled with ashes he was afraid of infection. The slightest infection could prevent the tendon from holding, and it could slip away, leaving Judy crippled.

Penicillin had just been released to the hospitals as a new drug, and he planned to try it on Judy, hoping it would keep the wound clear of infection. My anxiety over Judy's accident kept me awake night after night. Judy was terrified of the doctors when they came in with the large syringe of penicillin twice a day. But the tendon held, and eventually Judy's fear of doctors faded when she was home again and in her own familiar room. She had to learn to walk again, and her foot flopped at every step. I found the jagged, broken coke bottle in the ashes where Judy had fallen on it and admonished the help again about putting dangerous articles in the trash.

Ed was frantic when he got the news, but there was little he could do. Communication from Anson calmed him.

———◄◉►———

Nana had become ill again. She had suffered from arthritis for years and the pain and crippling bowed her legs so badly, they made a perfect circle when she stood. Besides constant arthritic pain, the cancer had returned and spread, making her weak and sick. Edema filled her stomach and from time to time the fluid had to be drained. We could only watch as Nana began to slip away from us until it was finally necessary to hospitalize her. The family was with her when she died early in August, 1944. It was terrible to lose her, but we were glad her suffering had ceased. Ed's surgery had given her four more years of life, and for this we were grateful.

———◄◉►———

Hudson, now Bill, was finishing his last year at Culver Military Academy, after attending both the winter and summer sessions. Mother and Dad had rented a cottage on Lake Maxinkuckee, where the school was located, so Bill would have a place to be with his friends and family on weekends. They had grown to love the lake. When they noticed a completely furnished house for sale on the East Shore, Dad decided to buy it that August. He felt it would give Mother something to take her mind off Nana's death as well as provide a permanent summer recreation place for the family.

The cottage proved to be a wonderful investment. Mother was busy fixing up the house more attractively with fresh upholstery and curtains, and Judy, Ann and I drove up to be there for awhile. The cottage was really a very large house with enough bedrooms to sleep up to fifteen people. It was a place to relax at the lake front, swim, ride in the new Chris Craft

[168]

motor boat which Dad had purchased, and enjoy the lovely summer breezes. We all loved the change, only about one hundred miles north of Muncie, an easy drive to a different environment.

After Bill graduated from Culver, he joined the Navy, and was sent to the Naval Air Station in Jacksonville, Florida and trained as a tail gunner of SB 2C (two seated Navy dive bombers). His college education was delayed until the war was over, and then he enrolled at Indiana University and majored in Business Administration.

—————◄◉►—————

Ed could not give me any information concerning the war, but one day in December I received a strangely worded letter that only meant one thing to me. The *Comfort* was returning to Los Angeles! The letter made no sense at all except for my interpretation. He wrote: "How nice that you will be spending Christmas with Betty Brown in California! You mentioned being at the Ambassador Hotel about the twenty-second and will visit her either in San Francisco or Los Angeles for a couple of weeks. Have a good time and write me all about it."

Tremendously excited, I made train and hotel reservations right away. I thought it safer to go to Los Angeles first. Then, if the ship returned to San Francisco, it would only be a delay of another day to meet him there. I had one week to plan and pack.

My parents were very much against such a fly-by-night trip. They said I should be with the children for Christmas, and how could I be sure the letter meant the *Comfort* was coming in? I knew I had to take the chance.

I felt guilty about leaving Judy and Ann with the family, but I boarded the train on the nineteenth, and on the twenty-second I arrived in Los Angeles, nervous, terribly excited and a trifle unsure.

I spent the entire day in the hotel room, pacing the floor, biting my nails, anything to keep from staring at the phone. I could do nothing but wait and hope. I didn't dare leave the room for an instant in case the phone might ring. I couldn't sleep, eat or read. I simply agonized, dreadful thoughts and disappointment overcoming the optimism I had felt before.

It was 6:30 in the evening when there was a soft knock on the door. I was ready to faint when I opened it, but there he stood!

—————◄◉►—————

The two weeks flew by on golden wings. We spent Christmas Day with the Bill Forrests in San Fernando Valley. Bill, a classmate of Ed's when they were in school at Exeter, was so handsome he modeled for Arrow Shirts after college. He also had aspirations to become an actor, a profession very much against his parents wishes. After an unhappy first marriage, he finally came to Hollywood and spent the rest of his life happily playing bit parts in movies. Bill told us M.G.M. wanted to make a

[169]

leading man of him, but he didn't want the notoriety associated with stardom. He enjoyed his quiet, private life with Wilhemina, his second wife. She was a motherly person, enormously fat, with a plain, homely face. They made an odd looking couple but were very much in love. "Willie" was a wonderful wife for Bill, and they had three handsome sons, resembling their father. We visited with Bill and Wilhemina at least once on every visit to Los Angeles.

Charlie Clark flew to La Grange to see Agnes and was shocked to find her so huge she couldn't stand and so toxic she even had edema of the nose. He rushed her to a hospital in Chicago where a Caesarian section was performed and twin boys were delivered, seven pounds apiece. The babies were strong and healthy, but for Agnes, the toxemia and dangerously high blood pressure put her life in jeopardy for several days.

Our last day together, Ed and I went to Olivera Street for Mexican food, then browsed among the shops in the Mexican quarter until time for me to board the train home. The picture of Ed standing on the platform as the train pulled away will always remain in my mind. It was the last time I ever saw him.

CHAPTER THIRTY-THREE

MOTHER and I had been teaming up on her two little spinet pianos, which sat back to back in the playroom over the garage. She helped me learn the Grieg Concerto by playing the orchestral, accompanying part. We progressed to other two-piano pieces for fun and eventually played two programs in Indianapolis — one at the Propylaeum Club and the other at the Athletic Club, as guest artists for Matinee Musicale. I accompanied Mother in a group of Grieg songs, followed by the Grieg Concerto.

Robert Hargreaves, the music director of Ball State University, asked me to play the concerto with his orchestra for the Spring Festival, May fifteenth. I had never played with an orchestra before and saw it as an exciting challenge.

On April twenty-eighth, a Sunday morning, I was to perform a Bach Suite for Mr. Cramer's repertoire class in Indianapolis, but I awoke feeling very depressed. I tried to practice the Bach but was unable to concentrate, feeling worse every moment. Finally, I called Mother just to talk to someone. When I heard her voice, for no reason at all, I suddenly burst into tears, sobbing uncontrollably. Mother knew I needed her and said she would be right over.

I felt better after she came but was still listless, sad and full of a foreboding I couldn't express. I went to Indianapolis but didn't have the energy to play well for the repertoire class. Depression hung over me the rest of the day.

When I returned to Muncie on the train, I decided to stop on the way home and visit with Jane and Jack to help raise my spirits. Jane Hitchcock had been divorced from Bill Green and was now married to Jack Simpson. They were a handsome couple and fun to be with. Jack was funny, and I knew he would pep me up.

They looked surprised and not too happy to see me. I felt my gloom must be smothering them also, but they finally confessed they had heard some bad news on the radio. Rather than trying to tell me about it, they turned the radio on for Walter Winchell's news broadcast, whose first explosive report told of a kamikaze attack on the *Comfort* off Okinawa. Apparently the ship was on its way to Guam loaded with wounded men when it was attacked. Twenty-nine were reported killed and thirty-three wounded, but the ship was proceeding under its own steam, without assistance. Winchell said the kamikaze attack had come at 8:30 at night under a full moon. I was sure the Captain would have blacked out the ship and zigzagged to avoid a direct hit, as Ed had explained how the Captain had done it during the Battle of Leyte. So I thought the plane must have fallen on the stern where the wounded were bedded in the wards. Having been on the ship, I felt sure Ed would be in surgery, the safest section amid-ship, and could not have been injured. Nevertheless, I was frightened and concerned. Aware of the time difference between Muncie and Pacific zone, I now knew my unusual depression that day coincided with the time of the kamikaze attack.

I left Jane and Jack and drove on to Mother's where she was keeping the children. I couldn't bear to go back to The Pines alone. Judy and Ann were asleep, and I climbed in bed with Judy, holding her close for comfort and strength.

The next day, Dad called his friend, Eugene Pulliam, in Washington to try and get more information about Ed. Pulliam owned the *Indianapolis News* but during the War was a correspondent in Washington. Gene looked over the list of casualties sent in by the Comfort, and reported to Dad that Ed's serial number was not on it. I spent the next two weeks in a fool's paradise.

On May fifth we heard about the funeral service held in Guam and even saw it later on the newsreels at a movie house. I looked for Ed but couldn't single him out from the rest as Taps were played, and the crew stood at attention as the flag-draped coffins were lowered into the ground. It was one year to the day of the ship's commission and three years to the day when Ed reported for duty at Sheppard Field in Texas.

Could Ed have been one of the wounded? They were shown being carried off the ship on litters. There was a gaping hole in the ship's side, and film showed the plane's remains buried in the debris.

Time passed, and I heard nothing from Ed. Because the kamikaze was a deliberate attack on a hospital ship, it was considered a "war atrocity" and became news immediately. Apparently, the reason the Japanese attacked the *Comfort* was in retaliation for a Japanese "hospital" ship we had sunk, which was carrying ammunition instead of wounded men.

On May twelfth, there was a large dinner party at the Delaware Country Club given by Isabel and Ed Ball. During dessert Dad was called to the phone. A few minutes later, he beckoned me to join him outside. He was pale, and with tears and voice breaking, told me the phone call was from the telegraph office trying to locate me. My telegram, "with regrets to inform you," had arrived from the War Department. I remember Dad and I sat on the steps of the staircase leading out of the Club for a long time. Finally, he went back to the dining room to get Mother. We drove home to Westwood, and I collapsed.

I began getting letters from the men on the ship, telling me more than I already knew. They enclosed photos of the grave site, the cemetery in Guam, and pictures of the ship. M.G.M. sent me the movie reel of the funeral service, which I had already seen. I was grateful for all the information, but it didn't help to ease the agony. I felt dead inside. I went through the motions of life for the sake of the children, my only reason for going on.

The letters from Ed's shipmates told the true story of the attack. The new Captain aboard didn't zigzag or black out, which would have been permissible under attack. The crew stood on deck and watched the Japanese plane circle above the ship, taking aim before it dove five minutes later into the dead center of the ship, burying itself in surgery, which was adjacent to the main boiler. It passed through three decks into the operating room where it exploded and killed all the patients, doctors and nurses there. Ed and Charlie were doing a brain operation at the time.

After the attack, the men on board ran to the surgery, at first believing Ed was alive, as they found him standing against the wall — but the concussion had killed him instantly, the force blowing him to the far end of the operating room.

Less than three months later the war was over, and Japan surrendered after the nuclear bombing of Hiroshima. The futility and waste of those war years is even more evident to me now after forty years. At least then we thought the lives lost were not in vain, as we had won "freedom for the

[172]

world." How naive we were! The farce of the Korean and Vietnam wars followed, and we are still faced today with the monstrous disaster of World War III sure to come.

Hospital ship, U.S.S. Comfort

News article on kamikaze attach on the Comfort

JAPANESE BOMB
HOSPITAL SHIP

Wanton Assault Enrages U. S. Troops Upon Okinawa.

BY AL DOPKING.

GUAM, April 30.— (A°) — American doughboys, enraged over a Japanese pilot's suicidal attack on a helpless navy hospital ship evacuating their wounded buddies, fought doggedly today for two airfields—their immediate objectives on Southern Okinawa.

The fully-loaded, unarmed, unescorted U. S. S. Comfort was attacked and heavily damaged 50 miles south of Okinawa. Twenty-nine were killed, 33 wounded and one was missing. The killed included six army nurses and five army medical officers.

Was Easily Identified.

Although the 13,000-ton vessel was readily identified as searchlights played on the giant Red Crosses painted on her gleaming white decks and superstructure, the Japanese pilot made several runs at her preliminary to his Kamikaze (suicidal) attack, reported Associated Press Correspondent Vern Haugland.

Vice Adm. Richard K. Turner, commander of the Third Fleet Amphibious Force, stormed:

"My printable comment on this outrage is unprintable."

Lt. Gen. Simon Buckner, Tenth Army commander who was visiting Admiral Turner today, said, "This is terrible. Any comment I could make on this wouldn't go through the mails."

These other developments were reported in Fleet Adm. Chester W. Nimitz's communique today:

Total American casualties on Okinawa and nearby islands were 11,413, including 1,847 killed, through Friday.

The Japanese sent about 200 aircraft in wave after small wave against American forces off Okinawa for 15 hours Saturday noon until 2:15 a. m. Sunday. They "caused some damage to light units of the fleet"—at a cost of 104 attacking planes shot down.

[174]

Funeral in Guam

Ed's grave in Guam

CHAPTER THIRTY-FOUR

I tried to pick up the pieces of my life, which now had little meaning. Judy and Ann gave me the courage I needed, and everyone, particularly Mother and Dad, gave me such wonderful love and support, I had to try and stay strong.

I had had two rehearsals with the Ball State Orchestra playing the Grieg Concerto before the telegram arrived. Naturally, I was unable to do the performance or ever play the concerto again.

I was very concerned for Agnes Clark. She was on the verge of a nervous breakdown and couldn't reconcile the fact that Charlie had saved her life, only to lose his own. The twins she had given birth to, now seemed a burden. Her physical health was poor, as she still suffered from high blood pressure and exhaustion after her life-threatening pregnancy.

I decided to invite her to join me at the lake. Perhaps we could help each other through this tragic experience. We met at the cottage toward the end of May. She brought Henry and Lyman, her handsome twin babies. Judy, Ann and I made up our little group. We spent the month of June together, alone. We did help each other. I felt Agnes's outlook had softened, and I began to look the future in the eye.

Ed and I had been close, not only physically, but also spiritually. He was a very religious person and felt God deeply. When we lived in New York, he attended church whenever he was free after his Sunday rounds. I sang in the choir in the Madison Avenue Presbyterian Church, and he usually appeared just in time to hear Dr. Buttrick's sermon.

About three weeks after the kamikaze attack, I was sitting in the den at Mother's staring into the glowing embers of a dying fire. suddenly I was aware of Ed standing beside me in his uniform. He spoke to me softly, saying he had been trying to come to me all this time to tell me not to grieve for him. He said he was all right and would always be near to watch over the three of us. He was there for a few moments, and I felt and saw his presence.

Ed appeared to me a number of times after that. He had said it was hard to get back to me, but he was going to stay for as long as I needed him. The last time he came was in Culver. I was almost asleep when he appeared, as always, in his uniform. He stood there, looking sad because I was crying so hard. He told me he felt he upset me too much by appearing in this way and said he would not come any more unless I really wanted him to. But he wanted me to know he would always be there if I needed him. I called out that I always needed him, but he was gone and never did return from then on except in my thoughts. It was true that instead of bringing me comfort, his appearances had been agonizing torture. But I am convinced from the experience that there is life after death.

Agnes Clark, Henry and Lyman

Ball Cottage at Maxinkuckee, Culver, Indiana

Judy and Ann hunt turtles with Alan Albright

Bill Ball skiing on Lake Maxinkuckee

Judy, Ann and Lucina at The Cloisters, Sea Island, Georgia

*Colonel Wright Hiatt
boarding train for Kansas*

CHAPTER THIRTY-FIVE

ONE of the doctors on the *Comfort*, Lee Maris, lived in Attica, Indiana. Gladys, his wife and I, had exchanged telephone calls during the terrible interim of waiting before my telegram arrived. Lee had been severely wounded and flown to the hospital in Guam. He lost an eye and the use of one arm in the kamikaze attack. Now he was home, recuperating from his injuries, spending weekends in Culver, where his family also owned a cottage. While Agnes was with me, Gladys and Lee joined us several times to visit and discuss the tragedy that befell us all.

During that summer I met a very interesting man who was head of the Cavalry School at the Academy, Captain John Carter. He had been wounded in New Guinea early in the war, and at first, was believed dead. Half of his face had been shot away, and he lay on the field, conscious, but unable to move. When two medics leaned over and said, "This one's gone," John summoned all his strength and closed his one eye. They gasped, hurriedly placed him on a litter and removed him to the hospital. He had one operation after another to rebuild his face and was sent to Hawaii for further treatment and therapy to improve his vision. He was taught how to needlepoint to improve his depth perception and became so involved in the art, he created designs of his own in petit point. Many of his pieces were hunting scenes. He would sit at the end of our pier and study the cloud formations, stitching them in free hand. His work was detailed and beautiful.

John loved to play golf, telling me it had been the most difficult sport to accomplish with one eye, but he beat me easily every time. He also played tennis, excellent bridge and was a wonderful dancer. He took me to the Culver dances on weekends. He was a man of many talents with a brilliant mind, and handsome — a rugged, solid male. It was far from true that he thought his glass eye made him repulsive. The doctors had done a marvelous job of skin grafting and plastic surgery. I admired him tremendously for his courage.

I knew for certain I had to return to New York where I felt more at home than anywhere else. I wrote to John Melvin and asked him to find an apartment for me, but it was going to be a long wait as apartments were very scarce following the war. In the meantime, I planned to be away from Muncie as much as possible as "The Pines" was a lonely and stifling place.

Judy would be going to school in another year, and I decided to "follow the sun" and travel before settling down when Judy began her education. I made reservations to go back to Sea Island for the winter, although I knew all the beautiful memories would be painful. I loved the resort, however, and couldn't think of a better place for the three of us to be. I needed to be close to my memories, even if they hurt. We stayed in Culver well into the month of September and then returned to "The Pines" to pack for Sea Island.

———————<◉>———————

The Cloisters was still the same lovely place. Our little room was in the Annex across the driveway from the main building. A cot was added for Ann, and it was quite comfortable for the three of us. We had a small, sheltered balcony overlooking the fishing creek, which was a nice place to sit and sun. An enormous closet not only accommodated our clothes, but made a nice playroom for the children.

Sitters were available for them, but I seldom made use of the service. There was an early dinner hour for children, giving me time to put Judy and Ann to bed and see that they were asleep before going back to the hotel for entertainment. There were shows and dancing and I often played ping pong with other guests, sometimes large "round robin" games, which were hilarious. I became quite expert at the game and could beat almost everyone.

During the day we played on the beach, if the weather was nice. I was amazed how many days of beautiful weather there were during the winter months. I remember swimming in the ocean on New Years Day, but I was the only one who braved the cold water!

The three of us thrived in the climate and outdoor living. The children were becoming beautiful little girls, captivating the guests at The Cloisters. Judy with her sweet manners and poise and glowing red hair was a bright jewel in my life. Ann was a charming tease, her softly curling, blond hair framing her face, making her irresistible to all. Both girls would grow up to resemble Ed, but Ann is his image. She shares his hazel eyes, identical hands and finger nails. Both girls also grew tall and slim with figures like Ed's, features I've always envied, as I am short and squat. I was bursting with pride for both girls as they learned to play unobtrusively among grown-ups, without the loud demands and whines of most of the other children there.

Mr. Aufmordt was an elderly German gentleman who spent his winters at The Cloisters, bringing his two daschunds along. He played golf every day, and when Mother and Dad arrived, Mother, who was a "sure shot" golfer, joined him. She told me it was amusing to play with Mr. Aufmordt as his two little dogs were his caddies. They were trained to find the golf ball, and as soon as he drove off, the dogs would run to the spot where the ball lay and stand at attention until he arrived. Mr. Aufmordt, however, was a lecherous man, and when he propositioned Mother, she gave up the golf games.

He hung around me a good deal and once asked me to be his partner at

[181]

bridge. Enjoying the game, I was glad to join the foursome. As we sat down at the table, Mr. Aufmordt announced he never played for less than ten cents a point. The remark went over my head as we dealt out the first hand. Then I slowly realized he had not said "a tenth of a cent a point" the stakes at ten cents a point were one hundred times the amount I had ever played for! No one commented on the stiff gamble, but as we played, I became extremely nervous at the position in which I found myself, recalling Mr. Aufmordt saying he paid for his fare back and forth to Europe playing bridge.

I couldn't believe it when the score tallied precisely the same for both sides at the end of the rubber. I felt I had played my part coolly and excused myself from the game "to see about the children." Mr. Aufmordt had kept score, and I strongly suspected he manipulated the game to cause the even score. Even scores are extremely rare.

Many service men came to The Cloisters on their terminal leave for R. and R. (rest and recuperation) before re-entering our "brave new world." Lloyd Hull was one — a very attractive fellow and fun to dance with. I saw a good deal of him later on in New York.

Another very nice man was Charles Chappell. He also lived in New York, and we became good friends and still correspond today. One night there was a special party at The Cloisters with a buffet and show around the pool area. Chuck asked me to join him for the party, and before the buffet, we went to one of the cottages for cocktails. The host made martinis, and, though I never was fond of them, they tasted rather good this time. Before we could finish one, the host passed the pitcher around, topping off everyone's drink. I didn't realize what was happening to me until we all stood up to go to dinner.

I was staggering After I put on my coat, I whispered to Chuck to take me home. He tried to encourage me, saying I would be all right after eating, but I knew I couldn't make it. I was barely aware of getting back to my room. Chuck paid the sitter and disappeared. I was "gone" until the next morning and embarrassed when I saw Chuck later, apologizing for spoiling his evening. He was a perfect gentleman, giving me credit for recognizing my condition and for taking steps to avoid further embarrassment. Chuck and I remained friends, and he even came to visit me in Muncie later that year.

Wright Hiatt swept me off my feet. He was a tall, red-headed, Army Colonel, stretching up to a height of 6'5", a lanky, avid tennis player, looking for a good time at The Cloisters. A graduate of West Point, he was an engineer in the regular Army, enjoying leave with his beautiful sister and her husband.

It so happened the Hiatts were originally from Winchester, Indiana, a

[182]

tiny town a few miles from Muncie, and we had many mutual friends. Marge Booker, Hi's sister, was simply gorgeous. She had a way of piling her beautiful, thick, auburn hair up high on her head then twisting in pearls or chiffon scarves to match her clothes. She was not only stunning — she had a lovely, warm personality.

Hi and I became more than friends. We became engaged. I fell head over ears for him with all his charm, wit and intelligence. He loved Judy and Ann as well as me and persuaded me to leave Sea Island a month earlier than I had intended. He and Marge were going to Palm Beach, Florida for a wedding, then back to Atlanta, where the Bookers lived. He wanted me to take the trip with them, and after a few days in Atlanta, said he would drive me home to Muncie.

Mother and Dad had come to Sea Island for the Christmas holidays, and my brother, Bill, came up from Jacksonville, Florida, where he was stationed so we could all be together. On January second I left with Hi and Marge, and my parents took Judy and Ann back to Muncie with them in Dad's plane.

As we traveled to Palm Beach and then to Atlanta, I learned more about Hi and began to feel there was something wrong, something unbalanced about him. The first hint was his jealousy. He was strangely jealous of Ed, and hated to hear me speak about him. It was unnatural for me to hide my feelings, and it made me very uncomfortable. I saw several sides of his nature. One day he would be the normal person I had grown to like, and the next day, a stranger. His moods changed like a chameleon's. I grew disturbed and was uncertain whether it would be wise to marry him.

We saw a great deal of each other over the next six months. He was stationed at Fort Leavenworth, Kansas but was allowed freedom from duty for some time after the war. He had seen heavy action overseas and helped to build the Burma road to China. The longer I knew Hi, the more concerned I became with his moods, trying to understand him. I felt it might have something to do with his war experiences, but he told me little about them, his thoughts a closed book.

That summer he planned to come to Culver so we could make a decision about marrying. After several postponements, due to his duties at the Fort, he called to say he would be delayed yet again. I was irritated and told him I felt he shouldn't bother to come at all. He became very angry and yelled over the phone, "If that's the way you feel about it, then goodbye!"

Within a month, I received a letter from Marge telling me Hi had stormed out to Jackson Hole, Wyoming, met a girl there and married her two weeks later. I knew then my concerns over his emotional outbursts had been justified.

[183]

Ed Cox had been stationed in Los Angeles during the war and stayed on after his discharge from the Army. He came to Culver one weekend and asked me again to marry him, but again, I had to refuse. He was a wonderful friend, but I could not visualize myself married to him. He told me he would never marry anyone but me and hoped some day I might change my mind about him.

Summers in Culver were filled with fun and friends, who arrived for visits. Fourth of July weekend was the highlight of every summer and always included Jane and Jack Simpson and Mary and T. J. Ault. There was a festive fireworks display shot over the lake at the Academy pier, and their three-masted schooner sailed around the lake with the Naval School Band on board serenading the cottagers. To show appreciation for the concert, the piers and homes around Lake Maxinkuckee were lit with candles in sand-weighted paper bags. The effect was magical. Sparklers and small firecrackers resounded along the lakefront, and, after dark, many boats converged in the middle of the lake to get the full benefit of the extravagant fireworks display at the Academy.

Bill and I began the water skiing craze at the lake. I drove the boat while Bill, an experienced skier, clowned behind the boat in crazy clothes (a long skirt, blouse, floppy hat and parasol). He did a strip tease act, discarding his clothes into the lake, which was hysterically funny. Another boat followed us to collect the clothes before they sank. Bill also built a ski jump. Flying through the air with skirts flying and parasol waving, he looked like Mary Poppins coming in for a landing.

It wasn't long before everyone wanted to try water skiing, and Bill became the lake's instructor. He had learned the skill at Cypress Gardens, while stationed in Florida. I've always considered Bill one of the most beautiful skiiers I have ever seen. At 58 his form is still perfect, and he looks very handsome, as on one ski, he slaloms behind the boat.

I never tried the sport because if I put my head under water, I have sinus and allergy problems. I knew I couldn't learn without being "dumped" a number of times into the lake. So I was content to drive the boat, an important job in any case. We spent hours on the lake, taking on one after another would-be skier.

One morning after breakfast, I was sunning in the back yard and Mother was playing solitaire at her desk overlooking the lake. She was watching Judy and Ann playing with Alan Albright as they searched for turtles at the water's edge. The girls, now three and five, loved catching turtles and collected a water tub full of different varieties every summer.

I suddenly heard Judy cry, "Mommy!" the sort of call that sounded an alarm. I jumped up and ran around the house to the lake front, but Mother was already there, wading into the lake, her long robe dragging in

[184]

the water. Little Ann was lying on her back, submerged by the lake water and completely still, her yellow hair floating around her head in graceful waves, her hazel eyes wide open and calm.

Mother reached her before I could, lifting her up out of the water, stumbling to her knees and tripping over her cumbersome negligee. She handed her to me, and I laid her on the ground and gave her artificial respiration. Ann finally choked, then cried a little. Fortunately she had not taken in any water.

Somehow, unconsciously she had held her breath from the moment she went under. When I asked Judy what had happened, she said, "Ann was sitting in the water and just laid back down." Alan said, "I thought she was a turtle."

Mother never got over the incident and had an iron fence put up at the water's edge along the sea wall with a gate to the pier that couldn't be opened by children.

Judy, Ann, Mother and Lucina at Jokake Inn,
Phoenix, Arizona

James Drain

[185]

CHAPTER THIRTY-SIX

I still had had no word from John Melvin concerning an apartment for me in New York. So I decided to spend the winter in Phoenix, Arizona at Jokake Inn after the Christmas Holidays.

In the meantime, we returned to "The Pines" after Labor Day to resume the routine of life in Muncie, and I met Jim Drain.

Isabel and John Drum introduced me to Jim. He was from Pittsburgh, Pennsylvania, and his business was in coal mining. He had been a friend of John's for many years. Very nice and very serious, Jim was fifteen years older than I. He fell in love with me and peppered me with attention, writing melting poetry and letters and phoning me often. I was attracted to him, not really in love, but flattered by his attentions. He was wonderful to Judy and Ann and sincere in his love for them. I knew it would be good for the girls to have a father and a normal life growing up, and was torn, thinking I would never love anyone again as I had loved Ed.

Time after time we made plans for marriage, but I was always unable to take the final step. Although it was unfair to Jim, I kept putting off the date and disappointing him over and over.

Early in December I had a telephone call from Sam Moxley in Indianapolis. I had known him slightly ever since I was a student at Tudor Hall, but because he was six years older than I, we were never in a group together. I knew him through his uncle, Barret Moxley, who was a good friend of my family. I always called him "Uncle Barret" as younger people do, showing affection and respect.

Sam called to invite me to the Traders Point Hunt Ball, and I was delighted to accept. It was always the best party during the Christmas season. I had no idea why he had chosen to ask me but suspected it had been arranged by Uncle Barret and Mother.

In any case, we had a wonderful time. Sam was a beautiful dancer, and we enjoyed the party and each other's company.

About two weeks later he invited me to go to an ice hockey game. Sam told me he was trying to decide whether to accept a job in Mexico City, and we spent a great part of the evening discussing the probability of such a venture.

He had spent his terminal leave from the Navy in Mexico City with friends of his parents, the Axel Wenner-Grens. In fact, Axel Wenner-Gren's wife, Marguerite, was a distant cousin of Hayes Davis, Sam's stepfather. Axel had offered Sam a position with Lecheria Nationale, a milk pasteurization plant, and Sam was wrestling with the decision of accepting, or continuing his job with Uncle Barret's wholesale drug firm, Kiefer-Stewart Company. It was an important decision for him to make, as it would mean starting a completely new life in a foreign country.

That night I invited Sam to come to Muncie for my New Year's Eve party, and when the day arrived, Father Time protested with a severe ice storm covering the roads with sheets of ice. People had difficulty getting to our house, and I was very surprised when Sam showed up. He arrived quite late, saying he had driven "sideways" for two and a half hours all the way from Indianapolis. He only spent an hour at the party before going back to Indianapolis. I told him he was insane to drive any more that night, and asked him to stay over, but he insisted on leaving. He told me he had only come to say "goodbye" to me, as we were leaving for Phoenix the next day! I thought it was a pretty silly risk when he could have easily picked up the phone to say goodbye!

———————————◆————————————

Dad bought a twin-engine Cessna airplane after the war, and we flew everywhere. Dick Whitney was his pilot, who made us feel safe and secure. I was beginning to fear airplanes but felt less tension knowing Dick would not fly in uncertain weather. Mother, Dad, Judy, Ann and I flew to Arizona January second. Jokake Inn was an attractive, Western-style, adobe cluster of buildings set in the desert, where a view of Camelback Mountain reared up in the distance. The nearest habitation was another swanky resort, Camelback Inn, down the road and out of sight. The two resorts were alone and unchallenged in the great expanse of desert as far as the eye could see. Being there gave me a feeling of loneliness.

Judy, Ann and I stayed in one of the cottages, which were named for Indian tribes. Ours was The Navajo House. Mother and Dad stayed a few days to help us get settled and then flew back to Muncie to face the winter.

The climate was cold, dusty, windy, and we didn't like it. I would have given it all up and gone home except both girls got sick right away from the change of weather and continued to be ill throughout the month of January. By the time they were well enough to travel I didn't want to expose them to the drastic climate change again in Indiana.

Our little house was not heated properly, and I finally persuaded the management to provide us with an electric heater. I was concerned about the children with their croupy coughs and fevers, and the doctor became a familiar face in our little adobe hut.

I met Helen Thomas, a tall, statuesque blonde, who was the social hostess at Jokake. She made my time there much more enjoyable, arranging bridge games and introducing me to the other guests. She was originally from Huntington, Indiana but now lived in White Plains, New York, where she taught Hygiene at the high school. We found we had many mutual interests and became lifelong friends.

[187]

Life at Jokake was dull compared to Sea Island, but eventually, the weather improved, and the children could play in the playground, where there were swings, a slide and see-saw, and, of course, plenty of sand. We used the lovely pool toward the end of February, when the sun warmed us more comfortably.

A letter arrived from Sam Moxley saying he had made the decision to move to Mexico City. He had bought a trailer to haul his belongings behind his Buick convertible and said he would be leaving soon. At the end of January, I was surprised by a call from him in San Antonio, Texas. He wanted to fly to Phoenix to see me once more before he crossed the border and asked me to make reservations for him at the Inn for one night.

He arrived late in the afternoon after the long flight from Texas. We had a quiet evening together, and it was good to see him. I was sorry he was moving to Mexico, where I had no expectation of ever seeing him again.

The next day was bright and sunny for a change. Judy and Ann played in their "sand pile" playground while Sam and I strolled along the path beside it, enjoying our time together before he had to leave.

The management of Jokake was excited about the entourage of Saudi Arabians who had arrived to spend a few days. Prince Faisal, who would be king at the death of his father, King Saud, was visiting the western United States to learn more about our oil production and management. He had with him a retinue of three or four bodyguards and advisors.

We were startled to see the group of arabs coming down the path toward us. As they approached, Sam and I moved off into the playground with Judy and Ann to give them room to pass.

Prince Faisal stopped to admire the girls, They were wide-eyed with interest at the flowing robes and turbans of the dignified strangers. Suddenly the Prince leaned over and scooped Ann up in his arms with a warm, fatherly gesture. After a minute or two, with a kiss, he put her down again, nodded, smiled at us and walked on silently with his retinue trailing behind him.

Sam and I were excited for Ann to have had this experience. She was unimpressed. We asked her what it was like to have the Prince pick her up and kiss her. "He smelled like a camel," was her only answer as she resumed her play in the sand.

———— ◆ ————

February at Jokake was a little nicer when the weather warmed up, and there were activities planned by the management. The best evenings were the occasional chuckwagon suppers out in the desert. Trucks would drive us and the food to a spot near a pile of rocks, where we could climb and find comfortable perches to watch the sunset while a huge fire was built and supper was cooked. The children loved it, running around freely with the other children and petting the horses a few guests rode instead of going by truck. I missed riding but did not like to ride Western style on the awkward, uncomfortable (for me) Western saddles.

After a ravishingly beautiful sunset, we sat on the rocks with our drinks, dressed against the chilled evening air in wool shirts, jeans, and jackets with hoods. After dinner we listened to the tall tales of the cowboys lounging around the fire, laughing at their jokes and drinking huge, hot mugs of coffee, unwilling for the evening to end.

—————⚬—————

Mother and Dad arrived to spend our last ten days at Jokake Inn with us. By then the pool area was popular, and the girls loved paddling in the shallow children's section while I picked up a tan. Dad, always full of nervous energy, couldn't stand such inactivity. He and Dick Whitney flew off to Los Angeles and returned two days later with Ed Cox.

We left Jokake on March first and flew back to Los Angeles to take Ed home. I remember Dick trying to take my mind off the ugly, jagged mountain peaks by teaching me to fly as we soared over the Sierra Nevadas.

We stopped at Palm Springs to have lunch at the gorgeous, new Tennis Club. Then we continued on to Los Angeles and spent a few days at the posh Beverly Hills Hotel. I felt Ed's hopes had risen again for a future with me in it, but the last night we were there, I made it clear it could not be. He finally understood, but an aura of gloom hung over him making us both uncomfortable. I said he should find a girl and get married. He shook his head, and I remember him saying, "I don't care how many men you marry, I'll still be waiting for you."

Dear Ed had a stroke during the 1950's but rallied and learned to walk again, returning to his job after months of effort. Then he developed circulation problems in his legs. First one and then the other had to be amputated above the knees, and he was confined to a nursing home, choosing Clearwater, Florida to be near his sister Margaret.

CHAPTER THIRTY-SEVEN

A FTER returning home to Muncie, I received a letter from John Melvin with the news that I could have one of the furnished Volney apartments by April first. I was excited and anxious to return to the city I loved and began making plans immediately.

Since I didn't need furniture, I even left my beloved piano behind, intending to rent a small spinet in New York. Packing was simple this time, and The Pines was left holding my possessions in storage.

The Volney was a perfect solution for me and the girls. Being an apartment hotel, there was maid service and a good dining room on the ground floor, or room service if we wished, in our apartment. I rented two adjoining apartments in order to give us three rooms, two baths and a tiny kitchenette.

The children used the large bedroom. I slept on the sofa bed in the living room by the door opening into their bedroom. The third room, which also had a sofa bed and its own bath, I used as a guest room. I put my rented piano there, and, with a large desk, the room served nicely as a study as well.

I bought a little electric stove with an oven attachment for the "closet kitchen" in order to cook simple meals at breakfast or lunch. The kitchenette was really just a bar with a small refrigerator, but it came in handy as a place to prepare food when we didn't want to go out for a meal. It was a good living arrangement, and I was glad to have such good friends as Ruth and John Melvin living in the same building. John was the Volney's manager.

Ruth and I resumed going to the symphony concerts and theater, and I found a delightful elderly lady to stay with Judy and Ann when I went out on dates.

Penny, our wire-haired terrier, came with us to New York, as she had become an important member of our family. She was well behaved and took to the leash nicely. We were only a block from Central Park and spent a great deal of time there, strolling along the paths in the pleasant weather. The children loved the zoo nearby, where they watched the animals by the hour and rode the carousel again and again.

———————◆———————

I discovered soon in my widowhood I had to be on the alert for men seeking amusement without serious intent. New York was full of such men, and I had to be "on guard" at all times. One incident I cannot recall without laughing, but for many years had to keep it a secret.

Soon after we moved into the Volney, I had a call from Fabian Sevitsky, who was in New York. It was the Easter season, and he called to invite me to share Russian Easter Eve with him at midnight mass in the Russian Orthodox Church on the lower East side of Manhattan. We would also attend an earlier service at the Cathedral across from St. Luke's Hospital on Amsterdam at 113th Street.

Fabian had ordered the two traditional Easter cakes, kulich and pashka, from a Russian woman on the far northwest side of the city and asked if I could pick them up for him as he was busy during the day auditioning prospective members for the orchestra. After the church services we would celebrate the advent of Easter with the cake at a party in his apartment at the Gotham Hotel.

It sounded like an interesting evening, and I was glad to pick up the cakes for him. I couldn't imagine how many people might be joining us for the party. The two cakes were large enough to feed twenty people easily.

That evening we taxied from one end of New York to the other to attend both services. They were impressive, solemn occasions. The Russian Orthodox Church on First Avenue was small and unpretentious. We climbed to the balcony and were fortunate to find seats on little, wooden benches along the railing, where we could look down on the sanctuary. We were there almost an hour before the service began, to insure ourselves seats and a good view. There were no seats in the sanctuary, and only the church members were allowed there, standing throughout the service.

At midnight the mass began. In absolute silence the church filled to capacity with worshippers. Many of the congregation wore Russian dress, scarves covering the heads of the ladies. The priest's robes glittered with golden threads, and the swinging of the incense filled the air with musky aroma. Somewhere a choir chanted from the recesses of the church, and the effect was both eerie and deeply moving.

Easter arrived in majesty and reverence, but when the service was over, the congregation came alive, hugging and kissing each other to celebrate and rejoice.

Fabian and I returned to his suite at the Gotham, where a fire crackled in the grate. On the coffee table in front of the large sofa beside the fireplace, were the pashka, kulich, plates and glasses for two. Champagne in a bucket of ice waited to be uncorked. I suddenly realized the "party" was a tete-a-tete.

Fabian opened the champagne with a flair, cut the cake and served us. The pashka was a delicious, soft confection made of cottage cheese, and the kulich was a rich cake full of fruit. We toasted each other and the advent of Easter, and soon after, Fabian began making advances. Resisting, and ignoring, I stuffed more cake in my mouth.

[191]

He wasn't deterred. He made a definite proposition that I should spend the night with him. I declined firmly, saying I had to return to my apartment and release the sitter. I had to go — now!

Finally, realizing I was not to be persuaded, he drew himself up to his full height, posing with one arm on the mantel, the other on his hip. He looked down at me sternly under this thick, bushy eyebrows and said in his heavy Russian accent, "You weel regret thees! One day you weel say to yourself, 'Yust think! And I could have had — *Seveet-ski!*'"

Nearly choking on the cake with impaired laughter, I hastened to leave as quickly as possible. I hurried down in the elevator and grabbed a taxi for home. It was the last time I ever saw him privately, and it was much later before I learned of the many affairs he indulged in.

About ten years later, Maria divorced him, unable to tolerate his Casanova life style any longer. He became involved in such a scandal in Indianapolis with the harpist in the orchestra, that he was summarily dismissed. But after the divorce, they were married and apparently lived happily together until his sudden death in Athens, Greece, while guest conducting the Athens Symphony.

<hr />

Jim Drain came to New York often and continued to talk of marriage. At one point, I even went so far as to buy a dress for the wedding, but I couldn't bring myself to marry him because I did not love him enough.

I wanted Mrs. Childs to meet him and took Jim to her apartment for a visit. I had confided our plans to marry and my indecision. I felt very close to Mrs. Childs and needed her advice and perceptive vision. During our visit, in the course of conversation, Mrs. Childs remarked quietly, "Marriage is a life of relentless intimacy."

I could not forget what she said. She must have been aware of the very thing I was afraid of.

When Jim and I finally said goodbye to each other, I was desolate and lonely. I saw him only once again after our final parting. I was at the theater with Duncan McQuaig. The play was *Medea*, starring Dame Judith Anderson. She gave a performance so electric and powerful Duncan and I were too weak to move out of our seats when the curtain fell. We sat several minutes in a daze of emotion, but when we finally started walking up the aisle to leave the theater, I saw Jim ahead of us. He saw me also but gave no sign of recognition.

It was pouring rain outside, and no taxis were available. Duncan and I huddled under his umbrella and walked for blocks. It didn't matter that we were drenched with rain. My tears flowed and mixed with the rain on my face. Duncan, of course, assumed I was still crying over the play.

Duncan was an ear, nose and throat doctor, tops in his field. He was a confirmed bachelor, but we dated often and had very good times. He removed Ann's tonsils that fall. She had constant colds that developed into nights of croupy coughing. Removing the tonsils, however, did not help Ann too much, as she continued to have one cold after another.

Judy was also sick occasionally. Once the doctor gave her penicillin pills to cure a chest infection, and she became very ill with a high fever and violent rash. Dr. Jackson realized it was an allergic reaction to the penicillin. Poor little Judy had already had as much penicillin as her body could take to save her leg. It was a hard way to learn that she could never take the drug again.

The children had so much illness that winter I thought of taking them to a warm climate during spring vacation. Mother and Dad suggested we all fly to Nassau in the Bahamas in March.

That fall Judy had started school. I chose The Brearley School, the best private school for girls in New York, and it was a good choice. Judy loved her teachers and made friends with her classmates. The Brearley bus picked her up and delivered her to our corner at 74th and Madison every day. Ann and I enjoyed walking with her to meet the bus in the mornings and greeting her after school in the afternoons.

———————⊰◉⊱———————

I saw quite a bit of Helen Thomas when she came in from Westchester on weekends. She stayed in my "guest" room several times. Once she introduced me to a young Frenchman who was in New York on a prolonged stay. His English was quite broken, but we got along well, and he asked me out a number of times.

On our first date he invited me for dinner, but Mother and Dad had just arrived in New York and had also asked me to have dinner with them. I asked Dad if it would be all right to bring along my new French friend. We all met at the Versailles Restaurant where Edith Piaf, the French chanteuse, was the featured entertainer. The Frenchman was delighted to be included. At the table he announced he knew Edith Piaf personally and said she was ill. She had the measles.

We were astounded, and I remarked if she had measles she certainly would not be performing that night. He looked perplexed, fished for words, and finally said. "I theenk I make wrong word. I theenk you call it seephilees." Mother, Dad and I sat in shocked silence. This was not the kind of conversation we usually engaged in at the dinner table. When Edith Piaf appeared to sing her French songs, I'm afraid she was not as appealing as before the remark.

———————⊰◉⊱———————

Sam Moxley and I had not corresponded, but when I moved to New York, I wanted him to know where I was. I sent him a Christmas card with a message and news of my activities. He answered in January with a long

[193]

letter telling me of his exciting, new life in Mexico. He was loving the challenge of his new job and was living at the home of the Wenner-Grens.

I responded in February with a funny Valentine asking him to be my Valentine in absentia, and he answered almost immediately with another Valentine, saying, "I don't want you to be my Valentine in absentia. I'm coming in person to see you and will be in New York February twenty-six."

The card arrived on the twenty-sixth! I was eager to see Sam, but I had a date for that evening and wondered how I could manage to see him and keep the date with Bill at the same time. Bill Hewitt had called me from Cleveland two weeks before, saying he would be in New York and wanted to see me, but he never showed up. To this day I don't know what happened, as I never heard another word from him.

The story about Bill is so interesting, I want to recount it. It sounds like a scenario for a movie. I met him through Dorothy Sarnoff, my friend from our singing days with Queena Mario. She came to Indianapolis on a Bond Rally the summer the war ended, and Bill Hewitt was part of the show in the campaign. Knowing Bill was at Fort Benjamin Harrison, an outpatient in the hospital, she wanted us to meet. He had undergone many operations to rebuild his left hand, burned badly in the war. He was lonely and discouraged and needed a little social life.

Bill was trained to be a pilot during the war, although he was 2 inches too tall to fit into the cockpits of the fighter planes. He was 6'4" but determined to fly despite his size. He proved himself to be such a good pilot, regulations on his height were overlooked, and he was assigned a B-17, the largest of the bombers.

They were on a bombing raid over Brussels when the German anti-aircraft fire hit Bill's plane. Fire broke out and Bill ordered everyone to bail out, telling the crew not to open their chutes until they were 100 feet from the ground, hoping they would not be seen by the Germans and would have a chance to escape before they were caught.

He was the last to bail out. He broke through the cockpit, and just as he cleared the plane, it exploded. He didn't realize he had been burned until he landed and was unable to get out of his parachute. The other crewmen opened their parachutes too soon and were taken prisoners by the Germans. He opened his chute very late and felt, if he hadn't been burned so badly, he would have had time to escape, but unable to free himself of the chute, he was finally found by the Germans and taken prisoner also. His face and left hand were burned badly, but he was given good care by the doctors in the prison hospital. Curiously, they worked assiduously on his face and it bore no evidence of scars or injury, but they didn't pay that much attention to his hand. Bill suspected they didn't intend for him to have a useful hand, which might be used against them in the war. His hand must have been a terrible sight after it was almost burned away,

[194]

because when I saw it, a year and twenty operations later, it was a badly crippled hand, frozen into a bent position. Bill said he told the doctors he wanted a hand that could hold a golf club, and this is what they gave him. But he would never have mobility in his fingers again.

As Bill recovered in the German hospital, the Americans were beginning to infiltrate German occupied Belgium. The Germans decided to move the hospital farther behind German lines, and set up a hospital train to transport the prisoners. American planes appeared along the road, and began strafing. In the confusion, Bill saw his opportunity, and with two other American prisoners, jumped from their truck and hid in the woods along the road.

If they were missed, at least they were not found, because they finally came to a farmhouse and hid in the barn. They were still in Belgium, and the farmer who found them helped them to the underground station. A few months later, Bill reached England and from there was sent home.

The army sent him to Fort Benjamin Harrison in Indianapolis where the best surgeons reoperated and formed a new hand for Bill that looked more like a human hand and could be serviceable.

Bill had undergone intense pain and suffering throughout the operations and slow recovery following each one, but at the time I met him, he said he only had two more to go before the hand would be as good as it could ever be. I admired him for his great courage and we saw each other quite a lot before I moved to New York.

—————◆—————

The day I expected both Bill and Sam to phone, passed without a word from either of them, but when I returned from church choir practice that night, Sam was waiting in the lobby of the Volney. It was so good to see him! I invited him in to my apartment, and we spent the evening catching up on the past year and a half.

He left for the weekend to visit his sister and her husband in Fairfield, Connecticut but told me he would return on Sunday evening and asked me to go to the theater with him.

All day Sunday I was a bundle of nerves. The day seemed endless. Somehow I anticipated Sam's visit with more eagerness than was usual for me.

He had tickets for *Mr. Roberts*, starring Henry Fonda, which was a great play. As we hadn't had time for dinner beforehand, Sam suggested we go to El Morocco for supper and dancing after the theater. El Morocco was one of the top night clubs in New York, ultra-sophisticated and lavish with zebra-striped decor. After a wonderful evening, we returned to the apartment, said goodnight to the sitter, and sat in the little guest room having a night cap. Without preamble, Sam asked me to marry him.

[195]

I was at once expectant, and yet, surprised. Suddenly everything came together in my head, and I knew we were right for each other. I said, "Yes," without hesitation. Instinctively I knew Sam was right for me, as I'd known with Ed.

Judy's seventh birthday party in Nassau

Lucina in New York

Judy, Ann, and Penny, 1947 — a photo portrait by Aunt Mark Eckerson

PART THREE
CHAPTER THIRTY-EIGHT

BY sheer coincidence, Sam had planned to fly to Nassau to join the Wenner-Grens after his business trip to New York. My family plans were to leave for Nassau on March twentieth, when Judy was out of school. The dates coincided so closely, Sam decided to stay the extra days in New York and fly down with us. We had three weeks to make plans for our June nineteenth wedding.

The night of our engagement was also a funny coincidence — Leap Year, February twenty-ninth! We celebrate this event every four years, giving it even more importance than our wedding anniversaries.

Sam came back to my apartment the next morning, and we called our families to announce the news. Mother and Dad were pleased, but surprised, and Bill added, "She hardly knows him!" The succinct remark was very true. We became engaged on our sixth date in a year and a half.

Sam called his mother in Louisville, Kentucky, and his Uncle Barret, who was vacationing in Naples, Florida. We learned later that Uncle Barret had a party that very night to celebrate our engagement, celebrating to the extent that he fell down the porch steps and broke his collarbone. That same day Sam told me he had a call from David Moxley, one of Uncle Barret's sons. David phoned him at the Biltmore to tell him I was living in New York, and it might be nice to call me and get acquainted. Sam told him, "I already know her. We're engaged." He heard David drop the phone at the other end.

I wanted the children to know Sam a little better before breaking the news of our engagement to them. So I asked him to have dinner with us. I made a simple supper of lamb chops, peas and potatoes on my little stove and served ice cream for dessert. I remember the menu because Sam gave the children a Spanish lesson at the table naming the food we were eating in Spanish. The girls were fascinated and picked up the accent quickly. I realized I would have to begin lessons myself immediately. After dinner I put the girls to bed, but it wasn't long before Ann began coughing in her sleep. Sam and I hurried to their bedroom, and, while I brought out the cough medicine, he propped Ann up against his shoulder to try and stop the spasms. As he patted her on the back, Ann gazed up at him sleepily and murmured, "Mommie's so nice. — And she's a good cooker too!" Sam was always amused by Ann's endorsement, thinking she was trying to promote me.

———⋅⟨◉⟩⋅———

Soon after moving back to New York, I found a small, needlecraft shop on Madison Avenue not far from the Volney. I noticed ladies in the back room doing piece work and thought it would be a good way to occupy my free time. I asked Mr. Mazaltov, the owner of the Art Needlework Shop, if he needed anyone else to help. He gave me a pair of slippers to make the petit point center and said he would pay me $2.50 for the job.

I worked on them at home and finished the pair about a week later. When Mr. Mazaltov saw my neat work, he paid me and gave me something else to do in petit point. I continued making the detailed work for the shop until I left New York, but Sam was horrified to learn of the stingy amount I was paid for such fine work. He asserted he *had* to marry me to get me out of New York and the sweat shop labor income. He figured out I was receiving ten cents an hour to compensate for the eye strain.

———————⋙◉⋘———————

I soon met Sam's sister, Polly, and her husband, Pete Bassick. We spent a weekend in Fairfield. Sam's mother flew in from Lousville to meet me, bringing THE RING, which had belonged to Sam's Aunt Martha Moxley. (Originally Sam had wanted the diamond reset by Cartier's in New York, but he surprised me with a new ring — three beautiful diamonds set in a row, instead of a solitaire.)

I felt very much at home with Sam's family. I loved them, and Polly's three children, Marshall, Candy and Barret, were near the ages of Judy and Ann, which was fun for the children.

———————⋙◉⋘———————

The time to leave for Nassau finally arrived. Dad's plane was a seven-passenger Twin-Beechcraft, leaving one extra seat for Uncle Barret, who we picked up in Naples en route. Several members of the Moxley family had also planned a Nassau vacation, and we all converged there March twentieth for a gala party.

As we flew in to the small field in Naples, Florida, Uncle Barret was waiting for us with other family members, among them Irving Jones, Uncle Barret's sister, the matriarch of the Moxley family.

Once in Nassau, we went to the Fort Montague Beach Hotel, a large impressive establishment, where all but Sam would stay. He was across the bay on Hog Island, owned by the Wenner-Grens, in residence for the winter. Today, Paradise Island, renamed from Hog Island is a Mecca for vacationing tourists and covered with high-rise hotels.

Our large, combined family group had been invited for dinner that evening by Axel and Marguerite to celebrate our engagement. Besides Mother, Dad, Uncle Barret and me (the children remained at the hotel) Polly and Pete, Doris and Scott Moxley, Irving Diven and Kitty Robb were all on hand. (Irving and Scott were Uncle Barret's daughter and son. Kitty was their cousin from Boston.)

A launch from Hog Island came to fetch us at the hotel pier, and in full evening regalia, we traversed the short passage to the Island. From the launch, we were driven to Shangri-La, the Wenner-Gren's estate, not too far from the landing.

Axel, Marguerite, her sister, Gene Gauntier, and Sam greeted us at the door of the gorgeous mansion, a palatial home, centered in a beautiful garden of tropical flowers and trees.

We became acquainted over cocktails in the spacious living room. The cocktails were named The Southern Cross. I was to learn it was the only kind of drink the Wenner-Grens ever served before dinner. They tasted something like side cars and were named for the Wenner-Gren's yacht, now the property of the Mexican government — their donation to the war effort in 1942.

Marguerite always reminded me of Fanny Brice in looks, but certainly not in personality. She was tall, big-boned and had rather coarse features, managing a stunning appearance simply because of her unusual clothes. She wore "costumes." Her evening clothes were extravagantly elaborate, and she was always loaded with jewels. Tonight a necklace of cabachon emeralds the size of pigeon eggs hung around her neck. The necklace was so long and heavy it had to be draped down her back so she could hold her head up. Several rings adorned her huge hands, the jewels spanning the width of more than one finger. Long emerald drops matching the necklace fell from her ears. I was told she had been an opera singer before she married Axel. This I scarcely believed, as her speaking voice was raw, husky and brash.

Axel was exceedingly handsome. Thick, white hair topped his tall, dignified stature, and penetrating, bright, blue eyes lit up his face with great expressiveness. I liked him immediately, admiring his keen intellect and congeniality. I also knew he could be cold as steel, and, perhaps, ruthless in his business dealings.

The dinner party was elegant, served by two waiters who stood at attention throughout the meal. The centerpiece was an extravagant flower arrangement of tropical flowers with the Swedish and American flags flying higher than the birds of paradise.

Dessert was a stunning ice block carved into a shell shape and filled with multi-colored sherbets. A "wedding" cake accompanied the sherbet, exquisitely decorated by their chef.

During dinner, many toasts and skoals were raised to us. It became apparent that Marguerite had drunk a little too much. I saw Axel look at her with his eyes a steely blue, and speak to her in Swedish. She immediately put down her wine glass.

After dinner, Marguerite, saying she wished to talk to us, steered Sam and me out to the veranda. We were served our coffee there while the other

[200]

guests sat in the living room with Axel.

Marguerite began questioning us, saying she thought our marriage was a bad idea. She turned to Sam, and asked him point blank what he saw in me. She asked why he wanted to marry a woman with two children? She thought I would be a detriment to his career. I was not that attractive anyway, she said, and I was too fat.

I was struck dumb by her rudeness and by Sam's negative reaction. He only replied meekly, "I like her that way." How could he sit there and listen to her without protesting? I boiled with fury at both of them.

I stood up and went back to the living room to thank Axel and say goodnight. Axel understood something was amiss, and knowing how blunt Marguerite could be, knew she was at the bottom of it. He ordered the car to take us to the launch, and the party left as he said gracious goodbyes to each of us.

We had all been invited to return the next day for lunch. this time Judy and Ann were included, but I had no intention of going back to Shangri-La. I was furious. What right had Marguerite to question our motives or to say my children would be in Sam's way!

After confiding her insulting remarks to Mother and Dad, we pondered whether to return for the luncheon or not, finally deciding it would be more insulting to Sam and Axel if we didn't go. So we bundled the children into the boat, and all of us went back to Shangri-La.

Again Marguerite, Axel and Sam met our group at the door. The first thing Marguerite said to me in greeting was, "Why, you've lost weight!" This was as close to an apology as she could come. Undoubtedly, Axel had wormed the conversation out of her and warned her to be more polite to me. I must add Marguerite never again said an unkind word to us. We got along very well, even though the barbs she tossed at me that first evening always stuck in my craw. I had to be nice to her because of Sam, since we would be living in Mexico. She could have made life impossible for us if she had cared to.

On March twenty-six, Judy was seven years old. The girls had made friends with several children in the hotel, and we asked them to her birthday party. The next day Sam and I left for Mexico to find a house. Mother and Dad stayed in Nassau for the remainder of the vacation and would meet me in New York on April second with Judy and Ann. Sam and I would have just five more days together until he returned to Indiana for our June wedding. It seemed a long time to wait.

I well remembered our trip to Mexico nine years before, recalling it as the only place I had ever visited I never wanted to see again. Here I was, about to embark on a life there — for an unknown length of time and in a country where I knew not a word of the language. Not wanting to be pessimistic, I told myself Mexico was probably changed from the dirty place I remembered and consoled myself with the knowledge that Sam loved Mexico and everything about it.

Sam and I flew to Miami, changing planes in Havana, Cuba, where we stayed overnight, and the next day we flew on to Mexico City.

We had the most wonderful evening in Havana. Sam had been there several times before on business and knew just where to go for the best entertainment. I don't know why we even had hotel rooms. We stayed up the entire night, not wanting to waste a minute of exciting Havana. We had dinner at the Sans Souci, an outdoor garden restaurant and night club with an extravagant floor show, dancing and a gambling casino.

We spent most of the evening and into the early morning at Sans Souci. Then Sam remembered a night club in a questionable neighborhood, which had a marvelous band of black entertainers. The place was called Chori's and was certainly unpretentious. Bare, wooden tables were placed around a small dance floor. The room was dimly it, and I felt a little nervous as the clientele were all black and more than a little drunk. Sam seemed to be well acquainted with everyone. We sat at one of the rickety tables, and he ordered drinks for us and the musicians, who drank rum and vinegar! No wonder the place smelled funny!

When the music began, it was fabulous. Chori, the drummer and owner of the establishment, didn't have a drum, but with his drumsticks he used everything in sight to make rhythms — the table tops, chair rungs, bottles and glasses — even the wall! He was a full orchestra by himself. We were fascinated and spent the rest of the night listening to the trio belting out the latin rhythms the Cubans had made so famous.

The patrons danced with liquid hip variations of the rhumba, entertaining us as much as the music itself. At one point in the evening there were voodoo dances, and one of the voodoo "specialists" came to our table to cast a spell over us. She placed sprigs of mint behind our ears, said an incantation and pronounced a life for us full of happiness. Her spell came true, and my little sprig of mint is still in a locket, dried but recognizable.

We returned to the Hotel Internationale in time for breakfast and to pick up our luggage for the airport. There was plenty of time to sleep on the plane.

———————⋖◉⋗———————

Sam registered me at the Reforma Hotel, a familiar landmark, now freshly redecorated, and he went on to 390 Paseo de la Reforma, the Wenner-Gren's home, where he lived. Coming in from the airport, I looked carefully everywhere for the signs of squalor so noticeable in 1937 but saw nothing reminiscent of those days.

Later Sam arrived at the hotel, and we went to an elegant restaurant for

[202]

dinner and from there to a night spot in Lagunilla, a section renowned for its local dives, mariachi entertainment and flamenco dancers. It was all very exciting.

The next day Sam and I drove around the residential districts of Mexico City, and I saw lovely homes hidden behind high, impenetrable walls cascading with bougainvillia and plumbago. We visited Margo and Bruno Pagliai, whose home was for sale. Margo was a beautiful brunette and charming as well. Bruno worked with Axel. A clever Italian, he made money hand over fist on side ventures of his own. Later Bruno divorced his stunning wife and married another beauty, Merle Oberon, the famous movie actress.

We liked their house but wished to see more before making a decision. So we drove farther from the Lomas de Chapultepec to another, newer house in the Lomas Barrilaco, a section just beginning to be built up as a suburb. The house we looked at was owned and rented by Mario Rabell, Sam's boss at Lecheria Nationale. We loved it and made arrangements with Mario to rent it.

The address was Sierra Amatepec 649, only one of a few houses built along the street following the edge of a hill. The house overlooked a compelling view of rolling hills where goats and cattle grazed. A deep gully fell from the brick wall in the back yard to rise again across the land owned by collective groups of farmers outside Mexico City. Blue mountains tipped with traces of snow were the faraway backdrop against the cloudless sky. The air of peace and privacy made us know this location was for us.

Good friends of Sam's, Kay and Don Thorburn, gave a party for us in the garden of their San Angel home. I met people who later became our closest friends. Kay's brother, Stewart Skidmore, was a salesman with Parker Pen Co. His wife's name was Fifi. His sister, Trudy, not yet married, was a delightful, vivacious girl. All had been born in Mexico of American parents.

Two other attractive American couples were Roberta and Ed Sherman, who was with R.C.A., and Kay and Gordon Benedict. Gordon managed a frozen food plant owned by his brother-in-law, Charles Montgomery. We were surprised to learn Kay's brother and father were acquaintances of my father's. The year before, Mr. Montgomery was driving to Florida to join his family there on vacation but never arrived. After searching for weeks for traces of him near his abandoned car, the police finally found his body outside of a small southern town. The sheriff's son was seen wearing Mr. Montgomery's shoes. upon investigation, the boy confessed he had encountered the man on the highway with car trouble and offered him a lift to a garage for help. On the way he shot Kay's father, stole his clothes and left him dead under a bridge near a lonely road. He led the police to the

[203]

body, which was positively identified later. Kay was still recovering from shock.

CHAPTER THIRTY-NINE

BACK in New York my life began to accelerate. Besides making the arrangements for our wedding, which we planned to have at the cottage in Culver, I needed to make purchases to add to the furnishings I would be shipping to Mexico.

I began a Spanish course at the Berlitz School, planning an hour of conversation a day for the remaining time I would be in New York. Judy would finish her first year at Brearley before we could return to Muncie on May twenty-fifth. We needed passports and immunization shots before moving to Mexico.

My allergist, Dr. Will Cook Spain, had been my doctor since I was married to Ed. Naturally, I turned to him for the necessary shots for the three of us. We had our small pox vaccinations and then the typhoid and typhus shots. Dr. Spain decided to give me a skin test before injecting me with the normal three immunization shots for typhoid. That night my arm was red and swollen from the minute skin test. When I reported my reaction, he said it could not have been that severe as I was not sensitive to any ingredient in the serum, but he would give me another skin test to be sure. That night, I really had a small case of typhoid fever, complete with headache, temperature, and a very sore, swollen arm where I had the scratch of serum.

Dr. Spain was concerned. He said I was either immune to the disease or violently allergic to the serum. In either case he did not want to give it to me. But as I could not live in Mexico without the immunization, Dr. Spain divided the three normal doses into thirty, and I was given an injection of the vaccine every five days until the series was complete. The tiny amounts subcutaneously did not affect me at all but it was nip and tuck to have the series finished in time. I had my last shot in Muncie the day we began our drive to the border, five days after our wedding. If I had been given one normal injection of typhoid serum it probably would have killed me. I am grateful to Dr. Spain for his caution and care.

I also had to have typhus shots. To be on the safe side, Dr. Spain divided the vaccine into five for me. I never again want to go through a series like that!

Everything was on schedule until Judy put a fly in the ointment by coming down with chicken pox! I had never had it. I brought out the

[204]

calendar and figured even if I escaped catching it from Judy, I might catch it from Ann, who most certainly would get the disease.

To avoid being a pockmarked bride, Mother hastened to New York to take Ann home to Muncie. With luck we might both escape the virus. Judy was still broken out with blisters, but we had to apply for our passports and have our pictures taken before Ann could leave. Judy's passport picture showing her poxed face made an amusing memento. I was surprised the official in the government office didn't spot her condition and put us all in quarantine!

Two weeks passed, and Mother phoned one morning to ask how I was. I said I was fine. "That's good," Mother said, "Ann is broken out all over with chicken pox." I breathed a sigh of relief because I had no telltale spots. My relief was short-lived, however, as later that day I noticed a little blister. Before long I was a mess of blisters.

I called Reg Conklin for advice when the itching became unbearable, and he ordered pyrabenzamine, which saved the day. Seven-year-old Judy was my nurse. She felt so guilty for giving me those nasty itchy blisters, that she would fix breakfast for us before the doorman helped her to the school bus. She helped in other ways sympathizing after having had the same miserable problem herself.

With ten lost days of precious time, I had to redouble my efforts to accomplish everything as soon as I was well enough to be seen in public. I started spending two hours in Spanish class every day to make up the minimum course of sixty hours. It was a tremendous effort to concentrate that long on the language. I came out of each session with a raging headache. I felt I learned a basic approach to Spanish even though I only had one Mexican teacher in all that time. I learned some vocabulary not used in Mexico as well as different dialects which were only slightly helpful later on. But I learned the feel and pronunciation of the language, which was invaluable when I was finally confronted with it in Mexico

---

Judy and I finished our "schooling" at the same time, and we were packed and anxious for the coming excitement in Muncie. We arrived a few days before Ann's fifth birthday.

Later Sam arrived to join in the pre-wedding festivities. He brought china poblano costumes from Mexico for Judy and Ann, as late birthday presents, and they loved to dress up in them and dance.

After the details of blood tests and the wedding license applications were completed, we drove to Culver to prepare for the wedding. We had planned a small wedding but in making out the invitations the necessary guest list grew and grew until our original modest guest list of fifty turned into more than one hundred and fifty. All members of both our large families consider an invitation a command performance. We had a full compliment of guests.

Our bridal dinner was at the Maxinkuckee Inn, where most of the guests stayed. The entire weekend was a delightful party. Jane Simpson was my matron of honor and Uncle Barret was Sam's best man. Judy and Ann were flower girls, dressed in dainty, white organdy dresses with appliqued pastel flowers. With flowers in their hair and little bouquets to carry, they made a perfect picture to add to our happiness and memory book.

June nineteenth dawned cool and windy. The pink tablecloths were nearly blown off the tables, and the little sailboat decorations lining the pier almost took to the sea in the high wind. We were married in the arch of the front door facing the lake, the porch providing a lovely simulated altar filled with flowers.

As we stood facing Dr. Milner, our Presbyterian minister from Indianapolis, my knees began to tremble. Sam felt me shaking, and he began to shake, the two of us carrying on a St. Vitus dance throughout the ceremony. He could hardly put the ring on my finger.

We drove to Chicago for the rest of the weekend to the accompaniment of rattling hubcaps and streams of toilet paper trailing behind. There were a number of jokesters among our guests. We had to stop along the road to remove the noisy rocks.

Sam had lived in Chicago during the war while he was in Naval Intelligence and knew all the nooks and crannies for fun in the city. His favorite restaurant, and mine too, was Don the Beachcomber's where we went for dinner. It became a ritual for us to go to Don's every time we were in Chicago. Sam said he felt he owned a plank in the building he went so often.

———————◆———————

We stopped in Culver for another night on the way back to Muncie. The shipment of furniture at "The Pines" had been packed up earlier in the month and was awaiting last minute additions before shipment to Mexico. Sam and I brought the last of the wedding gifts from Culver and placed them on the tailgate of the van in Richmond, Indiana, just before it pulled out on its journey.

A sad and upsetting note was injected into my happiness. When we returned to Muncie, a letter arrived from Washington stating the cemetery in Guam was to be disbanded as a National Cemetery. I had three choices for the disposition of Ed's remains. He could be moved to a family plot anywhere in the United States, to Arlington National Cemetery in Washington, D.C. or to Hawaii Punch Bowl National Cemetery.

I felt it was no longer my decision. I was now Mrs. Sampson Buchanan

Moxley and would not even be living in the United States, I thought Ed's mother should be the one to make the choice. I called Mrs. Eckerson at her summer home in Twin Lakes, Connecticut and read the letter to her. She was shocked also and told me she could not go through a funeral service for Ed after three years. She decided to have him buried at Punch Bowl Cemetery in Hawaii.

I was more than a little disappointed he would not be brought home but understood her feelings completely.

"With this ring," Dr. Jean Milner, officiating

Two flower girls, Judy and Ann

We cut the cake

[207]

Roberta and Ed Sherman

649 Sierra Amatepec, Mexico City

Sailfish catch in Acapulco

CHAPTER FORTY

S AM and I were on our way! Dad had given me a new Buick for a wedding present, and we drove it to Mexico. Penny went with us, but Judy and Ann remained with Mother and Dad until the house could be set up after the arrival of the furniture. In the meantime, Sam had rented a small furnished apartment for us in the Latino Americana on the Paseo de la Reforma.

We stopped in Little Rock, Arkansas and liked the Jack Tar Motel so much we stayed an extra day. A wall-eyed black maid took care of our room. The second morning she turned to Sam and said, "Ya'll's been freshly brided up, ain't cha?" A box of rice had been poured into our suitcases, and a few grains had spilled onto the floor.

The drive went well except for a couple of incidents. We stopped in Monterrey at the main hotel. As we prepared for bed, I went into the bathroom to brush my teeth. Marching around the basin in single file came a parade of cockroaches nose to tail. I couldn't locate the beginning or the end of the parade. I backed out into the bedroom following their trail. Aha! There they were, still marching, skirting the headboard of the bed intent on a search for what? Us?

Closing our just opened bags, we fled. If no other hotel was available, we were prepared to sleep in the car rather than in that infested hotel. Fortunately, there was a place across the street that was clean and satisfactory.

The next stop, before beginning the long mountain climb into Mexico, was in a motel that was modest, to say the least. As we approached in the darkness, we saw the roofline outlined in bright red and blue neon lights, obscuring the rest of the building, but a flickering MOTEL sign announced this as the last possible haven for many miles.

Having heard of scorpions in Mexico, I had my eyes peeled and kept my shoes on until the last moment before getting into the double bed with Sam. As he pulled the covers back to welcome me, the center of the bed revealed a gigantic beetle Sam had not even seen!

He could not coax me down into bed because the beetle scurried away out of sight, and we couldn't find it again! I stood in the middle of the bed, afraid to lie down and afraid to walk on the floor! Poor Penny was curled up on a little rug sound asleep, an unwary victim of crawling night creatures!

I decided Mexico was going to present a life full of adventures. We passed tiny villages on the roadside, children running naked in front of homes that were little more than a square of adobe mud with straw roofs. The people were so poor! The mountain driving was not unexciting. Twisting bends around the precipitous turns had no safe shoulders. We became used to the ubiquitous road signs warning us unnecessarily of "camino sinuoso!"

A week's driving finally brought us to Mexico City and the Latino Americana apartment. It would be a month before the van arrived with our furniture. I began haltingly to speak Spanish, but found I had forgotten most of what I had learned and had to start from scratch, listening carefully for the meaning and correct pronunciation as the Mexicans rattled away, unconcerned whether I understood them or not.

I had only taken conversational Spanish and had never seen the language written. So I naturally spelled words as if they were in French, a language I understood. I learned to pick out new words from signs on the street and tried reading the local newspapers. Eventually, I learned how to spell correctly, but for a long time the French language interfered. When I finally mastered Spanish, I had erased all my French and was unable to speak it any longer.

We went often to see our house far out in the Lomas and discovered there were no light fixtures in the house at all. Bare wires protruded from the ceilings and walls where fixtures should have been. I went on an expedition searching for light fixtures.

I had been having dizzy spells and feeling heart palpitations since we arrived in Mexico City and decided the symptoms were due to the 7,300 foot altitude. Not knowing the city and nervous about driving in the wild Mexican traffic, Sam arranged for a driver from Lecheria to take me to the electrical shops.

I saw some pretty lanterns in an open shop downtown and directed the driver to stop. There was no place to park the car, and the traffic was hectic and noisy. The driver indicated in sign language he would return. Conversation was impossible above the din of blowing horns.

I purchased a lantern for our front porch, and as I paid the lady, felt a dizzy spell coming on. She helped me to sit on one of the tall bar stools at the counter and disappeared behind a curtain of hanging beads. I was about to faint when she returned. Wordlessly, she pulled open the front of my dress, and without ceremony, spat a mouthful of Yardley's lavender water down my front. The surprise, chill and strong smell brought me around in a second.

At that moment the driver returned. I thanked her and jumped in the car with my lantern. We drove to the Latino Americana where I fell into bed, too weak to bathe and wash off the cloud of lavender that clothed me. I had to laugh over the incident. The woman in her zeal certainly blew out a strong spray!

The erratic heart beats and lightheadedness persisted until I finally saw a doctor. He said I was pregnant, but I knew he was wrong. I would wake

[210]

up in the mornings feeling normal, but after breakfast the dizziness overcame me, and I had to go back to bed.

I recognized the dizziness because three months after Ed was killed I had had the same symptoms and spent a few days in the hospital for tests. The doctor had diagnosed the lightheadedness and erratic breathing as a delayed shock reaction to Ed's death. After medication for a few months I felt well again. I also had switched from coffee to tea. Remembering this, I stopped drinking coffee in Mexico and felt much better right away. Now I knew the altitude affected me adversely.

I wanted to have a baby for us, however, and soon, because I wasn't getting any younger. I was thrilled when I realized I had become pregnant early in September.

To get me out of the altitude and to see more of Mexico, Sam and I took weekend trips to lower areas. We went often to Taxco, stopping at least one night in the charming Vista Hermosa resort, which had once been a sugar plantation during the time of Cortez. The swimming pool was one of the most gorgeous I have ever seen. It was the size of a small lake, with stone fountains shaped into the forms of Aztec gods, spitting streams of water back into the pool. An aqueduct of old stones crossed overhead, joining an ancient water wheel, which had been part of the sugar mill. Bougainvillia bushes and flamboyant trees framed the area in a blaze of color. The water was perfect for swimming — a clear blue, and refreshing under the hot Mexican sun.

In Taxco we always stayed at the Hotel Victoria, perched at the top of a steep cobblestone street. The view from the terrace was spectacular. Stretching from the red tiled roofs of the houses scattered in random fashion over the rugged hills, the view extended to the zocalo, where twin peaks of the cathedral pointed to the center of town.

Taxco was where Leslie Kitzelman Figeroa lived. After the death of her husband, A.L., she came to Taxco as a tourist and married her young guide, Fidel, twenty years her junior. She perservered with Fidel, forcing him to study until he became a bonafide artist, then sold his paintings from their gift shop in their home. She also ran a lucrative tourist business, showing her "historical" home on a hillside and charging admission. Theirs was a strange union, but each seemed to have found happiness. Marjorie, as I mentioned earlier, died soon after we arrived in Mexico.

We found a little house to rent in Cuernavaca, on the corner of Motolinia and Netzhualcoyotl, and we shared it with Kay and Gordon Benedict, alternating weekends with them. Sometimes, on long special holidays, we shared the house, enjoying the warmer climate and congenial company of each other. We had a small pool, but the water was icy cold, coming straight from the nearby mountains. It was seldom warm enough to swim, but it didn't matter. We sat around the pool, drinking long, tall rum drinks, which Sam had a great gift for concocting. After Sam and Gordon built a brick barbecue, the men enjoyed grilling our steak dinners.

Recalling my thirtieth birthday in Cuernavaca, I was happier than I could ever be, but I cried all day for reaching the dreaded age! I was entering "old age," my childhood gone forever. Sam laughed at my silliness, but I couldn't be consoled. I was glad I got over my sensitivity to old age so long ago, as each subsequent milestone has passed without a thought of regret. Now I am content with each passing year, hoping to fill it to the brim, every day counting for something.

A caretaker and his wife lived in a separate little house on the property to keep the house and grounds clean and safe from intruders. A high wall and barbed wire contained the corner lot, which was high above street level. Nevertheless, we were robbed once, fortunately when we were not there. The caretaker reported two men climbed the wall and held him and his wife at gun point while they ransacked our closets. We kept summer clothes there for the weekends but no valuables. The robbers were interested in Sam's new wardrobe and stole his nice jackets and slacks. He hated losing the snappy, red linen ones.

We loved the house, and when the Benedicts moved back to the States, continued to rent it, sharing it on the same basis with Roberta and Ed Sherman. Unfortunately, the house was riddled with termites, or we might have bought it. The heavy beams holding up the ceiling and tiled roof must have been almost hollow. Every morning we woke up spitting out termite chewings. The bed clothes, as well as the rest of the room, were covered with the "sawdust" leavings. We could even hear them eating away during the night and were in fear of the beams dropping on us some night, putting us away for good.

If we stayed in Mexico City for a weekend, we loved to browse around the flea market in the Lagunilla district on Sundays. There was a maze of sidewalk shops and streets filled with merchandise set up in an impromptu fashion. Block after block of every kind of ware from home made crafts to kitchen utensils were displayed.

Someone told us about a shop where a man made crystal chandeliers to order. We found him in Lagunilla, and I saw his work in finished products, as well as sketched designs. He laid one out on the floor for me, placing the crystal pieces in a shape with eight branches. I chose the crystals and the prisms and asked him to make the dining room chandelier and two side brackets to match for the wall. The result was stunning and cost a mere hundred dollars. He used old, Bohemian glass — perhaps a cut glass jelly dish or a set of goblets minus their stems, to create his masterpieces. He

[212]

hung it for us in our dining room, and it enhanced the living-dining area with its graceful sparkle.

———————————◆———————————

The furniture finally arrived. It was fun arranging it in the house, after planning it all on paper. Decor, another one of Axel's business ventures, was an excellent furniture and decorating shop. They made curtains for the windows and reupholstered the furniture in fresh, sunny colors.

It was customary for every family to have a staff of servants, unless they were very poor. It was unthinkable for a housewife to lift a finger, and each type of work necessitated a different servant to do the job. In other words, a cook would only cook — not serve the food, nor clean her kitchen. Fortino, one of the Wenner-Gren's housemen, offered to find servants for us. Fortino's nephew, Julio Ramos, came from Oaxaca to be our "house and garden" man. From the time we rented our house the previous March, Julio had lived in our empty house, without electricity, sleeping on the floor in his serape. Friends brought him food from quite a distance. After four months of living like this, he was delighted to have a bed to sleep on and a room of his own with furniture. We were forever grateful to Julio for his loyalty and service to us.

After we moved in, Julio's sister, Ana, joined us as our maid. She also came up from the country near Oaxaca, where life was primitive indeed. One night we left the house to go to a party and told them not to wait up for us, but just turn out the lights in the living room. They disobeyed the order about going to bed. Julio, as usual, was at the gate when we came home at two a.m. swinging it open for us so Sam would not even have to slow up to enter our driveway. He seemed to be able to detect the sound of the Buick approaching and never failed to be on hand to unlock the gate.

The next evening at dusk, we were having cocktails before dinner and Sam reached over to light one of the lamps. No lights. He tried one switch after another, but none worked. We knew the power was on as lights in the rest of the house were burning. Sam called Ana, and she ran in, going from lamp to lamp twisting the bulbs till they all came on. Then she brought in a ladder and climbed up to screw in the bulbs in the ceiling fixture. When Sam showed her how all the lights came on from one switch on the wall, she was amazed. All electric lights she had ever seen had to be turned on and off from twisting the bulbs.

Our search for a cook caused some difficulty. The first woman we tried was old and set in her ways. Celia would not accept my ideas or suggestions about the menus or cleanliness of preparation. We soaked all raw vegetables in potassim permanganate to kill the potent germs rampant in Mexico. We also drank bottled water, as water from the tap was pure poison. Celia would soak the salad greens in the germicide, but then rinsed them off under the tap, making the whole procedure ineffective.

[213]

She couldn't understand why we crazy Americans did such silly things anyway. We could not take chances with our health and Celia had to leave.

Then Balbina came to us. How lucky we were to have such a lovely person in our household! Balbina Ortega and I were the same age, and her two daughters the ages of Judy and Ann. Lola and Alicia lived with their aunt while Balbina lived with us. It was customary for all servants to live in quarters provided by their patrons.

I had noticed Julio speaking to the young nursemaid over the connecting wall between us and our neighbors. I wasn't too surprised when he told us we should have a laundress. Agustina next door had given notice to her patrons, he said, and would like to work for us. I told Julio I would speak first to our neighbor, Mrs. Muench.

A few days later I walked next door to introduce myself to Eleanor Muench. A vicious Doberman pincer stood at their gate, barking fiercely and forbidding me to enter. The mozo removed Dora with the bared teeth from sight, and I ventured into the house. Eleanor was cordial but when I asked her about Agustina's references, she had no idea Agustina intended to leave the job as nana to her children. I was very embarrassed. It was no way to initiate a good neighbor policy. Eleanor said, "Take her with my compliments. I wouldn't have her another minute after she went behind my back that way."

So Agustina came to work for us, and our household was then complete. She fitted in beautifully with the others, and eventually she and Julio married, raising two girls of their own, Mercedes and Frances.

CHAPTER FORTY-ONE

MOTHER and Dad brought the children to Mexico in November. By then we were well adjusted to life there and were anxious to have the girls join us. Dick Whitney flew them all down in Dad's new plane, a twin-engine Beechcraft.

We had an exciting reunion and showed them our new home with considerable pride. I broke the news about our baby to come, though, as yet, I had not visited a doctor.

Dad wanted to go to Acapulco. We took off for a few days and stayed at a lovely hotel on top of a hill, The Americana. Mother stayed with the girls while the rest of us went deep sea fishing, and I was thrilled when a beautiful sailfish took my hook. It was quite a struggle to bring in the fish as it was six feet long and weighed over one hundred pounds. It looked magnificent as it leaped into the air, fighting my line, its lapis lazuli blue body and dorsal fin glistening in the sunlight; but when I finally reeled it in, the dying fish lost its splendid blue color and turned a dull, gunmetal gray. The excitement turned sour within me, and I was sorry I had killed the courageous creature.

After the severe heat of Acapulco at sea level, we flew back to the cool climate and high altitude of Mexico City, and Mother and Dad prepared to fly home. We gathered up their luggage while Dick had the plane serviced, then returned to the airport to see them off. They got as far as immigration but returned to tell us they were not allowed to leave. Since they had brought in two children, they had to leave with them! This predicament required quick thinking on Sam's part. He called a lawyer acquaintance, Lic. Possi, who came to the airport with a paper for Sam to sign making him responsible for the children while they were in Mexico. Finally, after a delay of several hours, my parents were given permission to leave the country.

The day had been unusually strenuous. It was cold at the airport, and we had been under nervous tension. I, particularly, felt exhausted and went to bed as soon as we got home. Whether it was the abrupt change of climate, altitude, exhaustion or my strenuous fishing adventure, we will never know, but I miscarried that night. Dr. Chavez met us at the hospital, where I stayed a few days recovering from the subsequent operation, shock and disappointment.

Life resumed in a normal fashion with our family enjoying the routine of the foreign country. We found our existence in Mexico a complete revolution from anything we had known in the States.

It was not just learning a new language, though that in itself was a challenge. The routine of daily activities was quite different. Breakfast was an early, simple meal, but lunch was the heavy meal of the day, after which the siesta followed until four p.m. Businesses were closed from noon until four and then reopened until eight o'clock. Supper was served no earlier than ten.

We had to compromise a little on the late meal at night and had our supper at nine. If we were going to a dinner party, we would eat something light with the children because we knew food would not be served at the party until at least eleven o'clock.

The weather was a subject never discussed as it was always perfect. We knew the temperature between day and night would not vary more than twenty degrees all through the year. It was perpetual springtime. In the rainy season, the rains would last for ten to twenty minutes every day, and you could set your clock on the time. Every day the rain started a little later than the day before, until it passed into the night hours and eventually disappeared. We loved the rainy season because then the mountains

[215]

turned green and wild flowers grew in fields of color everywhere.

Our life in Mexico was idyllic. I often compared the difference between life there and life in the States by saying one lived in Mexico but one existed in the States. To me, it was that simple. Life there was unhurried, contented, easy and inexpensive. The enjoyment of perfect weather, interesting continental friends and acquaintances from all nations, gorgeous scenery, and colorful atmosphere made life a continuous pleasure.

Nothing is perfect, however, and there were things to contend with, such as the food and water, which had to be sterilized before eating, and there were dangers to health which inoculations couldn't prevent. The perennial joke about the tourist affliction, Moctezuma's Revenge, or The Aztec Two-Step, is not so funny when it strikes. We kept sulfaquinadine handy and a prescription of Hayes's, which was infallible. None of us had problems, but we were always careful.

There also was financial insecurity and risks in business greater than in the States, but the high interest return of twelve to twenty percent on investments compensated for losses in many cases. There were no taxes, no pressures, but there was a great deal of bribery and political flimflam. A tip could bribe almost anyone for anything. But happiness was reflected in everyone's face, even the very poorest of peons. They were content as material wealth was secondary to their religious faith and family closeness. Their acceptance of poverty as well as their ingenuity at eking out a living made them proud, industrious and independent people.

By contrast, I felt life in the States was always full of pressure, with the need to fill every hour with busy work. Our competition in business and the constant drive to make more money, then pay more taxes, creates health problems the Mexicans seldom have. Hypertension and ulcers, heart attacks and mental breakdowns are often the results of living too hard and too fast. Even our leisure has to be spent torturing our bodies with rigorous exercise to offset hours sitting behind a desk.

The following is a comparison between the costs of living in Mexico and the United States at that time. In Mexico we rented two houses owned two cars, and fed and supported six servants, two children and three dogs. The total cost of our living expenses including vacations, entertaining and medical bills came to just the amount of the monthly rent on my Volney apartment in New York. The difference was incredible considering the value received in the enjoyment of a gracious life.

I vowed that when I returned to Indianapolis to live I would not be caught up in the hectic tempo of American life again. But in spite of my resolution, it wasn't long before the rhythm and pressures of everyday life dragged me back into the eddy of speed, and the need to "accomplish it all *today*." We learned to appreciate "*mañana*" in Mexico. What couldn't be done today could wait until tomorrow. My Dad remarked he only knew two words in Spanish. "*Mañana* meant tomorrow and pyjama meant tonight."

In business, Sam felt he could get just as much work done under the Mexican system as he could in the States, without the pressure to be on time or the mental stress of a set routine. Life flowed in an easy fashion in both the social and business worlds. The siesta break in the day was a very real need in the rarefied air of Mexico City, and the hot noon sun of the lower communities in the country.

Soon after we arrived in Mexico, Axel asked Sam to take over the management of five companies. Sam had been placed on the Boards of Directors of several businesses in trouble, and five of these were silver factories. Sam's expertise in business, which Axel recognized, was his ability to reorganize failing companies into profit-making ventures. The dairy, Lecheria Nationale, was now making money, and it was time for Sam to take over another weak link in Axel's chain of investments.

Sam reduced the five silver factories into one operation, Conquistador S.A. and built the business into the top silver making industry in Mexico. Conquistador made most of the holloware sold in shops around the country. Sam became so interested in the silver business he bought a forty-nine percent interest in it for himself, while Axel retained the other fifty-one percent.

Mother and Dad returned to spend Christmas with us. They brought Bill and a friend of his, Jack Murray. Mildred Nottingham, my aunt, and Dick Whitney, Dad's pilot, completed the group. Having only one guest room, we could not accommodate everyone. So they all stayed downtown at the new luxurious Del Prado Hotel on Avenida Juarez.

Christmas was especially festive with such a large group gathered at the table for meals, around the tree on Christmas morning unwrapping packages, and later, singing carols around the piano. It was a very happy time.

When I packed my furniture to ship to Mexico, I had not forgotten my doll house, stored in Mother's attic, plus other old toys and a tricycle. Judy was now old enough to have the doll house, but Ann was still too young to care for the delicate miniatures, which were becoming antiques.

Sam found a carpenter who built a new house for Ann on the same scale as mine, and we furnished it with less destructible and valuable appointments. Ann's doll house was a charming Spanish replica. It had a stucco exterior with a tiny Mexican lantern hanging over the front door. The carved wood staircase and balcony over the living room was typically Spanish, as well as the little upstairs porch and domed windows. We were

[217]

thrilled with the result of the Mexican craftsman, Rodriquez.

I had a wonderful excuse to play in the doll house again and loved exploring the shops for Mexican miniatures to put in the new one for Ann. We placed the two doll houses side by side in the children's playroom and kept them hidden until Christmas morning.

Judy and Ann loved their doll houses and played with them almost every day. A short time after Christmas, Sam and I were amazed to overhear the girls conversing entirely in Spanish, as they played with their family of dolls. They were having a tea party, and though the Spanish was spoken in short phrases, they had heard enough in six weeks to pick up idioms and good accents.

The children's favorite names for their dolls were Mrs. Cabachon and Mrs. Vichyssoise, the heads of the doll house families. The conversation ran something like this: "Mas te, Señora Cabachon?" "Si, gracias, Señora Vichyssoise. El dia es muy bonito, verdad?" "Si, mucho, Señora." "Pues, entonces, ya me voy a casa." "Adios, Señora." "Hasta luego, Señora."

Not having begun school as yet, Sam and I were impressed with the amount of Spanish the girls had absorbed in just a few weeks. Judy and Ann did not start school until the first of February since, in Mexico, the long vacation of the year begins November first and ends February first. Therefore the schools do not have the expense of heating the building during the colder months. Also, there are many important holidays during this time.

The girls attended the Latin-American School, where they learned Spanish quickly. Half of their curriculum was in Spanish, the other half in English. Ann was in the pre-primer class, comparable to America's first grade. She learned to write (not print, as children do in the States for the first three grades) and began academic subjects. At the end of the year, she announced proudly with a Spanish accent, "I graduated and they gave me a di-plo-*ma*."

The schools, as in Europe, were two years ahead of American schools academically. They didn't waste time teaching subjects better taught at home. Basic academics were stressed because the majority of Mexicans did not go beyond the sixth grade, as they needed to work. Mexican law requires all citizens to be able to read and write before they can stop their schooling. Thus, the curriculum is accelerated to teach all children as much in the first eight grades as our schools teach through the twelfth. We admired the educational system. The children came back to the States head and shoulders above their classmates at Tudor Hall, speaking two languages fluently and receiving a solid background in "readin', writin' and 'rithmetic", as well as Mexican history.

———————◆◆◆◆◆———————

Life for me was almost too easy. I really didn't have enough to do. Four servants took care of all the menial work. If the senora picked up a dust cloth or tried out a new recipe, she lost a little respect from the staff. She was supposed to tell them what to do, not do anything herself. I spent many hours reading, sewing and making beaded pictures, and playing the piano. I refused to have a "nana" for the children, as most housewives did, because I wanted to care for Judy and Ann myself and be with them as much as possible. All too soon they would be grown up and not need me any more.

I began teaching them to play the piano, following in the footsteps of their first teacher in Muncie, Ellen Remington. I gave them each a practice lesson every day. I also gave Betti Ann Speissinger lessons. Betti Ann lived next door to us and had a great desire to learn music but had no piano. So she came to our house every day for a lesson.

There were quite a few children in our neighborhood, eight of them immediate neighbors on our street. Judy and Ann were not lacking in playmates. We had large parties for them on their birthdays, usually costume parties.

On Judy's eighth birthday we had a circus party, hiring an organ grinder with his monkey to play circus tunes. Balloons in great bunches were tied to the walls around our property, and of course, there was a piñata in the form of a life-size clown hanging from a tree. At the end of the party, the children gathered around the pinata, and blindfolded, took turns trying to strike it with a broomstick. Once broken, the clay pot inside holding all the candy, fruit and toys would spill out on the ground. A mad scramble would ensue as the children grabbed all they could to fill their paper sacks with the fallen goodies.

The children came to the party dressed as cowboys, acrobats, clowns and lion tamers. Judy dressed as a tightrope walker in a ballet tutu, and Ann and Jackie Whitehouse, a neighbor boy, went as Mr. and Mrs. Tom Thumb, dressed as bride and groom. The guests formed a parade, taking turns acting out their part in the circus, and the one who showed off his costume to the best advantage, received a prize.

For refreshment, Sam barbecued hamburgers and hot dogs on our outdoor grill, and everyone got a picnic supper. The parents enjoyed the party as much as the children. It was a huge success.

———————⋖◉⋗———————

November first, Sam's birthday, is also an important holiday in Mexico, being All Saint's Day and is celebrated in quite a different way than we celebrate Halloween in the States. After mass, the Mexicans take a picnic basket to their families' cemetery plots. The baskets contain realistic sugar skulls made in bakeries, with the names of the dearly departed glued to the foreheads — perhaps Rosalba, Jose, or Maria in shiny, colorful letters. They also include round loaves of a special bread called "the bread of the dead,"

[219]

reinforcing their picnic lunches with bottles of pulque or tequila. The family spends the day at graveside eating and drinking pulque with toasts for the departed ones, having a wonderful time and getting drunk as lords. The skulls are eaten as a final tribute to the departed aunt, grandfather or sibling.

As the Mexicans do not celebrate Halloween as we do, we thought it would be fun to have a traditional Halloween party American style, to celebrate Sam's birthday. Many of our American friends had not been to a Halloween party since childhood, so it was a bit of nostalgia for all of us.

The party began early with cocktails, and everyone came in costume. Sam wore his mariachi outfit, and I became Captain Bloodybeard once again, recalling my youth as a pirate. I blacked out my two front teeth to enhance the effect and wore jewelry, khaki shorts, riding boots and a bandanna around my head. I carried one of Sam's antique flintlock pistols thrust in my belt.

We dressed Julio as a skeleton. Sam painted luminous paint on a suit of long underwear dyed black, which looked very realistic after dark. We even found a skeleton mask with movable jaws. The effect transformed Julio into a man of moving bones. He served drinks from bottles labeled with skull and crossbones. Ana and Agustina were ghosts, flitting among the guests serving canapes.

After cocktails, we sent everyone away on a scavenger hunt to return by nine o'clock with as many items on the list as they could find, such things as a live flea, broomstick, skull, witch's wig, a book of ghost stories, a mariachi band and a Halloween pumpkin. The winning couple received a gallon of rum for their efforts.

We were amazed by the ingenuity of our guests when they came back with some of the things we thought impossible to find. There were plenty of fleas! Sam spent a good part of the evening flushing them down the toilet. We were also surprised when five mariachi bands arrived. The neighborhood was regaled with the different groups blowing their horns, trying to outdo each other. Finally, we persuaded them to band together and play one piece at a time!

Don Thorburn came late to the party after we had finished dinner, bringing along an uninvited guest, whom no one seemed to know. Her name was Mrs. Kerr. The two were not in costume but arrived having had at least as many drinks as the rest of us. Mrs. Kerr, dressed in a Scotch tartan suit and red gloves, immediately sat down at the piano, removed her shoes but not her gloves, and began to play. Those red-gloved hands played until after the last guest left in the early hours of the morning. She only stopped at brief intervals for a swallow from her Scotch hi-ball. I don't think she spoke a word throughout the evening, and we never saw or heard of her again, but that evening she kept the sound decibels high until we finally persuaded her to leave so we could go to bed.

Judy and Ann in their traveling clothes

Ready for take-off to Mexico: L. to R. "Ball Line" co-pilot, Judy, Ann, "Mimi," "Pom-pom" and Dick Whitney, 1st pilot

Christmas in Muncie: L. to R. Mildred Hawke, Judy, Ann and Aunt Mildred Nottingham

CHAPTER FORTY-TWO

I became pregnant again. This time I was more careful and sought the advice of Dr. Chavez immediately. Everything went well for the first five months, and then I had a bout of bronchitis. After a week I was well again, feeling fine. I had felt well all through the pregnancy. So I was surprised one morning, about ten days after the bronchitis attack, to awaken feeling nauseated and tired.

I slept until noon when I awoke feeling very ill. Balbina phoned Sam, but he was already on his way home for lunch. By then I was running a high fever and began to have labor pains. As soon as Sam arrived, we hurried to the hospital.

By the time I was in bed at the hospital my pains were severe. The nurse was out of the room calling for Dr. Chavez when I delivered the baby.

I don't think I ever was so ill and despondent. Evidently the bronchitis had harbored the deadly nephritis virus, killing the baby girl at least twenty-four hours before I became sick myself.

The next morning I was awakened by a nurse carrying a new-born baby into my room, and in my sleepy state, thought my baby didn't die after all. But the nurse went past my bed, excusing herself, and through a doorway into a room adjoining mine. I went into shock as the full realization of my loss struck me. I cried hysterically for hours, inconsolable in spite of the competent, sympathetic nurse who sat with me and helped me face my traumatic loss. She was furious with the nurse who had thoughtlessly entered my room with another woman's baby.

Penicillin cured my body of the acute nephritis, but nothing helped to cure my sorrow over losing our second baby. Now I was afraid of another pregnancy. I didn't want to jeopardize my health when I already had two lovely children and a wonderful husband to care for. Sam agreed we should not try to have another baby.

Judy and Ann came to see me in the hospital bringing a basket of pine cones, which they collected on the hospital grounds. The cones looked so pretty, representing the love the children felt for me. I still have them in a basket by the fireplace.

My convalescence took a long time. I had been quite ill and remained weak and unable to get out of bed without hemorrhaging. I stayed in bed at home taking medicine around the clock, but a month went by and I was not much better.

One day Balbina and Agustina came to my room and begged me to let them try and help. They said they knew a cure if I would agree to try their medicine. I would have agreed to anything by that time. They went out into the hills beyond our house and searched until they found a certain herb, boiling it into a tea for me to drink. It tasted very bad, but I sipped it down, not to disappoint them, feeling somewhat nervous about drinking an unknown weed.

After the tea was consumed, Balbina and Agustina stood on either side of my bed with a sheet, which they folded into a long strip, looped around my ankles, and pulled tightly, holding the pressure for a few minutes. They then moved the sheet up my legs slightly, repeating the process up my body until they finally had the sheet looped around my stomach and waist. This time they pulled against the sheet with all their strength until I felt squeezed as if in a too-tight corset.

At last they were finished. They thanked *me* and retired. I couldn't help but laugh, amused at the ignorance and superstitions of the Indians. However, I was grateful for their consideration and attention.

The tea and sheet treatment miraculously did the trick. The bleeding stopped, and I was able to get out of bed without any more trouble. I told Dr. Chavez what the girls had done. He, of course, laughed and sputtered about "those crazy Indian teas," saying, "They have a weed for every illness." But I knew his Vitamin K and ergot pills had done nothing to help me for weeks following the miscarriage. Superstition or not, I was grateful to Agus and Balbina for their knowledge and experience in such matters and thanked them for curing me.

———————◆———————

Judy had her troubles also. After a bout of severe stomach pains, the doctor advised us to have her appendix removed. In a small child, he said, it was often difficult to diagnose appendicitis, and it was much safer to remove it before a rupture. He operated, appearing later with Judy's appendix on a piece of gauze for us to inspect. "You see," the surgeon said, "It was perfectly normal after all." Having never seen an appendix, I presume he meant it was not swollen or discolored. The two inches of little white worm could have been anything on the gauze. Unfortunately he had made such a poor incision, which later became infected, that she had an ugly scar, twice as long and wide as the average.

I stayed with Judy in the hospital overnight, and when the nurse brought her breakfast the next morning, I was both amused and disgusted to see the food on her tray, a cup of coffee with milk (cafe con leche) and a pile of refried beans with a tortilla. Beans after an appendectomy? I gently asked the nurse if she could bring Judy some orange juice and a soft boiled egg with a piece of toast instead. She looked surprised but said she would try. Sometime later another breakfast arrived, but Judy laughed wanly as she tried the egg. It was full of shells! She couldn't eat anyway, she said, as she hurt too much.

Later that year Judy became very ill. She vomited constantly, and after a

[224]

few days and many consultations with Dr. Gonda, our pediatrician, he saw she was becoming dehydrated and advised us to put her in the hospital. He had not been able to diagnose her illness, but we could see she was becoming weaker and sicker by the day. In the British-American Hospital, they started intravenous fluids, and Judy responded to the treatment almost immediately. The next morning Dr. Gonda called us, laughing, to say, "Well, I know what's wrong with her now! She has turned yellow to the eyeballs. It's hepatitis." We weren't laughing. We knew how serious the disease is. But Judy recovered quickly with the proper attention in the hospital. Dr. Gonda told us Judy had acute infectious hepatitis, which meant the rest of us could catch it. But with our knowledge of the symptoms, prompt medication, and a careful diet, we should not become too ill. There was an incubation time, and I carefully watched Ann for symptoms as well as myself, checking the whites of our eyes for a change of color. Ann and I both got yellow eyeballs, and we began medication right away. Neither of us had further problems, but we were on special food for months. I had been on a particular diet for nephritis and barely had finished that regime when the diet began for hepatitis. It seemed to me I had one health problem after another in Mexico, but it was nice to be thin!

◄◉►

Sam's parents, Leona and Hayes Davis, came to Mexico to spend Thanksgiving with us. They came several times when Hayes took time off from his practice, but they always stayed with the Wenner-Grens. One weekend we were together at Rancho Cortez in Cuernavaca, where Margurite and Axel had a palatial home amid twenty acres of rolling, landscaped gardens full of tropical flowers and trees. They had elegant dinner parties here, as well as in their home in the city, and could seat twenty-four people at the massive dinner table. The silver service (made by Conquistador) shone under the candlelight from the tall, silver candelabra that dominated the center portion of the table.

Before dinner, the Southern Cross cocktails were served in the richly furnished living room before a huge fireplace. Marguerite's great love, having no children on which to lavish affection, was her pack of chihuahua dogs, which clustered around her and the guests at cocktail hour. Each guest was given a towel to put on his lap so that the dogs would not tear or soil your dinner clothes when they jumped up for attention. I love dogs, but in my opinion chihuahuas are nasty little dogs with bad breath. I always dreaded any intimate contact with one of them. She had twenty. So my chances of avoiding them was slim.

Dinners at the Wenner-Grens, even when there were no guests, always required full dinner attire. Once, when Leona and Hayes arrived for a visit, Hayes' suitcase missed the plane connection, and for the first night he had no dinner clothes for the evening. Axel insisted he wear one of his tuxedos. Hayes, being a much larger man, was miserable, choked into the tight trousers and coat, the sleeves ending far above his wrists. But he was dressed for dinner!

Hayes was a doctor and an excellent diagnostician. His temperament was easy-going and quiet — a loveable man. He was also a student, always reading and learning something new. He was particularly eager to speak every foreign language, studying Russian and even Chinese. He understood languages much better than he could speak them, having a quavery voice, which was halting, even in English, but he worked tirelessly at his hobby and engaged any foreigner in conversation. He was a patient man and one of Louisville's most respected doctors.

Leona, on the other hand, was a fiery vivacious woman who took control at parties and entertained everyone with clever repartee. Her great love in life was entertaining and being entertained. She loved people, talking to them and about them. Hayes and Leona were strangely matched, but a very happy couple. They both loved the visits to Mexico, where Hayes could meet people from many countries and Leona could enjoy the extravagantly beautiful dinner parties given by Marguerite and Axel.

Almost every weekend we left the city, and, if we did not go to our house in Cuernavaca, we explored other sections of Mexico. One of our favorite resorts was San Jose de Purua. It was a spa situated midway between Guadelajara and Toluca, about a two-and-a-half hour drive west of Mexico City. The resort was famous for its "radioactive," therapeutic waters, which came from underground springs, and people came great distances to take the baths, said to cure everything from arthritis to acne. There were two, large swimming pools full of this special water, one very deep for adults, and a shallow pool for non-swimmers and children. There was some danger as the water was opaque and the color of burnt orange. It was impossible to see anything beneath the surface. Sam saw to it that Judy and Ann learned to swim, and he taught them at San Jose de Purua.

The place was always crowded. People sat around the poolside covering themselves with the thick, orange mud, which was passed around in buckets by the pool boys. For a few pesos one's body could be completely covered. The mud was said to improve the skin. It was comical to see people sitting or lying about coated with the oozy stuff, looking like badly molded statues. When the mud was completely dry, they would dive in the pool and wash off in the murky water.

A different type of spring water was fed into the private baths adjoining the pool. Here, for an expensive treatment, one could sit in a large tub similar to a jacuzzi and be sprayed with clear water as in a shower. This was called a champagne bath because the water was gassy and tingled your skin to a bright pink flush. After one of these baths, people declared they never felt better in their lives.

The hotel sprawled over a great deal of land, beautiful rolling terrain in a valley surrounded by mountains. A waterfall spilled down one of the mountains near the pools, adding to the scenic beauty, and the climate was always hot and dry. There were cottages for rent belonging to the hotel, but we always stayed in the main building. The food was particularly good, and pitchers of spring water were placed on each table. At first we were afraid to drink it thinking it might affect us like the Pluto water at French Lick Springs, Indiana. Gingerly we tried sips of the water, which tasted like a refreshing lemonade. When we were assured it would have no laxative effects, we drank more and more of it until we were consuming several pitchers of the liquid at every meal.

—————◆—————

After a dinner party one evening in Mexico City, someone in our group suggested we all go to a Turkish night club where he had been recently. He said the Turkish coffee was excellent, and there was the added attraction of a good belly dancer. It was after midnight, but we thought it would be fun to join the others for a cup of Turkish coffee before bed. Our friend led the way in his car, and the three other cars followed behind until we reached the night club well beyond the outskirts of Mexico City.

The coffee was good and so was the belly dancer, but we could scarcely see anything as the place was almost in total darkness. Flickering candles lighted the tables dimly within multi-colored glass lamps.

When we got up to leave, Sam and I were the last ones out the door. We saw the red tail lights of the last car in our group wing around the corner and disappear. Quickly, we jumped in our car and tried to follow, but the car was gone. We had no idea where we were or how to get home. Houses were blacked out for the night and not a street light nor street sign gave us our location. We were in total darkness and silence.

We drove up one street and down another, becoming more and more confused in our directions and ended up, first, on a dirt road dead-ending into a group of adobe shacks. Backing out of this cul-de-sac we tried another road, only to find it ended in a brick wall in front of our headlights. After a half-hour of driving in circles and getting further into the country instead of toward the city, Sam stopped the car, turned off the headlights, and stood staring at the sky. Stars by the millions twinkled away, laughing at us in the black, silent night.

Sam found what he was looking for. The Big Dipper pointed to the North Star, and with this to guide us, Sam drove us home, navigating by the position of the star. He made frequent stops at intersections to relocate our direction from the star and to decide which way to turn. Eventually we found a paved street, then a familiar street sign and finally we were on the Paseo de la Reforma enroute to Sierra Amatepec.

[227]

I never got over Sam's ingenuity. Even having the inspiration to think of finding our way home by the stars was incredible to me.

———————◄◉►———————

One of the best weekends we ever had was the one in Acapulco when we entertained the U.S. Naval Fleet during its cruise to Mexico.

Hugh Caldwell, our Naval Attache at the U.S. Embassy, organized the party, asking Sam, Stewart Skidmore and Don Thorburn, all Naval Reservists, to assist him in Acapulco as a welcoming party for the Fleet. He proposed we all rent a house and share the expenses, using the place for a reception and as a base for the officers who might want to come over for a swim or a drink.

Hugh and his wife Tita drove to Acapulco in the embassy car with their chauffeur and maid, bringing groceries and liquor for the weekend. At that time Acapulco was just a sleepy village with a few resort hotels studding the hillsides. Most food was flown in from Mexico City or Guadelajara. The markets in Acapulco did not have much besides sea food and some local produce. So we brought food to last us through the weekend.

Kay and Don Thorburn brought Kay's sister Trudy, and Fifi and Stew Skidmore brought their young son, Monty, who was near Ann's age. We flew down, taking the children and Balbina to do the cooking for everyone.

Fifi and Stew met us at the plane to drive us to the house we had rented sight unseen. They grumbled with dejected looks that the place was a mess, the cockroaches so big you could put saddles on them. They continued to describe the disaster we had rented until we arrived. We entred an unpretentious wooden door set in a stucco wall after parking the car in a small garage on the street. Surprisingly, a flight of steps took us immediately down the hill, which was so overgrown with bougainvillia and other flowering bushes we could not see the house.

Arriving at the house below street level, we looked around in surprise. The house was completely open on all sides of the living room, making it an enormous lanai, or terrace, furnished with the typical ambience of Mexican living — swooping comfortable chairs, hammocks, large, low leather tables and the inevitable beautiful tiled floor, polished to a high gloss. It was cool, breezy and inviting. Only the bedrooms were enclosed, but they had large windows which could be opened to the sea breezes.

Beyond the house was the ocean. We had our own private beach, fenced to the water's edge on both sides to insure privacy. It was an absolutely gorgeous spot! How could we have been so lucky to have found such a perfect house for our weekend? The Skidmores had been teasing us with their gloomy stories to see our surprised reaction. They loved the house too.

We were excited about the arrival of Jane and Jack Simpson, who were

[228]

flying down for a visit with us. We met them at the airport the next morning when they landed in Dad's Beechcraft with Dick Whitney at the controls. After their arrival we had a full house of fifteen, not counting the servants.

The U.S. Fleet arrived, entering the harbor with two destroyers and a brand new snorkel submarine. The Captain issued an invitation to Hugh for all of his party to board the submarine for inspection that afternoon.

We responded eagerly, climbing down the vertical ladder to the infra-red lighted recesses of the ship below the water. It was eerie and looked oily from the shining polished metal below decks. I was impressed by the engine room and quarters of the crew, but I breathed a sigh of relief when I climbed up again into the bright sunshine of Acapulco Bay. Claustrophobia would have been a problem for me if I had to live enclosed in such a place under water.

That evening we had the reception for the Naval officers of the three ships, as well as all the Naval and Military officers of Mexico, who were in the Acapulco area. The governor of the State of Guerrero and the mayor of Acapulco and their wives were also invited.

It was a great party. We hired some bartenders from the neighboring country club to help serve the drinks, and our buffet table was sumptuous. The party continued well into the night, but about two a.m., Hugh noticed a small commotion at the fence line back of the bar and went to investigate. The caretaker of our house was really taking care. She had forced the three bartenders back against the wall with a machete and was holding them there when Hugh arrived. She explained the bartenders had been tossing bottles of liquor over the wall to a compadre who received them neatly and stored them in cartons ready to be carried off after the party. The caretaker had noticed the hanky-panky and immediately took action. Hugh retrieved the liquor behind the wall, paid the men off and told them to leave.

After a taxi called for the bartenders, Hugh's chauffeur learned about the incident. He hurried off in the embassy car, overtook the taxi and forced it off the road. Holding the men at gun point, he demanded the return of the money Hugh had paid them for the evening and gave it back to Hugh, explaining the men should not have been paid for trying to rob from him. Hugh was grateful for the loyalty of his chauffeur, and we admired the courage of the elderly caretaker who came to our defense. It was an exciting finale to the evening. Most of our guests were unaware of any unusual occurrence and continued to enjoy our hospitaility awhile longer.

The next afternoon there was a reception on board the destroyer, hosted by the captain of the ship. The Mexican Navy and Army officers and wives were invited, as well as other political dignitaries in the area. We dressed

[229]

appropriately, the men in their white dress uniforms and the women in their prettiest summer dresses, and were escorted across the bay to the destroyer in the ship's launches. The deck was full of guests by the time we arrived. Judy, Ann, Sam and I climbed the ladder. As we reached the deck, we heard the shrill piping sound of the boatswain blowing his whistle, standing at attention as Sam stepped board. Sam realized he was being given the honor of being piped aboard. As it happened, he was the senior officer of the entire party, a full Commander. He was surprised no one there held a higher rank.

Sam later said he was so taken aback, he could not remember which to do first — salute the flag or the quarterdeck. But he played his part correctly and enjoyed the party as honored guest.

We have never forgotten the details of the three-day party. Swimming in the ocean on our private beach, dancing the mambo on the tiled terrace, drinking tall, cool rum drinks and lying in the hammocks lazily chatting with our congenial group of friends were great pleasures to be enjoyed in our thoughts long after.

One indelible picture in my mind is of Fifi Skidmore at our reception. Barefooted, she was dancing on the terrace when someone saw a scorpion near her and called out a warning. Instead of moving a safe distance away, she straddled it, a bare foot on either side, and leaned far down to inspect the poisonous creature more closely. It was a *guerro* — a sting by this white scorpion can be fatal. They move with lightning speed when alarmed, but Fifi had had enough to drink not to care. Someone came with a broom and killed it while she never moved from the spot, mesmerized.

Dick Whitney flew us back to Mexico City, and the Simpsons continued their visit with us a few days longer. We had a wonderful time showing them the sights of Mexico and our favorite haunts in the evening. When they left for Muncie, we flew back with them for Christmas with the family.

I remember how frightened we were when we finally landed. The weather had closed in as we flew over the midwest. Dick attempted to land at St. Louis, but the airport had closed down before we could arrive. We were in deep fog and very low on fuel when we reached Indianapolis. Dick called the tower for permission to make an emergency landing, as that airport was closed also. We circled over the field many times, coming in low with visibility near zero, but Dick could not see the runway well enough to land. Jane and I gripped hands together and prayed. Finally, on one of his turns he approached the runway dead on, and we landed safely.

There was a group of commercial pilots gathered at the gate to greet us as we walked off the plane. They shook Dick's hand saying, "That was a great instrument landing you just made." Dick responded he had no blind instrument landing equipment on the plane. They shook his hand again!

———◄◉►———

Judy and Ann were as exited to see Mimi and Pompom again as we were. From the time Judy was a baby she had called Mother and Dad "Mimi" and "Pompom." Not only the children, but nearly everyone, referred to them by these names from then on. Mother and Dad loved their nicknames and even used them for each other.

The house was decorated beautifully with an enormous tree in the living room trimmed with all the favorite ornaments I remembered and loved from my childhood. On Christmas Eve, after the children were in bed, the rest of us, including Bill, sat around the tree and arranged the unwrapped surprise "Santa Claus" gifts for Judy and Ann on Christmas morning.

Mother said she thought it would be fun for each of us to open just one present apiece — the most special gift, so that we could enjoy it for itself before the deluge of gifts the next day. She wanted me to open a gift from her first of all.

The box I opened contained an exquisite figurine of Royal Copenhagen. It was a little girl gathering flowers, the second figurine Mother had found to begin my collection. The figurines were made in 1936 to celebrate the King of Denmark's seventy-fifth birthday.

I had ordered cocktail napkins for Sam with his monogram embroidered on them. As a child, he had drawn his initials to resemble a cartoon of the rear end of a cow. It was such a funny, clever design that I wanted to capture it forever. We all laughed heartily when he opened his package.

Bill's best present was a fancy camera, then Pompom found a beautiful pair of cat's eye cuff links from Mother in a tiny box.

"Now, Mimi, it's your turn," we all said. Mother looked but found nothing for herself alone. We had brought gifts of silver for both Mother and Dad but nothing for them individually. We looked at Dad questioningly. He said he had already given Mimi her gift. We asked, "What was it?" "Where was it?" But he wouldn't answer, Mimi searched among the packages and finally found a small box sent to her from a cousin in St. Louis. All of us were feeling uncomfortable as she began unwrapping the package. She said, with a little laugh but tears in her eyes "I do believe it's cheese." It wasn't cheese but a little fruit cake. All of us sat in miserable silence, and then I asked Dad, accusingly, what he had given Mother. He replied defensively, "I gave her the only thing she said she wanted. I stopped smoking."

We agreed it was a big gift to give, and Mother quickly spoke up to say it was true — she didn't want another thing from him — but we all felt he

[231]

could have given her *something* to unwrap — at least a pair of stockings. She got nothing else from Dad that Christmas, but he never smoked again.

In spite of our embarrassment over the situation, Christmas remained a memorable one. The next day there were ten at the dinner table as Mildred, Chauncey and Ethel had joined us. Charles, our beloved servant of many years, carried in a huge tray bearing — not the turkey we were all looking forward to, but an entire roast pig! Mother had decided to surprise us with something different, and we were shocked into stunned silence. Sam was asked to do the "honors" of carving, and we all watched and grimaced as he sliced into the juicy, fatty body, which looked almost alive. The head with little beady cranberry eyes stared accusingly at everyone, but the apple in his mouth prevented him from squealing.

Finally Judy broke the silence in a small voice, "I suppose we'll have snout hash tomorrow," she said. It broke the tension, We all laughed, relaxed and ate what we could of the animal. But it was the last time Mother put pig on the menu.

Marguerite Wenner-Gren   *Axel Wenner-Gren*

Bomar Cramer's portraits of Ann and Judy

CHAPTER FORTY-THREE

T HE year 1950 was one of happy and sad events that ended with an abrupt change in our lives. There were many parties and excursions to other parts of Mexico. We entertained often ourselves, and during one dinner party I was suddenly struck with the realization that I was listening to the conversation of our guests in six different languages. I sat back and thought about the interesting, cosmopolitan atmosphere of Mexico. I had not realized how many foreigners we had met during our brief time there. That night we were entertaining a group that included Swedish, Hungarian, Austrian, French, Cuban and even Australian friends, not to mention other Mexicans and Americans. All were conversing in their own languages to others who understood them. I felt it was a great privilege to be able to live in such an atmosphere.

One of the best dinner parties we ever attended was both typically continental and unusual in that it was a completely Parisian meal prepared by the mother of our host, Luis Brosier. Luis was the manager of Parisina, a jewelry-making company owned by Axel. The occasion of the party was in honor of Luis's parents, who were visiting him from France, and to celebrate his father's seventieth birthday.

We were invited for nine o'clock and assembled in Luis's home with the other guests for cocktails preceding dinner. Precisely at ten, the twenty-four guests were ushered into the dining room and seated at one long table. We were the only Americans but were able to converse in Spanish with the others. The elderly Brosiers, however, spoke only French. I was sitting near Mrs. Brosier. I found my lost French before too long and was able to talk to her, if haltingly. There was a babble of conversation in all directions, bits of Swedish, French and Spanish tangled in the air as the first course arrived. Mrs. Brosier, herself, had prepared the meal, not trusting Luis's Mexican chef to the delicate processes of French cooking.

A light soup was served and then a delicate fish course, followed by a patty shell filled with chicken and sweetbreads. After this came a salad of asparagus vinagrette and then the entree of duck a l'orange. During the dinner a different wine was poured with each course, and at dessert an ice mold of a swan was brought in with appropriate ceremony. It was filled with ice cream, a candle burning in the center. After the ice cream the pièce de résistance arrived. The birthday cake, aflame with seventy candles was a replica of a French chateau. It was quite a tribute and called for many toasts with champagne to Mr. Brosier, who was overcome with emotion as he made a hesitating thank-you speech, half in French and half in Spanish. Coffee and liquors were served as we continued to sit conversing with our neighboring table mates.

The dinner had been served so smoothly and expertly, we felt no sense of passing time or the uncomfortable feeling of eating too much. Everything had been so easy and pleasant we were amazed to discover we had been eating steadily for four hours! It was two a.m.!

———————<◉>———————

Anita Rabell had given us as a wedding present a splendid boxer puppy we named Guerrez. But as she grew to full size, she had an insatiable desire to explore the world and would scale our seven-foot wall, which was topped by barbed wire, from a standing position and take off for parts unknown. She also had a yen to play with Dora, the Doberman next door, and we would find them romping together at the Muenches. It finally became too difficult for us to be on the chase for her, and when Joe Rauschbauer, a silversmith at Conquistador, admired her to distraction, we presented her to him. The dog became so attached to Joe that she saved his life. They were crossing the street when a car appeared out of nowhere and would have run Joe down except that Guerrez, in a flash, jumped on him, knocking him out of the car's path, and she instead, was hit and killed.

We acquired two other dogs from friends when they moved away from Mexico. One was a little Maltese terrier named Gito who belonged to the Benedicts. The other was Sandy, a beautiful sable collie, given to us by our neighbors across the street when they moved away. We loved Sandy, but he also loved to run away and would take off whenever the gate was opened.

Penny accepted these intruders with good grace because she knew she was the favored pet. She suffered from ear problems, and it was necessary to take her to the vet more and more frequently. She possibly endured as many as ten operations to remove tumors, which I felt were indeed malignant, although the doctor insisted they were not. Penny lost her zip, and we knew she was ill. One morning I awoke to find her close to my side of the bed, asleep forever. As hard as it was for Sam, he carried her out into the yard and buried her in a remote corner under a flamboyant tree.

———————<◉>———————

Sam had been thinking for some time about returning to the States in order to start his own business. He had traveled to Kansas City and Dallas to look over some wholesale drug companies for sale, but none of them suited him or his pocketbook.

He heard of a firm in Des Moines, Iowa, and this time we all went with him. We left Judy and Ann with Mimi and Pompom and picked up Uncle Barret in Indianapolis to accompany us to Des Moines. Sam wanted his uncle's advice about everything, particularly in business. He adored Uncle Barret as a father, considering him the greatest influence in his adult life. Sam's father died in 1947 in King's Daughters Hospital in Shelbyville, Kentucky, where he had lain almost totally paralyzed by Parkinson's disease for twelve years. Sam and I stopped to see him for the last time as we drove to Mexico after our wedding. He could speak to us with

[235]

difficulty, but he could not move a muscle of his body without extreme difficulty and great tremors. His eyes sparkled, however, and conveyed an active, intelligent mind that had not succumbed to the imprisonment of his body.

When we returned to Indianapolis, disappointed with the company in Des Moines, Uncle Barret remarked about a mutual friend, Keller Brock, who was the owner of the retail Haag Drug chain in Indianapolis. He advised Sam to make a courtesy call on Keller before returning to Mexico. Sam had worked for Mr. Brock in the past and knew him well. Keller was convinced he had cancer, though a medical report at Mayo's Clinic had been negative, and told Sam he would have to retire from business. Sam made an offer to buy Haag Drug, and Mr. Brock accepted. We stayed a few days longer to settle the negotiations, then returned to Mexico in a flurry of preparations to move back to Indiana. We had the summer to finalize our plans for the move and make the necessary arrangements to change our lives. We planned to leave Mexico on August first, as Haag Drug Company would be turned over to Sam August twenty-third.

In June we had a welcome visitor, Bomar Cramer. Bomar had moved to Dallas, his original home, and had given up the piano for art. He was an accomplished artist, using water colors as his media, but now was painting oil portraits on commission and becoming quite successful. He had become disillusioned and bitter about his inability to make a name for himself as a concert artist. A brilliant pianist, he was his own worst enemy, having a nervous, tense disposition, along with a persecution complex. He made himself sick, worrying about his career and finally gave the piano up in disgust, as well as his teaching career. With art he was able to release his emotions and relax as he painted. He loved Mexico and came down as often as possible to paint and enjoy the ambience of the good life. Through correspondence I persuaded him to visit us and paint Judy's and Ann's portraits, with the promise that he would give me piano lessons while he was there. He agreed, and I was delighted with the prospect, settling down to the piano with a vengeance.

Bomar stayed with us for six weeks. He chose our sunlit library off the terrace for his studio, set up his easel and palette and began painting right away.

While he was there, Ellen Remington from Muncie came to Mexico for her vacation. She had been the children's piano teacher when they were three and five years old while we lived in Muncie. A remarkable woman, she invented a system of harmony games to compliment the study of piano, giving a thorough foundation of music to her students. She had studied with Mrs. Day, my first piano teacher, and realized the potentials of a system Mrs. Day had merely touched upon. Ellen Remington created well over a hundred games, which had appeal for preschool children and adults alike. Judy and Ann had learned quickly with her system, and

[236]

before we moved from Muncie to New York, I studied with "Rem" to learn her method so I could continue to teach my children. I never understood why Mother didn't know of Miss Remington when Mrs. Day left Muncie. If I had studied with her in the early days, I would have been a more knowledgeable musician and more thoroughly prepared instead of wasting over ten years with inferior teachers.

Miss Remington stayed in a small, comfortable motel, which I found for her in Polanco, a residential and commercial suburb not far from our home, but we entertained her for dinner and helped her with sightseeing. She and Bomar both had their birthdays during the month of July. She was seventy and Bomar celebrated his fortieth. We had a special party for them as their birthdays fell within a few days of each other.

———————◄◉►———————

Sam made another trip to Indianapolis that summer, and while there, followed up a plan we had made to build our own home on piece of property owned by Uncle Barret. After investigating the cost of our ambitious plan, he gave it up as too expensive. We had drawn a floor plan of our dream house, thinking it would be modest enough, but discovered prices of construction in the States had increased almost twenty percent more than we could afford. So Sam searched for a house that would be a more reasonable investment.

He called one day to tell me he had done a very scary thing. He had bought a house for us without me seeing it! I knew his judgment would be the same as mine and told him not to worry, but to give all the particulars of the floor plan, number and dimensions of the windows and so forth, and I would then be able to plan the details and buy what we needed before leaving Mexico. Prices were so reasonable in Mexico it would cost less to buy what we would need here and ship it home with our household goods than to buy in Indianapolis.

When Sam showed me the plan and described the house, it seemed very large indeed! But I had something concrete to work with and began the furnishings and redecorating in my mind. There were seventeen rooms in the four-story square brick house at 4106 Washington Boulevard. I would need to buy more furniture to fill all the space.

I had spent two years admiring Mexican crafts and now went on shopping sprees to collect the articles that had been my favorites. I had furniture made to go into a large Mexican playroom on the top floor of the house and bought serapes and hammocks, chandeliers and lamps made of hand-crafted tin. I even bought an enormous bolt of white material intending to dye it the appropriate color for curtains.

Our interlude of Mexican living was coming to an end. While the portraits were developing on their canvases, I was practicing all morning, but I spent the afternoons preparing and packing for our impending departure.

When the portraits were finally completed to Bomar's satisfaction, we were thrilled by his excellent reproduction of the children and his style of painting. To be truthful, I hadn't been eager for the paintings but felt it would be the only way I could entice Bomar to come to Mexico and give me piano lessons. But the portraits have remained a permanent reminder of him and those last lovely days in Mexico. The children, set in the time frame of their childhood and dressed in the organdy dresses they wore at our wedding are tangible treasures of the past.

Mother and Dad came to Mexico to help us with our move. When they left they took Judy and Ann, "Rem" and Bomar with them. Sam and I would have two weeks free to do the serious packing alone. Julio, Ana and Agustina had agreed to come with us to Indianapolis, and Balbina assured me she also would come if I ever needed her but did not want to leave Mexico and her children at that time. She had responsibilities to her own family. On August first, Dick Whitney returned to fly the servants to Indiana. The plane was full, as usual, Sandy filling the narrow aisle in the plane. Sam and I left soon after by car, hauling a small trailer behind us filled with more belongings. Until our furniture arrived, the children and servants stayed in the Culver cottage, but Sam and I "camped out" in our new house while work was being done to renovate it.

CHAPTER FORTY-FOUR

L EAVING Mexico I was fraught with mixed emotions. My relaxed easy life there would be exchanged for a hopped-up, over-active existence. We would miss our newly-found friends but would be among old friends at home. There would be the assurance of good medical care in the States and finances would be more stable with a better opportunity for the growth of Sam's career in business. Business risks were always great in Mexico. The war in Korea had begun, and we were concerned about our country's position in the involvement. Sam was still a reserve Navy Commander and could be called into service in the conflict.

Sam has always been happy in every job he was called upon to do. He looked back at his experiences in World War II as "a piece of cake," feeling it was a fortunate turning point in his life and that luck had followed him throughout his five years of active duty. Three years of his duty was spent in the Solomon and Mariana Islands in the Pacific as aide to Admiral Greer. He was attached to the land base of Fleet Air Wing 19.

He felt confident about managing his own business. When he took over Haag Drug Company the thirty-three stores were doing a five-million dollar business. Sam proved his ability by expanding the chain to forty-seven stores doing a fifty-million dollar business before his early retirement in 1972. He was regarded by his friends in business as well as his competitors as outstanding, keen, straightforward and farsighted, and was well respected and admired. His community spirit and generosity has made him a person sought after for friendship and advice.

—————◈—————

The house on Washington Boulevard was truly a dream house but needed some cosmetic work to improve it from the white elephant that it was. It had been unoccupied for years except for the realtor and his wife, who stayed there part time as custodians. My cousins, Lucy and Alvin Owsley had rented the house for a year when they were recalled from ministerial duties in Ireland in 1942 — the only tenants in a fifteen-year period. The house was dismal, dark and drafty — and the roof leaked. The interior was a hangover from the twenties with walls painted a muddy brown, and the fixtures, plumbing and kitchen were of vintage elegance. It was necessary to rewire the entire house for electrical safety and replace the old slate roof with new roofing. The rooms were enormous with twelve-foot ceilings, and once painted and papered in happier colors, airy, spacious and gracious.

The house was designed by the famous architect, Sanford White (his mistress's husband shot and killed him — a 1920's scandal.) It had a very unusual floor plan, with the large living room and sleeping porch (which we converted to a tropical-style bar) on a half-level between the first floor and the bedroom floor.

There were eight entrances to the house. The main entrance was a double door facing Washington Boulevard, which we seldom used, preferring the handier "carriage entrance" off the winding driveway. This porte-cochère had steps leading to a side door. It was called the carriage entrance, as originally, horse-drawn carriages had stopped here to let off their passengers. Its big, double doors opened into an entrance hall. Beautiful walnut panelling covered the walls, extending into the large main hall. From there archways opened onto a beautiful sixteen by twenty-four foot dining room. A room on the opposite side of the hall was used as a formal parlor, and a small, enclosed porch off the main hall and opening into the dining room through French doors, was filled with plants and our aquarium tanks of tropical fish. From this grand, open reception hall, a flight of stairs with a graceful walnut balustrade led up to a landing, from which two more steps led up to the sixteen by forty-foot living room. A high, carved cement fireplace was centered in the wall opposite the stairs, and to the left was a big bay window with a semi-circular window seat following the base of the windows. My two grand pianos filled this space later on when Mother gave me her nine-foot Steinway to accompany my Chickering when I found a two-piano partner. This end of the room became my "studio" in 1951 when I began to teach piano professionally.

[239]

Turning the corner at the landing, there was another half-flight of stairs to the four bedrooms, placed around the landing hall, which I used as a library. Bookshelves lined the walls, and I had my desk there.

Our bedrooms were so spacious they were the size of the average home's living rooms. The two largest ones were joined by a bath, which the children used. We also had our bath adjoining a guest bedroom. The children had a small playroom and study separated by a lavatory off their bedroom.

The back hall, reached by following the balcony around the staircase, led into our "tropical" bar down a few steps, or to a flight of stairs down to the kitchen or up another flight to the top floor of the house. This room had no doubt been used as a ball room in earlier days. It was almost the size of the entire house, fifty-three feet square with a hardwood dance floor, three dormer windows set in large alcoves and a high twelve-foot ceiling. The room contained a pool table and an old square piano. It became our Mexican playroom, which we used many times for parties. Also on this floor was a small bedroom and bath — Julio's quarters for as long as he was with us.

I hung the four eight-branched tin chandeliers from the ceiling, used a pair of twin beds end-to-end as a couch against one wall, hung our many Mexican pictures, tin masks and hammock, placed serapes on the floor, added a ping pong table and the room was transformed into a bit of Mexico. The children's dolls houses sat in the recesses of the dormer windows. After dinner we could sit here watching the new invention, T.V. or just play records and dance. We played many games of ping pong and pool, with Sam as our expert pool teacher. The parties we gave in this room varied from square dances to Halloween parties, New Year's Eve suppers or high school proms for the girls.

There was a dumb waiter built into the wall, which we pulled up by stout cables from the kitchen, bringing food and supplies to the bar or playroom and serving it on the pool table, laid with a large colorful cloth.

The dining room was used for more formal gatherings. It was a beautiful room with old French scenic wallpaper, depicting a fox hunt of the 1800's, hung above a panelled dado. We loved the paper, realizing its value, and had it restored to a fresher look by having the sooty sky repainted with pale blue water colors and repairing the frayed parts where the paper was wearing away. We hung our Mexican crystal chandelier over the dining room table, which could seat twelve when fully extended. Mother gave us the lovely antique table and eight Chippendale chairs.

Beyond the dining room, double doors opened onto a porch at the side of the house, and at the end of the room, French doors opened into the breakfast room, and from there, into the kitchen. The breakfast room was directly beneath the living room in the bay window area and had its own bay window, also. This bright, cheerful room led out to the porch and to the back yard from another door. The yard was full of old, tall beech trees and a small pond.

The kitchen was enormous, boasting a serving entry with a German silver sink, many cupboards for dishes, and an entry from the kitchen to the reception hall, containing more cupboards and drawers for linen and silver storage. There was so much room in the house that we needed the three servants from Mexico to look after everything. Agustina and Ana had their own apartment in two rooms connected to the three-car garage at the rear of our property. We furnished it as comfortably as possible and added a bath and heating unit, with space for relaxing when they were not at work.

When the furniture arrived in lift vans from the railroad station, we discovered it had been so badly packed much of our household goods were broken. There was not a chair that remained with all four legs intact. The customs official sympathized with us over the loss and charged us nothing on the new items we had purchased in Mexico. We gave him one of the three lift vans for his children to use as a play house and used another as a dog house for Sandy, fencing an area around it beside the garage. We gave the third lift van to Scott Moxley to use as a tool shed on his property. The furniture repairs were done at great expense, but there was no rebate from the Mexican insurance company which was owned by Axel.

After everything was in place, we couldn't believe the transformation of the house. It was not only elegantly suited for entertaining, but it was also an intimate house where we could enjoy privacy without being overwhelmed by its size. I was sorry we didn't take "before and after" pictures.

The children began school at Tudor Hall in the second and fourth grades. The school was conveniently near us, at 32nd and Meridian, and Sam dropped them off on his way to work. I picked them up when school was over at 3:30. The first winter was a drastic change from Mexico with unprecedented snow and sub-zero temperatures. There was snow on the ground from the first of November to the first of April, and I was amazed our three Mexicans weathered through it. Our house was not insulated, nor was there a damper in the fireplace to keep the heat from being sucked right up through the chimney flue. We burned fifty-five tons of coal that winter with Julio and Sam shoveling coal into the hopper three times a day. After that first winter, we insulated the house and caulked the windows. I even invented a damper for the fireplace. All these improvements cut our coal consumption down to twenty-five tons a winter. But we had no real complaints. We loved our home and found Indianapolis cordial, busy and growing every day with cultural improvements for theater and concerts.

[241]

Fabian Sevitsky was conducting the Indianapolis Symphony Orchestra, and it wasn't long before I auditioned and was accepted as a member of the Indianapolis Symphonic Choir, which sang with the symphony when a chorus was required for a performance. I sang with the choir for twenty-five years before I became too busy to continue the weekly rehearsals, and Sam wished to travel more after his retirement. I watched it grow from a small amateur group of sixty members into a prestigious group of one hundred and eighty outstanding voices, under the competent leadership of several different directors throughout the years.

I recall an experience I had with Fabian and the orchestra. We were in rehearsal at the enormous Butler Field House in preparation for an Easter program with our choir and two other choirs from Ball State and Butler Universities, making a total choir of four hundred and fifty voices. We were seated in the bleachers behind the orchestra, which was set up on the gymnasium floor. The row in which I sat was so high and far from the orchestra, the players looked like midgets below us but the acoustics were excellent. In the middle of the dress rehearsal of "The Battle Hymn of the Republic", I was suddenly aware of Fabian at the podium calling my name. "Lucina!" he called several times. I stood up raising my arm and he finally saw me and said, "Come down!"

I crawled over the long row of singers and down the bleachers, tier after tier, until I finally reached the podium beside Fabian where he ordered me to sing "In the lilies." (The second verse of the hymn-begins "In the beauty of the lilies.") Frightened half to death by the unexpectedness of singing a solo, I managed to sing the verse, and he told me I would be singing it as a solo the next night at the performance. It went very well in spite of the short notice I was given, but it was intimidating to sing with a microphone and in such an enormous hall. The place seats six thousand, and we had a full house.

Because of my affiliation with the choir, I found myself teaching piano. The wife of the bridge expert, Mrs. Easley Blackwood, sat near me in the soprano section. One night at rehearsal, she asked if I would take over her eight students since her health would not permit her to teach any longer. I thought it over for a few days and then decided to call the parents of the children to arrange the changeover. At first, all the parents told me they had already made other plans for teachers and I thought I was "off the hook." But a little later, two of them called back to say they would like me to teach their children after all. From those two students I was referred to others, and before long, I was teaching full time, many more students than I intended or really had time for. I have continued to teach steadily under a full schedule of twenty-five to thirty students for nearly thirty-five years and have a long waiting list, which I am never able to shorten.

I attribute my success in teaching to Miss Remington, whose system is a

[242]

perfect vehicle for teaching the basic fundamentals of harmony to anyone, particularly preschool children. The system is so good, I later helped Miss Remington put her music games in package form, and with instruction books to go with the four sets of games. We had them published. I try to convey to my students the love and enthusiasm for music, which I feel so strongly myself. I give them music appreciation along with the theory and practical application at the keyboard at the weekly private lessons, with the opportunity to perform at monthly group classes so they learn more about music in general and also learn from each other.

By 1951 I was eager to play more myself and looked for a partner to enjoy two-piano repertoire. I love the ensemble work and need a goal for performance. I asked Dorothy Merrill Ritter, who was still the music director at Tudor Hall, whom she knew who might want to play with me. She was playing professionally with Louise Sparks. When I heard them play a recital, I was more interested than ever to team up with someone also. She suggested Virginia Campbell, and subsequently, we were introduced. We arranged practice times together once a week and began to work. Virginia lived just a few blocks away, but not having two pianos, she always came to my house for the sessions, which we found ourselves enjoying more and more. Until Mother gave me her Steinway, we practiced at the Jordan School of Music at 34th and Pennsylvania.

Cousin Frances Ball, Arthur's wife, had asked me to store her Mason and Hamlin piano for her, and it was moved from Muncie and lovingly placed in our parlor downstairs. Here, Judy and Ann were able to practice without interfering with my teaching schedule after school hours. Our home sounded like a conservatory of music!

4106 Washington Blvd., Indianapolis, Indiana

Sam

Lucina in China Poblana dress, reminiscing about Mexico

*Mother posing with
her portrait*

Maureen Clark, General Mark Clark, Mother

[245]

CHAPTER FORTY-FIVE

IN the summer of 1953 our entire family went to Europe. The trip was triggered by President Dwight D. Eisenhower's appointment of Dad to attend the ceremony of Rhodesia's independence from Great Britain as his special ambassador. Dad was working for the C.I.A. in Washington, D. C., and my parents had lived in Georgetown during Dad's two-year service. Dad, quite honored and excited by the appointment, accepted.

Our entourage left New York on the S. S. *Independence* and sailed to Naples, Italy. My brother Bill, Mother and Dad, Judy, Ann, Sam and I made up the family group. Judy and Ann were then ten and twelve years old, eagerly anticipating a European adventure.

Judy was at the stage where she could act like a young lady when under pressure, and in the evenings for the formal dinners, looked quite grown up in her best dresses. One day Sam saw her with a group of other children playing in the lounge, bounding around the furniture, jumping on the sofas, hiding behind the chairs and shrieking with delight. Sam spoke to Judy, trying to make her understand she shouldn't act like such a hoodlum on the ship. He told her she was getting too old for such antics. Looking up at him with a serious expression she asked, "But Daddy, can't I be a little girl in the daytime and be grown up at night?"

Sam and Bill left the ship at Genoa to pick up an Italian Fiat 1900 which we would drive throughout the trip and ship home when we left from Gibraltar on the S. S. *Constitution*. Sam drove it to Naples where we all converged when the ship landed two days later.

Sam did the driving because Bill was recovering from a head-on automobile accident. He almost lost a leg when the ignition keys penetrated his kneecap from the impact. The collision caused him to lose the cartilage and eighty-five percent mobility of his knee. With perseverance and exercise, Bill finally regained most of the mobility he had lost.

We saw Dad off in Rome on a new jet plane, a British Comet bound for Rhodesia, Africa. I was terrified of the roaring engines, the first jet I had ever heard, and was fearful for Dad. Less than a month later, the same Comet blew up in the air on the same journey to Africa, killing everyone aboard.

Squeezed into the tiny car were six of us. Sam, Ann and Bill on the front seat, and Mother, Judy and I on the back seat. Mother and I couldn't resist buying things that caught our fancy as we went along. In Italy we drove up into the mountains on the Amalfi Drive, stopping to admire pottery and pretty dishes displayed in a small, roadside shop. We each bought a set of dishes, which were boxed and tied on top of the roof rack, already full of luggage. More luggage was tied to another baggage rack over the trunk of the car. Small packages continued to accumulate in the car as we toured Italy, Switzerland, France, Spain and Portugal during the ensuing six weeks. Sam alone knew how to load all our baggage, approaching the challenge as a giant jig-saw puzzle. He loaded and unloaded thirty-one pieces of baggage every day from the car to the hotels and back again! The hotels refused responsibility for anything left in the car. Sam developed a new set of muscles hoisting the boxes and bags because he refused help every time.

We drove from Naples to Rome, to Venice, and from there up into the Alps of Switzerland. With the heavy load, Sam had to exert all his efforts to make the car perform throughout the mountainous journey. To keep the momentum going, he would gun the motor as we swung around the hairpin turns at great speed. Mother and I were in fear and panic on the back seat, biting our tongues to keep from crying out in alarm. Mother calmed us by peeling juicy Italian peaches, which we bought from roadside vendors, doling out sections as we drove. The only type of instrument which we had was a nail file, and Mother made do, becoming an expert. In Interlochen, Mother presented her no-longer-presentable peachstained dress to a hotel maid.

Bill remained in Venice, promising to catch up with us later. The Lido Beach and the attractive girls in their skimpy "teenyweenie bikinis" were a temptation Bill could not resist. Bikinis were the newest swim wear on the Riviera and had not yet infiltrated the American beaches.

<hr/>

Recalling his arduous pursuits for the opposite sex, I am reminded of an incident. Bill Ball and Bill Bone are lifelong friends. The boys grew up together as sons of Mother and Gladys Bone, who were also lifelong friends. One summer during their college days they struck out for Los Angeles to spend their vacation on the beaches. En route they visited fraternity brothers or spent the nights in Beta Theta Pi houses, wherever they could find them, to save their travel money.

Once in Los Angeles they were eager to meet beautiful girls, but found it was not easy to find girls willing to be "picked up" by two boys, albeit attractive. They devised a scheme to attract the girls with a monkey and took it to the beach. Leashed, friendly and full of antics, the monkey soon had a crowd of giggling bathing beauties clustered around admiring it. In no time at all the boys had "the pick of the litter," so to speak, with more opportunities for dates than they had cash to spend.

They devised another plan. Once a week they appeared at the local blood bank, parted with a pint of blood, and left with twenty-five dollars each — enough for a modest evening of entertainment with the girls of their choice. They discovered, however, after several weeks of late nights and blood-giving, their energies were so low they couldn't enjoy the evenings to the fullest.

After we were settled in our rooms at the luxurious Grand Victoria Hotel, Sam and I decided to explore the night life and get a little supper, as we had not eaten since our lunch of peaches. We were directed to a Weinstube by the concierge and walked two blocks to find the place — a large hall, packed with tables around a dance floor. We decided to order a Swiss cheese sandwich and a glass of beer, but couldn't make the waitress understand, as she spoke little English. She had no idea what we meant by Swiss cheese, and we had no idea what other name that good Swiss cheese with holes in it was called! We described a sandwich using hand signals and kept insisting on *Swiss* cheese. She finally shook her head in bewilderment and took off toward the kitchen.

To our amazement and mortification, she appeared bearing an entire loaf of French bread and a stack of Swiss cheese that must have weighed five pounds. We were embarrassed at such a pile of food for the two of us, causing our neighbors to stare at us wide-eyed with no little amusement.

We ate what we could, but there was so much left, I surreptitiously wrapped chunks of it in the paper napkins and stuffed them into my purse and coat pockets until they were bulging. At the end of the evening, the patrons near us were even more amazed to think we had eaten all of the bread and cheese on the tray! For several days our family had snacks of Emmenthaler instead of juicy peaches.

We learned in Interlochen that a general strike had begun in France where we were bound. All transportation and communication was at a standstill. There were no trucks, trains, buses or planes operating — no telephones or post offices. We were concerned we might have difficulty buying fuel for the car on our way to Paris if gas stations were closed also. So we stayed several more days in Interlochen, not minding the delay since we loved the little town and the comfortable Victoria Hotel.

The strike was still on with no signs of arbitration, but we were assured by news reports that many filling stations were in business. So we pushed on to France, Bill joining us in Zurich en route.

We arrived in Paris, practically empty of traffic — a surprising phenomenon for this city of crowded streets and impatient, honking vehicles. Mother insisted we go to the George Cinq Hotel as this is where we would meet Dad on his return from Rhodesia.

The only available rooms were suites. One of them accommodated us comfortably, and we settled down to wait for the strike to end so Dad could get to Paris. We took the children sightseeing, and Bill did his own kind of sightseeing — for attractive girls. He found one in the person of Choux Catoise.

Choux (a nickname meaning cabbage) worked at the Hotel Meurice selling perfumes. She was vivacious, charming and attractive with soft, fluffy blond hair. We took her with us to help locate an address for Mother who wanted to buy a French poodle.

Sam drove up one street and down another, looking for the elusive address, and finally asked Choux to ask directions of a passerby. She reluctantly complied, relaying the information that we were to drive sixteen blocks further on. We drove and drove, but the street did not appear. So another person was asked directions, who said we were going in the opposite direction. Again unsuccessful in our search, we asked several more people, including a policeman, and after an hour or more of endless turning and twisting, finally found the right street. Sam asked Choux with perplexity why she couldn't understand the directions of all those people? She said, "But, of course, they didn't know where the street was!" "Why then," he said, "didn't they *say* they didn't know? "Oh," she replied, "that would have been very rude."

After several days planes began flying again, and we welcomed Dad when he arrived from Africa. He was bubbling with news of his exciting adventure and reported he was treated as though he were President Eisenhower himself. As he stepped off the plane from Rome, he said, a welcoming band was playing "The Star Spangled Banner" in his honor, and he was escorted in a black limousine with a body guard everywhere he went. He told us Queen Elizabeth of Great Britain was there, along with many dignitaries from representative countries, and he was impressed to meet and talk with so many V.I.P.'s. He took movies of the ceremonies and felt the experience was one of the high points of his life.

Sam was running out of money. He had been paying for the six of us during the entire trip, and the exorbitant prices in Paris were draining his funds. He had barely enough money to leave France. The strike was preventing him from wiring for more money from the States. He did have his personal check book, if foreigners would accept a check when his travelers checks ran out.

My birthday had arrived, and Sam wanted to celebrate with a dinner party at the famous Tour d'Argent, a restaurant we had read about in Art Buchwald's tour guide of Europe. Buchwald suggested that tourists ask to visit the room at Tour d'Argent were they stored all the silver extracted from the diners. Sam knew it was renowned as the most expensive restaurant in Paris, but also one of the best, and decided to throw caution to the winds and take us there to dinner.

That morning at breakfast at the George Cinq, we indulged the children "just this once" in a deviation from the continental breakfast, croissant and beverage. The menu featured Cornflakes, Wheaties and Grape Nuts. Sam noted they were $1.75 a serving and reasoned it was a

[249]

long way to ship cereal from America. He said they could order what they liked. When the waiter arrived Judy asked, "Do you have Rice Krispies, too?" "yes," he said. "Then, I would like Rice Krispies, orange juice and hot chocolate." Anne ordered the same.

Sam and I couldn't resist having a glass of orange juice with our continental breakfast too. The bill came to thirty-two dollars for the four of us. The Rice Krispies were $6.50 a serving because they were not on the menu.

This type of rip-off was common in Paris. We were charged $125.00 for a small amount of laundry and pressing, and a surcharge of $60.00 for the phone bill. When Sam reminded the cashier there had been no phones working during our entire stay because of the strike, he replied, "But the phones were in your suite."

Thus, when Sam reserved a table at The Tour d'Argent, he was prepared for the worst. To complicate matters further, Bill, enamored of Choux, invited her and her parents to come along, and Dad asked two other men he had just met at a perfume factory to join us with their wives.

In all, there were fourteen of us seated at a long table. Sam, waiving away the proffered menus, asked the maitre de what he thought best for all of us. Delighted, he suggested a soup, aspargus vinagrette, fish course, duck a l'orange, baked alaska for dessert, followed by nuts and coffee. Sam ordered it all for everyone, then gave the sommelier an order for his five suggested wines, one to complement each course.

The dinner was superb, and Sam had made up his mind that if they would not accept his personal check in payment, he was prepared to wash dishes afterwards. But the bill for the entire dinner came to just $145.00, a miraculous windfall for Sam. He expected an astronomical price after giving the waiter carte blanche in the reputedly most expensive establishment in France. We thought it was either a gross error on the part of the management, or, more likely, the fact that half of our party were French. If all of us had been Americans the bill probably would have been much higher.

———————— ◈ ————————

Bill decided to stay in Paris to enjoy the company of Choux until it was time to board the ship in Gibraltar, leaving room for Dad to ride in the Fiat with us. After one look at the car with its cramped space, and Dad bought a Jaguar so that we'd all be more comfortable on the last stage of our journey. The cars would be shipped home with us and resold at Dad's new foreign car agency, Auto-Imports in Indianapolis. The plan was for us to drive ahead with the children. Mother and Dad would follow three days later and meet us in St. Jean de Lux before crossing the border to Spain.

Sam was anxious to leave Paris, which he had grown to hate, and we left to visit the chateaux in the Loire valley. We relaxed after the hectic pace of Paris loving the beautiful chateaux, which I remembered from our first European trip twenty years earlier. We meandered through the countryside of southern France and finally arrived at our charming hotel in St. Jean de Lux, a seaside resort town near the border of Spain.

My parents had not arrived. We had dinner and waited anxiously for word from them. At nine o'clock, Mother and Dad finally arrived, weary and nervous. They had forgotten the name of the hotel where we were to meet, and, to add to the problem, Sam had inadvertently carried off Mother's passport and no hotel would admit her without proper identification. For several hours, they worried and scouted various hotels trying to find us. Then Mother thought of inquiring at the police station where we would be listed from our hotel registry.

We rested a day longer in St. Jean de Lux, then set out for Spain late in the afternoon with the Jaguar trailing the Fiat. As we drove along the deserted road "the rain in Spain" began to pour. Night was falling, and suddenly the head lights and electric windshield wipers of our Fiat went out. We could no longer lead the way in the darkness. Mother and Dad exchanged places with us, and we drove slowly along behind the Jaguar following its tail lights. In order to see through the downpour, Sam drove with his head out the window, rain pelting his face.

It was very late when we reached the Parador in Burgos. We had made reservations there because of a high recommendation from David Moxley. We arrived at ten p.m., exhausted from the effort of the last stage of the drive, longing for a bath and a comfortable bed.

The desk clerk shook his head and denied we had reservations, saying we were supposed to have been there the night before. We discovered we were a day late and had lost track of the time because of the confusion caused by the strike in France. There were just two rooms available, provided the people who had reserved them didn't show up within the half hour. As for the third room, they called other inns, but there was nothing. Finally, he announced there was a "chalet" nearby with a room available. Sam and I eagerly agreed to go to the chalet which sounded quaint and charming.

Sam and I returned to our blacked-out Fiat and followed another car to the chalet, through a gate to a dark, two-story square house set in the middle of a mud wallow made by the rain. We waded through it to the front door, illuminated by the headlights of the hotel car. A light glimmered, and the door was opened by an elderly woman in night clothes. As we stepped across the sill, we were nearly knocked backwards by the nauseating smell of burned olive oil, which had apparently been building in intensity for years. Resisting the desire to hold our noses, we

[251]

followed her to the second floor where she showed us our room, facing the mud wallow. A bare bulb hanging from the ceiling gave us a dim view of the room. The sagging double bed had a colorful pillow decorating the headboard. It was appropriately, a large red, ladybug. An upright wooden chair was the only other piece of furniture.

We inspected the bathroom and were repelled by dozens of large, greenish flies, lazily flying around in drunken circles, most of them centered in the toilet bowl and wash basin. We could not wash or use the bathroom at all.

When we looked at the bed more closely, gingerly pulling back the covers, we saw gray sheets, unwashed and obviously slept on for a long time. We decided we had to lie down and rest, spreading our bathrobes over the bed, and keeping most of our clothes on. We considered slipping down the stairs again to our car to sleep, but the woman had bolted the door behind us and left the house in total darkness.

We had no sooner fallen on the bed, groaning in misery, than head-lights appeared again through our curtainless windows. We knew it would be Dad in the Jaguar.

Dad appeared at the door of our room, exclaiming, "I can't stay in that awful hotel! I've come over here to be with you!" We laughed and joked together when he saw how bad the situation was with us but he took it all with good grace, disappearing into the room across the hall. It wasn't long before our door opened again and something flew at us on the bed. It was another "bug" pillow — this one a bright orange with purple spots. Dad tossed it in to keep company with our red and black ladybug.

At first light, after a sleepless night, we crept downstairs and opened the door, hoping to sneak out to the parador. A huge police dog, not vicious, but vociferous, greeted us with loud barks and awakened the woman, who appeared to call off the dog. Too late! he had already jumped all over me, leaving heavy, muddy tracks all over my dress.

We found our way back to the parador, where I could hardly wait to take a cleansing shower in the children's bathroom. But there wasn't any water. The children couldn't even brush their teeth.

So much for Burgos. In retrospect we have recalled that night often with much laughter.

1953 was the first year Franco permitted tourists to visit Spain after their revolution. The country was very poor, and, in August, the land-scape was a dusty brown from drought as far as the eye could see. I remember Spain as an etching in brown and black. No flowers relieved the drabness, and even the people wore nothing but those colors, the majority of them in mourning black for some family member. The drive all the way to Madrid was depressing, and we were reminded of Mexico as there was much similarity in the homes and general atmosphere. But Spain was much more distressed than Mexico at that time. Few cars but many horses and carts traveled the highway, causing my Father to remark there was "nothing to see along the way but you and me and manure."

Madrid appeared as an oasis in the desert. It was a beautiful city, and we stayed at The Ritz Hotel, elegant and richly furnished. Here the service was good, and the staff got in each other's way racing to answer our calls. We loved Madrid, where the buildings were painted a fresh white, grass grew in the parks, and a feeling of prosperity was in the air. Compared to the prices in France, Spain was inexpensive. Our beautiful rooms at The Ritz cost three dollars a day. Today, the rate is one hundred and forty dollars a day.

We no sooner arrived in Madrid when Bill called from Paris. We were terribly excited, eager to learn if Bill had become engaged to Choux. Instead, he was excited about something else. He wanted permission from Dad to buy a racing sport car, a Sciata Spyder, which he had seen in Paris and asked if he could have it shipped home. Dad agreed that Bill could have the car and reconfirmed our schedule to meet Bill in Gibraltar in time to board the ship.

We drove to Lisbon from Madrid, traversing more of the brown, dusty terrain, which we thought dreary and ugly. Crossing the border into Portugal, the scenery changed dramatically. We saw homes decorated with bright flowers cascading out of window boxes, people wearing colorful clothes and no sign of drought as we drove across the country. The biggest change we noticed was in the people themselves. In Spain, everyone had been friendly, welcoming and humble. The Portuguese were hostile, suspicious and even rude. It began at the border when we were delayed a long time by the Nazi-trained police who inspected our credentials to each cross of a "t" and dot of an "i". They tried hard to find a reason why we couldn't enter Portugal as tourists. After a long wait in the heat, tired and uncomfortable from the journey, we were reluctantly permitted to drive on to Estoril on the coast.

We had been told the beaches at Estoril were the best in Europe, but in our estimation they were poor compared to the marvelous Lido beach in Venice. We also visited the great fortress monastery of Sintra, a little further north of Estoril, a castle we have returned to on every visit to Portugal since. It is one of the most fascinating and grotesque structures of medieval times I have ever seen, perched at the top of an almost inaccessible mountain with a breathtaking view of the surrounding country below its turrets.

We drove down the coast to Lisbon, and found it an interesting city, and from there continued our drive along the coastline to Gibraltar, Spain. On the way, we saw a young man hitchhiking. Because he was dressed in kilts,

I felt compelled to make Sam stop and give him a ride. He had been traveling through Europe and told us wearing kilts improved his ability to get rides. He was right. They made him look very handsome, and "an honest Scotsman." We took him to Seville where we had rooms reserved at the Alphonso XIII, but he told us he would find a room nearby, at a fraction of the cost of our rooms, and meet us in the morning to continue on to Gibraltar.

The next morning, he appeared and told us he had stayed right cross the street at a pension for fifty cents, including breakfast and the pressing of his kilts.

We left Spain reluctantly, liking it more the longer we stayed, and very sorry it was almost time to sail home. We found Gibraltar disappointing as a town, and the Rock Hotel, which was a stiffly run British establishment, a poor excuse for a good hotel. It was run down, but too "high class" to permit children in the open air dining room. The children made up for the insult by leaning out the window of their room to talk to us while we dined below. We were highly amused by the disconcerted staff as we were the cause of the loud talking in the otherwise silent dining room.

Bill had arrived, and the next morning we boarded a lighter, which carried us to the S.S. *Constitution*, and we were homeward bound.

Christamore Follies show: Lucina and Verne Bailie sing a duet

Virginia Campbell and Lucina Moxley two-piano team

The mule trip down the Grand Canyon

Agustina and Julio Ramos

[255]

CHAPTER FORTY-SIX

T HE years passed. Sam worked hard to strengthen and expand Haag Drug Company and was most successful. In 1951 he joined Affiliated Drug Company in New York, which met twice a year for seminars on merchandise promotion and displays to increase sales. Every spring, the National Association of Chain Drug Stores met in Florida at the Hollywood Beach Hotel for a convention. We attended every year to renew acquaintances and enjoy the social and business aspects of the meetings. Sometimes, after the convention, we extended our stay for another week of sunning in Jamaica, or Havana, or perhaps, just a leisurely drive home, stopping at Sea Island on the way.

The children were growing into young ladies and doing well in school at Tudor Hall, and I continued to be busy with my growing roster of pupils and two-piano programs with Virginia Campbell.

In December of 1958, Julio and Agustina wanted to return to Mexico and marry. Julio had saved enough to enable him to support Agustina so she would not have to work and Ana went home with them, not wanting to be left alone. I wrote to Balbina asking her to come and work for us. I insisted she bring her two daughters as I didn't want her to be without her family. The three of them arrived not long after the departure of the Ramoses. Balbina cooked for us, and Lola and Alicia went to school at P.S. 66, not far from our home. The girls, the same ages as Judy and Ann, became their good friends and companions, and Balbina was another mother to my girls. We were a happy family and worked together to keep our large house clean and in order. We all had chores, and I hired a man to do the heaviest work in the house and yard.

Every two years the Christamore Aid Society put on a benefit to raise money for the Christamore Settlement house, which they supported. It was a professionally staged and managed variety show packaged by Cargill Productions in New York. Scenery and costumes were shipped to us along with a staff of directors and a producer. Indianapolis supplied the cast and rehearsed diligently for two weeks prior to the production, which was staged at the Murat Temple. With the expert directing, the Follies turned into a polished professional show, attended by a full house of enthusiastic supporters. A great deal of money was raised.

I auditioned for a singing part, and sang in the last two Christamore Follies before the Society turned to other ways for their benefits. My solos were in the "production numbers." The first was set on the desert sands and I sang "The Shiek of Araby" in a harem costume of filmy chiffon. It should have been seductive, but I think I turned it into low comedy. Two years later I appeared with Verne Bailey. We sang a pretty duet and my

[256]

costume was glamourous. It was a hoop skirt covered with white velvet and strung with pearls and rhinestones.

I became a member of Christamore in 1960 and worked at the house for two years, helping the youngsters learn a little music. I found the time spent with the children both rewarding and discouraging, as several in my group were eager to learn, but the majority disrupted the class. After a few frustrating sessions trying to keep them quiet, listen to records and play the music games, I separated the serious ones and gave them individual lessons at the piano. I felt these few gained some music appreciation in the long run, but would probably never have an opportunity to develop their potentials due to the environment in which they lived.

———————◄◉►————————

During spring vacation in 1956, Wayne and Dottie Ritter and their three boys, Lanny, Dwight and Pete, joined us for a trip to Mexico. We were excited to revisit our most favorite place and eager to see our friends again. We stayed at the inexpensive Hotel Cortez, across from the fancy Del Prado Hotel on Juarez. We liked the colonial atmosphere of the old hotel which had been a monastery at the time of the conqueror, Cortez. The rooms ranged from poor to mediocre, but the outdoor patio where meals were served, was brilliant with flowers, flamboyant trees and bouganvillia on the pillared walkways surrounding the patio. In the center, an ancient stone fountain bubbled and beautiful hand-painted tiles decorated the base. In the evenings, charcoal grills were lit by each table to warm the chilled air during dinner, and after the meal, there was folk dancing and a fireworks display.

We saw the highlights of Mexico City, then drove to San Jose de Purua for an overnight visit. We also returned to our favorite resort between Cuernavaca and Taxco, Vista Hermosa. Dottie and Wayne fell in love with the place and for years afterwards spent every vacation there. The children loved swimming in the fabulous pool and took turns diving off the high aqueduct into the deep blue water.

We arranged a visit with the Ramoses, Julio and Agustina, who now had two little girls, Mercedes and Frances, ages two and one. They told us they wanted to return to Indianapolis as Julio's grocery store business was not as profitable as he had hoped. Ana also was eager to return, and the Ritters were looking for someone to work for them. Sam helped them process their immigration papers and arranged a job for Julio at Haag Drug Co. Ana came to work for the Ritters, and Julio and his family followed her to Indianapolis, where they still live today.

Ana worked for the Ritters for several years, but then decided to try her wings elsewhere. She went to New York City and worked for a doctor's family as nursemaid. She met and married Martin Schneider, a German immigrant who spoke neither English nor Spanish. We often wondered

[257]

how they communicated, but sign language can be very effective! When their daughter, Nancy, was born, Ana became fearful of crime-ridden New York and persuaded Martin to move back to Indianapolis, where they live within a block of the Ramoses. Although none of them ever worked for us again, we remain good friends and have seen each other often.

<hr/>

That summer we took Judy and Ann on a tour of our western United States and visited most of our National Parks en route. We piled into Sam's station wagon and headed southwest in June. The girls studied the tour guidebook and map on the way to figure out the distances we were to travel, and how long it would take us to reach our destination for the night. They also chose the motels and places to stop. Of course they always chose motels with swimming pools, which was agreeable to us as we were ready for a swim when we reached the motels.

We remember the trip as one of the best we ever took. We planned it for the complete enjoyment of the children but ended up loving every minute of it ourselves. If the girls wanted to stop by a mountain stream and wade in among the rocks for awhile, we did too, freezing our legs in the icy water and laughing with pain and pleasure. We only had a few reservations in key spots, such as the National Parks, and spaced our travel to arrive without pushing for these places.

Our first important stop was Santa Fe, New Mexico, where we drank in the atmosphere of Western Indian culture and shopped for Indian jewelry. We drove to Gallup and visited the Zuni Indian village, then moved on to view the Painted Desert, Petrified Forest and the awesome Grand Canyon of Arizona.

As I write, I am reading Ann's account of the trip — her diary and daily log of events. But her description of the muleback ride down into the Grand Canyon is somewhat different from our impression of that day. She wrote: "We got on the mules about 9:15 to go down Grand Canyon. I was behind the guide. When we first started I looked down and got dizzy, but I got over it. We had lunch at the bottom, and I fed a lot of squirrels and deer with bread. Then we started up again. We had to stop a lot so the mules could get their breath. It was a lot of fun. I think we are going to be sore tomorrow."

Sam and I remember riding at the tail end of the mule train. The dust was so thick we tied handkerchiefs around our noses and mouths to filter the air. It was frightening to look down, so we saw little of the magnificent view, intent as we were on keeping our mules on the narrow trail. All we really saw was the rear end of the mule ahead of us. Judy's mule was Captain, but we called him the Lead-Pee Mule, because he stopped every ten minutes to relieve himself. Every mule behind him had to go on Captain's spot, flooding the path into slippery mud. By the time we got to the spot, we were afraid of a washout and a slip over the precipice. At the hairpin turns, the mules would tuck their legs into a sort of pedestal and turn with heads and necks far out over the emptiness of space. The riders were also suspended in space at this point, as the rear end of the mule was backed into the rock wall behind him. This part of the ride caused intense excitement. We felt as a hang glider might, floating over nothingness.

The ride threw us forward into the saddle as we made our way down the two-thousand foot drop to a clearing where we thankfully dismounted and had lunch. The trek had lasted almost three hours. After an hour's rest, we had to face the return trip, an agonizing ascent, taking almost twice as long. This time the rest of our body took a beating as we were thrown backwards in the saddle. The width of a mule is greater than a horse, very much like doing the splits as you sit astride.

Sam and I hurried to our showers to be the "first in." After a barrage of hot water to wash off the mule smell and relieve our aches and bruises, we headed for the bar for doubles! We no sooner began to relax and appreciate the comfort of the soft lounge and a warming drink when Ann bounded in, eager and excited, "Daddy, I've just met some girls who are going on the mule trip in the morning! Please, could we go down again with them?"

Our trip continued on to Bryce Canyon and Zion National Parks and then to Las Vegas. At that time Las Vegas was just beginning to develop from a small western town into a city. Tourists were flocking to Nevada, where gambling was legal, to play the slot machines. Soon large modern hotels were built with the accent on gambling facilities. To draw trade, entertainment was added at dinner, and the hotels competed with each other for the most glamourous floorshows. We had an excellent dinner and saw a show featuring Peter Lynd Hayes and Mary Healy for a very reasonable price. We stayed at The Sands, brand new that year, inexpensive and luxurious.

We crossed Death Valley to California and drove up the coast, visiting Sequoia National Forest, marvelling at the immense trees, some two-thousand years old. Highly impervious to disease, they live on, continuing to grow for centuries, unless they fall, a victim of their own size and weight.

We reached Yosemite National Park on Fourth-of-July Weekend, the worst possible choice of dates to view one of our nation's most spectacular parks. It was jammed with humanity, long lines of people waiting for meals or the bathroom, and driving their cars in single file lanes snailing the mountainous roads for miles. We stayed at Camp Curry, which we thought not only crowded but dirty and uncomfortable. It was particularly uncomfortable to leave the warmth of bed and walk the trail to the bath house in the chill night air. The one redeeming feature of Yosemite was its

[259]

magnificent beauty, but it was hard to see it through the mobs of tourists. Every evening there was a fire-fall down the mountain waterfall. At one thousand feet above us, burning logs were pushed over the edge of the falls simulating a firework display of golden fire and sparks as they fell down the mountain, the waterfall extinguishing the fire at the floor of the canyon. It was a spectacular sight.

Because of the unpleasant congestion we left Camp Curry sooner than we had planned and drove to San Francisco. Here we spent a week revisiting our favorite haunts such as Julius's Castle, Trader Vic's and the Cliff House. The zoo and the aquarium pleased the children, and we loved the interesting city with the roller coaster streets. Ann became ill with a virus, but we stayed on until she was well enough to travel.

We left the pleasures of San Francisco regretfully, and headed east through the mountain passes to Lake Tahoe, Sun Valley and Jackson Hole, Wyoming. After showing the girls the wonders of Yellowstone Park, we drove on for a week's stay at the IXL Ranch near the famous Eaton's Ranch in Wyoming. Here we enjoyed the ranch activities of horseback trails, barbecues and square dances. It was a small ranch, unpretentious with a homey atmosphere. We had our own cabin, but meals were served in the main house. We were each assigned a horse for the duration of our stay and rode daily on short or long trips, led by one of the hands. Judy and Ann loved everything about the IXL.

The highlight of the week was an all-day ride up the mountains to a small clearing where we had a picnic. There were possibly ten in our group, and most of the day was spent snaking carefully around the narrow trails along precipitous paths, reminding us of the mule trip at Grand Canyon. Horses are not as surefooted as mules, and I was alert at every step, nervous tension prickling my spine, as we made our way in single file, brushing the rocky mountain wall on one side and viewing the chasm below on the other.

At last we arrived at a small plateau where we dismounted and had our lunch. It was pleasant to relax for awhile before starting back to the ranch. Deer grazed nearby, and some were brave enough to take our offerings of food.

We decided to leave when the sky darkened and a misty rain began to fall. We mounted quickly and started out of the clearing at a trot toward the steep descending mountain path. Judy was just ahead of me, and as my horse began to trot, I caught a flash of her yellow wind-breaker as it blew off her saddle horn. My horse caught sight of the yellow flash at the same time, and in an instant, sidestepped and left me on the ground still holding the reins. It happened so quickly the woman behind me did not even see me fall. It was an ignominious accident, since I was the only one in the group who knew how to ride! My finger was twisted painfully from the jerk on the reins in my hand, but otherwise I was not hurt except for the jar and shock of the fall. When I mounted the horse again, I prayed thankfully we were still in the clearing when my horse spooked. A small sidestep on the mountain path would have hurled us into space over the precipice. I was very shaken on the trip back, sore in every bone, my injured finger swollen and throbbing. Tears of pain, and yet relief over my narrow escape of serious injury overcame me as we rode back. To make the trip more exciting, the lead horse carrying our guide spotted a rattlesnake near the path. He reared up in alarm, causing the first few horses to react in fear. Ann was riding directly behind him. We were relieved to see how well she controlled her horse and kept him from bolting by turning him around to face our train. The guide shot the rattler while the rest of us quieted our horses as best we could, but two of the horses bolted and raced toward the ranch, which was in sight further down the trail. We were horrified to see that Judy was on one of the run-away horses, and we watched until she reached safety at the barn. She was terrified by the experience and vowed never to ride a horse again. Unlike Ann who loved horses as much as I did, Judy was timid and fearful of the animals.

The day proved to be exciting, and one I didn't care to repeat. Of all the times in my life I had fallen off horses, this was the first time I had ever been hurt. We drove to a nearby town the next morning to have an X-ray of my finger, discolored and bent out of shape, and very painful. I was relieved to discover there was no bone broken, but the capsule in the joint was broken. The doctor said the finger would never straighten, nor would I be able to flex it. Thanks to my piano playing and diligent exercise of the finger, manipulating and massaging the sore and stiff joint, it gradually began to move more normally. After a few years, it was completely normal. Tom Brady, our orthopedic doctor in Indianapolis declared it was the best recovery of a broken capsule he had ever seen. Only a slight thickening of the joint and a stiff feeling when I extend or bend the finger remains.

The children cried when they said goodbye to the ranch and the friends they had met while there. They thought the week at IXL was the highlight of the entire trip. Ann stopped writing in her diary as she considered everything that we did from then on an anti-climax.

There was a stop for two days at a delightful, out-of-the-way retreat in South Dakota. Palmer Gulch Lodge was a small resort hidden in the Black Hills. We had seen a clever brochure of the place, as we planned our itinerary for the trip, and thought it might be a good choice for an overnight stop. It advertised "pets welcome" under a picture of a buffalo. It was difficult to find the Lodge as it was on a winding back road through unmarked country, but eventually we saw a post and rail fence with a painted sign announcing the property. It was a place we will always remember as a comfortable resort, quaintly and attractively decorated with Victorian antiques, and the dining room serving the most deliciously prepared food. We were not prepared for such gourmet meals and thought them to be better than the exotic fare served in the best restaurants of San Francisco.

We have always longed to go back to Palmer Gulch Lodge, but the opportunity never presented itself. There were private cabins and a lake on the property. The establishment offered hiking, fishing trips, horseback rides and trips to "Them Faces," (the mount Rushmore Mountain where four of our great Presidents are carved into the rock face.) We visited "Them Faces" and were impressed by the enormous representations of Washington, Lincoln, Jefferson and Teddy Roosevelt. We also stayed an extra day to attend an important rodeo event celebrating the Gold Rush days.

Homeward bound, we reviewed our journey with great pleasure. We agreed it had been a trip of fun and education. But the best of all was the closeness our family gained by enjoying it all together.

Sam selects an outrigger canoe in Pago-Pago, Samoa

Equator crossing on the Mariposa. Sam's role — the judge

[262]

Alex Scovell with daughter Janet, 1947

Lucina, doing a hula, wins first prize in most authentic costume

CHAPTER FORTY-SEVEN

T HE travel bug had bitten us, and we began to dream of seeing other corners of the world. I had always longed to take a cruise of the South Seas and visit tropical islands and Australia. So we planned our first adventure on the S.S. *Mariposa*. It was an ambitious trip for Sam as he would be away from work for five weeks and felt he could little afford such relaxation or expense. But we were enamored of the brochure, which spun images of the "Butterfly," the *Mariposa*, floating us off to the South Pacific ports.

We asked Sam's parents to join us, and they eagerly accepted, loving the thought of a cruise as much as we did. Hayes was recovering from a heart attack, and it was mandatory for him to rest from his practice in Louisville. We planned the trip together for several months, savoring the anticipation of the long voyage on a ship.

A young teacher from Tudor Hall was kind enough to stay with Judy and Ann while we were gone, to drive them to and from school and do the marketing and errands while Balbina kept house. The arrangement went smoothly while we were gone.

Leona and Hayes drove to Indianapolis, and from there we took a train to Chicago and changed to the sleek vista-dome for San Francisco. The trip on the train through the Feather River Canyon was as spectacular as any trip could be. We wound through the Rockies and drank in the beauty of the fall colors painting the forests with their vivid hues. It was late in September when we left, and snow had already fallen on the higher peaks of the mountains. Sitting in the vista-dome compartment on the train's roof was an exciting adventure all by itself, watching the moving panorama of our Golden West unfold as we twisted and turned into tunnels and alongside rushing rivers.

At last we were at the Oakland station and transferred to San Francisco by ferry boat, a trip I loved, as it made the approach to the exotic city even more exciting. The view of the hills covered with buildings and peaked by the Coit Tower on its wooded hill is still impressed in my mind like a picture postcard.

The ship was beautifully decorated with South Sea motifs and murals in the lounges and bars. The deck was large with a pool and areas for deck games and ping pong. Our cabin was attractive and comfortable with a spacious closet to hold our large wardrobe for the trip. I can't believe we could have taken a foot locker apiece as our luggage, but we did! We carried overnight bags as well. Drip-dry clothes were not on the market then, and we had to take enough changes of clothing to last the forty-three days, returning home with our footlockers stuffed with clothes to be laundered (and room to stuff all the "collectibles" we picked up en route.)

[264]

The sailing from San Francisco was unforgettable and breathtaking. It was a magical time. I was in a daze as the band played and serpentines were thrown from deck to dock. The ship's great whistle boomed from the stacks announcing our departure as we detached from land and glided silently out into the Bay, heading for the Golden Gate Bridge.

The sun was setting and a red-gold light played over the water, reflecting the sky. We approached the bridge, our last connecting link to America, slowly, escorted by the boat that would pick up the pilot after we cleared the channel. We watched, emotion building, as we finally glided under the Golden Gate's shadow and looked up to the great supporting girders and the tiny cars traveling above us. We were now at sea.

I never again experienced the same intense excitement on sailing. It was a new experience, more romantic than sailing on the Atlantic and to unknown, far distant ports. I felt alone, dislocated from anything tangible except the ship, our only link to civilization.

I wrote detailed letters every few days to the family at home, telling them about our travels, which turned out to be my diary of the trip. Mother saved the letters and gave them to me for safekeeping. To remember this trip, I hardly need to glance at them, as my memory is as clear and crisp as if it were yesterday. Our return to San Francisco was as memorable as our departure. The four of us stood with tears on our faces watching the skyline of San Francisco grow larger as we passed under the Golden Gate. None of us wanted to come back. The trip on the Mariposa had been the highlight of our lives.

It was rough, as it almost always is, on the sea between San Francisco and Los Angeles. The roughness begins so suddenly one doesn't have time to adjust to the motion of the ship, and people become seasick quickly. We were not affected, having taken the precaution to try the new dramamine pills before sailing. We sailed all night to Los Angeles, where we spent the day.

We rented a car at the dock and drove into the city, visiting several Huddle Restaurants. Sam had just started a similar chain of Huddle Restaurants in Indianapolis to incorporate into the larger drug stores, replacing the outdated soda fountains. He bought the Huddle rights in 1956 from the chain in Los Angeles, using the same name and menu. His first Huddle Restaurant in Indianapolis was at 56th and Illinois, the largest drug store east of the Mississippi at that time.

My brother, Bill, was instrumental in finding the type of restaurant Sam was looking for. He had been working for Sam since his graduation from Indiana University School of Business, first learning the silver business with Sam in Mexico and living with us there for awhile. After Bill joined Haag Drug Company, he lived with us on Washington Blvd. until his marriage. He was working for Sam in Los Angeles when he spotted the

Huddle Restaurants and called Sam to fly out and see their operation.

———————◆———————

Sam and I stood on deck and watched until the last lights of San Pedro harbor receded into the blackness of the night sometime after midnight. As the ship rolled and pitched, we reveled in the excitement of a long sea voyage.

The next day on board was everything one would expect on the South Seas — balmy, calm and perfect for swimming and sunning. The weather gradually increased in warmth as we neared the equator. The day of the equator crossing was a day of celebration on the ship. I escaped from being a "victim" of Neptune's by taking movies of the ceremony, but all the neophytes who had never crossed the equator before were held prisoner within a cable net on deck, dressed in bathing suits. One by one, a "prisoner" was dragged out of the net to be painted with mercurochrome and lipstick, shampooed with eggs and shaving cream, "operated on" and smeared with catsup, then flung into the pool. Sam was appointed the chief justice, dressed in a flowing robe and white wig of the British courts. Wearing his dark glasses, a painted-on mustache and tennis shoes, he was both severe and comical. Sam read off the list of "crimes" of each victim, judged them guilty, then pronounced sentences. Needless to say, at the end of the ceremony, he himself was thrown into the pool by the crowd of "victims."

———————◆———————

It was a wonderful pastime to sit and watch the sea. The gorgeous, bright blue color was so different from the Atlantic's cold green. The blue, green, purple and red flying fish fooled me as I thought they were birds from nowhere. At night the sky changed from the northern hemisphere with familiar shapes of the constellations to a starry sky confused by a different distribution of astronomical sparks of light. A galaxy of the Milky Way spread itself across the heaven, and we looked fruitlessly for the Southern Cross. There is a false cross that is large and well defined, but the true Southern Cross is small and hard to locate.

Sam had told me of the beautiful phosphorescence of the water at night that he'd seen at sea during the war, but this time our ship was brilliantly lighted instead of being blacked-out as during the war. We couldn't see the greenish, eerie light the microscopic plant life made. The only way I could see it was to go in the bathroom, turn out the lights and flush the toilet. Then the water flared in the stool with the bright green phosphorescence for a split second.

———————◆———————

I turned out to be a heroine on the ship. I was the first American to win the ping pong tournament over an Australian or New Zealander. Those nations are expert in all sports, and I was proud to be able to beat an Aussie in the finals. I won both the tournaments held during the voyage and received a pikake ivory necklace with matching earrings for my efforts. On the return trip my prize was a bracelet with a charm depicting the itinerary of the voyage on a map of the Pacific.

There were several costume parties on various occasions during the trip. At Halloween time, Sam and I dressed as ghosts. A South Sea island party turned me into a Tahitian hula dancer. I learned how to manipulate my hips from hula classes on board and won first prize as the "most authentic" as I hulaed across the dance floor. We managed crazy costumes each time the passengers were called upon to participate in the entertainment, and I sang in the passenger shows.

Sam and I love to play bridge, and every afternoon we would join a group for a duplicate tournament, or just play with another couple to pass the time. Movies and dancing were on the agenda for the evenings.

Leona and Hayes joined us at cocktail hour before dinner, and we enjoyed being with them every evening. Koko was our lively Finnish waitress, who was so efficient and charming she made our meals thoroughly enjoyable. It was always festive in the dining room, and the food was superb. Koko became such a friend of ours during the cruise we invited her to dinner when we returned to San Francisco.

After a week of beautiful sailing, we arrived at Papeete Harbor in Tahiti. Sam and I were up at dawn to watch the ship approach land. The sun was rising over the island in gold and red flames, and I was surprised to see such mountainous terrain. I had always pictured an island as flat and sandy. Tahiti rose up from an ancient volcanic eruption in the sea. The mountains were covered with lush tropical growth with black sandy beaches at their bases. The feeling of the island, the air, the colors, and the soft graceful Tahitians always smiling and gentle, were the things that made up the beauty and essence of the place.

As we approached the dock, a boat filled with lovely Tahitian girls in grass skirts came aboard loaded with leis. They swarmed over the ship, dropping leis of frangi-pani around our necks, intoxicating us with their delicate perfume. A native orchestra on the dock played as a group of girls in their long grass skirts danced for us. The Tahitian hula is quite different from the gentle Hawaiian hula, which is an undulating dance expressed by the hands. The Tahitian hula is all vibrating hips, which causes the grass skirts to shake like aspen leaves in a storm.

As we left the ship, more beautiful girls stood at the end of the gangplank placing wreaths of frangi-pani on our heads. Everyone on the island wore flowers in his hair, a crowning wreath, or at least a single hibiscus pinned over an ear. A flower over the right ear of a man signified he was looking for a partner, but if it was over the left ear, he was already "taken."

[267]

The town boasted one ten-room hotel — the Grand — which could be seen prominently from the harbor on a little rise above street level. We learned it was far from grand but did not walk over to inspect it. Smaller frame buildings made up the village, with homes and shops lining the few streets. Everything was simple, relaxed and friendly, with the emphasis on friendly.

As we walked along the dock toward town, we were enchanted by the myriads of bright colored, tropical fish playing among the rocks on the wharf. We could have stood for hours watching the angels, irridescent tetras and striped zebras darting in schools to feed on the algae clinging to the rocks. All colors and types swam together in confusion, making our tropical fish aquarium at home seem like a pale replica.

We were pulled away by the urgency of boarding an open jitney-style truck, which would take us on a tour of the island. We drove all day over dirt or gravel roads, viewing the lush scenery, Robert Louis Stevenson's and Gaugain's homes, and Captain Cook's Point, overlooking a long, black, sandy beach with no bathing tourists to destroy the view. At one point we were amused by a memorial to one of the Tahitian kings. His grave was marked by an enormous cement replica of a bottle of benedictine. We were told the king was devoted to the liquor, died from drinking too much of it, and honored by placing his preference over his grave.

The highlight of the day's journey was the stop for a luau at the home of the agent for the Matson line. It was a beautiful, landscaped property on a beach where we swam before lunch. We were given lava-lavas to wear, since none of us had brought bathing suits. These were simply lengths of brightly colored cloths with nothing to fasten them together, but when expertly draped on us by the Tahitian men and women, they could not come off as we swam.

After a refreshing swim in the clear blue water we were hungry for the luau, cooking under a great pile of earth called an umu. A fire had been built in the pit and a pig and other food, wrapped in banana or coconut leaves to contain them and enhance the flavor, were then placed on the hot coals and covered with a shallow layer of earth and linen cloths to keep the heat underground. Aromas from the smoking pit whetted our appetites as we waited, drinking long, tall rum punches to pass the time.

A view of the neighboring mountainous island of Moorea loomed up across the water, making a spectacular backdrop for our party. We were entertained by a large group of Tahitian men and women who did such wonderful hula dancing that I doubted if the men could ever get their eyes uncrossed, trying to take in all thirty women doing their twitches. Sam and Hayes were busy with their cameras. When we showed our movies later on, there was one point when the camera seemed to lose balance in Sam's hands. The picture veered off dizzily as though Sam was about to faint.

[268]

The luau was the most delicious food! The roast pig was cooked to perfection and the accompanying vegetables were uniquely prepared in their banana leaf packages. Baked bananas, breadfruit and spinach cooked in coconut cream was so delectable we have prepared it this way at home many times. Even the lavender poi was tasty, quite unlike the gray glue-tasting paste of Hawaiian poi.

Since we were only the eighth cruise ship to come to Tahiti, the island was yet unspoiled. But we learned an airport was being built. We were glad we were in Tahiti before it became overrun with tourists. It was twenty years before we went to Tahiti again. We were so disillusioned by the transformation of the island we did not leave the ship except for a brief walk to the town that was now a city. We noticed the people had changed too. They were no longer smiling and friendly, but appeared spoiled, sophisticated and bored. The prices were astronomical, the famous Quinn's Hut had burned down and the landmark Grand Hotel had been torn down for a highrise building.

We spent two days in Papeete, dropping in at Quinn's Hut several times. No matter at what hour, Quinn's was alive and jumping with dancing and drinking. Watching the action on the dance floor as we sipped Danish beer, was a revelation. Tahitian girls in great numbers danced with crewmen from our ship, who usually had several attached to each arm. The Tahitian men were not slouches either. They danced, equally as agile as the women, and "ran their motors" constantly. In fact, we noticed the Tahitians were so imbued with an inner rhythm, they walked down the street, switching their hips in time to their own inward music.

Our last day in this paradise was spent poking our noses into the shops and buying silk screen materials and carved wooden tikis, interspersed with visits to Quinn's. In the evening the town threw a party in the park for the ship. It was an all-night ball, formal and festive, and lasted until the ship sailed at six a.m. But we didn't last. We went back to the ship at one a.m. and got up again at five-thirty to watch us sail away. Many were on the dock to see us off including "the girls they left behind." Our departing view was of a young man who had been a passenger on the *Mariposa*, walking toward town with a girl on each arm. He had "jumped ship" to remain on the island paradise. We hung up our wilting leis and crowns in the cabin. The next night there was a South Sea costume party. Sam wore his newly-acquired lava-lava and hung the now dead frangi-pani leis around his neck, and placed the crown of wilted brown flowers on his head. With a sign announcing he was "tiredest lei in Tahiti" he received recognition with a prize. I had bought an entire armload of shell necklaces from a little girl, gifts for my pupils at home, and carried them as I had seen the vendors do, offering them for sale for "one dollah." I wore a Japanese happi coat of Leona's, a Tahitian hat woven with palm fronds, and blacked out several front teeth to look more authentic (a great flaw in

Tahitian features is the obvious lack of dentistry on the island.)

We sailed on to Aukland, New Zealand for a day. Aukland, a hilly city topped with red-roofed houses, looked more residential than commercial. The town had a quaint, old-fashioned air about it, and the number of sail boats in the harbor indicated New Zealanders loved the outdoor life.

We hired a taxi to see as much of the city as possible before we were due back on shipboard that afternoon. The most amazing thing we discovered was the profusion of flowers and their extraordinary size. Every home was nearly buried under cascades of flowers that tumbled over the fences and walls between properties. Most unusual was that every known species grown in different climates in other countries, grew together here, so much larger and more beautiful that they appeared to be entirely new species. Rock gardens stuffed with misem-bryanthemum (the New Zealanders call it "pig-face") in all colors of purple, pink and white spread into the hillsides, not satisfied to be contained.

Driving up and down the residential streets, oh-ing and ah-ing over the colorful sights, we learned from prominent signs there was a city-wide contest for the most beautiful home garden. We stopped to take pictures of one particularly beautiful garden. Birds of paradise, huge delphinium and stock made a background for the shorter stemmed tulips, poppies, calsideria, iris, and tropical wonders we had never seen before. Cascading down a rock wall was a fountain of wisteria and bougainvillia. Tucked in at the bottom of the wall in their own bed lining the sidewalk were pansies the size of saucers. A car drove up beside us and stopped as Hayes was adjusting his lens for a picture. The driver asked us why we were bothering with this garden. "It's not even in the competition," he said. "Go around the corner where you'll see some truly good ones."

We visited the zoo and saw the funny, nocturnal kiwi birds and tiny blue and white penguins about a foot tall, which are indigenous to New Zealand. The botanical garden house was an unforgettable sight with its extravagant display of orchids. We were especially entranced by a section containing nothing but pots of "pocket-books," which were double puff balls in myriads of colors, each "puff" the size and shape of a coin purse. We had never seen anything like them.

We returned to the ship in time to see the Maori entertainment, a wonderful show of singing and dancing. The music of this earliest Polynesian culture is beautiful and melodic, like something from the college songs of one's alma mater, or a church hymnal. The Maoris' skirts are made of thin bamboo strips tied together with black tape and give a rattling sound as they move. The ladies use poi balls expertly bouncing them on their bodies almost like a juggling act, except the balls are attached to strings wrapped around their fingers. The Maoris' faces are painted grotesquely with black designs and black lips to frighten away the

[270]

enemy. But they are far from a frightening people, very gentle and friendly. The population was just beginning to grow again after near extinction by the white man, although today there are very few pure-blooded Maoris left. We learned a great deal about their origin and culture at the museum in Aukland, which contained marvelous artifacts and information about the Polynesians, Melanesians and Micronesians of the Pacific Islands.

———————◄❖►———————

Crossing the Tasman Sea was rough, cold and windy — not unusual for this notoriously rough body of water. It was during the three-day journey to Sydney, Australia that we received a cable informing us of the death of Aunt Bertha Ball, and the news grieved me very much. I had always felt close to her and wished I could have been with the family and helped my cousin Janice in some way. A cable also arrived from Alex Scovell saying he would meet us at the dock in Sydney. I was anticipating the meeting with Alex with great anticipation after the twenty-year interval since we had last seen each other.

We had met many interesting Australians on the *Mariposa*, one couple in particular. Shortly after leaving Tahiti, we were having our cocktail hour in the lounge before dinner and noticed a gentleman alone at a nearby table. We had seen him often with his wife, but they never mixed with the other passengers and seemed to be left out socially. Impulsively, I asked him to join us at our table for a drink. He thanked me, but said he was waiting for someone. I told him when his wife arrived to join us. He answered with his Aussie accent, "She's not my wife. She's my lydie-friend." The four of us exchanged looks trying not to show our shock and surprise. But a little later, the "lydie" arrived, and they joined us.

As we became acquainted, we learned they were just coming home to Sydney after a year of travel around the world. His "lydie," Edna Laycock, owned an apartment hotel in the suburb of Mossman, and Cliff Miller managed the garden and custodial work for her. Later we learned Edna's husband was confined in a mental institution. According to British law, she could not divorce him as he would be unable to contest. She could do nothing to terminate her marriage until he died. Edna and Cliff loved each other and were together for the rest of their lives. Twenty years later when we returned to Sydney and met them for dinner, I asked Edna about her husband. She told me he had died a number of years before. I asked why she and Cliff hadn't married. Edna said she had spoken to Cliff about getting married. "Good idea," he had said, "but who would have us?" Their humor and genial good spirits made them fun to know, and we continue to correspond.

As we approached the breathtaking beauty of Sydney harbor, Cliff and Edna told us they would like to show us their city on one of the days we had on shore, and we accepted with pleasure. They took us on an all-day tour

[271]

of the many famous beaches around the shoreline of Sydney.

Alex was on the pier to greet us. He was easy to find, towering over most of the people in the crowd and looking much the same as I remembered. We spent the five days in port with him as our guide, escorting us to many places of interest and enjoyed catching up with the news of our families over the twenty-year span. He had married after the war and had two daughters. His wife, Alison, had not come to Sydney as she could not leave the children at that time. His dear father had passed away, and his mother now was terminally ill.

He drove us to the Blue Mountain region seventy-five miles from Sydney, at that time suffering from a severe drought resulting in spontaneous fires in the forests. A blue haze of smoke obscured much of the scenery in the Blue Mountain area, but we loved the drive and the day with Alex.

We visited the marvelous zoo in Sydney, crossing the harbor by ferry to the zoo. We had never seen a zoo to compare with it. We arrived too late for the last tour group of the day, but the owner and director of the zoo, himself, escorted us around in his jeep. He was a philanthropist who had built the place and then given it to the city of Sydney.

The animals were the healthiest and strongest we had ever seen in captivity, and they were all obviously happy in their surroundings with large compounds in which to exercise. As we approached each group of animals, they would recognize their beloved keeper and hurry to the fence to greet him. At each stop, the director would enter the compound, pat the animals, and give them a "treat" from the recesses of his pockets. I remember the beautiful giraffes, which galloped up at our approach and nuzzled the director lovingly, stooping their long necks to be hugged.

When we came to the kangaroos and koalas, we entered their compounds with the director, and I was enchanted when he picked up a cuddly koala and gave it to me to hold. The little animal clung to me, snuggling into my neck, and I could hardly bear to give it up when we had to leave. Its diet of eucalyptus leaves made it smell strongly of the herb, not unpleasantly, but its fur was not soft as it appeared, but stiff and gummy. We fed the wallabies and kangaroos with branches of leaves. All the animals seemed tame and friendly, completely unafraid.

The zoo was full of animals indigenous to Australia, and we loved seeing the strange creatures at close range. The director went into the cage of the platypus and picked it up to show it off. This is dangerous as the platypus has poisonous spurs on its hind legs, and handling it could prove fatal. The oldest and strangest of all creatures, it is an egg-laying mammal that can live under water, its beaver-like tail propelling it through the water like a canoe paddle.

[272]

We enjoyed the day so thoroughly we were eager to go to the zoo the next time we visited Sydney. Twenty years later we were dismayed to find it in a sad condition of disrepair. The animals were dejected and thin, and the koalas were in a secluded caged area where one could see them only with difficulty and certainly "not touch." The great benefactor had died and funds were lacking to support the zoo. We were sick with disappointment at the transformation.

One evening Alex took us to an Indonesian restaurant called The Tulip. I admired the dinnerware, which was lapis lazuli blue. The plates were large and egg-shaped, perfect for curries or Chinese food, and the cups were shaped in the same way. We offered to buy a set of dishes and the owner agreed to box them up for us if we would wait until the restaurant closed for the evening. An hour after the last patron left, the dishes were packed. Then the owner offered to drive us to the ship in his station wagon as there would be no taxis at that late hour of ten o'clock! As we drove to Woolamaloo Pier we realized it was true about the taxis. The streets were deserted. We were amazed that a city of that size and importance would close up as early as the most provincial village. Not so today! Now Sydney is a city rocking with action around the clock.

Our five days in Sydney was ended. We sailed away with tears in our eyes, waving to Alex, Cliff and Edna on the dock. Never expecting to see that far-away country again, nor our dear friends. As we moved out of the harbor we noticed a large piece of graded land jutting out over the water, obviously being readied for some construction in the future. We were told it was to be an opera house. We thought a building like that would destroy the looks of the harbor and the famous Sydney bridge, one of the most beautiful sights in the world, and were glad we were there before it changed. Our visit in 1977 brought us face to face with the new Sydney opera house, enhancing the view spectacularly with its modern "flying" roof lines. Far from destroying the looks of the harbor, the opera house has made the view distinctive around the world.

———•—◄◉►—•———

We returned to Aukland again for two more days of sightseeing. This time we rented a little Morris Minor to drive to the Rotorura area, where there is thermal activity covering about one hundred-and-fifty square miles. It is similar to our Yellowstone Park as a natural wonder. Sam drove expertly on the left side of the road, barreling through pastoral scenery. The lush grass in the country grew thick and rich, blue-green in color. Norfolk pine trees were the giants that stood as tall sentinels in the background against the sky while hundreds of sheep grazed the deep green of grassy meadows. Stone walls or thick bright red hedges divided the paddocks.

As we drove dizzily along, Leona and I on the back seat were tossed this way and that as we swung around the bends. At sudden brakings to avoid collisions with trees, people or sheep, the seat separated from the back, sliding forward and throwing us backward, hats over our eyes. Looking down to adjust the seat, we could see the road zipping along below in the gap made by the separation. Leona and I were hysterical with laughter, yet fearful we would fall through the gap onto the road. Neither Sam nor Hayes paid a bit of attention to our predicament. Sam concentrated on his driving, and Hayes sat stolidly, eyes forward, camera ready to take pictures. They were irritated by our sudden shouts of panic, and at long last, Sam stopped the car to try and fix the offensive back seat. He explored a wire fence beside the road and finally found a loose piece long enough to fasten the seat to the back of the car. Wired in place, the seat stopped slipping, and we continued our mad dash to Rotorura.

There is a Maori village in Rotorura. Unlike Yellowstone, where the Government protects the geysers from tourists with fences, ropes and signs to "Keep Off," the Maoris make use of the pools, piping the natural hot water into their homes. They bathe in the pools and rivers and cook in the steam pots. We saw many Maoris with cloth bags filled with their meal — perhaps fish and vegetables. The bags were tied to long sticks like fishing poles, and they would sit or stand on the banks dropping their bagged dinners into the boiling, bubbling geyser, the steam rising like a cloud around them.

Our wonderful guide through the maze of geysers was Rangi. Sam was amazed to recognize her as she had been his guide when he came to New Zealand for a month on leave during the war in 1944. Rangi, born in 1896, began her career as guide in 1922, and retired in 1965. She was such a famous guide, her story has been documented in a book by Ross Annabell, with Rangi telling the story of her life. Her portrait hangs in the British Museum, and she has escorted people as important as Queen Elizabeth and the Duke of Edinburgh. Rangi's personality and earnest endeavors to describe the heart of her people to each visitor made her an unforgettable character, the reason why Sam remembered her after thirteen years. She autographed her book for Sam in 1968 when Polly, Sam's sister, went to New Zealand. On our tour of the village she took us to her own house and asked us to sign her guest book, proudly showing us the signatures of movie stars and other distinguished people, including Eleanor Roosevelt.

The visit to Rotorura was fascinating, and we left reluctantly to continue on to Waitomo for the night. We arrived in time for dinner at the impressively large Waitomo Hotel. Our rooms were comfortable, and the bathroom was large but contained no toilet. For that, we had to walk a good block of corridors to a separate lavatory.

After an excellent meal, we walked to the nearby Waitomo cave, famous for its glowworm grotto. The night tour was just beginning, and we joined the group at the cave entrance, descending into the bowels of the earth by many stone steps carved into the cave floor. We were intrigued by the many features of the cave and its history as we slowly moved along the narrow, illuminated passages. At last we came to a river which flowed through the cave, and following it, arrived at a large lake. We were not allowed to talk, or even whisper, as the slightest sound would disturb the glowworms overhead. Once in the boat, the guide extinguished the lights in the cave. In total darkness, we floated silently out onto the lake. Gradually, tiny blue lights appeared overhead like stars in a black sky. As we stared in wonder, the entire cavern shone with an iridescent blue light, so bright we could see each other in the boat. Suddenly, the guide clapped his hands. At once all the blue pinpricks of light vanished, and we were again in total darkness. It was the most beautiful and eerie sight.

We walked slowly back up the slick, treacherous steps to the entrance. Hayes and Leona walked more slowly. Hayes was careful of climbing steps since his heart attack. He would go up three, then stop and count three before moving on. We finally reached the cave entrance. The guide extinguished the lights in the cave by the main switch and padlocked the gate as the group dispersed. We looked around for Leona and Hayes, but they were not there. Excitedly we called to the guide who was heading for home, and alarmed, he unlocked the gate again, turned on the lights, and hurried into the cave to find them. They were sitting quietly on the steps far below waiting for someone to come. They had fallen back in our retinue, unable to catch up when the lights went out and had sat down where they were, waiting to be found. They were calm but we were badly frightened, imagining a fall on the slippery steps in the darkness.

The next morning we were awakened promptly at seven a. m. with tea and cookies served in bed. Soon after, we were on our way back to Aukland. By early afternoon we were aboard the *Mariposa* and enjoyed a bon voyage treat of Maori dancers as we pulled away from unforgettable New Zealand.

———————•◆•———————

Sam just missed having two birthdays aboard ship. We crossed the International Date Line on November second instead of November first, but we celebrated his birthday twice at the Halloween party on the thirty-first, and again on the first when we had a surprise cocktail party and dinner for him in the private dining room. We invited seventeen other passenger friends to join us for the evening. Koko, our Finnish waitress, gave Sam a gift, a coconut shell painted colorfully inside, which stood on three little legs fastened into the coconut "eyes," a little bowl for snacks.

Suva, in Fiji, was our next stop for the day. We admired the handsome Fijians, tall and straight and very black. They had hair like doormats, combed up into a huge, round bush. The stunning policemen wore uniforms of white lava-lavas with red British jackets and wide black belts. but no shoes. Barefooted, they directed traffic as though they were dancing a graceful adagio. The women wore "Mother Hubbard" dresses (a chemise introduced by the first missionaries to cover up the naked ladies in those days.) They were short, colorful dresses over ankle-length white petticoats. The Hindus were beautiful in their saris with bright jewelry, colorful stones stuck in their noses, and bindi spots. The sikhs in their white turbans, breechcloths and black beards looked dignified and important.

The streets were swarming with myna birds strutting about, picking up crumbs. I wondered if any could speak the many dialects they overheard on the street corners.

We taxied to the Grand Pacific Hotel for a drink in the afternoon to cool off in the large wicker chairs on the breezy veranda. Sam had stayed here during the war when he came to Suva to buy souvenirs as Christmas presents for the men to send home.

—◆—

We left Suva for Pago-Pago, Samoa, our next stop for just one morning. Frank Springer, Irving's husband, had written the American governor, Peter Coleman, and asked him to meet us while we were there. Frank told us a great deal about Samoa, a place he had longed to return to, and described the officer's club where he had lived during the war. We sailed into the harbor, passing the building which sat atop a prominent spit of land jutting into the harbor entrance. The building had deteriorated and was now an empty shell. Tall, green mountains loomed up into misty cloud formations. The island looked like the setting for a fairy tale.

The Mariposa docked directly in front of Governor Coleman's home on the main residential street. The homes were modest, frame structures, but beautifully landscaped. Governor Coleman and his wife met us at the dock, and we drove around the island to a village where there was an outstanding performance of dancing and singing in honor of the Mariposa visitors. The Samoans performed on a grassy lawn "stage" with a backdrop curtain of tapa cloth at least five feet high and easily fifty yards long. The tapa, (tree bark hammered into a thin strip with wood mallets and then dyed in shades of black, brown and white in beautiful designs,) is the most noted art form of Samoa. The Samoan dances and songs are unusual also, differing in style from the other Polynesian islands. The dances feature firebrands or knives, which are expertly wielded by the men as they dance.

In the main square of the town were impromptu shops set up just for the day with tapa cloths, baskets and carved crafts on display. Sam bought a three-foot carved outrigger canoe, which he later varnished and hung in our tropical bar at home. We also bought a large kava bowl and some tapa. We bought so much a native boy had to help us carry everything back to the ship. Our stateroom now looked like a jungle, filled with South Sea crafts, shells, and tikis, overflowing from the now-too-small closet.

Governor and Mrs. Coleman showed us many points of interest on the island, and after the tour, we returned to their home for tea before sailing. We enjoyed their hospitality and generosity, waving goodbye from the deck as the bow lines of the ship were untied on their front lawn.

Drifting out of the beautiful harbor, we passed under a cable car, a transit for passengers to ride to the top of one of the tallest mountains. Samoans were crowded into the cab watching our departure, waving and calling down to us. Suddenly we were deluged by thousand of colorful flower petals falling from overturned baskets, the confetti-like bits covering the deck amidship.

The sea was rough on the Pacific as we fought the headwinds on our way to Honolulu, our last stop before San Francisco. We were delayed because of the weather and were told the ship used an extra hundred barrels of oil a day pushing through the heavy seas. At last we reached the Aloha Tower; a landmark on the huge port of Honolulu.

Although Sam had been to Hawaii during the war, this was my first visit, and I fell in love with the charm and gaiety of the island. We took a tour of pineapple plantations and orchid groves and saw other points of interest. We also taxied on our own to Punch Bowl Cemetery, winding up to the top of the hill, where a gatehouse marked the entrance. We inquired for the location of Ed's grave, and following the guard's instructions, drove along the bending roadway where we found his grave beside the path, one of many thousand Americans lost during the war, victims of the Pearl Harbor bombing. The view was a sea of flat stone markers in carefully placed rows covering acres of grassy hillside. Below sprawled the city, the harbor and beaches fading into the ocean. I put an orchid lei on Ed's flat stone marker, stifling back tears for his loneliness in this place. We drove back to town while I fell silent, contemplating the past.

Twelve years had brought me happiness with Sam, a new and different kind of life from the one I would have had with Ed. I have always grieved for him, not just for myself, but for everyone he touched or would have touched if he had not been cut down so early in his life. A brilliant career was in store for him as he was the finest of surgeons. I've wondered often how different my life would have been, visualizing a more solitary one as Ed became more and more in demand at the hospitals. I would have missed the companionship, fun and exciting adventures I discovered with Sam. Judy and Ann would have grown up in New York with different personalities because of a different environment, and their futures can only be conjectured. I do know they were given broader opportunities, more advantages and a healthier environment because of Sam. Today, forty years after Ed's death, I realize more than ever how fortunate I am to have found Sam.

[277]

The memorable cruise ended on the docks of San Francisco. We said farewell to our newly-found friends, promising to "keep in touch," and for many years we exchanged Christmas greetings. Bill and his bride, Jeanne Peck, from Anderson, Indiana, were on the dock to welcome us home. They had been married nine months before, on February twenty-second. Both our families were happy about their marriage.

It was good to see them, and after passing customs inspection with our enormous pile of accumulated packages and luggage we drove to the St. Francis Hotel for the night.

We had invited Koko, our waitress on the ship, to join us for the evening, and she met us in the lobby of the hotel at dinner time. We took everyone to Trader Vic's for a sumptuous feast, and then Bill took us to the Hungry Eye, a new night spot he had discovered. Shelley Berman, a relatively unknown comic at the time, was making his debut, and as we sat at our table next to the stage, we were engulfed with laughter at his monologues. Unknown to us, he was being recorded that evening, and later the tape was put on his first record. Bill gave us the record that Christmas, and to my embarrassment, I could hear myself laughing louder than anyone in the audience. At one point Shelley Berman had leaned far over on his high stool, looked me squarely in the eye, and said, "I appreciate your laughing at my jokes, but, lady, this is ridiculous!"

After the hilarious two hours, Koko took us to a place she always liked, a night club on the wharf — a sort of fishermen's hang-out. We were not too impressed with the dark, rather sinister bistro. A questionable clientele frequented the dive, but a lively band cut the smoky air with bright dance music. We danced, had more to drink, and presently felt we had had enough of the entire evening and begged to escape to the hotel. Koko, however, was just going into high gear; we left her there at two a.m. with her friends.

Our evening in San Francisco had been a wonderful welcome home, and we were ready to board the train and head for Indianapolis.

Gold miners visit a saloon in Leadville, Colorado

Twenty-fifth anniversary party — the Bridge Club and husbands: L. to R. Back Row: Robert Eaglesfield, Barbara Anderson, Fred Anderson, Ruth Eaglesfield, E. Havens Kahlo, Frank Springer. Front Row: Irving Springer, "Punch" DePrez, Sam, Lucina, Ellen Kahlo, Jodi and Gordon Culloden, "Poody" Ruddell

Balbina Ortega

Alicia Ortega

Elena-Maria, Rosalba and Anabel's confirmation.

CHAPTER FORTY-EIGHT

W E discovered soon after moving to Indianapolis that our large house, ideal for entertaining, was a sought-after location by organizations. We were glad to be able to open our house for symphony parties, Christamore and Dramatic Club rehearsals, meetings and benefit functions for many groups. Virginia Campbell and I had teas or buffet suppers for friends after our two-piano recitals. We also had parties for Judy and Ann, entertaining their classmates with square dances, picnics and Halloween parties similar to the one in Mexico. It was all great fun, but it also took a lot of planning and execution.

"Punch" Harris and I started a bridge club, each of us asking three friends to meet for two tables of bridge every other week. Punch invited Jodi Culloden, "Taddy" Larsen, and Ann VanRiper. I asked Irving Springer, Ruth Eaglesfield and Jane Fortune. We met at our house at eleven a.m. one Thursday in 1959 and played until time for us to meet our children after school, breaking for lunch in the middle of the day. We have continued our club and this year celebrated twenty-five years of "together-ness" at the bridge tables, taking turns entertaining the group every two weeks. Although the members have changed over the years, we still have four original members, Ann VanRiper, Ruth Eaglesfield, Jodi Culloden and myself. The others who now play with us are Barbara Anderson, Mary Watson, Dorothy Messenger, Ellen Kahlo and "Poody" Ruddle. We added a ninth member to insure us of two tables of bridge in the event someone was unable to come.

Our card games and social congeniality have brought us much pleasure throughout the years. For me, it is the one day every two weeks that I can completely relax with my friends and enjoy a day with no commitments. I love to play bridge, and I love the girls in the group. Occasionally we have had large "pitch-in" dinner parties, including our husbands (who all play a good game).

Several times we have invited the members and their husbands to join us at the cottage in Culver for a weekend. We spend the days on the lake, boating and swimming, or just loafing on the breezy porch, enjoying drinks and conversation, and the evenings at the bridge tables. The highlight of these times was the weekend of Sam's and my twenty-fifth wedding anniversary. The lake, where we had been married, was a perfect place to celebrate with our friends. The group presented us with a beautiful silver plate, centered with two cardinals engraved in copper and brass, the State birds of both Kentucky and Indiana. We were moved deeply by the gift and the affection of our friends. A clever poem (printed below), written by Punch Harris, accompanied the gift with much celebration, laughter and champagne toasts.

[281]

POME

When "Shelville" met Muncie and Mexico beckoned,
Sam's very best computer could hardly have reckoned,
The twenty-five years of joy and a fullness of life
Since Sampson took Lucina to be his dear wife.

Piano lessons, and classes, and duo-playing,
Grandchildren and poodles — they go without saying
Bridge — duplicate and lessons from Easley Blackwood,
To Sam and "Cina" the Italian system seems good.

Beaded flowers, needlepoint and valances, too,
Always assured Lucina of something to do.
And Sam with his painting and culinary art
Added spice to Haag Drugs and computer so smart.

The Symphony Board, choir and contemporary art
Have felt their great interest straight from the heart,
Their interests and skills — I've just touched the surface
To mention them all, would make us all nervous.

Most people take trips for a month or so,
But Sam and Lucina, forever — seem to go.
Their latest acquisition is one that's a chancer
They returned with a new friend, a real belly dancer!

The mates within may not be ducky,
But they hail from Indiana and Kentucky.
So let's drink a toast to our Sam and Lucina,
To be with them — we all know there is nothing finer!

("Ducky" refers to the duck decor of the cottage in Culver)

Punch (Mary De Prez Harris) is a cousin of Pat De Prez, my classmate at Tudor Hall. Punch graduated in the Spring of 1933 before I arrived at Tudor that fall. Although I knew of her, we didn't meet until 1941 when she and "Bud" rented our lodge on the horse farm in Muncie. Bud managed the White River Tobacco and Candy Company there, a subsidiary of his business in Indianapolis, Hamilton Harris Tobacco Company. They lived in Muncie for two years until Bud joined the army, returning to Indianapolis after the war.

When we moved to Indianapolis, we became good friends and saw each other often, enjoying our foursome of duplicate bridge. Punch wrote a social column called "Punch Lines" in the morning *Star* for several years after Bud had a severe heart attack in 1954 and retired from his business. He remained a semi-invalid for the rest of his life. After a few years of inactivity, he began teaching sixth grade in public schools on a substitute basis. Eventually, loving the work and challenge, he accepted a full-time position at Public School #15, and after a few years, became the sixth grade teacher at Park-Tudor. Tudor Hall had merged with Park School for Boys on a new campus. Bud was an outstanding teacher there until another heart attack claimed his life in 1978.

The four of us had many good times together. Once in a while we would leave Indianapolis for a "bridge weekend" at a remote spot, such as Batesville, Indiana, where there was an exceptionally good hotel. Registered in a suite with two bedrooms and a living room, we would play bridge in the afternoon and evening, sandwiching a gourmet meal in between sessions in the excellent hotel dining room. We would leave for home Sunday after a morning bridge game and Sunday dinner.

We spent several weekends at Punch's family farm in Shelbyville, Indiana, loving the quiet, quaint Victorian home built over a hundred years ago. Once we went there in the spring and opened the house for the first time after the winter months. After climbing the steep, narrow staircase to our bedrooms, to our horror, we found the rooms filled with thousands of dead flies. They covered the bed covers, furniture and floors, making a solid black carpet over everything. Not one fly was still alive. It took us over an hour to sweep the house clean, laughing and joking about the "fly holocaust."

That night there was a thunderstorm, blacking out the lights. But we persevered with our bridge and played by candlelight.

One day Sam brought us a family present — a recorder for each of us — two sopranos, an alto and a tenor. They were very good quality, made of cherry wood. Sam thought we would make a quartet, Judy, Ann and the two of us, and it would be fun to learn how to play the instruments together. Unfortunately Judy and Ann did not fall into the plan as he hoped. But I started studying the alto recorder right away and enjoyed picking out the tunes in the instruction booklet. Later we became proficient enough with the instruments to join a group, practicing once a week at each other's homes for an evening of octet recorder ensembles. It was great fun and lasted for a couple of years.

Sam and I took the instruments to the lake on weekends and tried harmonizing, struggling to keep the sour notes out of the pieces, but it was tough going at first. We sat on the dock in our swim suits, playing at the end of the pier until the sun drove us into the water from time to time for a cool swim — then back to the pier for more "whistle tooting." We received many strange looks from people passing by in their boats. We must have looked like swamies or snake charmers without a basket of snakes.

One weekend we practiced so diligently we scarcely spoke to the rest of the family. Mother and Dad didn't comment about our offpitch efforts, but it must have been torture to their ears. We even took the recorders to bed one night, Sam blowing the soprano or tenor recorder and I on the alto

[283]

as we sat up in our double bed. Everyone else was bedded down except for Dad, who had driven into town for something. We were playing a duet when Dad came up the stairs, stuck his head in the door and tossed a package on our bed, saying, "Here, I want you to learn these." We opened the package to find two pieces of sheet music. One was "It Only Hurts for a Little While." The other was, "I Almost Lost my Mind."

We left the recorders at home after that.

In 1958 Judy spent a summer in Aspen, Colorado, at the Aspen Music School. She was progressing very well on the piano, and I was proud of her interest in music. We thought she would be inspired by the high quality of the faculty in Aspen and exposure to the many fine concerts and educational features there. She left by train for Glenwood Springs with a group of other students, and the Aspen station wagon met them to transport the group to the camp, some fifty miles into the heart of the Rockies.

Judy experienced five glowing weeks thriving on the inspiration of her teachers, particularly her piano instructor, Edith Oppens, who was brilliant and eccentric. With her uncombed red hair flying in all directions and unkempt clothes hanging on her gross shape she looked like an unmade bed.

Sam, Ann and I drove to Aspen at the end of the session in August to take Judy home. We fell in love with the old-fashioned village, up-to-date gourmet restaurants, and the imposing mountains. Ann begged to be allowed to attend the school and promised to practice diligently to be worthy of such excellent teachers. We agreed, and the next year both girls returned to Aspen for the five-week course.

While we were there, I passed another milestone — my fortieth birthday. Judy presented me with a card showing a silly looking man, shaking with surprise and shock, shouting, "FORTY? I could have sworn you were *much* older!"

Several friends from Indianapolis were visiting Aspen at the same time, and we all gathered to make the party an occasion for me. Mother and Dad flew out in their plane, "The Ball Line," but the flight over the mountains and landing in the fog and rain on that tiny airstrip was too nerve racking for my parents. They went home by train and let Dick take his chances on the take-off over the Rockies. Virginia and Al Campbell, Josephine Madden and Mary Mattison were also there for a few days of concerts. Great music was performed informally in a huge tent on a grassy field outside the town every afternoon and evening. The lectures and master classes were led by the world's top artists.

On our way home from Aspen, we drove through Colorado to New Mexico and saw the cave dwellings of the ancient Taos Indian tribe. That fall, Judy began her senior year, graduating in the spring of 1959.

———————◄◄●►►———————

There was a student in Judy's class at Tudor Hall, Jane East, from Richmond, Indiana, who was very gifted in music. Dottie Ritter was her piano teacher, and I gave her singing lessons. Dottie and I were both impressed by her ability on the piano and her lovely voice. We thought she should have the opportunity to attend Aspen, but scholarships were hard to come by. After writing the director of the Aspen Music School at Julliard in New York, we were advised Jane could possibly raise the money for her tuition by giving a recital.

Dottie and I planned the recital to include Judy and Victor Rosenbaum, a talented boy of their age who had won a scholarship to Aspen the same summer Judy attended. He had studied with Rosina Lhevinne. We had barely begun to plan the recital when Sevi Solomon, the wife of our new Indianapolis Symphony conductor, Izler Solomon, told us the Albert Tiptons of Detroit had offered to give benefit concerts for Aspen. Both Albert Tipton, flutist, and his wife, Mary Norris, pianist, were on the summer faculty at Aspen. The Solomons spent their summers there also as Izler was the Aspen Festival's music director.

So the "Indiana Scholarship for Aspen Music School" was born. We accepted the Tipton's gracious offer (which let the children off the hook) and formed a board, inviting fifteen women to join. The committee organized concerts to raise money for scholarships, followed by contests for Indiana students ages sixteen to twenty-five with all instruments and voice eligible. We were pleased with the success of our first concert by the Tiptons, raising enough money to send Jane as well as Michael Hatfield, a French hornist and a member of the Indianapolis Symphony Orchestra, on a partial scholarship. Jane and Michael attended the full nine-week summer session of '59 while Judy and Ann were there.

Since the Aspen Board was founded twenty-five years ago, we have sent fifty-five students on full or partial scholarships, raising over sixty thousand dollars. The majority of the scholarship recipients have become professional musicians due to their experience at Aspen, a springboard for gifted and serious students.

———————◄◄●►►———————

Sam and I yearned to be back in Mexico again. We planned the trip while Judy and Ann were in Aspen. We drove down and took Balbina and Alicia with us so they might have a reunion with their family. Lola had already returned the year before and was attending secretarial school. She had never adjusted completely to life in the States and was always a little homesick.

We entered Mexico on the new International Highway, a distinct improvement over the old Pan-American Highway, which we had driven on our honeymoon. Mexico had changed much in the years we had been away. Villages had become towns, and towns were now cities. Monterrey, where we spent the night, was a bustling, industrial city with residential suburbs and a choice of comfortable, attractive motels on the outskirts.

Deviating from the direct route to Mexico City, we drove west the next day to San Luis Potosi, where Balbina and Alicia took the day's trip by bus to Mexico City. We progressed more slowly to the capital, lingering in the historic towns along the way, as we had not seen this part of Mexico before.

Once we stopped to ask directions from a man selling hammocks on a street corner. I could easily resist the sales pitch of the roadside entrepreneur, because I already had enough hammocks at home, but then he pulled little packages of gems from his pockets and unwrapped garnets, turquoises and topaz to show us, I couldn't resist his energetic appeal for a sale. When he proudly told us his father had cut the stones himself while languishing in the penitentiary, I quickly picked out a package containing three topaz and Sam paid him the equivalent of two dollars in pesos.

In Mexico City I had the topaz set nicely in a ring and a pair of earrings, thinking the glass costume jewelry would be a nice addition to my collection. I was later surprised when I showed the jewelry to Mr. Petri, our jeweler in Indianapolis. I laughed apologetically when I recounted the story to him. After looking carefully at the stones, he told me they were not only authentic stones, but very good ones.

After leaving the Ortegas at the bus station, Sam and I drove on to Leon, where we stopped to visit Horatio de la Parra and his family. Horatio had been the assistant manager of Conquistador for Sam, but was now in another business in Leon. He was a special friend of Sam's, and it was a pleasure to visit with him and his lovely wife again. Their large family of eight grown children were all present to greet us when we arrived.

I often remember when they surprised us in Mexico City on our first anniversary. We were awakened at six a.m. with loud, brassy music playing "Las Mañanitas". We hurried to the window to see what was causing such a tempest so early in the morning, and on the street in front of our gate was a mariachi band, serenading us for all they were worth. The de la Parras were also there, waiting in their car until Julio opened the gate and invited them in. The band and all of us were served an impromptu breakfast, while the music continued, paso dobles and other peppy tunes further awakening us and the entire neighborhood. The de la Parras presented me with a deep, purple silk rebozo and a triangular, fringed, elaborate shawl, knit by Horatio's mother. Sam received a colorful, striped serape and a sombrero. These gifts, accompanied by an early morning serenade, are tradition in Mexico for newly-weds on their first anniversary. The custom began during the reign of Maximilian and Carlotta, sent from France to govern Mexico. On one occasion, Carlotta ordered musicians to play for a court wedding. Her orders were given in French, as she couldn't speak Spanish. "Marriage" in French was interpreted "mariachis" by the Mexicans.

———◦◈◦———

We were enchanted with the state of Guanajuato with its scenic beauty and picturesque villages. We spent two nights at the historic hotel, Castilo de Santa Cecilia, in the capital of Guanajuato. Sleeping under the domed, brick ceiling in our bedroom was an exciting adventure all by itself. We wondered how all those bricks had managed to stay neatly in place for so many years and fantasized that just one loose brick could cause the entire ceiling to fall and bury us in our sleep!

There are a number of historic towns in Mexico which are protected by law against modernization — tearing down the old to make way for the new. Guanajuato and Taxco are both protected as National Monuments, within village limits. Sadly, the destruction of old Mexico City and its rebirth as a modern metropolis, has defaced the once beautiful city, now the product of over-population and needless disregard for historical value. The gorgeous avenue stretching the length of the city, Paseo de la Reforma, once, to our thinking, the most beautiful promenade in the world, had been widened by eliminating the colorful oleander bushes and riding paths in the park-like divider of the avenue and paved to make way for a four-lane expressway. The old, stately Spanish mansions that stood behind wrought iron gates since Colonial times, had disappeared, replaced by high-rise apartments and hotels.

Smog hung in the air, stinging our eyes. Breathing was an effort with the combination of altitude and pollution. We drove up our old avenue, Las Palmas, to find our house on Sierra Amatepec. We had difficulty locating it as it was squeezed against another house, and the street was so dense with homes ours was lost in the maze. The once spectacular view of the barranca across the hill, which had been the grazing field for cattle and goats, was now thick with homes, a new suburb of Mexico City. The great landmarks of the distant volcanoes, Ixtacihuatl and Popocatepetl could no longer be seen through the haze clouding the atmosphere. So much change in just nine years!

We visited with Eleanor and Mason Muench who still lived in "the house next door." They were the one link in our old neighborhood that hadn't changed. We went to dinner together at our favorite restaurant, The Jena, and spent the evening recalling "the good old days."

After dinner, the Muenches took us to a new night club where we sat for awhile listening to the music. We sat in a booth, adjoined by another booth where two men sat, one of them behind Eleanor. I was suddenly aware that the man had turned around and was speaking to her, and that she was becoming irritated by his insinuating remarks. Very deliberately and calmly, she turned to face him, then ground out her cigarette on his cheek. From then on, the man focused his attention on his own companion. I was astonished and shocked by her style of rebuff. The man surely was burned badly, but Eleanor showed no concern, nor said a word about the man's advances to her.

I had always wanted to return to Chichicastinango in Guatemala, but during the time we lived in Mexico City, we had no opportunity to travel there, nor was it a safe journey. Guatemala was in political turmoil and revolution, communism terrorizing the country. But in 1959, the country was again settled, though communistically controlled, and I persuaded Sam to include a trip there as I wanted him to see the beautiful country and enjoy it as I had in 1937.

We flew to Guatemala from Mexico City and took the same drive to Antigua and Chichicastinango as my family had done over twenty years before. There were more changes and improvements everywhere, particularly the highways, which were now paved and straightened into more direct routes. We discovered the villages to be little changed except for the hotels, now modernized for the tourists. In Chichicastinango the Mayan Inn had doubled in size. We stayed in the new addition across the road from the original building. The charm and beauty of the village were still present, and local customs remained, but I was sorry to see that the beautiful costumes of the provinces were no longer worn. The men wore blue jeans and wide brimmed hats as any cowboy in Texas, and only a few women clung to their long skirts and rebozos, the material plain and less colorful.

We walked the cobbled streets and followed a steep path where there was a holiday celebration. We watched the folk dancing, intrigued by the natives' interpretation and grace. Men in white suits and grotesque masks portrayed the story of a Spanish conquistador, impressing the people with his white skin and strange animal, the horse. Behind him rode Satan, the instrument of death and destruction. The accompanying music was played on homemade, crude instruments, while the dance depicted the history of Guatemala conquered by the Spaniards.

In the central square in front of the white church, Santo Tomas, we later saw a mass wedding celebration. Over one hundred couples paraded in their finery around the zocalo. Priests led the procession up the steep steps to the church. When they were all assembled, a priest chanted the wedding ceremony in front of the church entrance and finally blessed all the couples in matrimony. Following the mass wedding there was dancing and celebration in the square, punctuated by firecrackers.

Chichicastinango had not lost its magic for me after all those years.

The Mayan Inn had retained its charm, and we were still awakened by a barefooted boy slipping into our room to light the fire in the early morning darkness. We drove back to Guatemala City with more memories to cherish of the mountainous village.

We returned to Mexico and changed planes for Oaxaca, a town far south in Mexico. We had never been to this part of the country and wanted to see the famous Mayan ruins there. Anita Rabell came down to be with us, and we enjoyed being together as we explored the ruins. The town was interesting with busy shops around the square. In the evening we sat on the park benches to watch the dancing and general merrymaking while a marimba band played familiar and traditional Mexican music. I loved the gentle rattling of the marimbas, and having played a marimba in our school orchestra when I attended Burris School, I decided it would be fun to have one. The best marimbas in Mexico are made in Chiapas near the Guatemalan border. They are hand made and intricately decorated with inlaid designs in the wood. We had one shipped to Indianapolis, adding to the Mexican decor on our third floor.

The marimba began our percussion instrument collection. From then on we brought home instruments native to each country we visited. Today a strange assortment from Ethiopia, Brazil, Egypt, New Zealand, Bankok, Turkey and Hong Kong hang on the wall above the marimba. The collection includes a steel drum from Trinidad, maracas and castanets, and even a ukulele made from an armadillo. This instrument originated in Argentina is called a charanga, but we have dubbed it an "armadelele." An autoharp, quica, thumb piano, poi balls and bongo drums — rico-ricos, apachi, and Samoan "fish" drum — African skin drums and one-stringed fiddles, make an interesting conversation center.

Back in Mexico City, we had only a few more days to see our friends before returning to Indianapolis. Balbina and Alicia came to the Hotel Cortez to join us for our departure, and we drove away, regretting the time had been too short in the city, but we continued our sightseeing through Mexico, going out of our way to visit Patzcuaro again, a fishing village near Guadalajara which is picturesque and noted for the unusual style of fishing. Unique nets like butterfly wings extend on either side of the canoe-like fishing boats. In the early morning with the sun rising over the lake, the many boats casting their nets look like large dragonflies hovering over the gold-tinted water. There are many shops selling native crafts and Patzcuaro is a lucrative tourist center. Of course, we had to buy more pottery dishes and jicaras (lacquered trays) and tempting jewelry. At the small town of Tlaquepaque we loaded the car with lamps made from stone Aztec gods, a cocktail table with an inset of carved onyx, and other irresistible treasures. No wonder we had five flat tires on the way home!

CHAPTER FORTY-NINE

IT was after our trip that Balbina made the decision to return to Mexico. She was concerned about her mother who was over ninety and blind and felt she needed to be with her. Alicia was heartsick about leaving the States. She wanted to stay with us and at least graduate from Shortridge before going home, but it would be another year and a half, and Balbina would not permit her to remain. We understood Balbina's need to go back to Mexico, but it was hard to reconcile the loss of our wonderful help and dear friends. I knew our home would be too large for Sam and me after the children were in college. So I began to search for a smaller "nest" for just the two of us. Balbina promised to stay until we could find another house and help us move.

We had taken a "college selection tour" in the spring of '58 for Judy, and she chose Pembroke College (coordinated with Brown University) from the many colleges we visited. Sam's sister, Polly, had graduated from Pembroke and later gave Judy an enthusiastic account of her experiences there.

Judy's senior class was the last to graduate from Tudor's location at 32nd and Meridian. An old estate had been purchased for the school between Marian College and Park School for Boys on Cold Spring Road. The property was thickly wooded with a lake and a large ivied mansion, which would be used as a residence for student boarders. A new school building was under construction for occupancy in the fall of '59. Ann's class was among the first to enter the new school.

All the departments of our life seemed to be undergoing change. Besides the new location for Tudor Hall, our Second Presbyterian Church had built a great Gothic edifice on 77th and Meridian Street and in October moved from the historic downtown church to the new site. Virginia and Al Campbell had also moved from their home near us to a distant farm outside of Indianapolis. She bought a second piano so we could practice at her house, and we alternated weeks at each other's homes. When I drove far out of town on North Meridian Street into the country beyond 86th Street and on to 116th west to their farm, I felt it was a great distance to travel. I couldn't understand why they had chosen to live so far from "civilization"! But their farm was in lovely country with a large lake in a basin below the house, giving them a beautiful view from their front window. Al bought a herd of cattle and also a pony farm on the adjoining property and enjoyed quite a different business along with his law practice.

I saw many houses but only a few were interesting enough to show Sam, and one Sunday I persuaded him to look them over. The first house I had seen was on 116th Street near the Campbell's, but I knew it would be too small for us with only five rooms, It was on a short, dead end street, just one of seven houses. The only thing that attracted me to the house was the living room, which was large enough to accommodate the pianos. Not one modern house I had seen had a living room as large as our downstairs parlor on Washington Blvd., and even though the house was far from the city, I took Sam to see it — the last house on my list that afternoon.

I was taken by surprise when Sam showed a glimmer of interest. The fact that the house was far too small didn't concern him, as he immediately envisioned the possibility of adding another large room behind the kitchen at right angles to the living room. This would create a huge living area and enable us to keep our treasured possessions.

Before I knew what had happened, Sam was negotiating with the owners and an agreement was signed. We would not be moving in until the addition to the house was finished, and the Bewes brothers would continue to live in the house while the work was going on. Our house was sold within two weeks after we put it on the market, a perfect home for the Cavanaughs and their ten children, only a block away from their church and Catholic school, St. Joan of Arc.

January first, 1960, was moving day. We hated to leave the home we loved so much, but I had decided long before that when the girls left for college, or if we lost our good Mexican help, we would have to move. Also the neighborhood around us was deteriorating and our house was vulnerable to thieves and easy to break into. I was fearful of being alone at night. The large house was expensive to maintain and taxes were high. The small house we had just purchased would cost one-fourth as much.

I selected furniture which we would be able to use in our new home in Carmel, and shipped another van-load of valuables to my parent's home in Muncie. The remaining goods were sold at an auction in our back yard. I spent that day practicing with Virginia and tried to forget what was happening at home as I could not have stayed there and watched my familiar possessions sold to strangers.

In December we had one last party — a big bash, which we called our "house cooling," since we thought we would never be able to entertain large groups in our new, tiny house. I could not envision having more than eight at a time for dinner without any help, or even continuing to teach piano. Who would want to drive miles into the country for a piano lesson? I dismissed all my pupils and sent them to other teachers. I thought I wouldn't have the time to teach in any event with all the cooking and housekeeping to do myself.

We said tearful goodbyes to Balbina and Alicia when they left for Mexico a few days before Christmas, and on New Year's Day locked the door of our house on Washington Boulevard and drove to Carmel, Rural Route 2 Box 411 E. I parted sadly from some of our treasures as they were not appropriate for our new house — mainly the lovely crystal chandelier and sconces which were made for us in Mexico. The Cavanaughs wanted them, plus the oriental rugs and large mirrors over the mantels. The Mexican tin chandeliers also remained on Washington Boulevard along with the pool table which had given us so much entertainment.

We felt like pioneers striking into new territory, and it was almost a year before we felt really settled in our new home. I worked hard, unaccustomed to household chores. Although I loved to make a new recipe now and then, making three meals a day was quite different. It was time consuming and sometimes frustrating to plan and execute a varied menu day after day. For several years, to ease the monotony of meal planning, I had taken my favorite recipe books filled with a collection of clippings from magazines and newspapers and organized them into sections. Every day we would try something new from a different section. If the family was unimpressed, I would toss the recipe out, but if it was good, I marked it to save for another time. I decided to try all the recipes in a section before repeating the favorite ones, but this was taking a long time as there were many sections and hundreds of recipes.

I always asked the family their opinion of the new dish, salad, appetizer or dessert, and would get noncommittal answers most of the time. Ann called them "Mom's inventions." Once I asked Sam how he liked the new casserole. He replied, "What difference does it make? I'll never see it again." "Oh," I protested, "But I *will* use it again when I finish all the recipes in the section!" "By that time I won't have any teeth left to chew with," Sam answered glumly.

———————<◦>———————

Not long after we moved, Mother and Dad decided to move also. They bought a home in Golden Hill next to Woodstock Country Club and a farm in Zionsville, six miles straight west of us. Mother and Dad moved to Indianapolis in the spring after giving their home to the Baptist Church as a recreation center for students and a manse for the minister and his family. We were delighted to have "Mimi" and "Pom-pom" closer to us, and they felt happy about being in Indianapolis where Bill and Jeanne lived also, and where Dad had his import car business.

The move to Indianapolis from Muncie was a great change for my parents but they adapted to new friends and activities readily. Mother was enchanted with her farm near Zionsville where she raised her poodles. She had an active business attending dog shows and winning championships, breeding, selling, boarding and grooming. Before long her kennels were full and had to be expanded to house more than one hundred dogs.

Bill and Jeanne were raising a family of beautiful children. Twin girls, Julie and Janet were born in 1958. "Chipper," (Bill Jr.) was born two years later and John came along the next year. Our families were close but their marriage, unfortunately, ended in divorce in 1973.

Even though I had not intended to teach any longer, I began again after six months, unable to resist people who continued to call and request lessons. Before long, the small class I had intended, expanded into the usual thirty students, but I loved being busy and productive. Virginia and I, now in close proximity, continued our practice sessions one day a week alternating at each other's homes. We gave programs for organizations when they asked us, and had three albums of records made, which we sold or gave to friends. We celebrated our twenty-fifth anniversary with a two-piano program for friends followed by a buffet supper, dedicating the evening to our patient, loving husbands who put up with so many years of hour upon hour of practice.

We continued to play together until Virginia began to have problems with her eyes. Retinal deterioration was beginning but was not evident until after a double cataract operation in 1974. Slowly, Virginia lost her sight, and it became increasingly difficult for her to read music. At last she was unable to play any longer, and by 1979 we were forced to end our partnership. It was a difficult time as our two-piano playing meant a great deal to both of us. We had had such good times together and had given at least eighty programs during those years.

I asked Dottie Ritter to team up with me, and since 1980 we have enjoyed a partnership and still play enthusiastically for anyone who will listen to us.

Mother with poodle

Dad

1408 Golden Hill Drive, Indianapolis, Indiana

11612 Williams Creek Drive, Carmel, Indiana, 1960

S.S. France *to Europe*

Bouk, Bep, Fani and Laurens Van Oosten

CHAPTER FIFTY

THE past twenty-five years have passed swiftly and happily for the most part, except for Sam's illnesses and continuing health problems. I think it all began 1962 when he came down with encephalitis with a light case of chickenpox.

In 1967 during a routine physical examination his electrocardiogram showed heart damage. Dr. Morris Thomas thought Sam had had a heart attack and sent him to the hospital for rest and evaluation. Sam had been working very hard at Haag Drug. I was concerned and suggested he think about retiring. During a second hospitalization that year, Sam finally agreed and appointed James P. Steele, the treasurer of Haag's, as the new president. Sam remained on the Board of Directors and chairman, but his activity in the business slowed down considerably.

By 1970 Dr. Thomas, still concerned about Sam's condition, wanted him to go to the Cleveland Clinic for heart catheterization. The test revealed scar tissue on his heart, causing an uneven beat and a bundle branch block, which the clinic thought was due to some kind of virus. There was no evidence that Sam had ever had a heart attack, but he was given precautionary advice on his activities. Since Sam's retirement, we have taken many vacations and interesting trips as Sam said he wanted to travel and see as much of the world as possible before he had to use crutches!

Unhappily, this nearly happened in 1979. Since 1974 he had undergone an operation every year for bladder tumors. Chemotherapy had not been effective in eradicating them. Finally the doctor ordered radiation treatments following his fifth operation in 1979. Sam was in the middle of this series of treatments when circulation suddenly stopped in his left leg, resulting in numbness and pain. He had an immediate emergency operation to replace the blocked artery.

Sam rallied and did very well with his DuPont artery, and the bladder tumors seemed to be controlled by the radiation, the treatment resumed after the arterial by-pass operation. But three-and-a-half years later, in 1983, we were two weeks away from flying to Italy when the same leg lost circulation again, causing intense pain.

I rushed him to the hospital, and the surgeon felt there was little hope of saving his leg. Two emergency operations were performed within twenty-four hours because, after the first operation, circulation stopped again.

Miraculously, they were able to save the leg, although they warned Sam that when this new by-pass failed (and they assured him it would fail) they could not save his leg again. It would have to be amputated. Since then,

Sam has had persistent sensations and numbness from the nerve damage in his foot, but at least he still has his leg.

———— ❖ ————

During these years, Judy and Ann finished their years at college (Pembroke and Centenary Junior College, respectively), were married to Bill Cummings and Jeff Strohm (respectively) and each had two children. Judy's daughter, Breck, was born on Ann's wedding day, August twenty-fourth, 1963, ten months before Ann's daughter Tracey was born on June 4th, 1964 (the same birthday as my brother Bill's.) The girls' second babies, both boys, were born two months apart in 1966. Scott Lockwood Cummings arrived on August 17, and Bryan Wesley Strohm was born October 13. Coincidentally, my birthday lies mid-way between Breck's and Scott's on August 21st, and Sam's sister, Polly's birth date is August 20th. We have had many family birthday reunions during this week of August over the years.

In the summer of 1962, my parents and I took Judy and Ann to Europe, and after spending brief times in London, The Hague, Copenhagen, Vienna and Salzburg, flew to Paris and left the girls at the University of Paris for a six-week course of study conducted by Sarah Lawrence College. We traveled to and from Europe on The France, the largest luxury liner ever built, and certainly the most luxuriously appointed. The France was so impressive it seemed to dare the Atlantic seas. The water was rough, but the ship cut through the waves without a bobble.

———— ❖ ————

Judy met Bill while she was attending Pembroke, and he was at Brown University. After he graduated, he joined the Navy for his compulsory two-year stint before getting his Masters degree in business at Columbia University. After their marriage they lived on the east coast, moving to several locations dictated by the Navy. After receiving his Masters Degree from Columbia School of Business, Bill took a position with General Foods, and they lived in Mt. Kisco, New York, until he changed jobs to go into partnership with a marina company in Southampton, Long Island. Finally, after thirteen years of living on the Atlantic coast, Bill, Judy and their children moved to Indianapolis where Bill joined the A-Star firm as vice-president. We were so happy to have them near us! Breck and Scott became close friends with their cousins, Tracey and Bryan, and all attended the same school, Park Tudor.

Sadly, in 1981, Judy and Bill's marriage ended in divorce, an unhappy time for all of us. Ann's marriage to Jeff had ended in divorce also, ten years before Judy's. Three years later Ann was married again unsuccessfully to John Stanley. Their marriage lasted two years before the final divorce. But today Ann is married happily to Michael Lach, and they live in Boulder, Colorado.

Both Judy and Ann were in college when Sam and I took another long, eventful cruise to South America. Sam's parents joined us when we boarded the Argentine cargo liner, *Rio de la Plata*, in New York. It was a comfortable, well-run ship with a congenial group of passengers. But we laughed at the old-fashioned, tasteless, overstuffed furnishings, the decor a mish-mash of figured prints and flowered cretonne curtains. There was just one lounge and bar to serve the hundred passengers, but there was a small pool on the deck, and the dining room below was large, well-appointed and served delicious meals. The outstanding ship's feature was the enormous staterooms and baths. They were so comfortable we spent a great deal of time in our quarters. Even the bathrooms were twice as large as most staterooms on a ship.

We were the only American passengers aboard and discovered no member of the crew and very few passengers spoke English, but this suited us very well as we wanted to recapture our Spanish. We discovered the skill was slipping away from us, with no occasion to speak Spanish except to Balbina and Alicia.

I was made Queen of the Equator Crossing, an hilarious day. With much horse play around the pool, the neophytes, crossing the equator for the first time, were treated to pies in the face and shampoos of whipped cream and raw eggs and their bodies painted with lipstick before being thrown into the pool by the group of pirates. The mayhem ended with a mess of garbage on deck and in the pool. The heat of the equatorial sun beat down without mercy and caused the eggs and cream to spoil, creating an evil smell which hovered over the entire proceedings. My "court" sat in a group under an awning, protected from the sun's rays, but the heat was even more stifling under the canvas. My fake eyelashes drooped and mascara ran in black rivulets down my cheeks, and my hair was soaked under the white "Madame Pompador" wig. But it was all done in a spirit of fun.

The ship stopped en route to Buenos Aires at Recife, Rio de Janiero and Montivideo. Hayes and Leona knew a couple, Gladys and Salvador Romeo, in Montevideo, and when we docked they were there to meet us. We enjoyed their hospitality while touring their lovely city bordered by miles of white sandy beaches. Our friendship has continued through correspondence ever since.

We shared mutual friends with the Davises in Buenos Aires also. It made our stay in the Argentine capital even more enjoyable, coupled with a bonus of five extra days there. The Argentine State Line Company began a strike on our arrival, and we were required to leave the ship and stay in a hotel until notification that the strike was ended. We were glad to have ten full days to see beautiful Buenos Aires and spend some time with our friends. The city reminded me of Paris with its tree-lined avenues and many statues and fountains gracing the parks and promenades. We loved the continental atmosphere and the friendly, hospitable people, even

[298]

though we knew Americans were the least welcome of all foreigners.

There was one unpleasant incident. We were driving by taxi to the home of a friend who had formerly lived in Mexico City and had been at Lecheria National with Sam. At a crossing, we were horrified to see a woman's dead body in the street, partially covered with newspapers. She had obviously been the victim of a hit and run driver, but no one paid the slightest attention to her. Under the Napoleanic Code, anyone in the vicinity of an accident becomes an accomplice and is jailed without bail, if caught. Thus, when an accident occurs, the witnesses or people responsible, disappear as rapidly as they can. Our taxi driver stepped on the gas to get as far away from the body as possible before it was found by the police. I think a law is incredible which makes everyone guilty at the scene of a crime or accident.

The *Rio de la Plata* informed us of their impending departure at last and we boarded for the return trip. We went as far as Rio de Janiero, and then debarked for a visit in that fabulous city, staying at the famous Cococabana Beach Hotel. As different from dignified Buenos Aires as night and day, Rio was a city for fun and frolic. There was dancing and music in the air at all times. As we walked along the streets, Brazilian rhythms in record shops blared out to tempt the shopper to buy. Of course, we couldn't resist, and came home loaded with peppy records of the Batucada and songs of the Carnivals. We also bought gems set in lovely jewelry. Brazil is famous for inexpensive precious stones. We swam in the refreshing water of the ocean, languished on the beach and watched the hordes of bathers and small boys selling unusual kites, which flew like great birds over the white sand. We loved Rio and its night spots and watched the liquid movements of the black entertainers as they danced to the strong, compelling Brazilian rhythms.

The cable car ride to Sugar Loaf Mountain was hair raising, and one I could never repeat, but we had to do it once for the experience. The trip was long and necessitated a change of cable cars midway to Sugar Loaf, on a lower hill in the harbor. We rode so high airplanes flew beneath us as they took off and landed at the airport. The view was the most spectacular of any I have experienced as the harbor and surrounding country is the most beautiful in the world. With heart in mouth, I rode along, praying we would arrive safely. A return cable car passed us with painters on the roof of the cab casually repainting the cable car! I could not conceive of anyone having the nerve to do such a dangerous thing and cursed myself and my chicken heart.

———————◦◉◦———————

High on a mountain west of Rio stands the white statue of Christ blessing the city, a monument of strength and peace. It seemed small until we drove up the hill to see it at close range, then climbed the 100 foot tower inside the Christ's body by elevator to the highest vantage point of

[299]

the Christ's head. Looking down at the shacks of the desperately poor, which are called favelas and comparable to the worst of tenements, the scene was hard to forget. Thousands of flimsy huts ranged down the hillside until they were suddenly cut off by the high-rise buildings and hotels along the coastline. The contrast between the splendor of the wealthy and the squalor of the poor was a cultural shock. We understood the government was trying to irradicate the slums by building good apartments to house the poor, but the poor, accustomed to their favelas on the hills, would rent their new apartments to someone else, return to the hills, and be able to afford a T.V. set from the income. Antennas stood on the roofs of most of the shacks.

The *Rio Jachal* took us back to New York after our seventeen day stopover. We visited Trinidad and Caracas, Venezuela on our northbound journey. Sam was able to accomplish more work in the ship's library than at any other time in his career. He worked every morning of the two-week voyage in preparation for his first computer at Haags. The innovation of the computer enabled Sam to reduce inventory $1 million and add 4 stores, and the quiet hours without interruption helped his concentration on the task. It was something he could never have done at the office with all the interruptions.

Aboard Rio de la Plata. Hayes and Leona Davis, Lucina and Sam

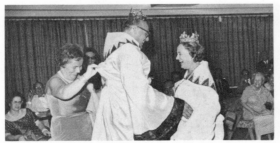

Crowning of the King and Queen of the Equator

Lucina as the Queen of the Equator

CHAPTER FIFTY-ONE

JUST one year later, Hayes became ill and died from cancer of the pancreas. It was a difficult adjustment for Leona, and a sad time for us as we loved Hayes so very much. We spent as much time as we could in Louisville, and Sam helped his mother adjust to her new solitary life as best as possible. In 1964 we took her with us on a cruise to the Orient. She loved to travel by ship as much as we did, and we planned a lengthy and leisurely trip, leaving home on New Year's Day and returning late in March.

Ann and Jeff flew with us to Chicago on The Ball Line (the family's name for Dad's plane) and saw us off on the California Zephyr with the vista-dome top, bound for San Francisco. We sailed for Hawaii on the *President Roosevelt*.

The five-day sailing brought us to Honolulu where we stayed at the Halekulani Hotel, the oldest hotel in Honolulu. Today it has been razed to accommodate yet another high-rise building. The Halekulani was a charming, graciously run hotel with a commanding view of Diamond Head jutting into the ocean. Cottages were scattered on the grounds snuggled under flamboyant trees and oleander bushes. The meals, we thought, were the best in town, and the facilities and location preferable to any place else in Honolulu. Almost every evening we sat under the shade trees on the lawn at the edge of the water drinking Mai Tais before dinner and listening to the gentle music of the Hawaiian entertainers, as birds at our feet begged quizzically for crumbs. The sunset spread out over the sky in glorious red and gold designs, changing to purples, blues and finally grays as the color melted into the ocean.

After four days in Honolulu, shopping and strolling through the International Market Place, dining with friends, and returning to Punch Bowl Cemetery to place a lei on Ed's grave, we spent the next day visiting the other islands of Maui, Hawaii, and Kauai. A guide met us in Maui and drove our group of eight tourists around the island in a large limousine. Most of the island grows sugar cane and pineapple, and we visited a Dole canning factory. At noon we arrived at the new luxurious hotel, the Sheraton-Maui where we were given rooms in separate cottages on the beach. From our vantage point we could watch the torchlighting ceremony performed every evening at sunset. A native, running along the spit of land extending into the sea, carried a burning firebrand high above his head. As he ran, silhouetted against the sky, he lit one torch after another until he reached the farthest point of rock. Then he dived into the sea, his firebrand falling with him.

We were loath to leave this dreamy, luxurious spot, but our tour's itinerary only gave us two nights in Maui before moving on to the island of

Hawaii. The island is so large it took us all day to drive the 150 miles around the coast from Hilo to Kona. Here is where the active volcanoes erupt from time to time and spread destruction from mid-island to the coast, covering the area with acres of black lava. Even so, the tropical growth persists, struggling up between the cracks where the land escapes the devastating flow of lava.

The orchids and other flowers were extraordinarily exotic but the day was long and tiring. We were grateful when we finally arrived at the historical town of Kona and our charming Naniloa Hotel. We spent two days, visiting points of historic interest from the days of Captain Cook, but preferring to wander around the village with its quaint shops and old buildings, sun and swim, and watch the hula dancing in the evening.

From Hawaii we took our longest flight to Kauai, flying over Oahu and landing about forty miles away from the most beautiful place I've ever seen. Driving over gorgeous, mountainous country, rich and green with heavy tropical growth, we arrived at the glamorous location where South Pacific was filmed, the Hanalei Plantation. The main building was on top of a high hill, and the cottages ranged down the steppes of the hill until the last one sat almost on the beach. We were put into the two cottages nearest the hotel at the highest point, which made the walking to the main building for our meals easier. The cottages were so close together, we could visit with sign language from our picture windows to Leona in the cottage above us.

The cottages themselves were unusual. The one room was furnished lavishly as both living and bedroom, completely enclosed with glass sliding doors. Curtains around the king-size bed could be pulled together for privacy, and curtains also could be pulled at the glass window-walls, but we could not bear to shut out the magnificent view, which was all around us.

The place was so magical, we spent an extra night as we hated to leave such a paradise. Kauai is an island famous for its abundant rainfall — more rain falls here than anyplace on earth, resulting in the lavish growth of vegetation and the freshest, greenest color imaginable. When we arrived, we had a misting of fine rain off and on, which did not deter us too much when we took a tour around the countryside and beaches nearby. We saw the mountain made famous as Bali Hai in South Pacific, and from our cottage, the beach far below us. We reached it by walking down the steep path behind the cottages. Once there the beach stretched around the rocky coast for miles. There was a rickety, rusty cable car which made the beach more quickly accessible, and we used it when we returned to the hilltop, but the ride was spooky. I decided the hot walk, pulling up the steep hill was a better choice than the uncertain, groaning and protesting transportation of the cable with its slipping gears.

We planned to do a number of things with the extra day we added to our "Bali Hai," but we awakened to peals of thunder and pounding rain. The glass windows were curtained with waterfalls, the view of the mountains across the cove blanketed in gray clouds. We could barely distinguish Leona as she peered through her cottage window toward us. A large golf umbrella was conveniently placed in our hallway, so Sam waded to Leona's cottage and brought her to our room where we spent the day watching the rain drench the landscape. Sam practiced his bartender skills and made tall rum punches, then called room service for meals which were delivered to us by well-hooded and rain-slickered boys.

In spite of the weather, we loved the Hanalei Plantation even more, enjoying our hibernation and torments of the storm.

The next day the rain storm was finished, and we left the Plantation after breakfast for a day-long drive touring the island. We visited the Fern Grotto, reached by a boat ride down three miles of river. We stood in the Grotto behind a natural screen of dripping ferns while the Hawaiian Wedding Song was sung romantically by a couple dressed in the traditional bridal dress of Hawaii. Many weddings are performed here in the Grotto, and the lovely song is a ritual that enhances the magic of the remote natural wonder of the cave. Waimea Canyon and the Kalalau Lookout were spectacular scenic points as well. We left Kauai with a longing to return another day.

———————◈———————

A few nights later, we boarded the *President Wilson* and slipped away from the Aloha Tower and the twinkling lights of Oahu. As always, I was full of mixed emotions watching the shores recede into the sea. Excitement and nostalgia compete within me as I am reluctant to leave lovely memories behind, afraid they will never be recaptured. Yet I am thrilled at the expectations of a future experience. The twinkling, fading lights beckoned me to return as they signaled their farewells.

The sea was rough, and the February wind bucked against us in gales of fury. The weather increased in intensity until we were pitching through forty-foot waves and seventy-mile-an-hour winds. I loved to stand on the forward, enclosed bridge deck, hanging tightly to the rail to brace myself watching the heaving waves rise to meet our prow. The bow was always awash, and I marveled at the crew as they worked, sometimes waist-deep in water to keep everything secure. It was a miracle none were swept overboard as we plunged down into the sea and each monster wave engulfed us. Each time the windows of the bridge deck where I stood would be splashed with a force of water so strong, it would be minutes before the wind drove the stream away to clean the glass.

One night, two days from Yokohama, we were having dinner. Suddenly, without warning, the ship rolled, throwing glassware and dishes across the dining room. A crash from the kitchen testified to much breakage and possible injuries. Our tables and chairs were secured to the floor, but we were alarmed at the sudden change of motion. We were accustomed to the pitching, but now, suddenly, we were rolling. An announcement to the passengers ordered them to proceed to their cabins.

On the way to our cabin, clinging to the safety lines in the passageways, we passed one of the larger suites, which boasted large picture windows instead of the usual round portholes. The door was swinging open and we looked in to see the room flooded, and the beds covered with broken glass. A wave had broken through, and it was fortunate the occupants were not in their cabin when it happened.

Soon after we were safely in our beds, three crewmen entered to batten the steel plate coverings over our portholes to prevent further damage from the waves.

At five a.m. Sam and I both wakened with a start. It was the silence that woke us and the unusual quiet rocking of the ship. Sam dressed hurriedly and rushed on deck to investigate. In a few moments he was back again, calling to me excitedly, "Bring the camera and come on deck! We're hove-to!"

A large, white Norwegian freighter, a dirty Japanese freighter, another small freighter and our ship were standing by, encircling a Greek freighter that was breaking up in the heavy seas and sinking.

The *Wilson* had responded to an S.O.S. from the Greek freighter, and the change of course had caused the sudden change of motion during dinner. The Greek captain of the freighter had appointed our captain to be in charge of the rescue operation as we had a hospital on board and could take the crew on to Japan after they abandoned ship.

We threw out oil slicks to calm the water, but the forty-foot waves were too violent for the crew to evacuate the ship by lifeboat. They were told to jump overboard, and the lifeboat would pick them up a few at a time and bring them to our ship. We watched the crew of the distressed ship working with the one lifeboat they would be able to use the one on the leeward side and finally it was lowered with two men to handle it. When the boat touched the water, the motor would not start. It was necessary to cut the lines to free the craft from the battering waves. Immediately the seventy-mile-an-hour winds blew the small lifeboat downwind as though it was under power.

Simultaneously the first eight men had jumped from the ship, but found themselves helpless to overtake the fast disappearing boat. Quick action by the captain of the Norwegian vessel caused his ship to turn broadside to the wind. He then let down many huge cargo nets that fell the length of the freighter. All eight men were blown into the nets and climbed to safety on deck.

In the meantime our captain, seeing their lifeboat in distress, let down our best lifeboat complete with first aid, ship-to-shore radio and emergency equipment, and set out to rescue the remaining crewmen on the deck of the sinking freighter.

Jumping into the sea from a forty-foot height is no easy feat. Many of the crewmen were unable to swim. All were reluctant to jump into the icy, stormy waters. They waited until a wave surged upward until it almost reached the deck, then jumped in and let the receding wave carry them down. How our crewmen could see the little orange dots of the life preservers in that turbulent ocean was a mystery to us. A bit of color would appear on top of a wave then disappear. Our hearts were in our mouths every moment expecting them all to drown. Miraculously each man was found and collected safely in our lifeboat, though it took an hour and a half to do it.

We watched the last two men on the deck waiting to jump — the captain and his brother, the chief radio operator. They waited a long time before jumping, but at last, they too went down on a wave from the deck like a toboggan ride. Later we learned the captain had to force his brother to jump at pistol point, as fear froze him to the deck, and he refused to jump.

After all the crewmen had been picked up here and there in the water, our lifeboat went to the rescue of the useless lifeboat, by then far out of sight beyond the encircling ships. But the men in it too were retrieved, and at long last, our boat returned and brought up the Greeks, black with oil. Some too spent to climb the rope ladder to the deck were placed on litters and hoisted up. We were on deck to greet them as they came aboard with cheers of welcome. One Greek, his face greasy black, knelt on the deck to kiss it, tears rolling from his eyes, crying, "I can't swim!"

There were no severe injuries, and later, cleaned up and wearing clothes donated by our crewmen, the Greeks were treated to a celebration unequaled on the ship. The passengers and crew contributed money to be divided among the men, as all they had had been lost on the sinking ship. We sailed away before it sank completely, but we noticed the Japanese freighter lingering on to salvage what it could of the wreck before it went down. They would also recover the two lifeboats which had to be abandoned at sea. Our captain explained it was too dangerous to bring the boats aboard with such heavy seas and gale winds.

We were two days late arriving at the port of Yokohama, due to the delay of the rescue and rough weather and were surprised to be met by Lou Standt at the dock, a friend of ours from nearby Zionsville, then living in Tokyo as head of the IBM division there. (Sam bought the first computer for Haags from Lou in Indianapolis.)

Lou went with us on a bus tour of Yokohama, and I remember only the discomfort of the freezing weather, the enormous Buddha at Kamakura and a lunch of octopus as we sat on small cushions on the floor around a long, low table. The floors of tatami mats were extremely cold, and inside homes and temples it was necessary to remove one's shoes. I remarked in my diary that "the bus was unbearable with all the smokers plus two chain-cigar addicts sitting fore and aft of me. The trip wore on from ten a.m. to three p.m., half of the time spent traveling in the bus. Japan is very colorless — unpainted houses, but interesting people to watch, especially the little children with their fat, round faces and rosy cheeks. The stores are full of junk. It felt good to be back on the ship in warmth and comfort. At least we had a nice visit with Lou, promising to meet him and Natalie on our return to Japan in two weeks. We sailed at six p.m. for Hong Kong and really slept through the night for a change in the calm waters."

For four beautiful days we sailed on to Hong Kong. The harbor, one of the most fascinating in the world, was cloaked in fog when we glided in to the dock in the early morning. Small sampans with eager boys crowded around our hull, calling to the passengers at the rail to throw them change. If the coins missed their boat, the boys would dive after them before they could disappear in the murky water of the harbor. They were unerring in recovering the money, exhibiting much experience in the game.

What fun we had shopping and sightseeing in frantic Hong Kong, one of the busiest cities I have ever seen and populated to the point of bursting at the seams! It was a happy time for the Chinese, being the holiday of Chinese New Year. The buildings were decorated with red banners and festive gold decorations adorned the shop windows.

Prices were so low it tempted us to buy everything in sight, but we settled for new wardrobes at the Hallmark Tailoring Shop, selecting samples of exquisite materials to be made into coats, suits and evening clothes. We were to be in Hong Kong while the *Wilson* sailed on to Manila, returning to Hong Kong in a week. But time flew as we found more things to do and buy, and more places to explore.

Sam said he was saved from bankruptcy by the the New Year celebration because shops were closed for three days honoring the Year of the Dragon. We were forced to abandon our shopping and go sightseeing instead.

The first morning of the holiday we were shatteringly awakened by loud cracks, booms and yells. In alarm, we flew to the window of our room in the new President Hotel and looked across to the opposite building. There was a string of firecrackers as wide as the width of a window hanging from the roof of a twelve-story building, reaching to the street below. A group of revelers had lit the bottom of the streamer, and for one half hour the

[306]

firecrackers sizzled and popped their way to the top of the building. It sounded like an enemy invasion, and at first, we thought a building had blown up. Firecrackers were the theme for three days, and we were constantly on tenterhooks expecting an explosion under our feet at any moment.

We saw many lion dances on the street and in the hotels, followed by crowds of merry-makers. The lion costume was worn by two men crouched beneath the silk coverings, the huge wagging head and shaggy mane resembling a dragon more than a lion with its great bulging eyes, the weaving motions as it moved along giving it a snakey appearance.

Our visit to the Tiger Balm Gardens is difficult to describe. Weird, brightly painted plaster statues of every known or imagined creature filled a hillside garden — a whim of the billionaire who invented the balm (a product similar to Vicks Salve) sold throughout Asia. The effect of the statuary in the Garden was unbelievably grotesque, as well as undeniably unique. The theme was supposed to represent every living thing from Adam and Eve to Noah's Ark, but the idea was carried into fantasyland. Walt Disney was represented by every character he had invented as well as ancient Chinese folklore personalities with their temples and pagodas. The thousands of "creations" here gave little room to squeeze our way along the paths between them.

Ferry boats plied to and from Victoria Island and the mainland of Kowloon every few minutes, and we crossed over several times to explore the island. Many hotels and businesses flourish on Victoria. Tall buildings nestle together resembling Wall Street in New York. For fun, we took a rickshaw ride to the Mandarin Hotel. It took two rickshaws because they were only two-seaters. Leona followed us in lonely splendor. The boys ran in and out of traffic without fear or trepidation, and we bounced and weaved along, holding our hats. Occasionally we looked back to see Leona, her face drawn in fear. She had noticed her driver was equipped with only one eye and was positive he could not see where he was going. She was afraid she would be separated from us or struck on his blind side as he veered through the tangled rush of traffic.

Our tour of Aberdeen Harbor in the sampan guided by a twelve-year-old girl, proved to be a memorable one for Sam. He was moved by the earnest endeavors of the little girl, who impressed him as someone eager for an education but who had little chance of ever going to school, relegated as she was to life on her family sampan, eking out a slim existence in competition with hundreds of others in the same circumstance. Sam almost changed her life by bringing her back to the States with us — to educate her and give her an opportunity for a better future. I'm afraid I stopped him before he was over his head in commitments.

[307]

She was a pretty girl and showed great skill in maneuvering the boat through the thick maze of sampans. Her two-year-old brother was safely anchored to the mast by a rope tied around his waist. She guided us to the floating Tai Pak Restaurant where we had a fairly poor dinner but a fairyland view of the harbor at night, lit with myriads of lights on the boats, blending with the thicker clusters at the harbor's edge and climbing up the buildings into the hills beyond.

Another time we enjoyed a delicious meal in a restaurant which we found after some difficulty. We were given directions by the owner of the Italy Shoe Shop where we were having new shoes made. It was the finest Chinese dinner we can remember, but the restaurant was very cleverly hidden. We were told to go to the Golden Dragon, but the lettering was in Chinese above a second-story window. We climbed the stairs, finding a rather plain, bare room with only one other table filled with diners — a Chinese family and their young children. Dubiously we sat down and wondered if we should stay. But the room was spotlessly clean, with a quiet dignity about it, and the table linen was fresh. We noticed the waitresses scurrying from drawer to drawer in cabinets looking for something but unable to find what they were looking for. Finally our waitress came to our table and in apology said she knew they had silverware somewhere, but it had been misplaced. We assured her we had no trouble eating with chopsticks and not to worry. She breathed a sigh of relief and began to bring our dinner, course after course of delectable food. Sam said it was the best Cantonese food he had ever eaten.

The next day on return to Hallmark for our last fitting, we told Gene Loo, the Chinese owner, about our wonderful dinner at the Golden Dragon. He reacted in alarm and said, "Who told you about that place?" We explained about the owner of the Italy Shoe Shop. He replied, "He shouldn't have sent you there. That restaurant is reserved for US — not for tourists!"

Time was all too short in fabulous Hong Kong. Before we realized it, the time had come to board the Wilson once more, and we were sailing back to Japan. A misty rain was falling, causing the view of the harbor at midnight to be a blur of rainbow lights. We watched until the last light glimmered on the furthest strip of land.

Kung Hei Fat Choy! Happy New Year, Hong Kong!

After three days of cold, rainy weather we arrived in Osaka, Japan. My impression of this port city was a sea of gray buildings. We visited Osaka Castle, an imposing fortress built high on a stone hill, and then drove on to Kyoto, the historically preserved town of Japan, formerly the capital of the country. Of all the places we visited in Japan, we found Kyoto to be the most attractive city. People there preserved its ancient culture and took pride in their temples and gardens. There was activity at night also, but after sightseeing all day we were too tired to venture beyond our hotel for nightclubbing.

Our guide for the three days in Kyoto and Nara was a handsome elderly gentleman who had been a professor of history in a university. Not wishing to retire completely, he became a guide, imparting his wonderful knowledge to tourists. We felt very privileged to have such a learned, cultured gentleman escorting us. He showed us everything in detail from the tea ceremony to tricks with matches.

During a walk through a park, we noticed a restroom. Leona and I decided to avail ourselves of this service, but to our chagrin discovered the restrooms in public places were not segregated. Men popped in and out of the open cubicles along side of us. The toilets were very different too, set flush into the floors, requiring one to stand over them. Seeing them for the first time was a shock, but they actually are more sanitary and practical than our western "saddles."

We found there were thousands of temples in the area of Kyoto and Nara, and our tireless guide wanted to show us each and every one. He felt they were all different with special characteristics, but they seemed very much alike to us. Our most painful experience was walking on the stone floors in our stocking feet. In February, the climate in Japan is cold and damp. I did what I could to protect my feet without shoes by wearing wool socks and extra slippers provided by the temples (but they were made of paper!) By the time our view inside the buildings satisfied our guide, our feet and legs felt they had changed to small stone pillars adhering to the stone floors.

Japan was the most uncomfortable place I have ever visited, as well as the least attractive. The gardens, which are a great source of pride to the Japanese are tastefully planted trees and shrubs on a gravel ground carefully raked to represent ripples in water. Boulders artistically placed among the firs and fruit trees provide the interest. Sometimes there are creeks with little bridges over them, but no flowers are planted. The only colors allowed in a garden come from the flowering trees which bloom in the Spring. I asked our elderly guide if the gardens were more colorful in other seasons of the year, but he said, no, it was the same year 'round. The red and gold of the painted temples relieved the starkness of the monotone coloring to some extent, but the overall drabness of the country depressed me.

Nick, our guide, recited poetry and told us interesting stories about the shrines we visited, and even presented us with his own sumi-ink drawings which were very artistic. He made the trip worthwhile with his wealth of information and delightful personality.

We rode by train to Tokyo on the Limited Express — a six-hour journey

[309]

at the speed of one-hundred-miles an hour. The train ran on a split second schedule and never varied its time table. Outside of Tokyo, however, we were delayed by a wreck on the tracks, and the train switched to another track to enter the station. So we were four minutes late getting to Tokyo. Later, at the hotel, a representative from the Japan Travel Bureau paid us a call to apologize for our late arrival in the city!

It was an interesting and comfortable train ride with the scenery made more beautiful by a snow-covered countryside. Meals were served by vendors passing through the train, offering food of all descriptions served in neat wooden boxes and tea in little pots with the cup resting on top. Telephone service was available, and by each seat was a radio with earphones to make the long ride more entertaining for the passenger.

We checked into the Imperial Hotel (one of Frank Lloyd Wright's first "creations," now torn down), and later Lou and Natalie Standt joined us for dinner. We found an outstanding restaurant in a beautiful park where we dined several times. The Chinzanso featured meals cooked at your table, each table fitted with a charcoal brazier, platters of raw food arrived, artistically arranged, and the kimono-garbed waitresses cooked the sukiyaki as you watched. The view of the park outside the paned windows was serene and woodsy with paths disappearing around the trees and bushes. On Sunday we were surprised to see a Japanese wedding reception outside the window by our table. The bride wore a traditional costume, a gorgeous gold and red damask kimono, the wide obi of gold silk around her tiny waist. Her headdress was the simple white, starched hat perched on top of her piled-up hair. She was gorgeous, and her new groom was resplendent in his cutaway.

Our tours in Tokyo covered all aspects of cultural life in Japan. We visited schools of dancing, flower arranging, sumi-ink drawing and origami (the art of paper folding). At the tour's end we were treated to the tea ceremony in a private home. It is very rude not to drink all of the tea one is served, and particularly gauche to make a face while drinking the thick, green, sandy, lukewarm "tea," which tastes and smells of fish. I spent a long while admiring the cup before I could get it down politely.

The Standts invited us for dinner, and I breathed a sigh of relief, announcing in their car as we drove to their home, how good it would be not to have to remove our shoes for once! But in their entry hall stood an array of shoes and slippers! I was embarrassed at my remark, but Lou just laughed and said they wouldn't be able to keep any servants if they didn't comply with the custom. The Japanese feel it is unsanitary to bring the dirt of the streets into one's home, and the tatami mats used as rugs are delicate and would be torn to shreds by rough shoes. The Japanese treasure these fine, intricately woven mats. They use little or no furniture, sleeping on futon mats, without central heating. Most of the homes are heated by charcoal braziers, which also serve as cooking stoves, centered in the

[310]

living quarters. The family rings around them to eat or sit. Beyond this bit of heat, the room is frigid. A Japanese woman explained they still cling to their traditional clothes of kimono and obi because they are able to wear many layers of wool clothing underneath to protect themselves from the winters' cold.

Charcoal heaters are a fire and health hazard, emitting carbon monoxide fumes, but with so little insulation in their flimsily built homes, there is generally enough air circulating to prevent asphixiation. The biggest danger in Japan is the constant threat of fire. Conserving everything, with land at a premium, the Japanese build their homes so close together that if a fire begins in one home, it takes only a few minutes for the entire block to go up in flames. I can't understand why, in these modern times, the Japanese endure such discomfort as they follow their ageless customs. With such ingenuous minds, why don't they have electric heating below the floors to warm them as they eat and sleep on the floor throughout their lives?

———————◆———————

Lou Standt told us a true story about a friend of his who had come to Tokyo on business. He had been warned always to have the written destination in Japanese on a piece of paper which he could show the driver when going by taxi as very few drivers speak English.

One day he wanted to return to the Imperial Hotel where he was staying and jumped into a taxi without realizing he didn't have the name of the hotel written in Japanese. But he fished in his pocket and found a package of matches which had the picture of the hotel on the cover, the name Imperial Hotel printed below. The taxi driver smiled, hissed, nodded, and they were off.

After awhile, the man became worried because the cab seemed to be taking a long while to arrive at the hotel. They drove and drove, and he repeatedly showed the driver the picture on the matchbook. The cabbie continued to nod his understanding, but they were going further and further from town, the streets becoming rutted and trailing off. At last the driver triumphantly drove up to a building, indicating they had arrived. It was the match factory!

———————◆———————

Lou invited Sam to give a lecture at an air base north of Tokyo concerning his experience in using one of the first computers to control inventory. Sam felt his talk was a success because the half hour allotted for questions after his lecture stretched to three-and-a-half hours of questions from interested and eager Japanese participants in the seminar.

The Standts were a great help to us while in Tokyo, showing us many points of interest tourists normally would not see. One weekend Lou drove us to the seacoast town of Shimoda on the Izu Peninsula. Natalie and their four sons met us a day later at a resort hotel. After bounding over rocky, terrible roads, we finally reached the breathtaking scenery of the peninsula and came to a hotel reminiscent of the Victoria in Taxco. It was perched on top of a hill overlooking the sea with the rugged coastline weaving irregularly in and out of coves. Lou told us this was the legendary spot presumed to have been the home of Madame Butterfly, immortalized in Puccini's opera. She was said to have walked to the edge of the cliff gazing out to sea in hopes of seeing her Captain Pinkerton's ship returning. We decided to take a stroll before dinner and visit the site of her lookout starting out at the reddened sky of sunset. Suddenly darkness fell and the mud holes and stones in the road were hazards as we made our way back up the hill from the coast to the safety of the hotel. Sam had a Japanese massage to recover, and after drinks and dinner, we fell into bed exhausted.

The Shimoda Tokyu Hotel was luxurious with separate wings for American style rooms (that is, furnished with beds and chairs) and Japanese quarters (futon sleeping mats — no furniture.) Lou preferred the Japanese style, but we chose the American way with central heating and comfortable beds elevated from the drafty floors. One adventure in a day was enough for us. But we did have a typical Japanese bathroom. There was no glass in the window by the tub. Sam managed to bathe in the freezing room with a snowflake shower coming through the open window, but I could scarcely use the bathroom long enough to brush my teeth in my overcoat. The winter wind blew in with a vengeance.

The next day we explored the area, driving along a gravel road until we came to a quaint fishing village at the water's edge. We could see it far below us straight down a cliff. We parked at the top and made our way by foot four hundred feet down a precarious path, over stones and foot-sliding portions until we reached the shoreline and the scattered fishermen's shacks. Some boats were pulled up on the rocky beach and fishermen and their wives were busy mending or drying the nets for their next outing. The villagers smiled at us toothlessly, wrapped in dark wool sweaters and caps. Some tried to speak to us, and Lou managed a little conversation, as he had picked up phrases living in Japan. We realized we were imposing on their privacy and did not stay very long, but walked on along the coast and found some unusual shells. I treasure these and have added them to our large collection.

It was as difficult to climb the steep path to the top of the cliff as it was going down, but we managed to get to our car without incident and soon were on our way to Hakone. The hotel boxed lunches for us, for the three hours of driving over mountainous, lonely roads. The route was chosen because of the splendid views of Mt. Fujiyama on the "skyline drive." Mt. Fuji is noted for its shyness, mostly hidden in the clouds, but on our drive, the sun shone, the sky was bright, and the mountain showed us its spectacular dimensions, snow draped around its cone. We were awed by the gorgeous sight.

We arrived at another elegant hotel, the Kowakien, where we met Natalie and their four boys. We had tea in their Japanese quarters, and later they came to our room for champagne. We were celebrating the fourth anniversary of our engagement! It was February twenty-ninth — Leap Year! What a wonderful way to celebrate and be thankful for all the blessings of our sixteen happy years together!

We drove back to Tokyo the next morning over snow-covered landscapes and mountainous roads. The lake below Mt. Fuji was stunning in a shimmering ice dress. We returned to the Imperial Hotel for another week before our final departure on the *President Cleveland*.

During our seventeen-day visit to Japan we met several Japanese people, were entertained in their homes, and saw many aspects of their lives and culture. We also saw some outstanding entertainment, both Western and Japanese, but one of our luckiest experiences took place during a tour of the Imperial Palace. We happened on a rehearsal of dancers in full costume preparing for a private performance for the Emperor. The Bugaken Dance is only performed for royalty, and we were allowed to watch this fascinating performance in rehearsal.

Another time we took a train for an all-day tour of Nikko. Our group arrived late in the morning and transferred to a bus. En route, we stopped at a rice farm and were taken into the farmer's home. The floor of the stable, filled with cows and oxen, was four feet below the floor of their dwelling. We stood in the stable among the animals and viewed the family at eye level as they went about their regular chores. Other than the difference in floor levels, there was no separation between the living quarters of people and animals. An ancient grandmother sat huddled around the brazier, her feet hanging into the pit over the fire where the charcoal burned. This plus the body heat of the animals were the only sources of heat serving the compound. The thermometer stood at freezing. The farmer, wearing a straw rain cape and large straw hat, showed us around his farm.

We scraped the mud, dung and snow from our shoes and climbed back into the bus. On we went, climbing snowy mountains over thirty-five switchbacks, finally reaching the dizzy heights in a heavy snowfall.

Our destination was the Toshagu Shinto Shrine at Nikko which was constructed in seventeen months in 1637 by ten thousand workers at a cost of twenty-three million dollars. It was a marvelous edifice, quite different from any other we had seen, painted bright red with lavish gold decorations. Here is where the famous monkeys "hear no evil, see no evil and say no evil" are immortalized in a bas relief freize around the cornice of the temple. The temple buildings set in a center of a group of pine trees heavy with snow, was a sight to remember for all time. The shrine was completely

[313]

isolated on the mountain top, reigning unchallenged. In spite of the freezing weather and heavy snow, Shinto visitors washed their feet and hands before entering the temple. I could feel the holiness and significance of the place.

The roads had become slick and hazardous, and we were told we were to take a safer route down the mountain by cog railway. The bus would meet us at the foot. It took us six minutes to descend, while the bus took one half hour to creep down the icy twists of the mountain.

The train to Tokyo arrived late in the evening, and we ended the day tired and cold, but it had been an exciting, beautiful day, well worth the discomfort of the weather.

We spent our last night in Tokyo on a night club tour with the Standts, beginning with a visit to a sake house, crowded and thick with the smell of boiling eels. After dinner and a good show, we ended up at a geisha house where we were entertained by the so-called, beautiful geisha women. They tried to look like porcelain dolls with their thick, white make-up, but to me they looked more like clowns. Their clothes and headdresses were gorgeous, but their childlike mannerisms and juvenile entertainment left us unimpressed.

The evening, however, was a perfect way to end our seventeen days of oriental life. We were ready to meet our homeward-bound ship, the *President Cleveland*, sister of the *Wilson*, at Yokohama harbor. We left Japan, appropriately, in the rain.

The *Cleveland* was familiar to us as it was almost identical in plan and decor to the Wilson. My brother, Bill, had been assistant purser on the ship in 1947. He had applied for a position with American President Lines after the war, thinking it would be good experience before entering Indiana University, but the job was not offered until he had been in school for two years. Although it interrupted his education for a year, Bill loved his experience and would have signed on for a longer stint, but he decided to return to the University for his degree in Business Administration.

Traveling east was as rough as traveling west. It seemed I was the only passenger aboard as everyone else stuck to their cabins, Sam and Leona preferring to "take it lying down." Movies and other events were cancelled because of the rough seas, but I felt fine and sat where I could watch the wave activity, curled up on a comfortable sofa with my needlepoint and a good book.

Our journey across the Pacific took twelve days, stopping for just one day in Honolulu. We lugged twenty-two pieces of luggage through customs in San Francisco and finally were on The City of San Francisco train bound for Chicago. The trip to the Orient began on New Year's Day, and we were home March twenty-first.

[314]

CHAPTER FIFTY-TWO

D ORIS and Scott Moxley lived not far from us, in fact next door to Virginia and Al Campbell on the adjacent farmland. Our favorite get-togethers were on New Year's Eves when they would come to our house for "a cold bird and a bottle." We would sit around a busy fire and plan exotic trips together.

One vacation we cooked up was spent in the Caribbean on a fifty-seven foot ketch. We sailed the beautiful blue waters in utter discomfort for a week, but it was a different trip and fun to be together. The blackbearded captain looked just like a pirate from my Captain Kidd books. His wife was the cook and bartender — most excellent, and a young blond Viking type was first mate. The captain laid down strict rules of conduct for the voyage. We were not allowed below deck while under way (he was afraid we would get seasick and ruin his upholstery). He also would not allow us to sunbathe or expose a fingernail to the sun more than ten minutes a day. Doris and I were made to sit on the stern bench, wrapped in robes and towels to cover every exposed area of skin. Umbrella hats tied under our chins kept our faces shadowed.

There was no drinking except beer until sundown when we were anchored in a quiet island cove, then rum drinks were served before dinner. I must say this was the best part of the trip. The nights were the most miserable trying to sleep in the narrow bunks — like sleeping on ironing boards. I had to be thoroughly awake before I could turn over as it took expert maneuvering to shift positions without cracking my head on the low ceiling. Even with care I could barely squeeze myself into the bunk without bruising some part of me. Water was rationed and bathing limited to the salty Caribbean with a fast rinse-off in the shower. The problem with the shower was that the water came out a drop at a time, but only when constant finger pressure held the button down. I have never been able to shower successfully with one hand.

Doris and Scott had different discomforts. Their bunks were the sofas in the salon, made into beds at night. They looked luxurious and roomy, but there was little ventilation, the nights hot and stuffy. A pet parrot of the captain's reigned in the salon. His large cage was next to Scott's bunk. At night, the parrot found a particular interest in Scott's toes, nibbling at them just as he was dropping off to sleep. Although we were not allowed to sleep on deck, Doris and Scott sneaked up when the crew slept and spent the nights under the stars in relative comfort, except for the mosquitoes.

In spite of the handicaps of sailing, the weather was glorious, the sailing brisk and exhilarating. Snorkeling in the coves was fun with the array of colorful tropical fish and vegetation in the clear blue water. While we swam, the captain and first mate stood guard with spear guns in hand in case a shark appeared out of nowhere.

Visiting the island and caves within the coves was interesting, and the captain's wife served delicious meals. We sailed in and out of St. Thomas, then an undeveloped, sleepy island village without much to offer a sophisticated tourist seeking a fancy hotel and swanky night life. In later visits to the island we have seen great development and progress for tourism. Shops and good restaurants now abound, and many beautiful homes stud the hills all over the island.

The sailing trip was just an initiation to bigger and better things. Our real adventure centered in Mallorca in 1967. The four of us dreamed up a romantic villa there for three months. The dream became a reality when Sam called his sister Polly in New York to enlist her aid in finding a house to rent somewhere in Europe for the summer. Polly, recently divorced from Pete Bassick, was living in New York and working for the Four Winds Travel Agency. She sent us brochures from At Home Abroad, and we selected one from a group of blurry pictures and sketchy descriptions. We thought it would be fun to be in Mallorca, a Spanish island in the Mediterranean. The cost would not be too bad if we shared the expenses considering the number of people we could accommodate for the price. The Scott Moxleys have three daughters, and Sam asked Polly and his mother to join us there also.

Polly and Leona flew to Mallorca together and arrived a day before us. Adamant about not flying over the ocean, I insisted we go by ship. So Sam and I crossed the Atlantic on the S.S. *Independence*, docking in Palma on May second. Polly and Leona met us with a rented car and drove us to the villa in Santa Ponsa, a new suburb seventeen miles outside of the capital city of Palma.

We couldn't believe our eyes and good fortune to have rented such a gem sight unseen! The house sat high on a cliff overlooking the Mediterranean Sea. Only a few houses were in the area, and most of them were in various stages of construction, but this one had been built some years ago as the landscaping and garden within the property attested.

The house was rented with a housekeeper and a gardener who obviously took great pride in the premises inside and out. The garden of roses and other flowers and plants were meticulously groomed, yet had a look of natural, spontaneous growth. In the center of the patio at the entrance were paths leading to a fountain.

The one-story villa had wings enclosing the patio entrance on either side and the construction was typically Spanish Colonial. Trumpet vines climbed up the stucco walls and threatened to curtain the windows.

Eusebia, the housekeeper, ushered us in. Beyond the entry we walked upon an expanse of elegant marble floors in black and white squares, covered with oriental rugs. Two crystal chandeliers hung from the ceiling illuminating a room richly furnished in antique Spanish Colonial. The living and dining room extended the length of the large house, separated by two steps up to reach the dining level. On the vast table were two magnificent silver candelabras and a pair of large silver fighting cocks. On a huge sideboard Madame Marades, the owner, had left her lovely tea service for our use. The appointments in the house showed discriminating and intellectual taste.

In the living room were sliding glass doors leading to a terrace the length of the house. The splendid view of the sea from our high lookout made a compelling backdrop of constantly changing colors and ships moving on the Mediterranean below us.

We had written requesting a cook for the household, even though the services of the housekeeper, her husband, gardener and handy-man were included in the rental; we felt the added expense of a cook was necessary. Their daughter, Martina, had been selected as our cook, and she came from Madrid bringing her husband, twelve-year-old brother and two-year-old son. The family of six were crowded into small quarters with barely enough room for Eusebia and her husband, but none of them had any complaints whatsoever. Martina was an excellent cook and Eusebia a fine manager and guardian of the villa.

Sam had just two "run-ins" with the servants. The first night we arrived, he went into the butler's pantry to make us cocktails before dinner. He found the glassware and a tray and brought them in to us as we sat on the overstuffed couches around a roaring fire of olive wood. It was cold in Mallorca and would remain cold until the first of June.

We were enjoying our drinks and conversation when Eusebia appeared and announced she would like to speak to "el senior in la cocina." There, in her domain, Eusebia wagged a finger in front of Sam's nose and in rapid Spanish explained that it was all right for Sam to make the drinks as they knew nothing about cocktails, but he must not carry them in. That was *her* duty. Sam, subdued and penitent, returned to our group.

Another time, we were sitting by the fire loath to go to our cold beds. It was about two a.m. and the fire was dying, the extra logs already burned. Sam remembered seeing a wood pile by the house and went out to get a few logs. In a few minutes Eusebia appeared requesting Sam's presence in the kitchen. Again she wagged her finger and explained that he was not to bring in the firewood. He was to pull the bell rope by the mantlepiece, and *they* would bring it.

Polly managed the house for us, took Martina to the market in Palma, planned the meals, and began Spanish lessons to help her cope with the language. Polly spoke fluent Italian, but had never learned Spanish and was eager to do so. She and Leona spent the entire three months in Mallorca, but Sam and I only stayed for six weeks. Doris and Scott came with Charlotte the day we arrived, stayed for two weeks, and then traveled around Europe, returning after we left. Sarah and Tina joined them after Park-Tudor was out in June. They remained at "Casa Marades" until the first of July.

While we were in the house together, we had a great deal of fun exploring the island a little at a time. The trips were varied, such as a day on a lovely beach with a picnic lunch, winging around the mountains to Formentor (the opposite north end of Mallorca) — the Drach caves, or a visit to Valdemossa where Chopin and George Sands spent a miserable winter. There was much to do, much splendid scenery to enjoy, and an ambience of life that included plenty of leisure as well as interesting places to see. It was fun just to stroll around Palma and shop. The town was quaint with old, historical buildings and a lovely walking street lined with benches and shaded by flamboyant trees meeting overhead.

Though the weather was quite cold, and the water unsuitable for swimming in May, Charlotte donned a wet suit and skied in Palmanova Bay. The sun was warm enough if one could find shelter away from the fresh breezes. We had a lovely terrace in a protected corner of the house which was perfect for sun bathing. French doors opened onto our own private porch from our bedroom. Sam and I used the large master bedroom with a huge double bed. The headboard of cast iron was painted with a picture of the Virgin and angels hovering about through clouds.

We were amused every night to see our bed turned down with my dainty lace nightgown lying beside Sams ugly red flannel nightshirt. They were laid out on the covers seductively. My gown had the waistline pinched in, and the bosom fluffed out. Sam's would also be laid flat, one red sleeve placed protectively under my gown and curled about the pinched-in waist. The first night we saw this display we laughed until tears rolled down our cheeks.

The only inconvenience in the house was the poor plumbing. The bathrooms were antiquated and to get hot water one had to fire a gas heater over the tub when it was bath time. Water had to be trucked up from Palma and stored in a large cistern. The water bills were exorbitant because we Americans kept clean. Eusebia was amazed at the amount of water we used. Evidently we ordered five times the amount an ordinary European family used in the same length of time.

There was a small powder room off the entry hall. The toilet was the kind made around 1920 — one of those "high rise" models with the tank almost at ceiling level and flushed by a long chain dangling from the tank. We discovered it seldom flushed properly and continued to gurgle unless someone climbed a ladder to adjust the chain at the top of the tank.

[318]

One day, Sam found the toilet gurgling away and thought he could fix it without calling for a ladder. He climbed on the washbasin to reach the tank, but his weight broke the basin right off the wall. It crashed down with him and water burst from the broken pipes, flooding the room and entry hall. Sam slipped and fell again while he tried to regain his footing, at the same time trying to stem the gushing flood by stuffing towels into the pipes.

Hearing the crash, we all rushed to the scene. The oriental rug in the entry hall was floating! Quick-thinking Eusebia opened the front door to direct the flood outside and called her husband. He quickly whittled pegs of wood and drove them into the broken ends of the lead pipes. In the meantime Sam had cut off the electricity to stop the water pumping in from the cistern, and the crisis was over. Most of the damage done was to Sam's pride and feeling of disgrace by his rash act. In a couple of days a plumber arrived to repair the wash basin, but Eusebia kept a watchful eye on Sam from then on.

When Sam and I left Palma, we arranged passage on the overnight ferry boat to Barcelona and found the trip delightful. We were sorry to leave Mallorca just when the sea was right for swimming and the weather warmed to a comfortable temperature, but our cabins on the Leonardo da Vinci had been booked, and we were due to leave from Gibraltar in just ten days. We planned to explore the Costa de Sol of Spain in the remaining time by going on a bus tour from Barcelona to Gibraltar. The tour would take a week, stopping in towns along the way to see the points of interest.

We were in Barcelona for the weekend and loved the city. On Sunday morning we decided to take a walking tour on our own in the vicinity of the hotel and set out along the lovely Ramblas promenade where families strolled together, children flew kites and carried balloons, and vendors sold toys and trinkets along the paths. Cages of brilliant exotic birds were set along the sidewalk for sale, and we enjoyed watching them peck and swing on their perches.

Presently we reached the cathedral and climbed the steps to enter the impressive building. It was noon and mass was over. We noticed several balloon sellers waiting for customers on the steps, and I was attracted to a group of musicians with strange looking instruments gathering on the platform at the base of the steps. We knew they were preparing to play and sat down on the stone banister of the steps to hear the music.

People gathered quietly, a few at a time, and from our vantage point we could see the entire panorama unfolding. When the music began, a group of six or eight people joined hands and formed a circle, first putting their coats and purses on the ground in the center of the circle. Slowly and gracefully the dancers stepped to the rhythm with the precision of a sixteenth-century pavane. It was a sardana! The ancient Spanish dance we

[319]

had read about that was still performed in Barcelona every Sunday in front of the cathedrals! This was a stroke of luck we never expected, and we lingered to watch for over an hour while more and more people found their way to the music. The instruments were ancient and were played beautifully in devotion to the custom. Strangers met strangers, joining hands silently as the dance continued without a break, until the square was filled with at least two hundred participants. The groups varied from as few as four in a circle to perhaps twenty, but the steps never varied, and not one broke the precision or missed the unison of the entire congregation. The dance had the formal solemnity of a religious rite, but gaiety and pleasure shone on the dancers faces. Groups of children and the very old blended their steps. Everyone knew the exact steps on each note of the music. Although the steps seemed simple, I could not learn by watching, the times to pause, reverse or stop.

A crowd had gathered and buses full of tourists were unloading to watch. It appeared the dances would continue for some time, but we were ready to move on and find a restaurant for Sunday dinner. Filled with pleasure and an utmost satisfaction from this once-in-a-lifetime experience, we wandered away over the cobbled streets, the music of the sardana still ringing in our ears. Rounding a corner, we entered an alley-wide street and spotted a restaurant with chickens on spits turning over coals at the entrance. It was exactly the kind of place we hoped to find. Wonderful paella served amid the old Spanish decor of a wine cellar, tables in cul-de-sacs lit by the gleam of candles on hanging copper pots, created an atmosphere of romantic adventure.

Our bus tour down the coast was much more delightful than our expectations. We found the passengers attractive and cordial, a group of British tourists, for the most part, from Australia, New Zealand and South Africa as well as England. We were the only Americans. We banded together on the bus and during the sightseeing as well as for meals in the hotels, where we stopped overnight and became well acquainted. The highlight of the trip was Granada where we had a magical experience.

We had been escorted through the Alhambra during our day tour of Granada and were impressed by its beauty, along with the ten thousand other tourists jamming through its corridors. We were hot and tired from bumping elbows with heel to toe humanity, but at the gate as we were leaving to go back to our bus, I noticed a small sign in Spanish which announced the Alhambra would be open that night at ten p.m. and illuminated. I nudged Sam to see the sign, and we decided to go back again after dinner.

At dinner we shared a table with the South African couple whom we liked very much, and asked them if they cared to join us for another trip to the Alhambra. They readily accepted, and we found a taxi to take us there.

We asked the driver if there would be any difficulty in finding a taxi near midnight to take us back to the hotel. He shook his head and said no taxis would be available, but he would wait for us, provided we came out at a quarter of twelve. He wanted to show us something else at midnight.

We entered and were greeted by two lonely guards. Not another soul was there. One of the guards elected to walk with us to explain the mysteries of the palace. The magic surrounded us immediately as distant, soft strains of Rimsky Korsakov's "Scheherazade" wafted through the loud speakers.

The guide could not speak English, but he was poetic in Spanish, walking close to me and whispering about the beauties of the Alhambra. He quoted Omar Khayyam from time to time and said how lucky he was to be able to work in the most beautiful place in the world. "And, just think," he added, "they pay me for the privilege!"

He led us through the gardens, illuminated by the playing fountains, and through rooms, which he described as the sultan's conference room, or harem quarters. "Just imagine," he spoke his thoughts aloud, "the sultan is sitting on his cushions back there by the pillared walkway, watching dancing girls in soft, transparent gowns. Above him along the grilled veranda are seated his veiled harem, looking through the tiny holes of the carved design above the pillars, to see but not be seen."

Artificial lighting throughout the palace made it seem bathed in moonlight, the floodlit corners looking like the moon itself. The mysterious, beautiful atmosphere captured our imagination, and we could only whisper and walk on tiptoe, hating to tread on memories of centuries past.

We have never forgotten the magic of that night and twice more have returned hoping to see the Alhambra lit at night. We have not been so fortunate. Today, illumination is only a few times a year on special occasions because of energy conservation.

The taxi was waiting for us in the otherwise empty parking lot, and we drove to another hilltop where we had a magnificent view of the Alhambra, bathed in subdued orange lights. We watched the imposing fortress with the lights of Granada below and the full moon above until midnight. At the stroke of twelve from distant bells in the cathedral, the lights of the Alhambra were extinguished.

———◆———

We changed buses in Sevilla for our last lap to Gibraltar. The new passengers aboard were British, and a little stiff. We missed our jovial new-found friends who had dispersed in other directions.

It was about ten o'clock in the morning when we reached Jerez de la Frontera and stopped to see the winery, Gonzalez y Byass, renowned for its famous sherrys. We were taken on a tour of the cellars where we saw enormous tuns of wine eight feet in diameter covered with dust and

[321]

cobwebs. Some had brass plaques identifying them for special patrons, one in particular was marked for Queen Elizabeth.

After the tour we were taken to a large warehouse where a long table groaned under a display of food — bread, cheeses and Spanish potato omelets, which they call tortillas. Baskets of fruit added color and variety to the assortment. We helped ourselves to the snacks and sat at tables set with five wine glasses at each place. Mozos (waiters) passed choices of wine, filling the glasses with different kinds for tasting. The glasses never seemed to become empty, being filled constantly as we drank.

Two hours passed before we weaved back to the bus and discovered the ice had been broken among the passengers. Even the bus driver joined the animated conversation, and before long the sound of music filled the air. Folk songs, show tunes and old-fashioned airs were sung in harmony with gusto. One little British lady who had been the shyest and stiffest, came to the front of the bus to lead the singing.

We stayed overnight in the same Rock Hotel that we remembered from our trip in 1953. It had been remodeled under a different management and was considerably improved since our earlier experience. We took the lighter to the anchored Leonardo da Vinci and had a pleasant voyage home on the lovely Italian liner.

N.A.C.D.S. *convention in Honolulu, Hawaii, 1969*

Ed's grave at Punch Bowl Cemetery, Honolulu, Hawaii

CHAPTER FIFTY-THREE

I had no intention of turning this book into a travelogue, but as I relive the years, I remember a great many high points during our vacation adventures that were significant events in my life. As we grew older and Sam had more leisure time, he wanted to see more of the world. We were now middle-aged and our children were on their own and busy with their families. Sam felt we could afford some time off each year to visit countries we had only read about. I was always willing but felt a responsibility to my piano students and hated to leave them dangling for long intervals. If we were away longer than two months, I arranged for another teacher to coach them during my absence, or planned a practice program to keep their interest and progress growing until my return.

In 1969 the National Association of Chain Drug Stores (N.A.C.D.S.) had its annual convention in Honolulu instead of Florida, and we spent almost a month touring the beautiful Hawaiian Islands before and after the four-day convention in April.

Because of my fear of flying over the ocean (or anywhere else in a plane for that matter), we included extra time for traveling by ship to and from Hawaii. But we flew to San Francisco because train travel was now a thing of the past. There were only a few passenger trains left traversing America.

We spent three days in San Francisco and then sailed on The *Lurline* for Honolulu. On the fifth day we awoke at five a.m. to see the black peaks of Coco Head touched off with bright beacons. It was the first sight of land. As it grew lighter and we eased toward the harbor, the lights on land became dimmer and buildings more distinct as the sun rose.

We landed at the Aloha docks and were met by Mary and Jim Steele, who had flown from Indianapolis to be with us before the convention. Jim was the treasurer of Haag's and had come to Indianapolis from Georgia after Sam bought the Jacob's Drug Store chain in Atlanta. They had become good friends of ours, and we anticipated a happy time together.

That afternoon we flew to Maui. We rented a car and drove to the Sheraton Maui and our cottage on the beach, which was the hotel we had liked so much five years before when Leona was with us on our trip to the Orient. We stayed three days in Maui, exploring the town of Lahaina, and swimming on the broad, white beach in front of our cottage terrace, then returned to Honolulu for the N.A.C.D.S. convention.

We stayed at the Ilikai Hotel, a new high-rise building, ultra-modern, sporting an all-glass elevator climbing the outside walls. Our corner room on the twenty-fourth floor gave us a panoramic view from Punch Bowl Cemetery to Diamond Head and the beach, as it spread in a semi-circle along the shoreline. At night the lights of the city and ships at sea created an exotic sight.

While Sam and Jim attended the meetings, Mary and I shopped or sunned on the beach, sometimes joining the men at the meetings but always convening with the entire assemblage in the evenings for dinner and entertainment. We also were treated to tours, including one to Sea Life Park. As we left the bus and walked to the entrance gate, we were amazed to see Polly escorting a group just ahead of us. Having no idea she was hosting a world tour, it was quite a coincidence to meet in this unlikely spot. Polly was as startled as we were. We arranged to get together later that evening at our hotel, after she was free from her duties.

After the convention, the Steele's joined us for a flight to the island of Hawaii, where we spent three luxurious days at the Mauna Kea Hotel. The slick, modern hotel was ultra-elegant, set in private grounds with a golf course, tennis courts and a private beach. It was beautiful, but my preference in tropical accomodations is the more modest, informal style with island decor.

We flew from Hawaii to Kauai for another three days at the Hanelei Plantation, the dreamy paradise we had loved so much. In the middle of the first night it began to rain, as it had on our previous visit with Leona, and continued until late the next afternoon. I think we would have been disappointed if it hadn't. We counted the cascading waterfalls down the mountains, ten in all, and just sat and watched the view from our picture window. Late that afternoon we met the Steeles in the Happy Talk Bar after the rain stopped and the sun shone again.

After our delightful visit to the Plantation, the Steeles left for their return to Indianapolis, but Sam and I flew to Molokai. For many years no one visited Molokai because it is where the leper colony was established after the white explorers brought leprosy to the Hawaiian islands. The colony is still there but has ceased to be a threat thanks to modern medicines and more scientific knowledge of the disease. We drove through the colony to see it at close range. The hospital, homes and people looked comfortable and cared for. We only saw a few distressed and deformed lepers.

The small Hotel Molokai was about the only one on the island. It was Polynesian in feel, rustic and charming, and set on a rather dirty beach in a quiet bay. The water was not suitable for swimming, and the beach was full of little fiddler crabs scuttling about, but they were fun to watch. We spent most of the day loafing in the dreamy spot and swimming in the hotel pool. Then the wind came up and blew us into our room, where we spent the rest of the day. The wind was so strong it blew the dust of the roads in whirlwinds, making it impossible to walk, breathe or see. We had cocktails on our little porch before braving the elements to go to the main building for dinner. We understood why Molokai is, perhaps, the least popular of the islands. The weather is uncertain and sometimes violent. We cut our time a day short as there was not much to do and flew back to Honolulu to our favorite Halekulani Hotel. We spent our last week seeing friends, poking into shops and wandering through the International Market, where there was a multitude of diverse entertainments, shops and restaurants.

My cousin, David Wierbach, was living in Honolulu then, and we saw him several times. He was playing with a small group of musicians in a night spot called the Hofbrau. Dave is an expert on the banjo but also plays sax, bass fiddle and piano, and has a good voice. He is a versatile musician, an asset to any jazz or Dixieland band. We spent one evening listening to the music at the Hofbrau, where the group called upon the audience to participate in singing the old, familiar songs as they played. David persuaded me to sing a couple of solos. It was fun.

On April twenty-eighth, twenty-three years to the day and almost the hour when Ed was kllled on The *Comfort*, Sam and I returned to Punch Bowl Cemetery to place a lei on his grave.

That night we went to the University of Hawaii for a concert by the Beaux Arts Trio. I had been studying with Menahem Pressler, the pianist with the trio, for several years at Indiana University. The trio is the most renowned in the world today. Menahem was astounded to see us at their concert, and it had been a surprise for us to find them in Honolulu also. Menahem and Bomar Cramer were the two most excellent piano teachers of my life. Each one of them gave me different aspects of interpretation and technique to balance and enrich my playing. I studied with Mr. Pressler for fifteen years, until their concert demands and his overflow of pupils (as well as my own) made it difficult for us to get together for lessons. I miss his direction and inspired coaching and often wish it were possible to study with him again.

We had lunch on our last day at LaRonde Restaurant, one of our favorite places because of the panoramic view of the entire city of Honolulu. As we sat in the tower of the revolving restaurant, we could see our familiar ship, the *President Cleveland*, waiting for us at the dock where we would soon board and sail for San Francisco. Our month-long vacation was at an end.

CHAPTER FIFTY-FOUR

I N the late 1960's, I became deeply concerned about the future of our country because of the increasing student uprising, black protests, riots and strikes. The Vietnam War had been dragging on for years, draining our wealth, military forces and moral fiber. It seemed to me we were not allowed to win the war because of political pressure on the Pentagon and intimidation by the public and the press. I felt our country's morale had never been lower. The young people were rebelling, protesting a war they didn't want to fight and "copping-out" with outlandish clothes, hair-dos and drugs. Their protests were reflected in their music, dissonant ear-splitting screams of defiance against society's order. Cults sprang up all over the country spreading the poison of pseudo-religious teachings to youths looking to escape the bonds of accepted social and religious order.

It was after the Kent State University disaster in Ohio and a weak-kneed letter from the president of my alma mater, Sarah Lawrence College, to parents and alumnae supporting a protest demonstration on the Sarah Lawrence campus, that I was angered to the point of writing a letter (see appendix). I sent copies to the editors of the Indianapolis *News* and *Star* and to several deans of major universities experiencing revolts on their campuses. My letter was printed in several papers in Indiana, and I received quite a number of supportive letters from the public and a few of the deans. However, I did not receive any response from President De Carlo at Sarah Lawrence.

Ann had been unhappy and uncertain about her life since her divorce in 1971, and we wanted to do something for her and her children that would give them something else to think about besides the break-up of their family.

We thought a summer trip to Alaska would entertain Tracey and Bryan, and perhaps Ann would meet companions her own age. We planned to take an escorted tour with Anita and Walter Farrell. Anita ran her own travel business, arranging Farrell tours and helping others plan their vacations.

Ordinarily we preferred making our own plans, but Anita's itinerary sounded interesting, and we thought we would take the tour with her then spend additional time in the Canadian West. We left with the group in July and flew to Vancouver, where we boarded an excellent, small ship, The Xanadu, for the sail up the Inland Passage to Skagway, Alaska.

The Inland Passage was a beautiful trip. We passed gorgeous mountainous country and stopped at Ketchikan and Juneau to visit the rugged, rustic towns. At the top of the Passage, farthest north, we anchored among the imposing glaciers and spent a half-day cruising among them in the ship's life boats. The children, then five and seven, loved the excursion, even though it was bitterly cold in the open boat. They even were allowed to walk on a glacier "island" with other passengers who dared.

When we disembarked at Skagway, we climbed on a narrow gauge railway train to ride to Whitehorse in the Yukon Territory. We chugged up the mountains all day in the puffing train, stopping midway for lunch at the railway station. The trip was an interesting, beautiful journey, interspersed with commentary from a loud speaker, a running monologue by our unseen guide — no doubt a recording.

After lunch the group divided — some returning to the ship on another train, and some staying on to climb even higher mountains to reach Whitehorse late in the afternoon.

If we had been smarter, we would have joined the passengers returning to the ship and skipped the journey through Alaska. We found the long uncomfortable bus rides on the dreadful roads hard to tolerate. The scenery was bare and uninteresting, and the days spent traveling were so tiring we couldn't enjoy the towns when we arrived. We could only fall in bed exhausted after dinner each night.

The towns of Whitehorse and Fairbanks were not very interesting, and when we drove to the base near the entrance of Mount McKinley Park, we thought, finally, the trip would be worth it. We stayed in an old train made into a hotel, which was unique and fun for the children and were awakened at four a.m. to begin the bus ride through the park. It was not dark. It was daylight forever at that time of year. No sooner did the sun set at midnight than it rose almost immediately to begin the dawn.

We continued our bumpy drive over the chuckholes and cracks in the road, hoping to see wild animals grazing the fields. With binoculars we could see distant caribou, and, once, a grizzly bear with her two cubs. A few snowshoe hare darted into the bushes, but the nearest animal life we saw at close range were a pair of mice running alongside the bus. The object of the trip was to reach the lookout point nearest to Mount McKinley. Nine days out of ten the mountain is obscured by clouds, as it was on this day. But we waited in the cold wind to see if the clouds might part for a moment to let us see a piece of the mountain at least. We were not lucky. We gave up and turned around to drive back through the Park, feeling disappointed and cheated.

On the excessively long days of driving through the barren land of Alaska, I tried to amuse Bryan and Tracey by reading to them or playing games. Otherwise they would have become restless annoying the other members of our group. We became absorbed by *The Call of the Wild* and other tales of adventure in Alaska. This gave the children an insight into the life of the early pioneers. Playing cards and coloring picture books absorbed them also. Bryan was a handsome child with a mop of blond curly hair topping his sturdy frame. At birth he weighed over eleven pounds and was estimated to reach a height of six feet eight when full grown. Today, at eighteen, he nearly attains the mark. Tracey, with her father's coloring, has dark fine hair that falls in soft waves and expressive black eyes. Always beautiful, she has grown into a striking woman of twenty with the figure of a professional model.

She is the only one of my four grandchildren with an interest in music, and I began to teach her when she was four. She was talented, but her temperament, like Ann's, was headstrong. She tended to fly off into tangents of emotion, first enthusiastic, then disinterested. She would stop lessons for a period of time, then want to resume. Her training, in my mind lacked the precision and concentration necessary to prepare her for a career in music, which she now wants. She attended Berklee Music School in Boston, majoring in piano and voice. Today she plays electronic keyboards in a combo searching for a future in production with radio or T. V. media.

Bryan spent one year at Rose Hulman Institute of Technology in Terre Haute, Indiana. After dropping out he started a partnership with a friend, Brian Seibert and is working on his invention of a revolutionary automobile transmission.

We had planned to go back to Fairbanks and continue our bus tour through Alaska and the Yukon Territory to Canada's Glacier and Jasper Parks. But the drive was too miserable to contemplate, and we continued with the Farrells to Anchorage where we flew back to Vancouver.

Ann and the children flew home, but we spent a few days in Vancouver on the lovely island of Victoria. The beauties of the Canadian National Parks are unforgettable. Sam and I have wanted to return and spend more time in the splendid Rockies — but not again in Alaska!

CHAPTER FIFTY-FIVE

I N 1972 Sam and I had the trip of our lives. It was the year Sam sold Haags to five of his junior executives and retired completely. We planned to see Europe in a big way, and in a leisurely fashion.

Sam's first cousin, Jack Collins, was a Brigadier General in the Army, and was then stationed in Addis Ababa, Ethiopia, as the Chief of Military Aid and Advisory Group. He and his wife, Virginia, invited us to visit them and bring Leona. Jack's tour of duty was almost over, so we made arrangements to include Ethiopia on our itinerary.

Sam, Leona and I sailed from New York to Boston, docking for the day,

[329]

on the twenty-fifth of March aboard the *Cristoforo Columbo,* an Italian liner. We spent the day visiting with Polly and Don in their elegant apartment overlooking the river, and later they drove us to the pier to see us off. Polly married Don Greer in 1969.

The next day was cold at sea, and it was spitting snow. It was also slightly rough, and as a precautionary measure, safety lines were strung across the public rooms, and the boat drill was cancelled. I didn't think the weather was bad enough for such measures, but evidently rougher seas were expected.

Although the rest of the ship was secured the dining room was not. Our table was near the center next to a large table for the captain and his officers. The fetters were not up around the table edges, nor were the chairs chained to the waxed, tiled floor. There were flowers on every table and a festive mood pervaded as we became acquainted with our three table mates.

We had just been served lunch when I felt a surging of the ship beneath me. It rose and listed to starboard. I grabbed the table edge and held on while I watched disaster strike. As the ship keeled over, Leona fell backwards in her chair and slid across the room out of sight. Flowers, wine bottles, and bodies flew by me as if on wings, and we continued to roll. I clung to the table with all my strength and watched in horror, feeling sure we would capsize, as we were now listing at forty-five degrees. The man across from me had fallen under our table, and I saw Sam next to me slowly tip over in his chair and fall to the floor. The only ones left in their seats, besides myself, were the couple pinned against the high side of our table. Tables, chairs, people, dishes, glasses and food covered the dining room floor. We hung suspended at this angle for several minutes before I felt the ship gradually settling back to normal. I continued to grip the table, expecting a return roll. But this did not happen, fortunately, and finally people were able to stand, and the waiters began to sweep up the garbage and broken glass which covered the room.

Sam slowly stood, finding he was unhurt, but the man across from me rose up from under the table with a foolish grin on his face, unaware that blood was running down his temple from a gash across his forehead.

We went in search of Leona and found her under a table and pile of over-turned chairs, just regaining consciousness. A purple bubble bloomed on her forehead where she had been struck, probably by a wine bottle. She walked with difficulty and in pain as we helped her out of the dining room toward the ship's hospital, but when we saw the long line of injured passengers waiting to see the doctor, we thought we should get Leona to her cabin and into bed. Inspecting her closer, we found another large bump on the back of her head where she had struck the floor falling backwards in her chair. Her legs were bruised badly where chairs had fallen across them, and she was moaning and complaining of a severe headache — a malady she had never experienced before in her life.

Eventually a nurse arrived to evaluate her condition. The doctor came much later. He was swamped with the injuries of the passengers and crew, treating everything from broken backs to cuts and bruises. Eight thousand pieces of glassware were broken on the roll, and for several days we were served on paper goods until a reserve supply of dishes could be brought up from the hold.

Leona was confined to her bed for the rest of the trip, in considerable pain, and we were quite concerned. The doctor was not able to do much for her, but when we arrived in Lisbon, the first port, she and eight others with the more serious injuries were taken to a hospital for X-rays. We were thankful Leona's X-rays did not show a fractured skull but were told she had a severe concussion and would have a continuous headache for a year. She did. She told us a year later that one morning she woke up and the headache was gone. It was a year to the day of the accident.

The captain reported our ship had been struck by a freak wave, "an act of God," under which, by law, no suit can be filed. But Sam felt the ship's stabilizers had stuck, causing the roll over without a reverse roll. However, officials stuck to their protective story, as the Italian Line could have been bankrupt from law suits if the incident was the fault of the ship. In fact, the *Cristoforo Columbo* only made one more run and then was retired. We felt sure damage to the ship had been extensive, that the stabilizers were at fault and the ship declared unsafe. But Leona refused to sue.

We were alarmed over Leona's condition and wondered how we should proceed on our trip. Should we cancel everything and fly her home or should we at least cancel the trip to Ethiopia? Leona would not be able to fly home alone now as she had planned after our visit with Jack and Ginny in Addis Ababa. As we continued on to Malaga, worries and indecisions plagued us. We spent Easter Sunday in Malaga. It was a beautiful day in Spain, and we were delighted by the pretty town and the people festively dressed for the holiday.

We sailed on to Naples, where another doctor examined Leona. We thought she had improved a little, but she still could not stand up without severe head pain and dizziness. The ship stopped briefly in Palermo and Messina in Sicily and then continued to our final destination, Piraeus, Greece, where we left the ship and drove to Athens by cab, registering at the Grande Bretagne Hotel.

Leona, exhausted by the debarkation and trip by car, went to bed, and again we were afraid she would not be able to stand the overnight flight to Ethiopia. Coincidentally, Doris and Scott Moxley were in Athens also, and we located them at their hotel on the outskirts of the city and explained our dilemma. They were flying home in two weeks and offered to take Leona with them when we returned from Addis Ababa. In the meantime Leona was determined to be well enough to make the flight with us as she had a great desire to see Jack and Ginny.

Every day was a small bonus, giving Leona more time for recuperation. Sam and I did some sightseeing while Leona remained quiet in her room. The Greek Orthodox Easter was one week later than the Roman Catholic Easter, so we were pleased to see another celebration of the holiday in Athens. There was a candlelight parade on the evening of Good Friday, and we watched the impressive procession from our balcony in the hotel room. Across the way on the hilltop stood the Acropolis, lighted in all its ancient dignity.

The evening arrived when it was time for our midnight flight to Ethiopia. Waiting for the airline bus, Sam discovered he had left his wallet, passports and all important documents for our trip in the lobby of the hotel. He rushed back, hoping he would find his briefcase intact. As he dashed into the hotel lobby, he didn't see the double glass doors and crashed into them head-on. The pipe in his mouth was knocked out, cutting his lip, and his glasses were smashed on his face. One lens fell out, and the frame broke in half, but he returned triumphant with his briefcase, his face cut and bleeding. He said he had never felt so foolish.

Flying over Athens at midnight was so breathtaking I almost forgot my fears. The lights on the ruins, particularly the Acropolis on its commanding site above the city, combined with the city and harbor lights, was a gorgeous sight. The moon was full, and we seemed to be flying alongside it. Later, in complete darkness, I could almost pick the stars out of the sky they seemed so close.

I slept very little in my excitement and watched the sun come up over the dry hills of Ethiopia. At dawn we landed in Khartoum for refueling, then took off again, arriving in Addis Ababa just before seven a.m. When it was light enough to see land, I was mystified to see small villages of thatched huts grouped here and there among the mountains, miles from each other, but not a road anywhere.

Jack met us at the airport and drove us to his home, where Ginny greeted us and we had a happy reunion. Leona, exhausted from the effort of the flight, went to bed and stayed there the entire week. She didn't seem to mind as we all convened in her room and gossiped. Beverley, Jack and Ginny's younger daughter, spent a great deal of time with her. Jack called the American Embassy doctor to examine Leona, and he advised X-rays of her legs, thinking she might have some broken bones, but the X-rays proved negative. Leona at eighty-four had never broken a bone, but she was in misery with her head and bruised legs.

The next day Jack drove Sam and me to the newly-established Awash Game Preserve, three-and-a-half hours from Addis Ababa. We stayed

[332]

overnight in side-by-side trailers, Jack in one and Sam and I in another. On the way we saw many herds of camels, goats, cattle and sheep driven by the Danakil tribal owners in the wilderness country. As we drove through the preserve that evening and following morning, we saw groups of gazelles, oryx, waterbuck and warthogs. I loved the little dik-diks that looked more like fox terriers than tiny deer. We followed a large family of baboons as they moved along, the huge males in the lead, and their mates bringing up the rear with babies clinging to their stomachs and backs. They were fun to watch, especially the young energetic ones, as they played tag with each other. There were kudus and ostrich, hippos in the streams and many colorful and strange birds. It was an exciting experience, although Jack apologized for the lack of real African animals there. Ethiopia does not have elephants or giraffes and is even short on lions. There were lions in the preserve, but we did not see any as they prowl at night and sleep during the day.

Near the trailers was a screened building, which had a lounge and dining room. There we had delicious meals served by tall, handsome Ethiopians.

Later that week we were invited to the Embassy for a dinner-dance given by Ambassador Ross Adair and his wife, Marian. The Adairs were from Fort Wayne, Indiana, and it was a pleasure to know them and be treated to such a nice party in the stunning Embassy home. A cocktail party preceded the dinner at the home of American Lt. Colonel Clyde Orr and his very attractive wife, an congenial and interesting black couple.

The Collinses had a party for us and took us shopping and sightseeing. Sam had new glasses made at a cost of four dollars, and we bought many souvenirs of good quality at very low prices.

We were surprised to learn we would enjoy yet another Easter. The Coptic Easter is a week later than the Greek Orthodox. While we were there, the Ethiopians, very religions people, were fasting, and we noticed how emaciated most of the people looked. For six weeks they scarcely touched food — no meat or dairy foods, subsisting mostly on grain and water.

On Easter, when Lent was over, we drove around the city and watched the celebration. We could hardly believe our eyes as we passed a field. There a group of men had just killed a steer, and were so starved they didn't take the time to skin it or cook the meat. They ere tearing hunks off the animal and devouring it with avid intensity.

Leona was much better when it was time for us to leave. Even she had enjoyed the visit, and the extra recuperation time there was good for her. We had a two-day stopover in Cairo on our return to Athens, expecting to see the fabulous collections in the Cairo Museum. We were disappointed to learn the Tut-Ankh-Aman treasures had been sent to the British

Museum in London for safekeeping during their war with Israel. Cairo was a city alert for war and signs of self-protection were everywhere. The streets, buildings and the museum were banked with sandbags. The one interesting thing we did was to go to the sound and light show at the Pyramids in the evening. Thrilling and inspiring, it told the story of the ancient Egyptians and the building of the pyramids.

We did not like walking on the streets because we were constantly besieged by beggars and vendors selling anything and everything. Shop-keepers hawked their wares and molested us unceasingly. The few things we bought and had sent home never arrived. They simply stole our money. Leona joined us on our brief walk and that evening had dinner with us in the hotel supper club. We rejoiced, celebrating her return to better health.

Back in Athens we called Doris and Scott, and the next day Leona joined them and flew home. We were glad she felt up to the long flight and more than grateful that Doris and Scott were with her. Sam and I spent another week in the city, loving Athens, the fascinating ruins of ancient times, the delightful people and lovely spring weather. Trees in bloom filled the air with the scent of orange blossoms.

The Greeks had a wonderful custom of community picnics on Sundays. We were lucky to see part of the proceedings as we drove to Delphi. For fifty yards along the roadside in the village there were glowing coals over which whole lambs were cooking on spits. The air was redolent with the aroma of charcoal and browning lamb as we drove past, longing to stop and join in the festivity. We visualized them dancing, joined in large circles, and imbibing great quantities of ouzo until late in the evening. The Greeks are a happy and proud people with many joyous customs.

One day we went to Paraglia on a cove near Praeus. Wandering along the quay, we watched activity on the freighters and yachts and were surprised to see the *President Wilson* tied up at the dock. We were compelled to go aboard and see our old friend, which fought the Pacific seas so bravely and brought the Greek crew to safety. As we walked through the familiar salons, we saw several crewmen whom we recognized. One of the sailors had been on the rescue team in the lifeboat and reminsiced about the exciting day of eight years ago.

Satisfied that we had seen Athens to our heart's content, we boarded the *Stella Maris* for a Greek Island tour. For four days we sailed from one beautiful island to another, stopping in Hydra the first night. Santorini was something of a tourist gimmick, but we did the tourist thing and rode donkeys up the steep mountain trail, twisting around the corkscrew path until we arrived at the hilltop village, hot and dusty. We found it not worth the effort and walked back down the road a somewhat less hazardous activity than the donkey ride.

We had a marvelous guide in Heraklion, Crete who showed us the 1400 B.C. Palace of Knossos and the museum housing the treasures of the palace. The tremendous ruin was still colorful with the red pillars and painted friezes depicting the life of those times.

Rhodes was interesting, entailing more donkey rides to the Acropolis, but Ephesus was the most fabulous place of all. The excavated ruins of the town revealed it had been an important port at the time of Christ. The Virgin Mary is supposed to have fled from Jerusalem to Ephesus, and we saw where she had lived until her death. This is also where the apostle St. Paul lived to the end of his days, started his church and wrote his letters, included in the New Testament. We were transported into the past and could almost see the ghost inhabitants walking the streets in their togas.

The last island on the circuit was Mykonos, famous for its scenic uniqueness, the old windmills scattered on the hills. We strolled on the square, looked into the shops of gleaming copper and brass and sat drinking ouzo as we watched the passing scene. That night we were treated to a Taverna dinner and Greek folk songs with dancing.

From Athens we flew to Istanbul, Turkey for a few days, staying at the modern Istanbul Hilton. We enjoyed the exotic city, the mosques, the Topkapi Museum (one of the most fabulous in the world) and the famous Bazaar. We bought a lovely, silk oriental rug to ship home. The one disappointment in Istanbul was not seeing any good belly dancers. The Turks claimed all their best belly dancers are in New York, and we thought they must be right. A friend of mine in the Symphonic Choir did belly dancing in restaurants in Indianapolis. She was better than any we saw in Turkey.

On May third we flew to Vienna and rented a car. We attended *Der Rosenkavalier*, which is one of my favorite operas. The opera house was right across the street from our Hotel Sacher, and after the production, Sam and I had supper in the hotel dining room. We were alone in the room until Leonard Bernstein came in with an entourage of about twenty people. I guessed he was in Vienna at the time making his T.V. series on the Beethoven symphonies.

I had always wanted to see the Spanish Riding School exhibit their famous Lippizzan horses, and this time had tickets, which we had ordered long before we left home. The show had barely begun when I started feeling tight in my chest. I was having an allergic reaction to the years of horse dander and dust accumulated in the great hall and could not breathe. I had to leave the show, choking with asthma. We went back to the Sacher, and I went to bed greatly disappointed.

[335]

We loved Vienna, even in the rain, but we left after a few days and drove on to Salzburg, winding through the schlosses (lakes). The hotel was across the river from Salzburg. All we had to do was walk across the bridge to be in the old town. We loved the beautiful gardens of the Mirabel Palace full of tall, fat, colorful tulips, and, later that evening, went to a chamber concert inside the palace, a most appropriate setting for Mozart's and Schubert's music.

After spending two days in Salzburg, and consuming wonderful food, such as the nocherl souffle at the Golden Hirsch, we drove to the nearby Schloss Fuschel, a charming hunting lodge. Sam had not been here, but I had been captivated by it when we came in 1962 with my parents, Judy and Ann. It was a small, square building with turrets, built on the very edge of a high point overlooking the exquisite Lake Fuschel. Some turreted rooms were furnished in Tyrolean style, others more elaborately with antiques. We were given the royal suite! It was the most beautiful room overlooking the lake. The furniture was nineteenth century French, the large bed piled high with double down puffs. Everything about the hotel was elegant and the cuisine matched. It had once been a famous hunting lodge for royalty, but during World War II, the high-ranking German of officials appropriated it for their living quarters. After the war it was turned into a hotel.

The entire time during our stay it downpoured rain. We were not able to row out into the lake, nor walk the forest paths. But it was a delightful place to be "locked in." We spent much of the time in our large living-bedroom suite in great comfort, and in the evenings joined the other guests in the lounge around a blazing fire in the large fireplace. The walls were hung with many heads and antlers of deer and wild animals shot during the hunting seasons of previous days. We ate in a large porch dining room, enclosed during bad weather, but open when the air was mild. In May, it was cold, and the constant rain and wind did not help the climate.

After we left Schloss Fuschel, we began our drive through Germany, touching Switzerland as we edged around Lake Constance, and seeing the most beautiful country along the way. The prevailing weather, rain and more rain, prevented us from stopping to explore towns until we came to Innsbruck, where we stayed overnight and were entertained by a Tyrolean group playing Swiss instruments, Alpine horns, zithers and cowbells. There was dancing with a maypole, yodeling and slap dancing. It all was done in a great spirit of fun.

We ferried across Lake Constance from Meersburg after browsing in the village and their fourteenth century castle and stayed in quaint Tyrolean hunting lodges until we arrived in swanky Baden-Baden, a town in Germany renowned for its spas. There we stayed at the Hotel Bellevue, a large impressive resort hotel surrounded by manicured lawns and gardens.

To reach Baden-Baden we drove through the famous Black Forest in the rain and fog. But as we climbed higher up the mountains, the rain changed into snow. The scenery resembled a Christmas card. The immense dark firs standing in thick formation on either side of the road were heavy with snow. We couldn't have wished for a more beautiful sight, a rather unusual one for May.

We saved time by taking the Autobahn from Baden-Baden, thinking to arrive at the edge of the Romantica-Strasse, where we planned to wander, but we were unable to find accommodations in either Ulm or Augsberg. We had not planned to go to Munich but found ourselves there for the night.

Driving on the Autobahn was frightening. To keep up with the rushing traffic, we were forced to drive at one hundred miles an hour. Even so, we were passed by trucks and cars as though we were tied down. Sam is no slouch behind the wheel, but even he thought we should stick to country roads after that day.

We arrived in Munich at dinner time and found a nice, modern hotel for the night. We could always spot a hotel in Germany because a prominent sign is posted in front reading *Eingang* (meaning Hotel Entrance.) At the back of the hotel is also a sign for the exit, reading Ausfahrt. We thought these names were funny, but it was easy to find our way in and out of these places, at any rate.

Thinking it would be fun to see Munich at night, we arranged for a night club tour. The guide sent around a sheet of paper and pencil asking us to write down our names and the name of our hotel where we would be delivered at the end of the tour. Often, he elaborated, people forget where they belong after a night of beer gardens, such as we would soon experience.

We sat quite a while until the list made the rounds, and the guide was satisfied all had signed. Once, he explained, he had neglected to confirm the tourists with their hotels. At the end of the evening a Japanese tourist had confidently written as his hotel, "The Hotel Eingang."

The best part of our trip through Germany was the Romantica-Strasse. We explored tiny villages and stayed in their inns, absorbing the history of the ancient walled fortresses. Rothenburg was our favorite town. We stayed at the Eisenhut Hotel, and walked to see every corner of the interesting fortified village.

The old walls still encircled Rothenburg. We climbed to the top of the ramparts and walked the length and breadth to view the buildings and scenery within and without the town. When the clock in the Market Platz struck the hours, a statue of the burgher appeared in the clock tower and drank three litres of beer.

We wanted to stay longer, but the hotel had been fully reserved. In fact, the entire town was sold out for the coming festival the next week.

Nürmburg was our next destination. I was eager to return to the lovely old town I remembered from 1932, but I was not prepared for the change. Nürmburg had been bombed and devastated during World War II. Shell holes marked the facings of the old cathedral and the few buildings that still stood through the bombardments. The old castle that fascinated me with its torture museum when I was fourteen had been repaired with a modern face and turned into a museum where World War II exhibits were displayed. After seeing a movie showing the disaster of the war, I left sick and depressed.

We stayed in a tiny hotel on the main square. It had no restaurant, but in the next block was a bratwursthausle. We ate on the terrace at umbrella tables, or inside, around an open wood fire braising bratwurts. It was the best we had ever tasted (at every meal) we ate the sausage, sauerkraut and potato salad and washed it down with beer.

Heidelburg was another disappointment. It was dirty and overrun with college students, scattering litter and beer bottles. Our hotel was poor and had no restaurant — the last choice in a town full of tourists. Our room was tiny and overlooked nothing. The only redeeming feature was the view from the castle on the hilltop, which was breathtaking even through the haze. We pushed on to the Rhine valley, stopping to get acquainted with Rudesheim and search for the Lorelei. The drive was beautiful all along the way with many castle ruins on the hills. Eventually we arrived in Coblenz where the boy had asked me for a dance years ago. I could not guess where we might have stayed then. The hotel could have been destroyed in the war. Most of the town had been reconstructed, particularly along the Rhine River.

It was painful to reminisce about my pre-war visit, and I no longer wanted to see anyplace where I had been in 1932. We skipped Cologne and hurried through Germany to the Netherlands.

—————<◦>—————

We had a good three-day visit with Bep and Laurens Van Oosten in The Hague, sightseeing through the Dutch villages and climbing up into the old windmills. We stayed at the lovely Wittenburg Hotel not far from their home, meeting them every day for meals and companionship. Of course we had to go to Schevenigen, but the huge wooden barn on the pier was gone. The entire section on the coast was a recreation-resort area with modern buildings.

Another three days in Amsterdam brought our Dutch tour to a close. We stayed at the Hotel Krasnepolsky on "hippie" square. It was interesting watching the hippies of all nationalities, who lived on the square. They sat alone or in family groups around the central fountain during the day. At night the police forced them off with fire hoses, cleaning their trash off at the same time. They were supposed to spend the nights in a designated building, but most chose other streets on which to sleep. It is hard to fathom why young people wish to drop out of life and live hand to mouth, unwashed and in rags, bearing illegitimate children and wandering barefoot in search of dope in seedy sections of town. What a tragedy and waste of human life! We were told it was their protest against society! But at whose expense?

Our stay in Amsterdam included the day and night tours on the canals, hours in the marvelous Rijkmuseum, a fascinating flower auction in Alsmeer, the Frans Hals Museum in Haarlem and much good Dutch food in picturesque restaurants.

After spending the rainy month of May meandering through Germany and Holland, we flew to London on June first. Bep and Laurens saw us off at the Schiphol Airport, handing us a gift-wrapped shoebox as we started to board. We were told not to open it until we were on the plane. Curiously we untied the box as we flew over the Channel and were amazed and shocked to see a familiar, exquisitely carved Indonesian goddess, a dragon at her feet with open jaws and "flaming," lashing tongue. Sam had admired the figure in their home as it stood on the mantel. They gave it to us with a note expressing nearly forty years of affection and friendship since Bep and I met in The Hague in 1935. We were deeply moved by the gift, as it was a real sacrifice for them to give up such a beautiful piece of art and memento from the country where they were born. We treasure the lovely reminder of our mutual feelings of friendship and have placed it prominently in our own home.

The first night in London, Sam called an old New Zealand friend, Dawn Arnal, whom he had met in Wellington during the war. She was now living in London, and we invited her for dinner. I had met her some years before when she and her husband visited us in Indianapolis when they lived in Canada. Now she was divorced and trying to make a living for herself and her son, Craig, who attended a prep school near Oxford.

During the evening we told her we planned to rent a car and drive to Cornwall's coast. Dawn suggested she and a friend might like to be our "English speaking guides," as her friend knew that part of the country well. She offered to pay for their room and meals if we would pay the car expenses and arranged for us to meet her friend, who, she said, worked in Bentley's Bar. We were to join them there for lunch the next day and make our plans for the excursion.

We arrived on time for the lunch date and waited quite a while, but Dawn did not arrive. We were languishing and starving for food when forty-five minutes later, Dawn showed up with her sister, apologizing for being so late. She had been trying to locate David. (We then learned her "friend" was male.) After another forty-five minutes David finally appeared. It seemed he had been very reluctant to meet us.

During lunch we discovered David Yellowlees had been living with Dawn for over a year, and their relationship was now a little off balance. Besides not wanting to be involved with us, he wished not to go on a week's tour with Dawn. Actually, David was a very attractive man. He was heavily built, tall and dark with black, penetrating eyes and thick, black hair. His attractiveness was matched by his intelligence and background. We learned he was from a wealthy family from Bath. His father had been a prominent surgeon in London's Harley Street and hoped David would become one also. David attended Oxford for a year, but the war began and he enlisted. When the war finally ended, he returned home, after long years of active service, burned out with life.

He refused to go back to school or work at any job and became dependent on his widowed mother for a small stipend. He was an adult drop-out. His job at Bentley's Bar was the result of a bet. His friends wagered he could not hold any job — even one sweeping out a pub after hours. Challenged, David applied as the "sweeper" and won the bet, sticking to it for over a year. When he met Dawn, he simply moved in with her to save his expenses. She, unfortunately, was in love with him, but he was more in love with himself.

We were somewhat embarrassed by their arrangement and felt put out, drawn into an awkward situation. We were not eager to embark on a journey with them but didn't know how to back out. Dawn was pressing the trip enthusiastically, but the atmosphere was tense between them, David slouching in his chair, drinking only beer for lunch while Sam and I threw silent, quizzical glances at each other.

Warmed by the beer, David became friendlier, evidently feeling we were not bad sorts after all and joined in the conversation, suggesting he would plan the itinerary, make reservations in the hotels and call Avis to order a car for us.

We left all the plans to them as we were leaving the next morning on a week's bus tour to Scotland. The tour was somewhat of a disappointment because it did not include stops at the many interesting places on the way, such as the beautiful mansions and castles, which I would have loved to visit. But this was a "Countryside Tour" from London to Edinburgh and back, circling through the western country of England's Lake Region, east from Glasgow to Edinburgh, and south through the eastern section back to London. The glorious rhododendron were blooming in bushes as large and high as the cottages along the way, in all shades from pale pink to deep red. We stayed in comfortable inns and were served excellent food. We also enjoyed the company of the other tourists on the bus, a very congenial group. Cold weather and rain continued to plague us. In fact, there were only about thirty days free of rain in the entire three-and-a-half months of our trip, but we were dressed for it, and hadn't expected it to be any better.

After our return to London, we joined Dawn and David for an evening of bohemian atmosphere at La Boca, a lively restaurant on the Thames just outside of London. We agreed to meet the next morning at the Avis office to pick up the car David had ordered.

Always punctual, Sam and I arrived at nine a.m. but it was nearly two hours later before Dawn and David showed up. We were irritated by the delay, and Sam, too angry to drive, asked David to get us out of the London traffic. He preferred to practice driving on the left on country roads.

It was at least a lovely day, warm and sunny as we drove south, stopping to see the marvelous Salisbury Cathedral. Through the vaulted chamber we could hear the fluted tones of a boy's choir singing and wandered in to find the boys rehearsing. We stood for quite a while listening to them in the splendid setting.

Driving on, we stopped now and then when Dawn would cry out as a pub appeared on the roadside. She had to have a beer in every pub we passed. Finally we decided it was time to stop for the night and asked David to direct us to our first hotel. But he had neglected to make reservations anywhere, thinking it wouldn't be necessary. Sam couldn't believe it because June is a busy tourist month. We tried one hotel after another, only to find them all booked. At one inn they were nice enough to call other hotels in the area for us, and we finally found one with just two rooms left on the outskirts of Exeter. It was a trifle seedy, the rooms up three flights of stairs, but it was adequate for one night. We always asked for a bath with our room, but Dawn said she didn't care about that. All she demanded was a double bed!

Except in the London traffic, Sam drove the entire time and, fearful of side-swiping an oncoming car, hugged the left side with great determination. The narrow, twisting roads of Cornwall were lined with heavy shrubbery, and I sat gasping in fear as the bushes scraped the car on my side. Sam said he would rather scratch up the car driving too close to the side of the road than hit a car head-on. I agreed, but telephone poles also lined the roads and whipped by with terrifying closeness. I sat and cringed while David, sat stolidly in front of me, keeping his fears to himself. Dawn was most unconcerned, sitting behind Sam and furthest from the danger. She chain-smoked her way along. This, of course, added to my discomfort and tension. Occasionally, Sam would hug the edge of the road so closely, he would ride up over the curbs. It was a miracle we survived!

We traversed the coast line and stopped to inspect interesting fishing villages along the way and then came upon Mousehole; tucked into a cove

[341]

with its narrow, cobblestone streets winding up and down hills. We fell in love with the quaintness of the town and wanted to remain, but there was no room available. We made reservations at nearby La Morna Cove on a hillside. It was a picturesque inn with low twisting stairs around corners and corridors, and our rooms were charming with little niches and crannies tucked under a low ceiling. There was a compelling view of the sea and wooded hills from our windows. We wished we could stay indefinitely and explore the surrounding area, but we only had one more day before we had to move on.

We drove to Land's End, but it was an unsatisfactory trip as the tip of England was cloaked in deep fog. We settled for a beer in "The First and Last Pub" in England. I simply couldn't drink the quantity of lager the rest of them were able to consume each day. Even one was too much for me. But I discovered mead, and settled for that while the others drank their lagers.

It was David's birthday, and we wanted to return to Mousehole for a special lunch to celebrate the occasion. Sam had noticed an old tavern called The Lobster Pot situated on a jutting pile of rocks off the cove in Mousehole's center. He roused the owner at eleven a.m. and ordered a table at the noon hour with lobsters and chilled champagne. It was a memorable meal!

That morning, after washing my hair and carefully combing it out after it was dry, we were walking along the sunny streets of the village. The air was full of screaming sea gulls, swooping over us to dive into the harbor for their catch. I suddenly felt a soft "plop" on top of my head. A gull had made a bull's-eye on my fresh hair-do! Sam and David, walking on either side, could clearly see the white blotch on top of my hair. While they were cleaning it out with a tissue, an elderly, toothless woman trotting along the sidewalk looked me up and down appraising the situation, and with a cackle said "Ha! You've just had a bit of Cornish luck, ain't-cha?"

We were so enamored of Mousehole, we delayed our departure as long as possible. But we had a six-hour drive that day to reach Taunton, so pulled away with happy memories. Mousehole (pronounced Mouzel by the British) seemed perhaps more attractive than anyplace else we had seen because, while we were there, the weather was warm, sunny and perfect. We had been in such bad weather for so long, perpetually cold and damp, we feared we'd begin to develop mold.

We wandered through Wells Cathedral, marveling at the splendid, historic edifice, and to Bath, where we were in awe of the extensive ruins built in 43 A.D. by the Romans. They were more fabulous and interesting to me than any ruins we had seen in Rome. Underwater pipes conveying the hot and cold water to the baths were still in operation, and much of the wall paintings were visible.

David's mother lived in Bath, and we were determined he should call on her while we toured the ruins. He was almost adamant about not seeing her, not wanting to explain his presence in Bath. At length, after much persuasion from Dawn, he left us, presumably to see her, but I privately suspected he may have sat out the time in a pub, (unless he needed to extract more money from her.) My unkind comment is only written to explain the true character of the man living with Dawn. He was a charming leech, a hypocrite with the culture and intelligence to fool a bedazzled, lonely woman. He returned to us with noncommittal remarks about his visit but seemed to be more relaxed and less guilt-ridden. Perhaps he really had seen her after all.

In Berkeley we went through the best preserved castle in England, still occupied by the owners. Here is where Edward II was murdered. From Berkeley we crossed over into Wales and spent the night in Newport. Again rain dampened our spirits for sightseeing. We didn't see too much except for some interesting ruins of castles. We pressed on again back into England.

Our twenty-fourth anniversary was spent driving back to London, stopping to sightsee in Worchester, Stratford-Upon-Avon, Oxford and the gardens of Blenheim Palace, the birthplace and home of Winston Churchill. We continued on to find Craig's school centered in five hundred acres of beautiful grounds with its own lake. Craig, Dawn's son and Sam's godchild, showed us around the school. We had a pleasant visit with him before returning to London late in the evening.

Back at the Mayfair Hotel, we walked across the street to our favorite restaurant, The Empress, for a late anniversary dinner. We had had a wonderful trip with Dawn and David, with many interesting stops, much pub-hopping and the drive ending more pleasurably than it had begun. Dawn told me later the trip had reunited her relationship with David, and she felt sure they would marry soon. As it turned out, this was not to happen. Within the year Dawn discovered he had turned his eyes on another blonde. Dawn "gave him the sack," and he moved out and married her.

We were in London three more days, moving from the swinging Mayfair Hotel, which we liked very much, to the Atlantic Hotel, one of the worst we have had the misfortune to encounter, to join a group from the Indianapolis Symphonic Choir. We were going on a Baltic cruise to sing concerts on the ship and, after the cruise, to perform in Dublin.

It was fun to be with the others from the choir, some of them friends already from long association at rehearsals. About forty from the roster of one hundred and eighty flew to London to make the combined vacation and concert tour together. Dr. Charles Webb, dean of the music school at Indiana University, was our very inspiring, competent director. He converted our rather amateurish choral singing to one of professionally high caliber. Organized to accompany the Indianapolis Symphony Orchestra, the choir joins the orchestra twice a year on their subscription concerts. Choir members included their husbands or wives on the trip, and Charles brought his beautiful wife, Kenda, and their three young sons.

Charles had planned tours for us, and we went again to the familiar landmarks of Windsor Castle and Hampton Court. In the evening we attended a concert of the London Philharmonic Orchestra with Vladimir Ashkenazy, the pianist, playing a Mozart concerto. The finale was the world premier of a symphony by Tillet, which I predict was the first and last hearing. It was horrendously loud with eleven percussionists working like mad. We left as soon as we decently could and took the underground back to the sleazy Atlantic Hotel in a remote section of London. The meals we had at the hotel were memorable for the slow service and mediocre food. Our room was in the rafters of the building, the bathroom down a darkened hall. We were thankful it was for one night only.

The next day we boarded the *Regina Magna* at the Tilbury docks. The ship was the old Bremen, a famous German liner of the thirties. It had been bought and remodeled by the Greeks very attractively as a cruise ship. We loved the cruise, enjoyed the enormous liner and had fun at our daily rehearsals. We shared tables at meal time and found time for bridge and ping pong when we weren't visiting port towns.

The cruise lasted two weeks, sailing the Baltic Sea from Amsterdam to Oslo, Göteberg, Stockholm, Helsinki, Isle of Visby and Copenhagen before returing to London. The itinerary was supposed to include Leningrad, but we were told the Russians had refused us entry at the last moment. Supposedly the ship was one inch too long to fit into the dock slip! Yet, *The France*, the largest ship afloat, made regular stops in Leningrad. The rearrangement of the itinerary, to include Göteberg Island, caused our scheduled concert in Stockholm to be cancelled as we arrived one day too late. However, we sang our concert on the ship and were so well received, the passengers asked for more. We complied, singing several more times for the entertainment of the ship.

We enjoyed the interesting ports of call. When we were in Amsterdam, we met Bep and Laurens again for lunch at the elegant Hotel Amstel and visited while our group toured the city. In Stockholm we took time to call at the Wenner-Gren's city home and were greeted cordially by the housekeeper, who gave us the latest news of Marguerite, then in Nassau. She said her health was failing. Later, due to circulation problems, her leg was amputated. Axel had died in 1959 of cancer, but his philanthropy lived on in the form of the Wenner-Gren University which he had founded and given to Stockholm.

We did not have time to visit the Wenner-Gren's Herringer Castle on the outskirts of Stockholm, but we had seen many pictures of the large estate, the hunting grounds and the massive mansion. We loved Stockholm and would like to return another day for a longer visit.

At the end of the delightful cruise, our group was driven directly to Heathrow Airport in London where we boarded a plane for Dublin, Ireland. We rehearsed and later gave a concert at the downtown Prostestant church of St. Anne's, which was well attended. The congregation graciously gave us an elaborate reception in the basement community room of the church. The people were all so very friendly, and, the ladies had made enough sandwiches, cakes and cookies for a group three times as large. We felt everyone liked us and our music.

The choir left in a body the next day for Indianapolis, but we stayed on to see a little more of Ireland. The night before the flight we had a medieval dinner in Limerick at Castle Knappogue, a fitting farewell celebration of our two weeks together.

We saw the group off at Shannon Airport then rented a car and drove around the Ring of Kerry, one of the lovely sections of Ireland. The day we chose to "ring-around" Kerry was thickly fogged. The narrow, twisting road around the rock edges of the Dingle Peninsula was a little hair-raising, especially when we couldn't see where we were going. But the weather added spice to the adventure, and after all, we were experienced by then at navigating in rain and fog.

Everything we saw in Ireland was a joy and a pleasure. We vowed to return another day. After a week, we flew back to London, collected the balance of our luggage, which had been stored at the Mayfair Hotel, caught the boat train to Southampton and sailed home on The France July thirteenth. The three-and-a-half months had been full of wonderful experiences, and we really weren't ready to go home.

[345]

Mousehole, Cornwall, England

Sam with David Yellowlees

'Cina, Sam and Dawn Arnall

[346]

House in Cuernavaca, Mexico — terrace

Scott and Breck in the pool

Stairsteps in front of Borda, Cathedral, Taxco

[347]

CHAPTER FIFTY-SIX

WE decided to add on a wing to our house. Ever since we had moved to Carmel I had disliked our small, crowded bedroom. It was so close to the living room anyone walking in the front door could see us in bed. I missed the spacious bedroom on Washington Boulevard and couldn't get used to the cramped feeling and obstacle course of furniture — even after fourteen years.

Since Sam had retired, he had no place of his own to work or even to store his files of paper and office furniture, which he needed to keep at home. He also had to parade through the living room to use the guest bathroom instead of the one near our bedroom because he preferred the shower, and I had always yearned for a real dressing room with good lighting for make-up and plenty of closet and drawer space. We were exceedingly cramped for closets.

We had no emergency exit from the house in case of fire and no shelter possible if a tornado struck. I wanted a doorway leading from our bedroom to the open terrace. The present window was covered with climbing roses along the outside wall, full of thorns, and to escape in case of fire, could be injurious.

For all of these reasons, we consulted with our neighbor, architect and friend, Roll MacLaughlin, who drew up a plan for us, suggested a contractor, and work was begun in the fall of '73.

The contractor began digging a basement, which would be under the entire new wing. Having a basement was also an improvement as we had missed a place for storage. Now it could also be used for a new furnace, water heater, storm shelter, and would include space for a workshop for Sam. Our ping pong table, uselessly stored in the garage could be set up, ready for a game.

With the new plan we would have a very large bedroom with walk-in closets, an office for Sam's private use, and, between the two rooms, a large dressing room and bath. It would be a spacious, comfortable addition for all our future needs. We also enclosed half of the terrace with screening and storm windows for dining. A door was cut through from our bedroom to the porch for an easy exit, and to join the wing to the rest of the house, doors from the two bedrooms were cut at the window sites.

By November we had to move out of our bedroom and close off that end of the house because the workmen were ready to drill into the walls to make the connection. We moved into the family room with our closets emptied and bureau drawers full of clothes. One end of the family room became a huge open closet. We bought aluminum clothes racks, where we hung our clothes and lived out of bureau drawers full of the rest of our necessities. It was fun "camping out" and sleeping on the sofa bed. We made it cozy and warm by keeping a fire burning in the big fireplace beside our bed. We loved going to sleep with the crackling sound and watching the flame-shadows dance on the ceiling.

We knew the work would continue throughout the winter, and we would soon become weary of the constant hammering, filtered plaster dust and the general confusion upsetting our household. We were hungry for a glimpse of Mexico and thought this would be a perfect time to get away. We arranged to rent a house in Cuernavaca for three months with the help of Kay Blair, (previously married to Don Thorburn) who lived in Mexico City.

We began our drive to Mexico right after Christmas, taking our little miniature poodle, Sophie, along with us. She would be happy away from home as long as she was with us. We decided to drive leisurely, stopping to see friends along the way, and taking the west coast route down through Mexico, as we had never been that way before. When we arrived in Tucson, Arizona, Ruth and Bob Eaglesfield joined us to be our first guests in Cuernavaca. We met them at the airport, and from Tucson, continued the trip together, down through Mexico, crossing the border at Nogales. We celebrated new Year's Eve in Guaymas at one of the many resort hotels, decorated with the usual paraphernalia of serpentines and balloons hanging from the ceiling. It was a colorful and loud evening, the mariachi band blowing as hard as they could on their horns — a perfect way to initiate a new adventure with our good friends.

We continued driving along the western coastline of Mexico to Mazatlan and almost to Puerto Vallarta. We wanted to see the famous new resort area as it was nonexistent when we lived in Mexico, but the hotels refused to accept us because of Sophie. It was the only place we encountered difficulty because we had a pet with us. We skirted around the snooty town and went on to Guadalajara, spending two nights in a very nice, modern hotel, resting after our long drive. We saw what the city had to offer, but our favorite place was on the out-skirts of town, a famous, fun-filled tourist trap of shops — Tlaquepaque. Just saying the name of the village is fun. The shops are jammed with arts and crafts from everywhere in Mexico — and Mexicans are fine artists, original, creative and love bright colors. You can always find something unusual, decorative and useful — textiles, pottery, basketry or wood carvings. The Mexicans also make beautiful jewelry, using their native silver, copper and semi-precious stones. It is easy for me to fall prey to the temptations of Mexican products.

Our last night on the road was spent in Morelia. I always liked the pretty colonial city, with its typical Spanish-style buildings and old-world customs. It didn't try to be modern but remained proud of its Spanish-Mexican heritage. The zocalo and city streets were strung with Christmas lights, and we walked through the park, crowded with merry-makers and children skipping about, holding balloons and ice cream sticks. There were parades of costumed people, bands and entertainers all in celebration of Children's Christmas on Twelfth Night, the day of gift-giving. December twenty-fifth is a holy day spent quietly in church, but the two weeks following are given over to parties, piñatas and gift exchanges, cluminating on January sixth, the night we arrived in Morelia

———————⟩◉⟨———————

We found our house in Cuernavaca delightful! We were amazed by the growth of the city since we had lived in Mexico. From the sleepy town we remembered, it was now a sprawling city. The house we were renting was in an entirely new, hilly suburb, owned by an American couple from Chicago who were in the process of a divorce.

Within the confines of the high, protective wall on the property were two buildings — the main house and the guest house, separated by a good-sized pool. The two-storied guest house had a bedroom and bath on each floor, the upstairs reached by an outside staircase. The main house contained the living quarters, large master bedroom and bath and a pretty shaded terrace overlooking the garden and pool. A cook and two house maids took care of our needs.

The noted artist Echevarria's home and studio was across the street from us. The day we arrived was the day of his funeral, and the street was full of mourners and curiosity-seekers. He was a painter who went in for enormous billboard size paintings. They decorated the studio walls with cubistic style murals, taller than the walls around his property. They made a rather ugly vista from our gate, and a striking contrast from the otherwise plain country dotted with modest homes.

We kept the guest house filled with family and friends for week-long visits. Doris and Scott arrived, soon after we did, and occupied the other bedroom in the guest house. The six of us drove to different spots, spas and tiny villages to browse and shop in their markets.

Polly and Don brought Leona the second week, followed by old friends from Mexico City, Anita and Mario Rabell. We urged my parents to visit us, but they declined. Mother had too many poodles to look after and Dad was afflicted with arthritis, making every movement painful. But one night, just before dinner, Dad called from a hotel in Cuernavaca. In great surprise, we learned he and John (the servant who looked after Dad) had flown down that day, rented a car at the airport and driven to Cuernavaca to find us. Unfortunately, he had neglected to bring our address along. So when they finally located a hotel, after much difficulty due to the language barrier and unfamiliar surroundings, Dad called Mother in Indianapolis to ask for our telephone number.

We were shocked to think of John driving through the demented

Mexican traffic and maze of roads, trying to reach an unknown destination in complete ignorance of Spanish. It was like being in a canoe without a paddle. Even reading the road signs along the way would have been impossible.

We brought them to our house for dinner, but could not invite them to stay as our house was already full. Polly's daughter Candy and her husband, Tony Rosenthal, had just flown in from Los Angeles while Polly and Leona were there. Dad did not intend to stay with us in any event, he said, because he was on his way to a well-known spa near Taxco that was sure to cure his arthritis.

John was terrified of embarking on the highways again. We assured him we all would go along in our car and lead the way. We saw Dad registered in a nice hotel, visited awhile and had lunch at the swanky spa-resort, then left to spend the remainder of the day in Taxco. Dad planned to take the baths for a week, then return and stay with us when a guest room would be free.

The next evening I called to check on his progress. He was not there; had checked out with no forwarding address! Frantically, I called the hotels in Mexico City where he had stayed previously, but no one had heard of him. Horrible visions of an automobile accident whirled in my head. I hated to call Mother and alarm her, but there was nothing left to do. Trembling, I told her Dad had disappeared without a trace and was shocked by her answer. "He's just fine" she laughed. "He's sitting right here beside me! He didn't like the spa." Dad had not even stayed overnight there. He had returned to Mexico City after we left him and caught a flight home.

This little anecdote about my father reflects much about his personality and instantaneous changes of plan. A whim was translated into action. It was sad to see my energetic father with all his vitality and sense of humor become imprisoned in a chair, suffering with the pain of arthritis and old age. He became cross and demanding, an entirely different person from the eager, fun-loving parent I had known. It was almost a relief when Dad died in 1980, no longer enjoying life and trapped in an ailing, frail body. I imagined his soul released to explore at will, as he so loved.

<hr />

Later on Judy, Bill, Breck and Scott flew down from Southampton, Long Island, to vacation with us for a week. The children had a wonderful time swimming in the pool, and we loved taking them to Vista Hermosa and Taxco, which Judy remembered well. While they were there, Balbina and Alicia bused down to Cuernavaca from Celaya to see us. Then all eight of us drove in two cars to Apizaco, to see Lola and her happy family. Lola had married Francisco (Paco) Brito, and they had a two-year-old daughter, Maria Elena, who was a beauty! Lola was again pregnant and would have Rosalba soon. She was destined to bear two more daughters

[351]

after this. Their fourth child was named Lucina, which made me very proud and happy. I was thrilled when Lola presented me with a large box full of beads, which had belonged to her grandmother. It made a great addition to my supply, and I needed many to make my flower arrangements and beaded pictures.

Apizaco is a small town high in the mountains near Pueblo. Paco is an engineer for a railroad company. Their home is small but very nice and also accommodated Paco's parents, who live in their own separate addition.

On our return to Cuernavaca, we dropped Balbina and Alicia off at the outskirts of Mexico City where they took a subway for the bus station and eventually returned to Celaya. Alicia worked for the Campbell Soup Company as secretary to the head of the research department. She is the highest paid woman employee next to the secretary of the company's president. We planned to see them again in Celaya and take them home with us for Alicia's vacation.

Marguerite Wenner-Gren had passed away only months before we arrived in Mexico, but we visited her faithful Frederick Alin and his family in their Cuernavaca home. He had come from Sweden with the Wenner-Grens on their yacht and had been the major-domo of the family ever since. He and his Mexican Wife, Josefina, were with Marguerite when she died and were the heirs to much of her estate. He wished to sell a quantity of her possessions, and we bought a dozen silver cocktail glasses that had served us many Southern Cross cocktails.

After the amputation of Marguerite's leg, she was never able to cope with the constant, agonizing phantom pain and disfiguration. She refused visitors, remained isolated in her home in Mexico City and literally drank herself to death.

We met new friends in Cuernavaca, and one elderly German lady invited me to use her fine Bechstein piano for practice. I accepted and was delighted to be able to go to her home every morning to practice the program Virginia and I were due to play in May.

The three months passed quickly, and before we knew it, we were driving away from the pretty house on our way home. We had only been in Mexico City long enough to pick up or deliver our guests at the airport, just once staying to have lunch at one of our favorite restaurants. The city had changed so radically since we had seen it in 1959, we were shocked and dismayed. Population explosion and pollution had made an incredible, terrible transformation. We drove the Periferico Highway circling Mexico City, supposedly avoiding much traffic, but we inched along the three lanes each way in dense, solid rows of cars, breathing the black exhaust fumes for two hours until we finally came to the Laredo Highway on the far outskirts of the capital. A pall of gray smog had hung over us,

[352]

stinging our eyes, but real tears mingled with the smog irritation as we deplored the present state of Mexico and what happens when "progress" is uncontrolled.

Kay Blair had invited us to spend the weekend at her home in San Miguel de Allende, and we were delighted to have another visit with her before leaving Mexico. Kay is a person of many talents. She worked as an interior decorator, is an artist and also an acomplished writer. She had designed the house creatively on its different levels and furnished it with stunning Mexican crafts. A few years later she and Don moved permanently to San Miguel.

We had a lovely, restful weekend with the Blairs, then pulled away to resume our drive to Celaya, where we stayed with Balbina and Alicia in their apartment. They entertained us royally with a dinner party, inviting the president of Campbell Soup Company, the research director (her boss) and their wives. Balbina prepared a delicious dinner, and we enjoyed conversing with their interesting guests. It was evident they highly esteemed Alicia, and we were impressed by the way she had elevated herself to a position of importance by her enthusiasm and winning ways. Not even a high school graduate, she had learned secretarial work with Lola's help, looked after Balbina, and gained valuable work experience beginning with her first job as the overseas telephone operator at the Hilton Hotel in Mexico City.

We were amused when Sarah Goodman, a friend of ours in Indianapolis, told us the following story. Sarah had put in a call to a friend on vacation in Mexico, and the telephone operator, receiving the call at the Hilton, greeted her, saying she remembered her as a friend of ours. Alicia told her who she was and asked her to please give "saludos" to the Moxleys for her. Sarah was dumbfounded by the coincidence and relayed Alicia's greetings to us with some excitement. She had never had such a "close connection" before! Alicia's knowledge of English was her entree in Mexico to all the best positions, as bilingual people are given preference in jobs.

Balbina and Alicia drove home with us and remained a week before returning to Celaya. We had had such a blissful time away from the construction at home, we had forgotten what a mess would confront us when we returned. We knew the wing would be completed by April first, but we didn't realize the entire house would be covered with plaster dust, which had blown through the furnace vents on every speck of space.

We intended for Balbina and Alicia to enjoy a work-free vacation, but they pitched in with gusto along with us, cleaned the house and straightened up the terrible disorder. It was like moving in completely. We placed the furniture in the handsome new addition and filled the closets with our dusted-off clothes. But it was almost time for them to return to Mexico

[353]

before the house was in livable condition.

I had never been under such pressure! As soon as we could dust off the pianos, Virginia and I set to work on our program scheduled for the last of May. My pupils resumed their lessons immediately on our return, and I was swamped with commitments.

We had barely said good by to our dear friends, the Ortegas, when Anita Rabell wired her intention of visiting us for the month of April. We had invited Mario and Anita to come "sometime" when we were in Mexico, but did not expect it would be so soon. Anita said she would be coming alone, however.

Virginia and I had practiced all day and were taping the program to evaluate our progress, when I noticed an irritating flash of light occuring just behind my vision. It kept flashing, but I couldn't take time to to locate the source of the bright light. I said nothing to Virginia as we continued the taping, and, frankly, I was too busy to pay much attention to it.

Anita was arriving that evening on a nine p.m. flight, and, as we drove to the airport, the darkness in the car made it easier to find that flashing bright light somewhere just behind me. I realized I could make it flash when I turned my eyes. Fear over-took me as I was afraid my retina was detaching, but I couldn't call my ophthamologist until Monday morning, and it was now only Saturday night.

We met Anita, had a late conversation before bed, and the next morning Sam left on a business trip until Wednesday. I called Dr. Thompson early on Monday, and he said I needed a retinal surgeon. He referred Dr. Rich and I made an appointment for Thursday. In the meantime, I was to "walk on eggs."

My knees shook as I realized my retina really was detaching, and I would surely have to have surgery. The flashes in my eye had stopped, but in their place, large "ink-blots" floated across my vision constantly. I wanted Anita to have a good time, and we were invited to a large dinner party Monday evening at the University Club. I thought it would be all right to go if I moved carefully, didn't lean over or stay too late at the party. I wasn't very happy about driving at night with one eye acting crazy, but I did, and it was worth it because Anita had a very good time. Anita is a beautiful woman, and, as I have previously written, almost a double of Dolores Del Rio. Although older than I by a number of years, she looked ten years younger and was sparkling and vivacious. She captivated every man at the party.

When Sam came home on Wednesday evening, I tearfully told him about the next morning's appointment with Dr. Rich. Although I had not lost the vision in my left eye, I saw weird "pictures" in it. Besides the floating black ink blots, a geometric screen like a tiny fly swatter mesh

[354]

filled my vision, each hole in the microscopic screen centered by a black dot. I saw this picture every time I looked into bright daylight. Small wormy objects crawled over my eyeball, resembling scraps of movie film. Although what I was seeing was fascinating, it was unnerving, and I was on edge with apprehension.

Dr. Rich looked into my eyes with a light so intense I thought I was blinded. But during his examination, I relaxed, feeling confident about his ability. He could see torn places in the retina which he said he would repair by a freezing technique.

After a day's delay, Community Hospital confirmed space for me and I was ensconced in a room, anxious to have the waiting over with. Anita decided to stay on and keep Sam company while I was incapacitated and unable to defend myself!

The waiting dragged on with one delay after another, but finally on Saturday at one-thirty I was taken to the operating room, a day later than scheduled.

Sam and Anita were there with comforting words when I awoke with both eyes bandaged. The next day the right eye was uncovered, but a patch was placed over the left eye with a tiny hole in the center, which I could see through. It was to keep my eye focusing straight ahead in one position to allow scar tissue to develop and hold the sections together.

After five days I was allowed to go home, but I had to wear the eye patch for another two weeks, stay home and do nothing for a month. The doctor encouraged me to watch television, which would keep my eyes focusing straight ahead. I could not read, lean over or do any activity, such as teaching. I was lucky the retina did not fully detach as that would have been much more serious, but I recovered normally and with an actual improvement in my vision. Judy developed a detached retina in 1984, which resulted in a greater problem for her at the time. Fortunately she recovered with normal vision also.

After Anita left us I began to practice and teach again. It was fortunate I had worked so hard memorizing the two-piano program in Cuernavaca! We played the program on schedule at the end of May with only two weeks of brushing up, and it went very well.

Life resumed its normal pace.

While visiting Balbina and Alicia in Celaya, we were impressed by Alicia's ability, ambition and charm. She was a competent, capable young lady, but when she talked about her career, we discovered she was not happy. As secretary to the research director, she felt she had gone as far as she could in the company, even though she had a chance for an opening as assistant to the research director in agriculture. This position, however, necessitated a degree. When Alicia asked Sam for his advice, he asked if she would like to attend Purdue University and finish her education with a degree in agronomy. Alicia was excited but worried she would not be accepted, lacking a high school diploma.

Sam began to work on Alicia's problem as soon as we returned from Mexico, sending for her transcripts from Shortridge High School. He also wrote the Dean of Admissions at Purdue, explaining the reason for Alicia's fifteen-year lapse in schooling, describing her job at Campbell's and including a resume of her progress after she left the States for Mexico in 1959.

The Dean was impressed by Alicia's ability to elevate herself with industrious and conscientious endeavor, and replied that Purdue would be glad to accept her, disregarding her non-completion of high school.

Alicia began her freshman year at Purdue in 1975, living with us when she was not on campus. Sam gladly paid all her expenses, board and tuition. We thought of Balbina's daughters as our "second" daughters, as, I think, Balbina felt about ours.

At age thirty, after a fifteen-year interim between schools, it was very hard for Alicia to return to academic life, but she struggled hard to overcome the difficulties and graduated in 1979, a victorious and happy woman. Alicia inspired Judy to return to college for her degree in journalism from Butler University in Indianapolis. Judy graduated in '83, exactly twenty years after her '63 class at Pembroke.

Alicia's natural, youthful and winning personality won her many friends at college, and the university, in turn, was very good to her. The faculty showed sympathy and consideration for her, offering help and extra tutoring when she needed it. Alicia's daily grades were high, but she fell apart during exams. She would become so nervous she failed nearly every test. After psychiatric help from a tutor, she found she was able to cope with testing a little better and made up her courses during summer school.

When Alicia returned to Mexico, she was given a position with the Mexican government in the department of seed exchange with foreign countries. Being bi-lingual, with a degree in agronomy she was able to get a higher-paying, more responsible job. Alicia rented an apartment in Mexico City for herself and Balbina, but it wasn't long after she returned that Balbina developed cancer. She battled her illness, slowly but surely losing ground over a five-year period. Our hearts ached for Balbina and the girls, feeling helpless not to be with them in their distress.

Lola Ortega

Alicia Ortega

Alicia graduates from Purdue University, 1979

[357]

Polly's family, West Hyannisport, Mass. Back Row, L. to R. Marshall Bassic and wife, Margo; Holly Rosenthal; Tony Rosenthal, Polly Greer, Leona Davis, Barret Bassick, Jill Rosenthal; Don Greer; Candy Bassick Rosenthal (in chair.) Front Row: Michael and "Rocky" Bassick; Melissa Rosenthal

CHAPTER FIFTY-SEVEN

W HEN Polly married Don Greer in 1969, he owned a large estate on Cape Cod in West Hyannisport, as well as a stunning home in the Virgin Islands on St. Thomas. They spent summers on the Cape in their huge frame house on the beach and winters in St. Thomas. We felt they had the best of both worlds, and visited them, taking Leona with us on several occasions.

One summer they offered us their home in St. Thomas for as long as we cared to stay. We were thrilled and spent six weeks of the summer in 1975, inviting family and friends to visit us.

We flew down after Ann's marriage to John Stanley on June fifteenth and took Bryan and Tracey with us. A few days later, the honeymooners arrived and spent two weeks. We surprised them by inviting Judy, Bill and their two children, Breck and Scott, to come at the same time.

We had such fun together! The children swam in the pool below the house or at the beach for long hours at a stretch. We used Don's sailboat (at his invitation) to visit the numerous islands near St. Thomas, picnicking on the boat or on the beach. The five bedrooms were occupied for almost the entire six weeks we were there.

My brother Bill arrived with his twin daughters, Julia and Janet, and stayed for awhile. Doris and Scott Moxley were with us when Julieta and Agustin Salvat came from Mexico. Later Marie and Vic Luther and Mary and Jim Steele arrived for a week. They were friends who had worked with Sam at Haag Drug Company and were now retired also. Our final guests were Billie and Charles Penzel, old friends of mine who had once lived in Muncie but were then residents of San Juan, Puerto Rico.

"Blue Rocks," the Greer's home, sat on the saddle of the mountain close to the top, where it commanded a magnificent view of both sides of St. Thomas. To our right lay the town of Charlotte Amalie, nestled into the protective circle of the harbor, where cruise ships lay at anchor and sailboats dotted the water. On the left, the mountain view dropped down to Megen's Bay and its extensive beach. Along the ridge beyond the jungle growth of tropical palms lay the unobstructed view of Drake's Passage through the British Virgin Islands, a most breathtaking sight.

Of all the places we have ever traveled with all the beauty and glamour of many sites around the world, never can a place compare to Blue Rocks. Designed by Frank Lloyd Wright, the house took advantage of every scrap of scenery, breath of fresh air and living comfort. The furnishings were luxurious, a combination of oriental and tropical style designed for relaxation. The living room, walled by sliding glass paneled doors, opened onto a deck where we could have cocktails, meals or just sit and revel in the view. The deck overlooked treetops and the gardens below, where we picked papaya, bananas, coconuts or mangoes every day. The vegetable garden contained everything we needed for the table, and Don's faithful French gardener and custodian, Theodore, saw we lacked nothing. Every morning a fresh bowl of fruit was placed on the kitchen table, and the refrigerator was always stocked with freshly cut vegetables.

The weather, cooled by the tropical winds at the mountain heights. was infinitely more comfortable than the stifling heat of the town at the shoreline. At night the balmy air carried the heavy perfume of the frangipani trees, and the view was magical with the lights below and the sky filled with bright constellations. We will always remember St. Thomas with love and nostalgia.

For eight consecutive years Sam drove Leona to Naples, Florida for the winter months of February and March. She rented a house in the old section of town, enjoying the change of climate and seeing her many friends. Polly and Don sometimes came for part of the time to ease Sam's responsibility with his mother, keeping house for her, preparing meals and running errands. I didn't like being away from home for as long as two months I felt a responsibility to my students and our house. I was afraid to leave the house in the dead of winter, vulnerable to common winter disasters, such as the furnace going off and pipes freezing. So I preferred to wait and join Sam and Leona for the month of March when most of the winter hazards were past.

It was seldom we could leave Sam's mother alone, but in 1981 we were able to be away for a week as Polly and Don had arrived to stay for the month of February. Leona at ninety-four was nearly blind and unable to do any cooking or housework in unfamiliar surroundings, although she still lived alone without any help in her own home in Louisville.

I flew from Indianapolis to Orlando on February twenty-fourth, where Sam met me, having driven up from Naples. We spent three days going through the remarkable exhibits of Epcot Center. Then we drove leisurely back to Naples via the east coast of Florida, stopping to spend a night with my dear friends, Jane Hitchcock Batzold, and her husband, Jack, in Palm Beach. It was the first time we had seen them since our visit years ago in Jamaica. Jane met Jack Batzold there after her divorce from Jack Simpson. They were married and lived in Kingston for many years until Jack's retirement from his business in the bauxite industry.

The next two nights were also spent in Palm Beach, with our other dear friends, the Chumleys, Mary Ellen (Bussy) and Norris, who were now living there most of the year in a newly acquired home. We had a wonderful time seeing our old friends and then proceded down the coast to Pompano Beach, for lunch and a brief visit with Mary and Jim Steele, before crossing Alligator Alley to reach Naples.

Polly and Don had planned a cocktail party for their friends in Naples the evening we returned from Palm Beach. It was their last night before leaving for St. Thomas. Two years before they had sold their home in Hyannisport and were making St. Thomas their permanent residence. They had completely redecorated the house and built a new kitchen, making the house even more attractive and commodious than before. We were looking forward to seeing all the improvements sometime in the future.

That night the phone rang before dawn. It was a disastrous message from the Greers' neighbor that their home was burning to the ground. At three a.m. a fire bomb had been thrown through the kitchen window, and the house was ablaze almost instantly, the mountain winds sucking the fire through the house as fast as through a chimney flue. The neighbor had been awakened by the mighty crash of the roof falling in, but it was too late for the fire department to check the raging fire, seen as far away as St. Croix, an island perhaps forty miles across the Caribbean. If Polly and Don had been sleeping there, they could not have escaped.

St. Thomas had been a hot bed of unrest and violence for some time. Once the house was broken into and Polly's purse snatched while she napped in the living room. Another time Don's granddaughter came close to being molested, but the intruder was surprised by Theodore and escaped over the wall before he could be caught. Although enclosed by a wall and a high fence with gates locked at all times, the property was still vulnerable.

Polly and Don were devastated by the loss of their home. They lost everything except for the contents of a small safe, which contained Polly's good jewelry and some important papers. The safe was found buried in the debris of charred beams and ashes, where it had fallen from the second floor to the basement. The only clothes they had were the ones they had brought with them to Naples for the month's visit. Polly was grateful they had not been there, and Don philosophically said it was almost a godsend to have the problem of living on St. Thomas at an end. They had become increasingly concerned over the erupting violence, muggings, rapings and robberies in Charlotte Amalie and the neighboring islands of St. John and St. Croix. Polly would not stay in the house alone when Don left on business trips. They both felt relief but great sadness at losing their beautiful home and all their possessions.

They left for St. Thomas immediately to assess the damage and recover one car that wasn't completely destroyed and returned to Naples to stay with us until it was time for our departure, April first. Then they rented a small apartment and bided their time, thinking they would "float" for a year before deciding where to settle down. As it happened, they found a charming house in Naples near the beach almost right away and bought it. They still live there and love the community of Old Naples. Naples has been the winter home of many Moxleys, Sam's Aunt Martha among the first gathering of "snow birds" to arrive in 1897. Aunt Martha's cottage was the eighth one built in Naples, about three blocks from the beach, looking the same as always except for new ones being squeezed in among the row of houses along Eleventh Avenue South, where it had once stood alone. Uncle Barret's cottage, "Mandalay," was on the beach at the end of the avenue, and next door to it was "Coquina," a cottage belonging to Sam's cousins, the children of Kitty Armstrong Robb. Another large piece of property farther south on the beach had belonged to Uncle Barret's mother-in-law, Mrs. William Scott.

Thinking back on our stay in St. Thomas, I recall how amused we were when the open jitney buses made their daily tour up the mountain hauling tourists from the cruise ships. The buses invariably stopped at the Mountain Top Hotel on the peak for the view and banana daiquiris. As they passed Blue Rocks, we could hear the spiel of the driver over his loud speaker saying: "Here we have a beautiful house built from the blue rocks found on the property. It is owned by rich Hollywood people who don't even live here."

Perhaps this kind of advertisement made the natives of St. Thomas believe the place was uninhabited and easy to rob — or to commit arson in their envy of people more fortunate than they.

Blue Rocks, St. Thomas, U.S. Virgin Islands

The end of Blue Rocks

The Moxleys and Steeles abord the Royal Viking Sky, *Circle Pacific trip,* 1977

Aboard the Prinsendam *with the Van Oostens,* 1978

[364]

CHAPTER FIFTY-EIGHT

I N 1977 we planned another long trip after Mary and Jim Steele raved about the new Royal Viking Line. The Norwegian cruise ships were making history on the high seas. The Steeles had taken a North Cape cruise on the *Royal Viking Star* and wished to take the Pacific Circle trip which lasted for seventy-seven days. They begged us to go along with them, and we were easily tempted.

The trip began on January twenty-third when Judy drove us to the airport for the flight to San Francisco. We shopped for two days, browsing in Chinatown and around Union Square, where we found a magnificent "tree" table, a slab of redwood we couldn't resist. It makes a stunning cocktail table for our "travel" family room in Carmel. We had visits with Barret Bassick, Polly's youngest son, and Betty Brown Fielding, who lived near the city and drove in for the day to be with us. It was good to see her after a lapse of many years.

The Steeles arrived the night before we sailed, and we toasted the upcoming voyage with Tongas at Trader Vic's.

Although the ship, the *Royal Viking Sky*, appeared elegant and was superbly designed for passenger comfort, I felt uneasy. Even in the quietest of seas, the ship wallowed and rolled. She felt top heavy. There were nine decks above the water line but only two below. I wondered how we would fare if the going really got rough.

———◄◉►———

The ship was delayed docking in Los Angeles by fog, and we hurried off by taxi to spend as much time as possible with Nita and Bill Nottingham in Long Beach. They had been living in California since Bill's retirement in New York, and it was good to see my cousin again.

Bill proudly showed us his workshop full of furniture to be caned. He had a thriving business having learned caning at the Blind School in Indianapolis in his youth. With more business than he could handle, he had taught Nita, and we were amazed and incredulous at the beautiful workmanship on the chairs. We had a lovely day with them, and they treated us to lunch in an excellent Mexican restaurant. We were so glad to have had the visit as it was the last time we ever saw Bill. Late in 1983, he died of a massive heart attack at age seventy-three. On a cold, rainy spring day in April, our family gathered in the little cemetery at Eaton, Indiana, to attend the burial service of Bill's ashes. Sam, Mother and I drove to Eaton from Indianapolis to greet Nita and Bill's sister, Corinne, whom we had not seen for many years.

The cemetery appeared to be almost a private one as many of the gravestones were inscribed with the names of members of Bill's paternal grandmother and her antecedents, the Adsit family. They had lived on a large farm adjacent to the churchyard in the early 1800's, and the burials dated back as early as 1827.

A rainstorm was gathering as our group of about twenty people shivered around the graveside. Anticipating a downpour, the minister led us in a brief prayer service, and then we hurried against the wind to reach our cars and drive away.

I felt much nostalgia as we drove past the farmland that once had been Orchard Lawn Dairy. The old schoolhouse (where the dynamite had been discovered) and the barns were still there, but painted an ugly bright yellow rather than the fresh white I remembered. Even the lodge, tucked in behind the rolling land was painted a matching yellow. We could only catch a glimpse of it down the lane as we drove along.

We met at Corinne's large Victorian house in the center of Eaton after the funeral service. As we entered the front door, Corinne said, You have to be thin to get into my house."

There never was a more literal statement. The moment we entered we stood facing a veritable museum of dolls from floor to ceiling. You could walk only in single file from the front hall to the living room, which contained hundreds of dolls, one a life-sized mannequin. They sat on the furniture, stood on the floor and tables and took up all available space.

The former dining room was converted into another collection of seven or eight doll houses completely furnished, as well as more cabinets and tables loaded down with dolls of all kinds. The only entry in or out of the room was a narrow passageway, just wide enough to allow a "thin" person to pass through. There was not a place to sit down in the house.

The rest of the house was filled to the brim with other types of collections and bric-a-brac, even to the kitchen. Overflow of many pieces of furniture and normal household items cluttered every conceivable space. Corinne said the upstairs was the same as the downstairs rooms, but the best of the collections were upstairs.

None of us had ever seen such an amassed assemblage. It was a bizarre and rather frightening effect to see so many doll's eyes looking back at you. Corinne had begun to collect the dolls only six years before, after the sudden death of her daughter, Mildred, at thirty-one, a lover of dolls.

The doll museum of over 10,000 was her memorial.

———••———◄◉►———•———

Before leaving on our cruise I had noticed something on the back of my calf which looked as though it could be an infected ingrown hair, but I was so busy I had no time to visit the dermatologist. I planned to have the ship's doctor take care of it. I had been made aware of my tendencies toward skin cancer when a small growth was surgically removed from my hand after

[366]

my retinal repair. Dr. Hibbeln had warned me about sun exposures saying the many winters I had worked so hard to get a "healthy" looking tan would only cause malignancies for the rest of my life. I had come home from Mexico with the best tan I ever had.

The Norwegian doctor on the ship was very attentive. I went to him every day for treatment as he requested, but it was obvious he didn't know what the "infection" was. I finally asked him to make an appointment for me at the first port with a good dermatologist. He arranged for me to see a doctor in Wellington, New Zealand.

Our first stop was at Moorea, Tahiti — the beautiful island with the significant hump of a mountain covering its base. We had only seen it from across the water in Papeete twenty years before. Now we drifted into its cove at sunrise and spent the day at the Bali Hai Hotel, languishing on the beach and drinking in the atmosphere of the exotic island. The hotel had bungalows perched over the sea with glass floors in the living rooms. We could sit and view colorful tropical fish swimming under our feet while sipping cool rum punches. Little bridges over the craggy rocks at the water's edge connected the bungalows to the beach. The bay was filled with beautiful fish and coral of many hues. Later on, we took tours beyond the reef in glass-bottomed boats in both Moorea and Papeete. We did nothing else in Papeete. The happy village of '57 was just another city now — a big disappointment for anyone who remembered its simple charm before the airport was built.

Tonga was our next port of call, somewhat disappointing because of the solid sheets of rain that fell all day. But this was where Sam had a vivid memory of his Tonga experience during the war. As he tells the story:

"In August of 1944, the area commander called me in to say there was nothing in Tulagi for the men to buy and send home to their families for Christmas. He ordered Ted Cummerford and me to go wherever we needed to buy one hundred thousand dollars worth of gifts to bring back in time for the Christmas mailing.

"I had made friends with the commander of a New Zealand Air Force PBY Flying Boat, Anti-Sub Patrol Unit operating out of Lions Point on Florida Island. I got him to assign a PBY and crew to me for a flight to the Fijis, and, if necessary, on to Hawaii.

"On our flight from the Solomons the crew gave us the red carpet treatment, serving tea with whitebait canapes, and I suspected something was up. There was another passenger on board, a tall, slim, golden-skinned officer in New Zealand Air Force Uniform.

"During the flight the pilot of the plane came back to sit with us while the co-pilot continued the flight. He introduced our fellow passenger as Bert Tupou and told me he was a Tongan going home on leave. He said it was very difficult to find a ship going to Tonga and asked if we would be in the Fijis long enough to release the plane in order to fly Bert to Tonga, a six-hundred mile flight from the Fijis. I told him I didn't know whether I could find the things I wanted in the Fijis or whether I would have to go to Hawaii, but would know by noon the next day. If I could order what was needed, I would then be able to release the plane with the time to fly to Tonga before dark.

"After the pilot returned to the cockpit, Bert Tupou invited us to fly with the plane to Tonga where we would be the guests of his family. Both Ted and I were very interested in the possibility of accepting the invitation.

"In Suva, we checked into the Grand Pacific Hotel for the night and had a late dinner. We were the last guests in the dining room, and, at the end of the meal, ordered after-dinner coffee. We were informed with much hauteur by the waiter that 'coffee was served in the lounge'. We went into the lounge and sat in large wicker chairs at the only vacant table in the room. The lounge was filled with British Colonials, dressed to the teeth, sitting in dead silence while they sipped their coffee. I said something funny to Ted, causing him to laugh. All the heads in the room slowly swiveled to direct their gaze at us, then slowly swiveled back. This struck me as being so funny, I began to laugh also, which shocked the entire assemblage. Several people rose from their chairs and departed in displeasure at the lack of decorum of the crude Americans.

"The next morning I found many shops manufacturing tortoise shell and silver jewelry, mostly run by East Indians, and was able to place the hundred thousand dollars worth of orders, to be filled within six days. We were then able to accept Bert's invitation and left on the plane for Tonga.

"Apparently the pilot had radioed our time of arrival, because when we landed in the harbor of Kikualofa and taxied up to the dock, we found a reception, including the Royal Band, to welcome us. That night there was a tremendous reception at the home of Bert's parents, where we met his father, a tall, slim, broadshouldered, ram-rod straight officer with an iron gray crew cut. He commanded the Tongan Military Forces. We learned Bert was the nephew of Queen Salote Tupou, and that he was not home on temporary leave, but for an indefinite leave to be inducted as chieftan of a group of the Tongan Islands.

"The luau was elegant, with the women serving all of the men first before they had their food. Later, while I was talking to an older Tongan couple and their daughter, one of the flight crew members walked up and joined us. After a short conversation the enlisted man proceeded to proposition the daughter for 'a little push-push in the bush.' They departed, hand in hand, leaving me standing with her parents, my jaw hanging open, too embarrassed to say another word to them.

"The next day I asked Bert about the episode and was told there was no disapproval of pre-marital sex in Tonga, which was quite different from

[368]

western culture, but, with a further difference that once a couple decided to marry and posted the banns, if either one of them was ever unfaithful to the other, the unfaithful partner would be exiled from the islands and forbidden ever to return. Bert pointed out with pride that this was quite different from our customs of disapproval of pre-marital sex, but with rampant cheating after marriage. He also pointed out their royal family was a matriarchy with the throne descending from the queen to her eldest daughter. This made the Tongas certain of their royal lineage, because, he said, 'You *do* know who your mother is'."

After our ship anchored in Nikualofa, Sam was determined to learn the whereabouts of Bert and asked a number of Tongans about Bert Tupou, but no one had heard of him. After being greeted by a group of performing dancers, we took a ramshackle bus to another dock and boarded an open launch for a nearby island where we would have a luau and entertainment. Almost there, the heavens suddenly opened up, and we were soaked to the skin and cold from the driving wind. We could do nothing but return to the ship in another enclosed launch to dry out and change clothes. We missed the luau and a good time but it turned out to be a fortunate mishap.

After a hot shower and shampoo we went to the ship's dining room for lunch. A handsome Tongan stood at the doorway, looking lost. Sam asked him if he could be of any help. The young man thanked Sam and explained he was arranging a table for lunch for a group of Tongans from his Department of Tourism. Sam then asked the same question about Bert Tupou's whereabouts. The Tongan shook his head. Sam continued by saying Bert had been a New Zealand flying officer. The Tongan's eyes brightened and he said there had been only one Tongan in the New Zealand Air Force but his name was Baron Vaiea and he was his boss. Baron Vaiea was the Minister of Commerce and Industry. We felt this man had to be Sam's friend.

The Tongan phoned his office to make an appointment with Baron Vaiea, and we were to see him at three p.m. after the Baron attended a cabinet meeting. The young Tongan insisted he would take us personally to the government building and return us to the ship after we had seen the Baron. I did not want to appear at the office of a minister, even in Tonga, with my hair in curlers, hidden under a scarf, but I had no other choice. My curiosity was stronger than my pride, and I felt I must meet the man I had heard so much about.

We had a nice informal visit and the Baron informed Sam that when he was inducted as a chieftain, his name had been changed during the ceremony. He remembered Sam vaguely, but when Sam asked about his three sisters who played the piano and reminded him of the music he had sent to them via Leona, he became very cordial. The Tupou family had responded to the gift of music by sending many beautiful tapa cloths to Sam in care of Leona in Lousiville. We have them in our house in Carmel today.

Our self-appointed guide returned us to the ship, but not until he had given us a special tour of his own, showing us where Baron Vaiea lived and stopping at a market where we succumbed to another tapa cloth. He lingered on the ship and stayed on the docks waving good-by to us as we sailed away.

We had a rough night sailing from Tonga to Aukland, but at six-thirty we were up on deck watching the approach under a flaming sky with lights twinkling from shore. It was Sunday, and we had planned to attend the horse races at the track in Aukland, but were disappointed to hear the races that week would be held in a town far from Aukland. We were only in port for the day. I took a poorly conducted tour around the seedy side of Aukland's outskirts instead, while Sam rested on the ship.

The roughest stretch of water on the entire trip was our sail around New Zealand from Aukland to Wellington. We were tossed about in our cabin beds and were unable to sleep all night, but we arrived early in the morning miraculously intact and took a lovely morning tour of Wellington. We found it to be a prosperous city full of gorgeous gardens and charming homes. Sam had spent a month's leave here during the war and remembered it well. Here is where he had met Dawn.

We stopped for morning tea at a ladies bowling club and were served a real feast of home-made "goodies," a high tea that was really lunch. After our fill of the delicious food, the ladies demonstrated their skill at lawn bowling, and explained the intricacies of the game. Their bowling uniform was a white dress, white brimmed hat and white tennis shoes. They looked very pretty on the bright green grass, smoothly clipped so the ball could roll straight toward the goal.

We enjoyed the morning, but the afternoon was not so enjoyable. My appointment for Dr. Topping was at one-thirty. We walked upstairs in a modest office building to an old-fashioned reception room with an overstuffed, ancient sagging sofa and two matching chairs. The one window looking out over the park needed washing. My heart sank to my boots in apprehension wondering if this man was qualified. But when I was ushered into his surgery, I was immediately at ease by his manner and charm. The surgery, though a very small room, was immaculate with the very latest equipment. He looked at the offending spot on my leg and clucked, "Tsk, task, I certainly don't want to ruin your trip — or your leg, but something should be done about this." I told him firmly, not to worry about the looks of my leg. Just to get the thing out.

Dr. Topping injected the calf with an anesthetic, cut out the growth and showed it to me on a piece of gauze, saying he was sure he had gotten it out intact, It looked like a miniature brain, the size of a pea. He said he would wire the ship's doctor the results of the laboratory's examination. In the meantime, he wanted me to see the ship's doctor every day for antibiotic ointment and change of dressing.

I was so relieved to have that nasty growth gone, I felt like skipping down the street. It was a week later as we were crossing the Tansman Sea toward Sydney that Sam happened to be at the ship's reception desk when the wire arrived from Dr. Topping. Sam read it as it lay open on the desk. The "excised growth" was a squaamus carcinoma. Sam broke the news to me so I could cover my shock and pretend it was news when the doctor told me. He advised us to fly home just in case there was an early recurrence. He cleaned the wound and dressed it every day, watching it carefully for any change. I decided to continue on the trip as long as possible and then fly home from Tokyo, if he thought it advisable.

We docked at Christchurch the following morning and viewed the city from a tour bus. With its architecture and landscaping it reminded us of England more than any place else in New Zealand. Even a factory had a spectacular garden on its grounds, rivaling any botanical garden display.

That night we sailed under a full huge moon rising orange over the hills and sea. It had been a gorgeous spring day.

We were disappointed at Milford Sound, one of the features of the cruise, but the day was so eerie with fog, we could not see enough to know how very beautiful it must be. We were forced to turn around before reaching the climactic scenic wonder of Mitre Peak.

We sailed on to Sydney in the rain. During the cruise, we had been entertained by a series of lectures on operas by a delightful gentleman, Dr. Popper. His wife was an accomplished pianist, and she played themes as he described the various operas. In Sydney, our enthusiastic group attended the opera Aida in the fabulous new Sydney Opera House. Sam and I were interested in seeing the spectacular modern building, which was only at its inception when we were in Sydney twenty years before on the Mariposa. The building had taken sixteen years to construct at a cost of one hundred and twenty million dollars and was a bone of contention among the citizens of Sydney. But we were enthralled by its stunning appearance in the harbor and were excited by the opera house in its superb setting.

We met our friends, the Graeme Stapelfeldts for lunch the next day. They drove us around Sydney, and because we were eager to see it again, — to the zoo. We were bitterly disappointed by the change and run-down condition of the zoo. We had met Graeme on the *Mariposa* in '57, and at our invitation, he had spent Thanksgiving with us in Indianapolis as he toured the States. He was a tall, handsome, red-headed fellow, and we liked him very much. Now he was married to Frances, a lovely girl, and they had three attractive children. We also saw Edna Laycock and Cliff

[371]

Miller, who had dinner with us on board the *Sky*. We did not see Alex, as we were in port for such a short time, and an airplane strike prevented us from flying to Melbourne as we had planned. We phoned him from a post office in Sydney — the only way we could make a long distance call. It was a complicated procedure and would not have been successful if Graeme had not helped us put the call through.

Our weekend in Sydney was too short. It seemed the ship docked on weekends in every large port, when shops were closed and sightseeing curtailed, another disappointment about the cruise. We had arrived in Sydney quite late in the afternoon because of a typhoon at sea. Two days later we were delayed three hours loading on oil, and another four hours to avoid the persistent typhoon, which caused us to miss seeing the Great Barrier Reef at Cairns. By now we were used to disappointments on the *Sky*. There was nothing to do in Cairns but walk the deserted streets of the town and look into the closed shop windows. It was an outpost town and reminded us of a movie set of a western ghost town. We pulled silently out of Cairns Harbor at two a.m. on our way to Bali.

It was Leap Year, and February 29th found us passing the Torres Strait between Australia and New Guinea. We were supposed to have stopped at Lae, New Guinea, but trouble in that country prevented us from docking. We celebrated our engagement anniversary with a cocktail party for twenty of our new-found friends on the ship. The card room, reserved for us, had been decorated with flowers and candlelight.

The night before our arrival in Bali I hardly slept. I was up at dawn and peeked out our porthole to see a vision of sailboats against the rising sun leaving Bali's harbor for the sea. I rushed up on deck for a better view to watch the fishermen in their unique, homemade boats with brightly colored sails. I counted one hundred and twelve going to sea for a day of fishing.

We transferred to the dock on the ship's tenders and were welcomed by the graceful Balinese dancers, accompanied by a gamelin orchestra. The men sat crosslegged on the ground to play their marimba-like instruments, which are tuned in quarter tones instead of our western half-tones. The off-pitch sound reverberated with the oriental rhythms and quarter-toned scale form and created an unintelligible cacophony of sound at first, then became a stirring, emotional experience. The sarong costumes and headdresses of the dancers were incredibly beautiful, the cloth woven in bright colors accented with gold threads. Their make-up was rather grotesque with bright red color accentuating the eyes and white faces. They were marvelously graceful, especially their expressive hands. Their artificial nails were at least six inches long.

I could have stood and watched them all day, but we had to crowd into buses for a tour of the island. To our delight the scenery was as exotic as the dancers. Terraced rice paddies meticulously manicured covered the hillsides; crude, handmade bridges crossed wild, flowing streams where naked, laughing Balinese were bathing; huge tropical flowers and thick jungle growth tangled together in dense forests weaving a fabulous symphony of color and texture.

We stopped to see two marvelous hour-long dances illustrating tales from the Indian epics, the Ramayana and the Mahabharata. The Balinese are deeply religious people, living out the legends of their Hindu beliefs. Their arts and crafts are symbolic reflections of their faith, and they refuse to make anything that has no connection to religion. Consequently, their art is a dedication, a moving expression of their feelings with even the crudest rendering conveying a message.

It was a fabulous experience being in Bali. Here, there was no disappointment.

—————⋯—⟨◆⟩—⋯—————

We arrived a half-day late in Singapore, and all the day tours were cancelled. Being Sunday, the shops were closed and there was nothing to do but taxi with the Steeles to the famous Raffles Hotel for their Singapore Slings and lunch. Ball Corporation had recently bought a plant in Singapore that made well-head equipment for off-shore oil drilling. I decided to call Mr. Laurence, the president of the Avery Laurence Corporation, and introduce myself as a member of the "family." The Laurences were not in Singapore at the time, but his secretary, a delightful Chinese girl named Mary Yee, was very cordial and insisted on escorting us through the plant.

It was interesting to see the process of constructing an entire off-shore platform of housing and machinery for the drilling crew. There being no work activity on Sunday, we could see even more because we could walk into places which would have been dangerous during work hours. After Mary Yee showed us around the plant and then through the luxurious residental area, she took us to the Laurences' stunning apartment for tea.

Mrs. Laurence, we learned, was Japanese, and their home reflected her heritage. It was elegant, but simple, with beautiful Japanese objets d'art.

Forty of us left the ship in Singapore to fly to Bangkok, then catch up with the *Sky* three days later in Hong Kong. After the two-and-a-half hour flight, we arrived late in the afternoon at the gorgeous Dusit Thani Hotel. The twenty-seventh floor had a rooftop restaurant serving delicious food, and the basement level below the street was fllled with many shops. The lobby was extravagantly decorated with comfortable rattan furniture upholstered in rich purple shades and luxuriant tropical plants and trees. Parrots and cockatoos hung in cages. It was an exotic hotel, and also convenient and comfortable. It was easier to shop in the hotel than flnd your way on the heavily trafficked streets. I found a colorful piece of Thai

[373]

silk, which was made into a dress for me in less than a day.

Bangkok's great tourist attraction is a boat ride through the clongs, which are waterway canals like twisting streets in a town. Without our guide it would have been easy to get lost. We saw everything imaginable from the sampan. Floating markets of fruit and vegetables were bargained off to shoppers on shore, or in surrounding boats. Families lived on the river in shacks built on stilts. They bathed, washed their hair and clothes and even brushed their teeth in the dirty flow. Factories operated along the banks. Orchid growers, souvenirs of all kinds, and even monkeys, elephants and snakes were hawked from junks and sampans. It was an exciting, mind-boggling experience trying to see everything at once. Temples were everywhere along the banks, and we stopped to see one and marveled at the splendid, ornately decorated building filled with huge Hindu figures worshipped by kneeling, nearly prone Thais.

The next day was a long, hot, but interesting tour of Bangkok, including the King's Palace and grounds. Our guide throughout our stay was a darling, diminutive girl name Noi. Many of our group were overcome by the heat and had to return to the hotel, but Noi was most helpful and took time to look after them. After leaving the city, we lunched at a floating restaurant, where we had a good Thai curry, then visited a village where all sorts of handcrafts were being made. There was also a performance of dancing, sports and ceremonial rites. You could ride on elephants or hang a python around your neck. (I didn't.) It was a fascinating day culminating at the Pinon Restaurant for dinner in true Thai style, removing our shoes before entering. A colorful show of graceful dancing ended our evening and eventful visit to Bangkok.

We arrived in Hong Kong a day before the *Sky's* arrival, so our group stayed at the handsome Mandarin Hotel on the island. In '64 the hotel had just opened for business. Now it had a well-used look but it was still very nice. We had been awed by the immense crystal chandelier in the lobby dominating the scene. It was one of those extravagant creations from the Venician glass blowers. In 1964 it sparkled with all the fire and light as a great diamond would under a spotlight. The years without dusting had filmed the glass, and it now looked like an immense uninteresting blob.

We were treated to a cocktail party and evening tour after a dinner at the Tai Pak Restaurant in Aberdeen, which we also remembered. When my turn came to step off the sampan to the dock at the restaurant, a wave caused the sampan to back away, leaving me with one foot on the dock and one foot still in the boat. I had no leverage to pull myself up, but a girl fortunately had taken my hand to help me. I was in panic, terrified of falling into the filthy water of the harbor, particularly with the still-open wound on the back of my leg, which had to be kept sterile. I was in an awkward "splits" position when another girl rushed forward, grabbed my other hand and somehow they were able to drag me up on the dock. I was hurt in the process. My left leg had gone into the water but had not reached the bandage, and my right leg was scraped and bleeding, where I had been dragged over the wooden dock. I was frightened and shaking and hurried to the ladies room to wash the dirt away and remove my torn stockings. The attendant in the wash room was unable to understand my request for soap, as there was none, but someone finally brought a bottle of mercurochrome, which I applied after washing the dirt out of the bloody scratches, with, I assume, the same dirty harbor tap water.

My left white shoe was no longer white, covered with the goo of the harbor, and I nearly threw up with disgust and fear of infection. I limped back to the table too ill to eat anything, the strained muscles all over my body hurting more intensely every minute, but I was truly thankful I had not completely fallen in the water.

Instead of returning to the hotel after the meal, which our guide suggested, I stuck it out with the rest of the group, later sorry that I had. Told there would be more riding in the bus than walking during the evening, I felt I could last through the evening. But it seemed we walked for miles, and every step was agony. I discovered I had also wrenched my back in the accident. The evening seemed endless, but there was a good show of Chinese dancing at the Ocean Terminal, where the evening mercifully ended at midnight. Along with my other problems, I came down with Bangkokitis that night. A kind soul gave me a lomotil to relieve the symptoms temporarily as all our pills for dysentary had been left on the ship.

Back on the *Sky* I battled the effects of Bangkok food for a week with the help of the good doctor. My muscles and strained tendons flnally returned to normal, but the best news was that after one month, the bandage came off for good, and the wound healed with a scab. I was finally able to shower without one leg sticking through the shower curtain.

The voyage continued through the Sea of Japan to Nagasaki. A welcome ceremony by city officials complete with band and fireworks made an auspicious docking. The Steeles joined us for a three-day overland tour that afternoon, and we departed with eleven other passengers on an up-to-the-minute mini bus, touring through beautiful scenery, museums and the ninety-nine islands of Saikai by boat. The trip on the launch was gorgeous and no less interesting as we were shown the oyster beds where Mikimoto produced his fabulous cultured pearls. We drove up mountains, skirted bays and beaches and passed through little villages and big cities. At night we were treated to cocktail parties, dinner and geisha entertainment in our hotels.

On the last day at Fukuoka City we boarded the Bullet Train for Hiroshima, traveling silently and comfortably at 120 miles an hour. Here we were shown in great detail the aftermath of the atomic bomb, which ended World War II. The Peace Park with the mass graves of thousands; the eloquent statue to the children destroyed by the bomb; one building was left a bombed-out ruin to emphasize the destruction of the city, now completely rebuilt. The museum contained miserable exhibits. It was a horrible and sobering sight and brought back many memories of the futility of that war.

The Bullet Train carried us to Kobe where we were delivered to the ship late in the afternoon in time for departure to Yokohama. In Yokohama we left the ship and taxied to the Tokyo Airport.

My decision to fly home was based on common sense over fear. We were not eager to spend two more weeks at sea tossing about in rough weather in the North Pacific. We had had an interesting trip, quite long enough. My leg had healed nicely with no sign of recurrence, but still we were anxious to get home. I swallowed my fear of flying over the great ocean — and my resolves never to do it.

We sat for hours in the airport teeming with thousands of people but finally boarded a plane for Anchorage, Alaska, for the six-hour flight. We watched the sun rise as we flew at twelve-thirty a.m. and landed in the dismal, snowy, icy Anchorage airfield before six, Alaska time. A Northwest Orient plane gathered us up for the flight to Chicago, another long five-hour flight, and finally on to Indianapolis. We had left Tokyo at six-fifty-five p.m. — twenty-six hours had elapsed! (Only twelve hours in the air — fourteen hours waiting in airports.)

CHAPTER FIFTY-NINE

OUR dear friends, Bep and Laurens Van Oosten, had written us about their experiences since Laurens' retirement from the army. Loving to travel, but not having had much opportunity, Laurens signed on as ship's doctor on the Holland-American Line, taking Bep along. These were working-vacation trips for them, allowing Laurens to continue his medical practice and see the world at the same time. He signed on the Prinsendam, when it was commissioned, for a course around Indonesia. It was the first time the Van Oostens had returned to the country where they were born. Their enthusiasm spilled over to us when they described the journey and the comfortable ship. We wrote asking them to let us know the next time they would be on board so we could join them on one of the cruises.

The time arrived the year after our Royal Viking cruise. We arranged to meet the Van Oostens on the *Prinsendam*, planning an exciting excursion around the Indonesian adventure, including an extended visit to Australia.

We left home in October of 1978 and flew to Honolulu. My determination not to fly long distances over the ocean had been broken down at last, but I still did not enjoy the flights, suffering through long, cramped hours, tensely praying each flight would be a safe one.

We stopped in Honolulu for a day and night to help break the jet lag of the eight-and-a-half hour flight from Chicago and went to the Halekulani Hotel to sleep it off. The next day we wandered to our favorite spots, lingered in the shops and enjoyed our last stay in the Halekulani Hotel, soon to be razed for another high-rise building. This, more than anything else disillusioned us about the growth of Honolulu. The hotel had been literally crowded out by enormous buildings along the beaches. The raucous sound of jack-hammers and pile drivers split the tropical air continuously in every available vacant lot as ground was graded for future buildings.

Our thirteen-and-a-half hour flight to Singapore departed at midnight and was totally exhausting. We sat next to a pregnant mother and two-year-old child going to Korea. They had been flying for twenty-two hours and the child was so spent she screamed and thrashed around constantly throughout the night. The mother was too tired herself to control her. The little girl lay on the seat beside me, asleep at last, but twitching and kicking her feet into me in spasms. At four a.m. we landed in Guam to change planes and were put into an isolation room for in-transit passengers, where we sat confined for two hours, numb from lack of sleep and the freezing cold from the air conditioner. At last we landed at the Singapore airport at eight a.m., one day ahead of ourselves, but nine hours behind!

We taxied to the Shangri-La Hotel (a fitting name for the exotic establishment) and were told our rooms would not be ready until ten o'clock! There was nothing to do but sit on a backless bench in the lobby in a dazed condition and wait. Sam was miserable, suffering a fresh cold from the flight.

I was suddenly alert and awake when I saw an old friend from Indianapolis emerge from the elevator. I jumped up and ran towards him, greeting him in surprise, "Al Stokely!" He looked down at me bewildered. "And what is your name?" he said. No wonder he didn't recognize me in my disheveled state after a sleepless night. I responded, "For goodness sakes, I'm Lucina!" Then he too reacted in pleased surprise and told me to call Jeannette in their room and arrange a time when we could get together.

Jeannette also was surprised to learn we were in Singapore and invited me to go to the pool as she was just leaving for a swim. I replied if I dove in, I would surely sink. All I wanted to do was sleep all day, if we ever got a room. Later we could meet for dinner.

We had a good time with the Stokelys that evening, finally rested from the all-night flight, but not yet over the jet-lag, which lasted for several days longer. I was convinced more that ever that air travel is sadistic.

We learned the Stokelys had an appointment with two ladies from the Avery-Laurence Company to show them parts of Singapore. They asked us to join them. So again we enjoyed the hospitality of the Ball Brothers subsidiary in the persons of Mrs. Pepper and Mrs. Emerson. The delightful ladies escorted us to a handcraft center, where Jeannette and I chose materials of Thai silk for dresses.

We invited the ladies and the Stokelys to come aboard the *Prinsendam* that afternoon and see us off, which they did. We also located Bep and Laurens Van Oosten, and they joined us for a champagne send-off party in the cocktail lounge of the ship.

The *Prinsendam* was a small ship but well-appointed and excellently run. It was a wonderful cruise, and the tours were fascinating excursions, revealing the terrain, customs and crafts of the Indonesian people. It was especially nice to be with the Van Oostens again. We sat at their table for meals, and, although Laurens was kept busy on the ship with many patients, Bep was able to go with us on the tours, and her company was most welcome. Neither of them had forgotten the language, and sometimes the four of us went off by ourselves to see something of interest not included on a tour.

Penang was the first port, which was full of reclining Bhuddas and monkeys. Then we went to Belawan, on the island of Sumatra, for a long day's journey through the jungles. In the jungle's center was a village —

literally a mud wallow with houses built on stilts over the mud. We were shown through one building in which forty people lived. There was no privacy except for curtains separating their rooms. To enter and exit we climbed shaky ladders, reaching a long, dark hallway where we passed to the opposite wall. "looking in" on the lives of the poorest of people. Some had no beds or chairs but lived on the floor, cooking on little charcoal stoves. Most of the people wore cloth remnants or nothing at all. All lived in abject poverty, and many were ill, lying on straw mats and cared for by younger, healthier family members. It was a sobering, sad sight, and we felt great embarrassment for intruding into the privacy of their lives. Oddly enough, none of them paid us the slightest attention and seemed to take our tour group for granted.

We breathed a sigh of relief when we were on the ground again — even the muddy ground. We were told the village would be impassible during the rainy season, as the dried caked earth would become a morass of deep mud. There were dances at the outdoor village center, where swarms of people had converged from out-lying villages. The dances were interesting, but the experience was depressing and a little scary.

Sibolga was a dirty fishing village. We went ashore and rode in a pedicab (called Becaks) to sightsee. Bep was with us, fortunately, to fend off the beggars and keep us from being cheated by the driver. It was a hectic ride. We were relieved to get back to the ship via the tender.

By contrast, the island of Nias was enchanting. Nias, on the other side of Sumatra, was beautiful, primitive and rugged. We climbed steep steps to reach a village at its peak and watched a performance of gymnastic prowess by the men. Wandering along the streets, we were tempted to buy a huge trumpet shell from a street vendor, which is now proudly added to our collection.

Sam, still ill with his cold, did not leave the ship at Jakarta. I joined the crowded bus of passengers alone, as this time Bep also declined the tour. It was unbearably hot, but I enjoyed seeing the botanical gardens of orchids and the museum. We were in a batik factory when we were suddenly caught in a deluge of rain and were forced to head back to the bus, drenched and splashed with mud.

On the way back to the ship in heavy traffic, we were caught in traffic jams unequaled by anything I had ever seen. It grew later and later and darker and darker, as we inched through Jakarta. The ship was due to sail and had to keep on schedule. We arrived at the dock as they were about to drop the lines from ship to shore. The captain held up an extra hour for us, or we would have been stranded in Jakarta, necessitating a flight to catch the ship at the next port. Sam was hanging over the rail on deck, as were all the other passengers, anxiously awaiting our late arrival. We were more than relieved to board in the nick of time.

[379]

One of the passengers had attracted my attention. I was puzzled oy a nagging feeling of recognition every time I saw her on deck with her husband but could not remember where I had ever seen her. One morning I was passing the movie theater and heard the sounds of a piano. Someone was playing a Chopin waltz, practicing slowly and with precision. As it was time for a lecture to begin, Sam and I entered the theater. The lady rose from the piano bench, and I immediately knew who she was.

As she passed by on her way up the aisle I asked, "Aren't you Ruth Slencyznska?" She returned my question with a question. "Where are you from?" she asked. I replied that I was from Indianapolis, and she walked on without further explanation.

I was slightly put off, but more than ever certain that it was Ruth, and later in the lounge I felt compelled to speak to her again. I approached her and told her I was sorry for causing her embarrassment, but I had to know if she really was Ruth Slenczynska. I explained I had heard her play at Tabernacle Presbyterian Church in Indianapolis and had attended her marvelous workshop of the Chopin Etudes at Dr. Curtis Clark's house two years before.

She merely nodded in the direction of the gentleman reading beside her and said, "Meet my husband, James Kerr." Then we both smiled, and she couldn't remain incognito any longer. She finally explained. "Please don't tell anyone on board who I am. We are on vacation celebrating our tenth wedding anniversary. If anyone knew who I was I would be asked to play, and this is my time for a rest before I begin my concert season when I return home." Of course I assured her I would not let her secret out, but I was bubbling with excitement over meeting her. We became friends on the trip, and as I knew she would be performing again at the Tabernacle Presbyterian Church in April, told her we would like to have a party for her after the concert. She was delighted, and I made arrangements when we returned to Indianapolis.

Ruth Slencyznska was a child prodigy, born in California of a Polish immigrant father and American mother. Her father, a violin teacher, resented her rejecting his instrument in preference for the piano, but began to teach her when she was just three years old. He forced her, almost beyond human endurance, to practice nine hours a day with severe punishment if she missed a note or for any infraction of his rules. Her first performance was a recital at age four, and from then on he drove her to excellence and unbelievable endurance, exploiting her talent all over Europe and America. Her flrst concerto with an orchestra was with the Philadelphia Symphony at age eight, and her first solo recital of real importance was the same year at Town Hall in New York, 1934. We attended her Golden Anniversary recital there in November, 1984. She is the first woman artist to achieve a fifty year career of professional performance.

[380]

I learned about her when I was studying with Bomar Cramer. He told me about the amazing child prodigy, six years younger than I, but I never heard her perform until she came out of "retirement" as an adult. Ruth had escaped from her tyrannical father when she was sixteen and began a more normal life of her own, going to school and finishing her education. She then taught piano, flnally performing once again, more brilliantly than before.

She and her husband are both professors at the University of Illinois, Ruth as artist-in-residence and James, a political science teacher. We have been friends since the Indonesian cruise.

———————◄◉►·———————

I had a surprise party for Sam on November first, inviting a few friends for cocktails. The Van Oostens gave him an exquisite Balinese painting, which is now framed and prominently displayed in our "travel room of treasures." At dinner a group of Bataki singers came aboard to entertain the passengers, and they sang a special serenade to Sam for his birthday.

We were thrilled to be able to visit Bali again, which we think is the most exotic and interesting port in Indonesia. I was up at quarter of five to watch the fishing boats go out to sea as the sun rose.

This trip we were able to see different areas of the island, including the gruesome bat cave, where thousands of bats "hang out." We toured the handcraft centers and saw the fascinating Barong Dance. But our greatest experience was seeing the famous Monkey Dance that night on the former palace grounds. The only illumination came from the open flre burning on center "stage" and on small candlelit tables, where we sat to watch the dance. About fifty men and boys, their half-naked bodies glistening with oil, silently slipped in from the dark shadows. They seated themselves cross-legged around the fire leaving room in the center for the dancers. The chorus began a rhythmic chant, soft but insistent, imitating the voices of chattering monkeys. The dancers depicted the story as the soft syllables of the chant grew in volume and intensity. We were hypnotized and carried along by the drama as the story unfolded. Never have we seen anything to equal the emotion and precision of the villagers reliving a story they had believed in since childhood, caught up and transformed into mystic monkeys.

Surabaya was our last port of call around the islands of Indonesia. It was an attractive, interesting city with many things to see — among them, the zoo and flower market and an exhibition of a trance dance. In the afternoon, we ferried to Madura Island for the bull races, a different sort of entertainment. Being with the Van Oostens on the comfortable ship and seeing the wonders of fascinating Indonesia made a trip that was unique from all others we had taken. There were sights we could never see anywhere else, such as the Komodo dragons (giant monitor lizards) that

[381]

live only on the island of Komodo, east of Java. We saw several of the huge beasts from the safe distance of the bus as we toured the mountainous jungles. They looked like those I remembered from the pictures in my fairy tale books.

The cruise had been most rewarding. Two years later we were shocked when the *Prinsendam* burned up and sank off the Alaskan coast. Everyone was saved, mercifully, but many elderly passengers were stranded in life boats for twenty-four hours before they were rescued, exposed to the freezing temperatures of the Alaskan climate.

We spent three days exploring Singapore and Malaysia before making another long overnight flight to Brisbane, Australia. It was an uncomfortable eight-and-a-half hours, but eventually we landed early in the morning and checked into The Gazebo Terrace Hotel.

Brisbane is an attractive, enterprising city, lying on a wide, curving river that seems to embrace the town. The city, illuminated at night, was a sparkling sight from the roof garden of our hotel, where we dined in preference to other restaurants.

A cheerful, attentive chauffeur-guide showed us the environs of Brisbane. One day he drove us to the Gold Coast, a plush strip covering many miles of magnificent beaches along Australia's eastern coastline. On the way we stopped to see an extraordinary bird sanctuary, where birds live freely in their natlral habitat, but are contained by high tents of mesh screening.

We also visited my favorite animals, the koalas, in their sanctuary. Here we could hold the cuddly creatures and view them in their natural setting. Kangaroos, emus and exotic birds were also protected here, and we were allowed to feed them. Australia has many animals indigenous only to that country. We were fascinated to see so many weird species.

The highlight of our Australian experience was the unusual excursion on the *Elizabeth E*, a small cruiser, which had been a sub-chaser in World War II. We flew to Mackay (pronounced Mackeye by the Austr"eye"lians) on the coast of The Great Barrier Reef area where she was berthed, boarding her with about twenty other passengers. The tiny cabins below deck were adequate for the week's trip. All of us shared a mutual shower room, but two toilets were assigned for "ladies" and "gents."

The crew consisted of a seasoned captain, flrst mate, stewardess and an outstanding chef. They were attractive young people, expert sailors who kept us entertained and comfortable.

Our fellow passengers were in the middle-age bracket, with one couple considerably older. Even though they were octogenarians, they were more alert and ready for adventure than anyone else. There were about six of us

Americans, the balance Australian, except for one German lady who had difficulty with the English language. She also had difficulty maneuvering around the narrow passages on deck because of her Humpty-Dumpty shape. We became a congenial, merry group before the voyage was over.

The sailing was rough on the open sea, but in the lee of the cluster of islands of the Great Barrier Reef, it was calm and the weather perfect. Each island was interesting with special features. A few were posh resorts, or tried to be, others were mere strips of land with beaches full of washed-up coral and sand flies. Between Whitsunday Island and Hook Island was a marvelous underwater observatory, where we could watch the myriads of colorful fish living among the bright coral formations and plants.

When we left the sanctuary of the island to cruise open water for the Outer Barrier Reef, we could not sleep all night for tossing on the rough seas. We anchored at six a.m. at the edge of a barren atoll. Walking on the reef was touted as the real purpose of the cruise, and this was the place the captain had chosen for the adventure. Although it was low tide, it was not low enough to anchor very close to the reef. We were taken, a few at a time in the dinghy, and left in knee-deep water to walk the rest of the way to the beach — perhaps one hundred and fifty feet. All of us were wisely wearing tennis shoes to guard against the sharp coral underfoot — all of us but the German lady, who had not brought protective foot covering. As she stepped barefooted into the dinghy with us, I warned her not to come unless she wore shoes. We were delayed a little until the captain found a spare pair of ragged tennis shoes for her to put on. We noticed the other passengers having difficulty wading through the water, moving very slowly to keep their balance, but they had all reached the beach by the time we arrived at the reef's edge. The game octogenarian couple were in our dinghy also, and they climbed out of the boat, holding fast to each other, and waded through the now murky stirred-up water toward the dry land. Sam and I each grabbed a fat hand of the German, knowing she was uncertain on her feet and would need assistance.

The distance to the beach seemed endless. We picked our way through the moving water unable to see where we were stepping. Coral formations of all sizes and colors blurred under our unsteady feet. We tried to pick firm places to step, but the "stepping stone" we thought we were on, would collapse into mush and we would sink down into a lower level struggling to keep our balance. I was desperately afraid of falling on the poisonous coral, which could cut the skin at the slightest touch and cause deadly infections. Our hands and knees were not protected as our feet were; so it was of utmost importance not to stumble and fall. The dead stone-like coral looked just like live coral, but it was very soft, and the many varieties and wavy water made it impossible to distinguish our footing. Nearing the beach, I flnally saw a broad "rock" and raised a foot to place it down for my next wobbly step. I caught myself just in time — the water calmed enough for me to see a giant clam a yard long below the surface with its shell mouth gaping open. I had almost put my foot down inside the enormous clam's jaws! I could have been imprisoned there or lost my foot in the process!

Completely unnerved and shaken by my narrow escape, I reached the beach, trembling and upset for having been stupid enough to have taken such chances. I was angry at the captain who permitted his inexperienced passengers to take such risks. Once we had walked to the beach through the deep, treacherous water, we had to return to the dinghy — another fifteen frightening minutes. I was more angry than ever when we discovered there was nothing to see on the reef except fast, scuttling crabs, stranded by the low tide.

We sighed with relief when we were safely back in the dinghy. But as Sam climbed aboard, he looked down at the edge of the coral shelf into the eyes of a giant moray eel staring back at him just a foot away. Below the glass-bottomed boat was a bottomless pit of fathomless depths. We toured the area looking at the sea below us and became more alarmed as we realized how many dangers lurked below the surface. Many sea snakes were writhing in schools near the reef. They are very poisonous and love to hide among the coral plants, where they feed on small organisms. I shuddered to think of all the things we could have stepped on or just disturbed, as we walked on the crumbly, collapsing bed of coral.

The first mate was the only one injured in the adventure. He had seen his daring captain walk barefoot on the coral and thought he could do the same. He received a deep cut on the bottom of his foot for his foolishness. It promptly became infected and rendered him useless for the rest of the trip. He probably had the infection for many months, as they are difficult to cure.

Except for this scary experience, the week's cruise was pleasant. The captain apologized for letting us "greenhorns" off in unusually deep water. He said usually it was very low tide when the boat came in to the reef, and he didn't like to disappoint the passengers when the walk on the reef was the high point of the trip. It certainly was the high point of adventure for us, but we could have done without it.

The young chef prepared delicious, varied menus and there were good snacks served with tea before breakfast, mid-morning, four o'clock tea, and before retiring at ten p.m. We laughed when we overhead two Australian ladies conversing in the lounge. They were commenting on the good time and the good food, but one added with some indignation, "I hate not getting a cup of tea whenever I want it!"

———————◄◦►———————

The week was over much too soon. After the rough trip back to Mackay, we flew to Melbourne for a week's visit with Alex and Alison Scovell. Alex met us at the airport and drove us to his pleasant home in the suburbs. The change of climate was abrupt, from the heat of the northern continent to crisp, cool weather in the south. We enjoyed our reunion tremendously and that night curled comfortably under electric blankets. It was the first time we had met Alison, whom we found as hospitable and delightful as Alex. Two decades had passed since we had seen him.

Alex became our tour guide in and around Melbourne. The city, unlike Sydney, is more conservative with a feeling of colonialism, despite the modern buildings and big businesses. It has the atmosphere of a small community with the advantages of its importance to the country, historically and commercially. We loved the city and would like to return for a deeper exploration.

One memorable experience was our trip to Phillips Island. Alex drove us two hours farther south on the coast to watch one of the world's natural wonders. Every evening at dusk, tiny fairy penguins come in from the sea to nest in their rookeries. The penguins are a miniature variety, about a foot high, and completely oblivious to the thousands of spectators who gather on the beach every evening to watch the migration. They are also oblivious to the floodlights turned on after dark and make their way, coming in from the sea by the hundreds, marching up the beach, never deviating or hesitating until they find their individual rookeries, fllled with chicks clamboring for food. Although the baby penguins have been left alone all day, they do not stray from their nests, and when their parents return from the sea, craws filled with food, the youngsters become very agitated, jumping up and down and uttering squeals of excitement. By some uncanny instinct, each penguin finds his rookery among the many hundreds hidden in the marsh grasses and rocks inland from the sandy beach. If someone happens to be standing in their path, the homing penguins just walk over his feet, barely noticing the intruder.

Before the penguin "invasion", we were told over a loud speaker not to move suddenly from our positions and not to talk or make noises. Above all, we were not to interfere with a penguin's migration or try to change his direction. We assembled on grandstand seats back of the beach before dark, and, as the sun set, the first penguin led the others in from the sea. As the light quickly darkened, the floodlights were turned on to illuminate the beach, showing us countless more appearing and beginning their waddles in all directions toward their nests for the night.

We found many nests of baby chicks before it was too dark to explore. They seemed to be quiet, if not sleeping. But as the light waned in the sky, anticipating their evening meal, they became restless, tumbling over each other in the nests. As the adult birds spilled out on to the beach, the nestlings were beside themselves with excitement, squawking and falling out of their nests into the reeds and running around in circles.

[385]

The chicks were fuzzy little gray balls of angora-looking fur. How I longed to pick one up! It was also tempting to try to catch one of the adults and make friends with it. They were adorable. But we were also very much in awe of their life-style and wouldn't consider interrupting their busy schedule for a moment.

As we walked back to the car, parked far behind the beach in a large lot, we were amazed to see many more rookeries secluded in the bushes as far as there were reeds to conceal them. They had been so well hidden we were unaware of their existence until the appearance of the adult birds created the confusion in the nests. Many of the nests were at the very edge of the parking lot, practically under the wheels of the cars.

Our visit with Alex and Alison was a welcome break from the tourist life we had been leading. It was restful and comfortable to be in their home and meet their family and friends, who were invited to dine with us. Alison was a wonderful cook and tempted us continuously with her rich offerings. We were sorry to leave our good friends when the week was over. It had been a pleasant interlude. I hate to think we might have to wait another twenty-one years before meeting again! This seems to be the mystic number for our reunions. 1936, '57 and '78 were the years that brought us together.

Sam and I left them to fly to Canberra, the capital of Australia. The city is modern and quite beautiful, but inland. Without the coastal winds to blow them away, Canberra is infested with millions of stinging, biting flies. We were tormented by the swarming pests that refused to be brushed off our clothes and skin. They always gave us a nasty bite before saying goodby.

The World War Memorial was an outstanding museum as was the Aboriginal Historical Museum. We took a launch to a small island on a serene lake centered in Canberra and enjoyed the time we spent sightseeing. We loved everything about the city — except for its sticky flies!

From Canberra we flew to Sydney and again had a reunion with Edna Layock and Cliff Miller. Cliffs health had deterioriated, and he was very crippled with arthritis. His love for dancing was a thing of the past. He was on crutches, walking painfully, but his sense of humor was still bright and optimistic. They were a loving couple, and, I felt, short-changed by circumstances in life, which prevented their marriage. By the time Edna's husband died, they were too old and accustomed to their single existence.

We spent another day with the Stapelfeldts, our other friends from the Mariposa cruise of '57. We toured the magnificent Sydney Opera House and had dinner together in the elegant dining room that evening. We browsed the Argyle Shopping Center near the docks during the day. It was an entertaining place to explore, with many handmade crafts for sale. The

[386]

stores were built in nooks and crannies on several levels, following the rock formations. The area was extensive, covering several blocks, but connecting all the shops under one roof, as shopping centers often do. We spent hours wandering, had lunch in one of the nooks and looked for good buys.

Our wonderful trip was nearly over. We sailed from Sydney on the *Mariposa* — her final trip before retirement. The cruise was a nostalgic one for the crew and passengers, yet the air was festive, the food marvelous and the service top-notch. We consider the *Mariposa* the finest passenger ship we have ever been on, after experiencing twenty-seven different liners.

Suva, Fiji and Honolulu were the only stops we made en route to San Francisco. The final voyage of the *Mariposa* came to an end as we crept under the Golden Gate bridge entering San Francisco harbor, December 14, 1978. The dawn was foggy and the air chilly. Moisture was in the air and in our eyes as we left the ship. Our country's last cruise ship would be sold at auction within the year.

Cudding a koala in Australia

The Mariposa

Lucina and Ruth Slencyznska

S.S. Royal Viking Sky, *North Cape Cruise*, 1980: *Sam, Lucina, Breck and Tracey*

The view of our ship from Dalsnibbe, Norway

[389]

CHAPTER SIXTY

I always had longed to attend the Edinburgh Festival of Music in Scotland, and Sam offered to take me the summer of 1979. The important festival is so popular a year's notice is required to assure reservations. I was delighted by the prospect. We also decided to take the North Cape cruise on the *Royal Viking Sky* preceding the week in Scotland.

In the meantine I began to think more and more of our granddaughters, Tracey Strohm and Breck Cummings, who were now fifteen, budding and beautiful. I remembered my first trip abroad when I was fourteen and how much it had enriched my life and longed for the girls to have the same experience. After much thought, I broached the idea to Sam that we take the girls along with us. Dear Sam, always generous and amenable, agreed, and we reserved another room at the Hotel Caledonia in Edinburgh and a cabin for them on the *Sky*.

Our plans were set, but I wasn't satisfied. Why go all the way to Europe and see only a corner of it? I thought the girls should see as much of Europe as possible, while the opportunity existed. Eventually, with much hesitation, I suggested to Sam that we venture on "The Grand Tour" with them.

He groaned inwardly, but we re-organized our plans to set out much earlier in the summer to include, not three weeks, but, eight weeks of travel with the girls. Tracey and Breck were beside themselves with excitement and enthusiasm. We were slightly less optimistic, worried over the strenuous schedule and possible weariness of our aging bones trying to show the young, energetic pair the maximum in the minimum time. We were afraid the girls would be bored with our constant company and dreaded the thought of having to stay up late in the evenings to "entertain" them. We also were afraid they would resist our efforts to show them the great masterpieces of art and architecture in the museums and cathedrals and balk over the constant trudging necessary to "take it all in."

We planned to include much leisure, yet have them see the most important places in the countries we were to visit, which meant returning to the capital cities which we had no interest in seeing again. We nearly scrapped the cruise on the *Royal Viking Sky* because of the expense and the additional two weeks on our agenda, but Anita Farrell, our friend and travel agent since the Alaskan venture, pointed out we would be so tired by the end of the first three weeks, we would need the rest on shipboard, where the teen-agers would be free to "do their own thing." We felt she could be quite right about this and left the cruise in mid-position on the itinerary.

I finally received the agenda of the Edinburgh Festival, but was frankly disappointed to see no artists or concerts which especially interested me for the week we planned to be there. I visualized battling the crowds and traffic alone to a few of the concerts while Sam and the girls tootled off to the Highlands, preferring not to attend "the dull performances." We would all be tired of sightseeing after seven weeks. So I suggested a change of plans again — scrap Scotland and take a "castle" tour of Ireland instead. Our plans changed from concerts to castles, and I took considerable ribbing from Sam.

From the date of our invitation to the girls to accompany us on this Great Endeavor, the dollar began to decline in value, as America sank into an economic recession. The alarming prospect of a severe depression made our ambitious, expensive venture seem ludicrous. The cost of the trip for four quadrupled as summer approached, and Sam and I thought of cancelling the trip entirely. But we felt we had an obligation and didn't want to disappoint the girls. We also wanted to share the experience with them. So Sam closed his eyes to our greatly devalued dollars and resigned himself to pay heavily for the trip.

No one could have been more surprised and pleased than we were when the excursion turned out to be a great success. Everything had been well planned in advance and thus ran smoothly in operation. The girls were enthusiastic about everything we did. Far from keeping us up at night, they were more willing to stop than we were, and were up, ready to go in the mornings to meet our scheduled tours. (Sometimes Breck seemed to drag, giving us some anxious moments and fears of delays, but she always appeared on time, miraculously.) The four of us were congenial, cooperative and considerate of each other. The girls, very different personalities, nevertheless got along well enough together, closer than they had ever been in their lives. They began to understand the need to integrate their preferences and temper their whims to others — sometimes winning, sometimes losing, but always cooperating to suit the majority.

We flew to Paris on an all-night flight and checked in at the Hotel Cecilia early in the morning. The hotel was my idea. I had yearned to stay there again since my fond memories of our 1932 sojourn at the Cecilia. Anita Farrell had discovered the hotel was still in existence, and nearly the least expensive hotel in Paris. We decided to take a chance and were not disappointed. In fact, the small hotel and its pleasant manager turned our previous animosity toward the French into a more cordial feeling for the whole country. The management couldn't have been more friendly or helpful. Sam relaxed and enjoyed the week in Paris, admitting he was a convert.

Hotel Cecilia was in a convenient location on one of the streets spoking out from the Arc de Triomphe, a block from the monument and within easy walking distance to the shops on the Champs Elysee. The weather was lovely, cool enough for a sweater but bright and sunny. It was fun to

[391]

sight-see, lunch in sidewalk cafes under the big umbrellas and poke into the glamourous shops to look, but not to buy.

Of course we had to show the girls Paris night life. The barebreasted, nearly nude show girls shocked our young teen-agers, but the shows at The Lido and The Moulin Rouge were fabulous none-the-less. The Lido was not far from the Cecilia, and the streets were open for "business" after dark. We passed groups of prostitutes in outlandish costumes hawking their trade with pseudo-sophisticated posturing, bored and carelessly draped along the walls of the buildings. The Cecilia was next door to another hotel, which seemed to be their central headquarters. One night quite a group of the "ladies" was assembled, talking to several young men near our hotel entrance. The crowd gave way as we elbowed through, trying not to show our nervousness. The "girls" were attired in leopard leotards, bright clashing colors of hot pink, purple or "the wet look." With hair dyed orange, purple or green, they looked like they had all been "struck by lightning" (as Dad would have expressed it.)

The concierge unlocked the hotel entrance for us, and, once safely inside, Sam breathed a sigh of relief. He was extremely nervous with the responsibility of looking after three females, and the walk made his hair stand on end. He showed me a pipe probe that became a four-inch long stilleto. He had carried it sticking through his fingers in a doubled-up fist to protect us from a mugging.

The night we went to Moulin Rouge, Tracey alarmed us by developing a pain in her side, which might have been an appendicitis attack. Though it turned out to be a false alarm, we were concerned. We taxied to the night club for fifteen francs, but when we left to return to the hotel it was after midnight, and the streets were swarming with revelers, sending off firecrackers under pedestrians' feet and creating a great disturbance. Bastille Day, the fourteenth of July had just begun. We tried for more than thirty minutes to flag down a taxi, but none paid us the slightest attention, although the street was full of parked, unengaged taxis. At last Sam persuaded one of the drivers to take us, but it cost eighty francs, which is one reason Sam can't abide the French. They are quite adept at bilking tourists and show contempt at the same time. Except for this single incident, however, our ten days were very pleasant, contrary to our earlier experiences in Paris.

Trips to Versailles, Fountainbleau and a dinner cruise on the Seine filled much of the four days in Paris. We managed to show Tracey and Breck the outstanding features of the city and its museums without becoming weary. We left Paris for three days on a bus tour of chateaux in the area of Mont St. Michelle, Angers and Tours.

The old abbey castle of Mont St. Michelle was fascinating to explore. We climbed to the turret tops 'til our knees went to water. The drive

[392]

through ancient Normandy and the Brittany villages was breathtaking, with whole fields bright with poppies and wild flowers lining the road sides. Medieval, half-timbered homes of the thirteenth century were sheltered by the shadows of the fortresses and the homage of the townsfolk.

We toured several interesting castles and gardens each day along the circling route and absorbed the history and beauty of the many varied architectural styles of the period. We enjoyed visiting the residence near Amboise, where Leonardo da Vinci lived his last three years and where he died. An exhibition of models made by I.B.M. from Leonardo's drawings of his inventions was most interesting. The chateaux of Cenonceau and Chambord, which we had seen years ago were the final glorious monuments of the past on the tour before we headed back to Paris.

From the balmy air of Paris we were struck by the stifling heat in Spain and struggled in the frantic atmosphere of the Madrid airport to transport ourselves and our eight bags to the Ritz Hotel, where we had stayed before in 1953.

Things had changed in Madrid since then. Tourists had taught the Spaniards how to charge for service. The Ritz Hotel in the fifties had cost us $3.50 a night for our beautiful double room with luxuriously large bathroom. Our accommodations were exactly like the ones we had in '53, but each room cost $115 a night. The hotel was still lovely, but twenty-five years had taken the fresh look of luxury from it. The gorgeous deep-pile carpeting throughout was faded, and the pile worn thin. After the excellent late lunch on the plane, we were not hungry for another full meal, but we entered the elegant dining room for a snack before retiring. We had cold gazpacho soup and flan, the simplest and most common fare in Spain, and the bill was sixty dollars.

We spent most of the week on a bus tour to Granada, Sevilla and Cordoba. We remembered the bus tour we enjoyed so much in '67, but this Atesa Tour did not measure up to our previous one. It was a nine-hour grind in the heat to Granada with only a couple of "coffee" stops and a paella lunch. The scenery over the mountains was spectacular, but all looked bone dry above the tan and red soil under miles and miles of olive trees. Acres of sunflowers and hills of grapvines added some color to the landscape.

Of course, our great disappointment in Granada was to find the Alhambra closed at night. We took the girls to the Caves instead and watched the flamenco dancers perform. The day trip through the Alhambra was excellent, fortunately fewer than usual tourists, so we had a better view and more leisure to see its details. Breck and Tracey were enthralled by the castle and its magnificence, but we were sad not to see it

[393]

again with the magical effects produced by the night lighting and Sheherazade music.

The five-and-a-half-hour drive brought us to Seville and a nice hotel with a pool on its rooftop where Breck, Tracey and I had a cool swim. Another flamenco dance program entertained us that night. We had a fabulous tour of Seville the next day, but at the end of it were so weary, we were content to stay in our rooms, rest and forego the night life.

Cordoba's weather seemed hotter than anywhere else in Spain, but the tour through the city was excellent. We loved the marvelous mosque built over three centuries with the Catholic cathedral in the center of it and the old Jewish quarter with the remains of the synogogue. A two-thousand-year-old wall and ramparts had surrounded the city, the remains still in evidence.

Back in Madrid we did little else but rest in the Ritz. The Prado Museum next door held little interest for the girls, so we spent a minimum of time there. We dismissed the idea of going to a bull fight as Breck put her foot down and said she did not want to see "the gore."

We discovered it was quiet Breck who braved the barriers of the foreign languages intrepidly. She ventured away from our group time after time to speak to anyone in order to hear their language and try to converse with them. Tracey was timid and shrank from becoming involved in conversations with anyone, even English-speaking persons. We thought this a funny reverse of their characters — at least what we had previously observed about them. The girls both studied Spanish in school and were quite fluent, having heard the language spoken most of their lives at home. But it was Breck who spoke it, Tracey refusing to say even "*si*" or "*gracias.*" We were amazed as we had thought Tracey to be much more sophisticated and outgoing than Breck. Breck tried to speak every language in every country we visited, even Norwegian. She picked up phrases and used them whenever there was an opportunity and was not intimidated by the language barrier at all. Later, while at Hanover College, Breck majored in geology and minored in Spanish. During this time she went to Peru and again to Spain with her class, living with families there, improving her ability to speak Spanish and understand the customs of the people.

————————————◆————————————

Our Italian experiences were extensive and fun. We spent more time here than either France or Spain. We saw a great deal of Rome, staying in a delightful hotel, the Londra and Cargill. It was modern, well-located, and the meals, all self-service buffet style, were delicious. We toured by bus to Italy's "heel" seeing Naples, Pompeii and Sorrento. We were trying to gratify Breck's wishes to "see ruins." She really longed to go to Greece, but it was impossible to go that far on this trip. We had to compromise with the

[394]

ancient ruins Rome and Pompeii offered to satisfy Breck's appetite for "old stones." She was ecstatic and could have explored every ruin indefinitely.

The worst part of the stay in Italy was the tremendous influx of tourists. Hordes of them gathered at the same time and in the same place in dozens of buses. There were line-ups for sites of interest, meals and toilets. The traffic jammed constantly, making us late everywhere. It also took extra time for the guide — he repeated everything in four different languages. One day seemed endless as we snailed to Sorrento and back. By the time we returned to the outskirts of Rome, there were five solid lanes of vehicles backed up for miles to get through the toll gate on the "expressway."

The one evening we ventured out in Rome was to attend a ballet performance of Don Quixote at the Baths of Caraculla. It was a beautiful night to sit under the stars in the restored ruins of the baths, the stage in front of a back drop of ancient stones and pillared walls. The ballet was lovely with the elegant costuming and excellent performance of two noted Russian stars, Katarina Marlova and Vasseilivitch. We were exhausted at the end of the long evening as it was one a.m. when we returned to the hotel — hard on travelers with a strenuous schedule!

On the heels of the late night, we were awakened at five-thirty the next morning to make the bus for Florence. The day was very hot, the bus not air-conditioned and we suffered intensely on the drive until we reached Florence at six-thirty by a round-about route in order to see more of interest on the way. The four of us slept through the day, buffeted by the hot air blown through the open windows. The scenery was lost on me as I only occasionally opened my eyes to glimpse an ancient castle ruin on a green hilltop. We stopped in Perugia and Siena, but we were all much too tired to do any walking and sat at sidewalk cafes for ice cream or a cooling lemonade. Assisi where we had a good lunch was a city that reminded us of Taxco. We sat on a balcony overlooking the rugged roofs of the town, bargained in the street shops and finally arrived in Florence, exhausted. We considered the day "a bad day at Black Rock!"

Two days in Florence allowed us to see a great deal of the city and its fabulous art. But pushing our way amongst the tide of tourists wore us out. Venice was the same — hot and crowded. It was worth your life to walk on the streets and hard to see anything through the crowds. Tourist guides led their groups of fifty to one hundred people by raising a colored banner high over their heads so the group could keep track of their leader. Brightly colored flags of all kinds and sizes fluttered in San Marco Square, the streets so jammed it was impossible to find a pathway.

We learned to do our exploring in the evenings after the tours were over. We loved Venice in spite of the crowds and sweltering heat. It was pleasant to relax in our hotel rooms (another Hotel Londra) overlooking the canal in cooler comfort during the day and venture out when the sun was down.

Then we would choose from many inviting restaurants for an early meal before the stampede for tables began. After dinner, we'd have coffee and liquor on the square and listen to lilting music played by large orchestras, or we'd take a quiet gondola ride through the dark canals, lulled by the lapping waters and dipping oars of the gondoliers. Shopping was fun too, with the windows full of Italian glassware and fine linen.

Of course we had a day on the Lido beach. Breck and Tracey must have been waterlogged from so much swimming. I was disappointed with the beach. Dressing rooms and restaurants almost obscured the sand. In '53 the expansive beach had been quite bare, pure and white. Today the millions of people had dirtied the sand and trashed the beach. Even the water looked polluted, which twenty-five years earlier had been clear and sparkling.

We decided to have one evening at the Danielli Excelsior where we had stayed before. It is the "top" hotel in Venice, a luxurious extablishment, and we thought it would be the evening "par excellence, "but it turned out to be the worst meal, the poorest service and the most uncomfortable evening on our trip — in addition to the most expensive. It was cold and windy on the rooftop dining room, and we were placed at a table without a view. Although there was an inside dining room, they refused to serve us there. Instead of leaving, as we should have done, we stayed and shivered and covered our shoulders with the large but inadequate napkins. When the food came it was also cold, the meat tough and tasteless. We left in disgust after paying through the nose for a bad evening. We all agreed even the little pizzaria on the back street of the canal was a better place to eat.

We said a regretful goodby to Venice, dripping with perspiration, but loving it in spite of everything, and flew to Copenhagen to board the *Royal Viking Sky* for the two-week North Cape cruise. Again we had an abrupt change of climate. Our perspiration froze to ice crystals. We wrapped up in coats and hurried off to the Tivoli Gardens as soon as we were checked into the Hotel d'Angleterre that evening. We knew Breck and Tracey would love the amusement park, and it was especially fun at night, lit up like a Christmas tree.

The cruise was the high point of the trip. We were delighted to discover there were many teenagers on board and a good program of entertainment planned especially for them. The junior director involved the young people in sports tournaments, parties in the disco, and get-togethers for banana splits or cokes. The youngsters entertained the adult passengers one evening with a rock and roll show of dancing and singing. The girls took part in all the activites, found the boys attractive and the girls congenial. Tracey even had the excitement of a "shipboard romance."

Besides the sports and diversions on the ship, there was always the supreme beauty of the scenery as we slipped along the outer west coast of Norway to the North Cape and back again among the islands and coastline of eastern Norway. We paused to visit the towns almost every day during the two-week voyage, each village or city having something unusual to distinguish it from any other. The nights became shorter and shorter as we neared the north Cape until finally, as we anchored there overnight, the day and night blended into one conflagration of sunset and sunrise from eleven p.m. to one a.m. It took the sun fifteen minutes to set and disappear into the sea only to rise again at once like a slow bouncing ball. All the while the sky was a spectacular shower of gold and red flames. The glassy sea reflected the shimmery lights of the sky and shadows of the giant pines along the shore to the peaks of the towering snow-capped mountains, showing their up-side-down reflection. Who could sleep through such a night? It was worth many sleepless nights to witness such a phenomenon of nature. The daylight continued for four days until we reached Bergen, sailing southward.

Far from resting on board, as we imagined we would, we slept less and exercised more than during our tours on land. There was such indescribable beauty everywhere we couldn't stop looking just to sleep! Mountains, snow fields and rushing waterfalls down the walls of the fjords with doll-like villages stuck on the hillsides made us wonder how the townsfolk made their way, and we marveled how they built homes on the cliff edges in the first place. In Geiranger, buses drove us all day up switch-back narrow roads to the village of Dalsnibba, where we overlooked the valley five hundred feet below us. The air was crisp with a warm sun, and, anchored in the bay at the foot of the drop, our ship looked the size of a thumbtack.

Hammerfest, near the North Cape, was completely rebuilt after the war. The Germans occupied the town during the war and leveled it in 1944 when they evacuated. Now it was a clean, colorful village boasting a lovely contemporary church, with gorgeous stained glass windows. Sam and I enjoyed strolling through the streets, finding it fun to mingle with the pleasant, handsome Norwegians. Our southward journey began here after hitting the peak of the north the night before.

From the beginning to the end of our cruise, the weather was springlike and delightful, except for three consecutive days of rain from Bergen to Oslo. We were told we were experiencing the best weather in over six years. Always there was a fabulous panorama of mountains, waterfalls, bright green pastures, farms and villages nestled on the hillsides or at the water's edge. The Lapplanders in the far north of Norway were interesting people to see, dressed in heavy, black wool costumes embroidered with bright flowers. Each family was identified by a different, unusual headdress. They were short, sturdy people with rugged creased features, reflecting the nomadic life they lead in the old, uncompromising climate of the north.

We made our way in and out of fjords discovering more and more breathtaking surprises in the scenery as we rounded the bends of the coastline. In Bergen the rain fell heavily all day but no one complained, as we paddled around the city and sloshed through the woods to Grieg's home at Trollhagen. But we were glad to return to the ship and exchange hot water showers for the cold ones that had been dripping down our backs. The rain continued to pelt down the next day in Stavanger, and the temperature fell to fifty-five degrees. It was hard to see the city through the streaming windows of the bus, but no one wanted to venture beyond the vehicle for the insistent downpour. The storm followed us at sea, and we were tossed about all night — the only rough weather on the trip. It caused us to arrive late in Oslo, but though the weather was cloudy, it remained clear while we toured the capital city, revisiting the Kontiki Museum, which we had seen in '72, and seeing other sights new to us, such as the most unusual statues by Vigeland in Frogenger Park depicting the human life cycle from womb to death.

We returned to Copenhagen, refreshed from the cruise. Breck and Tracey shed tears of regret, hugging their new-made friends goodby and promising to write. It had been a memorable experience for them — a taste of shipboard life and vistas of another culture.

Our only bad experience came that day in Copenhagen. We left the ship for the airport at 9:30 a.m., but our plane didn't take off for London until noon. As the plane rose up from the runway, I felt it suddenly lose altitude and I stiffened in panic. Sam said it was nothing, but a moment later we circled and returned to land. We were told to remain in our seats and that "nothing was wrong. We just lost an engine on the take-off!" We sat in the plane for an hour, then were given tickets for lunch in the airport restaurant, where we were to be paged when the plane was ready for boarding. By the time we appeared for lunch, the restaurant was nearly ready to close, and we were served a quick, cold meal. The hours passed. We were given no word or hint of what was happening to our flight. Finally at 4:30 the news reached us that the engine would have to be replaced, and we were to be put on another plane at 7:30! By that time we had turned into glassy-eyed zombies.

When we arrived at The Bailey Hotel in London, it was close to midnight, but even through sleep-bleared eyes we could see it was a dump. It actually looked like it had been bombed! The lobby reminded me of early 1930 hotels — dark, overstuffed, broken-down chairs lining a wall, an overhead brass chandelier converted from gas to feeble electricity. The reception desk surrounded a lone sleepy man, now suddenly alert, but obviously unaccustomed to doing business and bewildered by it.

We were led to our rooms on the second floor through dim hallways. Stacked on the floor at random was furniture, bathroom fixtures, plumbing pipes and lots of fallen plaster. "You must pardon the disorder. We are

[398]

renovating," our "guide" explained. Our rooms were cornered together at the end of the same hall where we managed not to trip over the old-fashioned toilet left standing in the way.

In our dreary, chintz-patterned room with the faded wallpaper, Sam said he would go out and find us another hotel. I said it was a silly idea at this hour of the night, well after midnight. I begged him to let us stick it out for one night, then search for new bunks in the morning.

Though Sam did investigate other possibilities the next day, there didn't seem to be another hostel in the city of London with two available rooms. The weekend was peaceful enough, but at dawn on Monday morning the workmen began their drilling, gutting a six-room section out of the building. Our teeth chattered with the vibrations.

Other than the renovating problems, we had no other objections to the hotel except for its decor and seedy appearance. It was, in fact, respectable enough, and the dining room was notable and served excellent food. We found the suburb of Chelsea convenient. The "tube" was just across the street from the hotel, connecting in moments to anywhere we wished. There were other good restaurants around the block for a change of diet, and we became used to stepping over debris and around the workmen and their tools as we went to and from our rooms.

We even entertained the Neely Aligs and their children, Marian, Frances and Fred, who were in London at the same time. Tracey came down with a bad cold and fever, and we thought it best to have the Aligs come to The Bailey rather than meet them elsewhere and leave Tracey all alone. We were highly amused when Emily and Neely appeared in the lobby and assessed our establishment with one horrified look. They had just come from a week in Ireland, staying in a friend's castle. In London they were renting a swanky apartment near Harrod's and told us about their lucky find with much enthusiasm. They were a little more impressed with the food in the old-fashioned dining room, and we had a good time together. They couldn't believe the trek to visit Tracey, as they stumbled around the obstacle course to her room.

The Bailey Hotel had been prestigious once — possibly in 1900. Vestiges of grandeur remained, a graceful stairway leading to the upper floor, which split away at the landing to form two staircases on either side of an impressive stained glass window.

In Stratford-Upon-Avon we saw a splendid production of *The Merry Wives of Windsor* — one of the best productions in our memory. It was done in the true spirit of Shakespeare, bawdy and vigorous. The girls loved London and all its sites steeped in history, as much as I did. Westminster, St. Paul's and the Tower of London were met with enthusiasm, as was the ritual of the Changing of the Guard at Buckingham Palace. We toured all the tourist attractions and loved them all, as we always had. We enjoyed a leisurely trip by launch to Windsor from Maidenhead — something I had not done before. It was a pleasurable ride on a beautiful sunny day, and the scenery was pretty on the Thames. After passing through two locks, however, the engine on the launch conked out, and we limped into a boat yard for repairs. They transferred us to another boat after quite a delay, and we "carried on" undaunted. This was my birthday, seeing the doll house at Windsor Castle, Hampton Court, traveling by launch and ending up with a show in London that evening — Sherlock Holmes done in great style, and terrifying sound effects — a production of *Crucifer of Blood.*

Three days later, when we arrived in Dublin, Breck celebrated her sixteenth birthday. We honored her at dinner at Fitzpatrick's Kilkenny Castle, where we spent the first night on our Castle Tour. Our chauffeur, Tony White, met us at the airport with his Mercedes limousine. He was our guide throughout the week, showing us the heavenly Irish countryside, and stopping for two nights each at the splendid castle hotels. They once had been privately owned mansions or castles. Tony turned out to be a non-stop talker and a jerky-foot driver, but even so, very nice and helpful. We found the week to be the restful one we needed before returning home to our respective busy lives. We did little else but drive during the days and lounge in the gorgeous hotels.

One of the loveliest of the hotels was Dunloe Castle, six miles from Killarny on a huge, pastured estate. Caramel-colored Haflinger horses grazed on the bright green pasture in front of our bedroom window, a dreamy picture to remember. The background of blue, hazy mountains in the distance framed the far side of the picture behind rows of trees, and a white fence encompassed the foreground. I fell asleep peacefully and cozily under down covers, wishing I could wear the comforter outside the next day, as the air was cold and nippy.

Breck and Tracey rode horseback at Dunloe and played with the small Haflinger horses as they grazed the field. They explored the woods and trails of the estate, while we sank into deep arm chairs and nursed our tea or Irish coffees by a warming fire in the fireplace.

We drove to Cong and spent another two nights at Ashford Castle, a bonafide castle with a moat and turrets. It was a huge gray mass of stone set in a green pasture near a sparkling lake. Exploring it was a must. The girls and I climbed up to the turrets and down stairs and along corridors, admiring the exquisite furnishings, portraits and artifacts in the castle rooms. We slept that night with music wafting up from the "dungeon disco." Our corner bedroom overlooked a lovely rose garden, hemmed in by tall, colorful hydrangeas. Centered in the rose garden was a bubbling fountain. Beyond the red ivied walls and turreted fort was the lake, winding away and dotted with islets. We also could catch a glimpse of the opposite wing of the castle. It was an elegant and glamorous place to languish, with one drawback. Castles are cold and drafty.

The next day we rode around the lake in an old tender from the *Q.E.II,* stopping at one of the islets. There were two ancient churches there of Celtic origin and a graveyard boasting the oldest stone in Europe, 409 A.D., inscribed in ancient Gaelic. It was while we were at Ashford Castle that, just sixty miles away, Lord Mountbatten was murdered. His fishing boat had been set with a time bomb. All of Ireland, as well as we, were shocked by the sensless, cruel murder — another brutal act by the I.R.A. terrorists.

We left Ashford Castle with regret and continued our drive to New-market-on-Fergus, seeing the usual sheep farms behind stone wall paddocks, fields of cows and thatched cottages. The last night of our journey was spent at Dromoland Castle, set perfectly between lakes and green-swards. The castle was smaller than Ashford, but was done in impeccable taste. The girls rode horseback again in the nearby village, while I enjoyed the luxury of the lovely living room, sewing on my needlepoint piece. That evening we did the "tourist thing" and had a medieval banquet at Bunratty Castle. It was fun and raucus, filled with dinners at long tables and lined with benches where we sat crowded together on either side. The mead was too much for Tracey, and she giggled mightily throughout the meal. The entertainment was excellent with appropriate Renaissance costumes, and the dinner good — eaten with one knife and your fingers. It was a fitting close to our many experiences with our precious grandaughters. We wouldn't trade anything for that journey together.

Breck at the summit of the North Cape

Haflinger pony nuzzles Tracey's hand — Dunloe Castle grounds, Ireland

[402]

Samburu tribesmen

Giraffe with backdrop of Mt. Kilmanjaro

Masai women

"Jambo" from Africa

[403]

CHAPTER SIXTY-ONE

WE took our great African adventure the next year. I had always been fearful of going to Africa but had a great desire to view the wild animals at close range. My fears were coupled with a vivid imagination, having seen many movies of Tarzan and blood-thirsty adventures of treachery and intrigue in the bush! Cannibals boiling missionaries, safaris venturing into unkown territories, where lion and hyenas roamed through the campsites — elephant stampedes and so on. All these pictures juggled around in my mind with the dread of finding myself in the heroine's shoes in the middle of the jungle, a deadly snake coiling up a tree behind my head ready to strike. Perhaps I might come down with malaria — or cholera, and lie helpless with chills and fever in a tent with only a witch doctor to chant get-well wishes over my head! My worst fear of all, of course, was flying the great distance to reach the Dark Continent!

Putting common sense and curiosity over my rank stupidity, we planned a two-week safari with Anita Farrell who was organizing a tour for late October. We had been properly inoculated against the rampant diseases prevalent in Africa, though nothing for snake bite. (One had to take one's chances once in a while.) I planned to keep my eyes open for the critters at all times.

Thirteen of us gathered at the airport on the seventeenth of October, 1980. Except for one bachelor from Newark, Ohio and a couple from Palm Beach, Florida, the thirteen of us were from Indianapolis. I am not really superstitious about the number thirteen but was relieved when the other three mentioned joined us at Kennedy Airport in New York for the long flight.

After a five hour "sit" at Kennedy, we finally took off at 10 p.m. for the overnight stretch to London. Anita thought we would need a proper bed to sleep off the rigors of the flight, so we were taken to a nearby motel for a day-long rest. I managed to sleep an hour-and-a-half before our next grueling all-night flight to Kilimanjaro Airport in Tanzania. The flight took eleven hours, including one fuel stop at Lacana, Cypress, mid-way on our journey. We reached the Kilimanjaro Airport and immediately had a remarkable view of the famous volcano mountain, covered in snow, welcoming us to Arusha. We were lucky to see Kilimanjaro at all, since it is generally obscured by low-hanging clouds.

The Tanzanite Hotel (named for the purple gem found in the hills of Tanzania) was a thirty-minute ride from the airport on the out-skirts of the small town of Arusha. It was a pleasant, rustic motel compound with cottages scattered on rather bare ground and a central building for dining, drinking or loafing. An outside veranda set with tables and chairs provided a good view of the animals enclosed, thankfully, by a fence. Here was our first close-up of Real, Live, Wild Animals in their natural surroundings, where samples of the tamer varieties were kept, such as giraffe, zebra, ostrich, condor and eland. A pretty man-made lake provided the roaming animals a proper water hole, and the grassy stretch outside the fenced-in grounds was filled with bright flowers in well-tended beds. It was a pretty view and stimulated our desire to see many more animals on our trek-to-come.

We reveled in a good clean-up in our rather bare cottage. Three days of living in the same clothing with no toothbrush is demoralizing. (I had neglected to think of carrying a change of clothing or cosmetics in my carry-on bag — an oversight which won't happen again.)

The next day, after a long, welcome sleep, our group left in three mini-buses, which were ours for the week in Tanzania. We drove for miles over incredibly dusty and broken down roads full of pot holes until we reached Tarangire National Park, where we would spend two nights in tents! As we drove through the park, we began to see herds of grazing animals by the hundreds. We were thrilled by the zebra, gnus and cape buffalo in great quantity. Elephants abounded, but we were shocked to see the evidence of their ravages. Whole forests were uprooted and trees mishapen, with branches and limbs torn away, robbed of their edible leaves. The park looked as if it had been destroyed by tornadoes. The guide explained the vegetation in the park could feed two thousand elephants, but eight thousand inhabited the area. The land was in peril of complete devastation.

In just the short time we drove around the park, we counted twenty-seven different varieties of birds and animals. The animals, which had already migrated from Serengeti National Park, were now eating their way on their migratory path through Tanzania to Kenya for the winter. In the spring, the migration returns to Serengeti, and the cycle continues year after year. Though the animals are supposedly protected, there is a great deal of hunting, especially by the natives, for food, and for pelts and animal parts as tourist souvenirs. An entire elephant must be killed in order to extract a few hairs from its tail to make "lucky" bracelets. A rhinoceros is killed for the aphrodesiac said to be found within its horns, and the powder is sold at an enormous price, as well as the horns themselves. The rhino is becoming extinct from the rampant killings.

We laughed at the silly warthogs, calm enough until we approached. Then, in alarm, their corkscrew tails unwound to spikes, standing straight up in the air as they ran for shelter. Many varieties of the deer and antelope family graced the landscape with their sleek beauty. We saw them all in large numbers, feeding in groups for protection against their predators. The predators were also in evidence, though the lazy lions seemed to be yawning sleepily under the shade trees after prowling all night for food.

[405]

The campsite was on the top of a cliff overlooking a valley of grazing land to the upsweep of mountain shapes, gray-blue against the cloudless sky. The central building with the public rooms and screened dining porch was near the parking lot where our mini-buses lined up, and we paraded through the building and down a dusty path at the cliff edge to our assigned tents. Ours was fairly far from the main building, but I was glad there were two more tents past ours. There was some comfort in having neighbors on either side. Mary Louise Moynahan had the last tent to herself on the row, beyond which was a tangled growth of shrubbery and trees, the edge of the "civilized" area. Anita and Walter Farrell were next to us.

The tents were permanently attached to concrete slab foundations but were, nevertheless, canvas tents, fitted with zippered flaps, which could be opened as needed for windows and doors, the openings well screened against insects. Behind each tent was a semi-private wash space. I can not glorify it by calling it a bathroom. It was another concrete slab with a cold water shower head placed over an ineffective drain. The toilet was simply a ten-gallon bucket with a toilet seat loosely placed on top. You had to be very careful when sitting or the entire outfit would overturn. Although curtained by tenting, most of this space was exposed, and the general public well informed of his neighbor's visits to the privy.

Inside the privacy of the sleeping tent, there was little space to move. A hard cot was placed on either side, allowing a narrow passage between them from the front "flap" to the back "flap," exiting to the slop jar and shower. A chest and a piece of furniture resembling a dressing table were placed behind the cots. There was a lamp, which produced a faint orange glow, but we were informed the generators supplying the electricity to the camp would be cut off from nine p.m. to six a.m.

We sat together with the Farrells and the rest of our group on our front "stoop" before dinner, watching the sunset and drinking cocktails with snacks, which the Farrells supplied. It was the eve of Mary Condit's eightieth birthday, and this called for a celebration. With binoculars we could identify the animals grazing far below us on the plain. It seemed so safe, so remote, so peaceful!

We trekked back up the path for a good meal on the large screened porch. Some sat until dusk, drinking coffee and nightcaps before returning to their tents, but Sam and I, still tired from the exhausting flight, walked back to our tent over the now scuffed-up dusty path. We had noticed it had been raked in neat wavy rows before our arrival. Now the trudging back and forth had messed up the design made by the rake tines.

It was a hot night, but a gusty wind blew around the tent. We opened our flaps to admit as much air and light as possible from the dying sky. The faint orange glow from the one bulb in the lamp made it hard to find our

[406]

night clothes. Reading was impossible, so we climbed into our cots, — but not before I checked carefully for spiders, scorpions or even a snake! In spite of the heat, I crawled under the load of covers, not wanting to loosen anything, in the event something besides Sam might want to share the bed with me and crawl in.

I was wide awake, listening to the wind now grown wilder, howling over the plain below me. I watched through the mesh screening as the moon rose in the sky from a dark orange ball to a silver one. My imagination flared and filled my thoughts with the roaming animals we had seen all day. The parade of animals marched on in my mind while I tried to sleep; then another thought nagged me. What if I had to go to the bathroom? I would never have the nerve to stumble through the darkness to find that wobbly slop jar or even to get out of bed in the first place! The night dragged on miserably, while Sam's snoring and those of our neighbors on either side penetrated the whistling, tormented wind.

I was just beginning to relax, sleep inches away, when I came wide awake from no sound at all. It became deathly still when the wind suddenly stopped roaring. Now I began to hear other things the wind had stifled. Stealthy footfalls and heavy breathing from something close by. My heart gave a lurch as a lion roared, followed by an animal cry sounding an alarm. It was picked up by another and another in quick succession until a cacophony of cries — three short panicky, high-pitched tones followed by a fourth on a rising glissando, increased in volume. I could tell when one was caught. The rising glissando at the end of its cry was cut off in mid-crescendo and was choked to silence. The hysteria of the herd was suddenly silent. I heard the kill fought over with growls and scuffling. It all sounded so very close! Cries issued near and far from the stalking or preyed-upon animals, but I could not identify many of the sounds. I lay stiff with fear and wished Sam would wake up, but he continued to snore peacefully.

Another sound from the direction of the parking lot sounded like an oil drum being overturned, then the crunching of shrubbery and sticks underfoot. The foot-paddings could only be ELEPHANT! I began to whisper, "Sam - Sam," trying to wake him, but not loud enough. I didn't want the intruder to hear me. Unmistakable plop sounds were so close, my eyes opened wide to see across the tent through Sam's screening and there, certainly, was his great shape white in the moonlight, looming on the path and coming straight toward us. This time, hysterically, I called to Sam (sotto voce) and he finally stirred, answering in his loud, normal voice, "What do you want?" "My God, shut up!" I breathed. "Look out the window!"

I braved the bare floor of the tent to get out of bed and clung close to Sam while we stared at the apparition through the tent flap. The elephant with great dignity and purpose walked on, barely making a sound, and paused beside the acacia tree at our front stoop. For fifteen minutes the great creature quietly ate up the tree, ripping a branch here, a branch there until nothing much was left of it. He looked white in the dark night with the moon reflected off him. At last I let myself crawl back to bed, exhausted, while Sam, now wide awake, continued to watch intently.

The elephant, finally satisfied with the yellow blossoms of the acacia tree, moved away, turned and headed right for me! I lay in bed looking up at him, holding my breath, lest the slightest movement cause him to investigate my whereabouts with his trunk. His knees were at my eye level, but I could see up to his tiny eyes. In all of Africa I never saw another elephant with tusks of his dimensions. They nearly dragged the ground! He walked by slowly, picking his way over the tent ropes and disappearing somewhere behind our slop jar.

I broke out in nervous perspiration. The excitement of the night's adventure had worn me thin, and I went limp as a rag. I finally slept but woke up again at dawn, my eyes opening on a beautiful serene sunrise.

The next morning, Sam pooh-poohed my account of the lion kill, but I stuck to my guns. Evidence supported me for there were cat footprints in the dust of the path in front of our tent. Also huge plops of the elephant were distributed along the way, and the spoor of lion or leopard marked the trail also. We dodged them all the way to the dining room. At breakfast we were told lions had killed a cape buffalo on the road just outside the entrance gate of the compound. I was vindicated. It had not been a nightmare or figment of my imagination. I imitated the animal cries I had heard, and the guide assured me I sounded just like a baboon.

We were not the only ones to have seen the "white elephant." Mary Condit woke her roommate, "Sparkle" Crowe, to announce, "An elephant's come to wish me a happy birthday!" "Well, for goodness sakes, zip up the flap before he walks in here!" Sparkle had replied.

Everyone else had slept through the night in blissful ignorance — even Anita and Walter, who were right beside us, but that night they were all able to see the "white elephant" when he appeared in the parking lot while we were having dinner. We were not allowed to walk the paths to our tents while the elephant munched away on the trees in full view. The servants banged on pots and pans to frighten him away, but until the elephant had his fill of tree branches, nothing would disturb him from the spot. After he slowly ambled off in another direction, we were driven to our tents in the buses.

I was nervous about repeating another night like the one just endured. But I was so tired, I slept soundly through a peaceful night. The only evidence of animal life near us were the tiny tracks of dikdik all over our dusty front stoop. For the rest of the trip we were housed in cabins made of sterner stuff. I didn't think my nerves would hold out for any longer than two nights of camp life.

———————◆———————

Everywhere we drove we saw animals by the hundreds. Everyone but us carried cameras and constantly snapped photos from the windows or stood up through the opened roof of the bus for a wider sweep with their telephoto lenses. We were not allowed to get out of the buses. Not interested in seeing the sights through a view-finder, we preferred the pictures in our minds instead of on paper, reproducing pale replicas of vivid memories. One could not reproduce the suspense or emotion of a moment when, for instance, a rhinocerous would be spotted, a new born baby at her side. It would be a moment of extreme caution and tense silence. Rhinos, though near-sighted, can hear the slightest sound and will move with lightning speed to charge, if threatened.

Those who favored seeing birds over the animals were put together in one of the buses and usually went in a different direction, but generally we were seldom out of sight of each other. The drivers, knowing best where the animals would convene, followed those routes off the main roads. In remote clusters of rocks or bushes, we would come upon a lion pride or a freshly killed eland, surrounded by hyenas.

We will always remember Clara Huntington and her husband, Paul, who rode with us. She was a fervent photographer and wanted to take shots of each animal we came across. Many rolls of film were used and much time was spent while she nervously focused and refocused to get it all just right. She wanted the animals to pose at just the right angles, urging them to smile or "look this way, please."

Once we came upon a magnificent pride of lions — the male, three females and their seven cubs. We drove into the center of this family scene, dividing the group with the male and one female on our right and the rest of the pride lying on a rock formation at our left. The adult females indolently watched us with their yellow eyes while their cubs worried over a half-eaten carcass. Clara, camera adjusted, leaned far over the top of the open-roofed bus, dangerously near and vulnerable, calling the lions to come closer! The male lion was already but six feet away, his orange, sleepy eyes staring at Clara. Clara fumbled as usual in nervous anticipation of the finest shot for her album. The animal looked at her with his hypnotic stare for so long that we kept calling to her in agitation, "now, Clara, — snap it now!" Still she fumbled. The lion was bored. He had posed long enough and began to amble away, his tail flicking up at Clara with disgust, waving goodby. She snapped the camera just as he squatted to relieve himself.

Another time she snapped an action shot, which was perfect. At last Clara had won with a beautiful picture. She sat down, inspected her camera and said with disgust, "I was out of film."

[409]

From the Tarangire Park we drove to Ngorongoro Crater over impossible roads built for Tanzania by Chinese coolies. There were holes big
enough to swallow the whole bus and barely room to skirt around them.
Up and down we jounced all over the country. The dust was so thick we all
wore dust masks, which we had purchased at home before we came. The
masks were the kind used by hay fever sufferers, pollen and dust-proof, and
they helped a great deal. We used a new one every day. The natives driving
herds of cattle must have thought we were creatures from outer space as we
passed them on the roads. The Masais were tall, thin and majestic
looking. They plastered their hair with red mud to keep it in place, and
their bare chests were adorned with wide-banded collars made of bright
colored beads strung on wire. They often stood like storks on one leg, the
other bent at an angle to allow the foot to rest on the opposite knee. They
seemed to relax in this position and stood erect and balanced without a
wobble. Seeing their mud and straw huts here and there on the vast
expanse of barren ground, we wondered how it was possible for them or
their animals to survive without any evidence of food or water. The Masai
consume a ghastly diet of mixed blood, urine and milk from their cattle.

Ngorongoro Crater Lodge was a mighty improvement over "tent city."
The usual central building of public rooms was surrounded by many
separate smaller ones for sleeping quarters. One very nice room and bath
had an enclosed porch, which served as a sitting room where we could
enjoy the view of the countryside in comfort. Rooms were joined together
as in ordinary motels and reached by sidewalks leading to all the buildings,
including the restaurant. Everything was open and we were warned not to
walk on the paths after dark unless attended by a Watusi, spear-carrying
guide for protection. We realized the necessity for this as a herd of cape
buffalo had taken up residence on the grassy slope just off the sidewalk
leading to our quarters. These animals are one of the most dangerous of all
types in Africa. They charge without warning or cause. We were forced to
pass them, much too close for safety, to get in or out of our room.
Everywhere on the trip we were fearful of the after-dinner walk to our
bedroom, but only twice did we find a spear-carrier to walk with us.

Our trek into the crater was another exciting day. We rode in four-wheel
drive land-rovers down a perilous track to the dusty crater floor five
hundred feet below, where animals of all kinds live, protected by the walls
of the crater. The animals are born, live and die here. We could see them
at very close range. This is where we saw the large lion pride, rhino and
new-born baby and herds of oryx, zebra and gnus. We also saw baboons,
vervet and blue monkeys in great numbers, as well as gorgeous birds —
ibis, ostrich, Egyptian goose and many others. All over Tanzania and
Kenya we kept a log of the species of birds and animals we saw on the
safari. At the end of the two weeks we had spotted forty-eight different
types of animals and one hundred and seventy varieties of birds. We were

disappointed not to see a cheetah, the shy, swift cats who are well-hidden during the daylight hours, but the first of the land rovers drove into our picnic spot that day in the crater and surprised five cheetah sunning on the rocks. By the time we arrived, they had dashed away like lightning bolts. We brought boxed lunches along as the entire day was spent in the crater, and left the vehicles to eat our lunches on the rocky rise beneath a grove of acacia and flambouyant trees. At the base of the rocky formation was a stream. It would have been pleasant to sit in the shade out of the heat, but our chicken bones drew a flock of kites, which literally attacked us to get at our food. We had to retreat into the land rovers and close the windows to protect us from the birds. One of the men was struck on the side of the head, the kite's talon raking his cheek. Flies swarmed around us, particulary the tsetse flies, who stuck to us and bit right through our clothes. Tsetse flies cause encephalytis and infections to animals as well as humans. We were besieged by them for the two days we were in the crater and at Lake Manyara. Tsetse flies made their way into our buses by the dozens. Spraying did nothing to deter them. The day at Lake Manyara was almost impossible to endure because of them. They covered the animals, sucking their blood and making them miserable and then transferred their nasty, tenacious selves to us, biting viciously.

The hotel at Lake Manyara was lovely, and its neighboring park was famous for the lions who showed their preference for sleeping up high on the limbs of the acacia trees. Perhaps it was to get away from the fliesl We were not lucky enough to see any lions in the trees but saw many thousands of birds, which the lake harbors in the center of the reserve. A great flock of flamingoes made a striking picture on the beach as we drove up. Our approach caused them to fly as one enormous pink umbrella over the lake. Crowned cranes, plovers, saddle hornbills, shrikes and pelicans hovered near the water and fished for food. Giant kingfishers and sacred ibis stalked the beach. We even saw the "go-away" bird. Of course, vultures were prevalent everywhere, swarming over carcasses or waiting patiently in trees for something to die. They were not ugly birds, but their beaks were wicked, hooked weapons made for tearing into flesh and bones.

The week in Tanzania came to an end when we returned to Arusha and the Tanzanite Hotel. It now seemed very civilized and tame after our exciting week in "the bush." We had seen and done many things unique in our experience and loved it all — even our flirts with danger here and there.

To enter Kenya, the law required us to leave Tanzania, as the border was closed between the two countries. We flew to the Seychelle Islands for a bisssful, clean, dust-free weekend. The Seychelles are one thousand miles away from the Kilimanjaro Airport, and Mahe reminded us very much of St. Thomas in the Virgin Islands. Situated in the Indian Ocean, two-thirds degrees from the equator, the Seychelles are havens for tourists, yet simple and unspoiled. The terrain is mountainous, and driving is on the left. The natives are black and their homes look much like those of the blacks on St. Thomas. Except for being a much larger island, we could have been in St. Thomas, but there is no hotel there to compare with the Mahe Beach Hotel. It is a modern, slickly elegant building built on a cliffside overlooking the ocean. The views were awesome. We reveled in the luxury, feasting our eyes on the most brilliant sunset that evening, recovering from our bumpy, dusty trek through Tanzania.

I longed to stay in the hotel the next day and do nothing but rest, but we were scheduled for a tour of the neighboring island of Praslin to see the fabulous giant tortoises and coco de mer fruit trees. It was a rainy day, and we flew by small plane at dawn to the island. It was more riding around on bumpy roads, with not much of interest to offset the discomfort and somewhat boring day. We languished most of the time at the Village de Pecheur, a small hotel on a nice beach where we swam and later had a very good lunch of freshly caught fish. There was not much to offer in the village itself but a few shops specializing in tortoise shell jewelry.

The tortoises, indigenous to the island, were enormous. Some were contained for tourist viewing, but we could enter the enclosure and feed, or even ride them if we cared to. I noticed one tortoise in distress. It had a long strand of leafy grass hanging from its jaw and kept opening its mouth wide in spasms. I called attention to it and our guide jumped over the fence and pulled the grass from its mouth. The creature was choking to death. Tears rolled down it cheeks as it looked thankfully at our guide then withdrew into its shell to recover.

The day was rather dull and uneventful, but the tour through the coco de mer plantation was interesting, and we learned about the unique coconut, found only on this island. It is of great size, growing into shapes larger than basketballs. If not opened at once when ripe, the coco de mer turns stone hard and is impossible to cut. At one time the species was becoming extinct. The trees take years to bear fruit. In order to save the rare plant, the government took over the forest, provided security against poachers and had each nut planted the moment it fell from a tree to insure the growth of a new one. Now there was every reason to believe the fruit would survive its near extinction, but it is still forbidden to eat the exceptionally delicious meat found in the coco de mer.

I was sorry not to have more time to enjoy the beauty of Mahe. We flew to Nairobi, Kenya at noon the next day. We saw the town of Mahe on the coastal edge only briefly as we drove through it on the way to the airport, but the aerial view was intriguing as we looked down on its rooftops from the mountain drive.

Nairobi is a thriving city. We were struck by the smooth, neatly landscaped four-lane highway leading into town from the airport. The center was planted with extravagantly beautiful tropical flowers, shrubs and jacaranda trees in full bloom. My favorite trees of all, the jacarandas, were in lavender profusion all over the city, and beds of well-tended flowers of brilliant colors in parks and gardens made the town look festive and prosperous. It was a striking contrast from the poverty of Tanzania. Nairobi sprawled for miles around with many posh hotels and important business companies bringing in world trade and tourist revenues. We stayed at the Hilton hotel buzzing with so much activity we had to wait long intervals before one of the battery of elevators would arrive to carry us up or down.

We began our second week of safari with an overnight at the famous Treetops. After the splendid week of seeing the animals in Tanzania in all their natural surroundings, this seemed to us a tourist gimmick out of proportion. Perhaps it would have had a different effect on us if it had been our first night in the bush territory, but coming from such a rich experience, Treetops seemed a watered-down version of animal life, theatrically presented to tourists.

We had lunch at the Outspan Hotel in Nyeri and were treated to African dancing before our transport in large, commercial buses to Treetops. At the entrance gate we were met by a "white hunter" fully garbed in khaki safari costume (probably provided by Paramount Movies) with a fifty caliber elephant gun "at the ready" in his right hand. With proper emphasis on the warning to "keep together," he led our close-knit group through the open ground toward a rustic log building a block ahead of us. We supposedly were exposed to roaming predators — true, but not too chancy, I felt. ("The most dangerous part of the trip," as Dad used to say in stressed, pseudo-frightened tones.) Occasionally, the guide explained, an animal would charge the group, and he would have to shoot it.

We arrived intact and proceeded up a flight of ladder steps to the main level of the building. The lodge was built from huge trees forty-feet above the ground, a protection against animal invasion, except for the monkeys who can climb anything. The place was full of them. We were given a tiny room with just space enough for two cots, heads to the window, a viewing place for the all-night vigil, watching animals convene at the waterhole. A floodlight, simulating moonlight, was turned on after dark to illuminate the small lake and muddy ground, the central action spot for night prowlers.

The huge building was packed with tourists, and the dining room was so long and narrow we couldn't see the end of it. There were long tables with benches on either side, where we crowded together for dinner. The food was served on movable dollies tracking down the middle of the table, and we helped ourselves as it passed. The atmosphere was noisy and

[413]

excited, everyone ready for night to fall and the vigil to begin.

On the roof of Treetops was a bar and many chairs and benches where people could see for miles over the bush. A forest of trees near-by was full of monkeys, who considered the roof of Treetops an extension of their home. A nursing mother cradled her baby in one of the comfortable rocking chairs, unabashed as her privacy was invaded. We were told not to feed the monkeys. They were not the tame "zoo" variety and could strike a wicked blow. Nevertheless, we noticed the servants at the bar giving leftovers of bread and crackers, fruit and meat in unlimited amounts to the animals as they poured onto the veranda, begging with longing eyes. The food was given surreptitiously by the natives, and we felt it was to encourage the monkeys to inhabit the roof, as they added an authentic touch to the scene.

We saw some animals that night and even a territorial dispute between a rhino and a cape buffalo. The buffalo finally conceded the rhino's superiority, backing reluctantly away as the rhino advanced with lowered head and menacing horn. A few elephants appeared to drink at the water hole, as well as impala, waterbuck and bush pigs, but nothing to compare with the numbers of animals we had seen in Tanzania. Our windows were heavily screened to keep the invading monkeys out, and once a peeping tom peered around for a view of us.

We left Treetops early the next morning and returned to the base at the Outspan Hotel, where we ate breakfast and then began our morning drive to the Masai Mara Game Reserve. Animals were everywhere. We were delighted to see a gerenuk for the first time. These are of the deer family but have extremely long necks and bodies. They eat from the low-hanging tree branches, standing up to graze on their long back legs, using their forelegs to help draw the branches down to head level, where they can nibble the foliage.

Many ostrich herds, reticulated giraffe and grevy zebra plus untold hundreds of magnificent and strange birds kept us continuously fascinated. Crocodiles crowded in slithery piles on the muddy river banks, and we counted sixty-five elephant in one herd as it crossed the river. Many in the herd were babies, following close to their mothers for moral support. We saw an oryx with her two new-born babies and once came upon a tiny gazelle alone, lying immobile beside the road. We stopped to see it more closely. Evidently it had just been born and was staring at us intently. Our driver, concerned that the gazelle was dying, left the bus to inspect it more closely. Just as he touched it, the baby sprang up like a jack-in-the box and leaped for safety out of our sight in seconds. We were sure this was the first moment of action in the baby's life. Later we saw the reason for the abandonment of the baby gazelle. The mother had used herself as a foil to attract a nearby lioness stalking in the long grass. As we approached the lion was distracted and moved away, and the adult gazelle returned to find her foal.

[414]

Time and again we witnessed the intimate life of wild creatures. Each place visited brought new experiences and sudden surprises. The hotel at Lake Naivasha was situated on a river and landscaped artistically with lush grass and flower gardens. We stayed in cabins rather far from the central building, which were quite luxurious. Our beds were fitted with mosquito nets, hanging from the ceiling and tied in a huge knot during the day. At night they were untied and flowed around the beds like great white parasols. It was fun to climb into the sanctuary of the cocoons and sleep in comfort, knowing we were safe from a malaria-carrier.

That night after dinner we were the first to leave the dining room and return to our cabin in the woods. We started to step down off the porch for the walkway, when we were stopped by one of the waiters. He quietly told us not to venture on the path as a hippo and her calf had come up on the lawn from the river and were grazing by the path. A mother hippo is quickly enraged and protective of her young. In spite of a sluggish-looking body, they can run very swiftly and attack with competence. We watched the pair, illuminated by the floodlights over the lawn, and presently the entire assemblage of guests and staff gathered at the porch railing. Some avid photographers ran out onto the lawn anxious to have close-up shots and came dangerously near the animals. With the protection of the crowd, we took advantage and dashed to our cabin, keeping a watchful eye out for other creatures of the night. There were many roaming baboons on the grounds, and a family of them used the roof of our cabin as their home. There was scampering and grunting throughout the night, but we were safe within our locked door and barred windows.

The next day was Sam's birthday, and he couldn't have had a better place to celebrate than at the Mt. Kenya Safari Club. It was one of the most luxurious places we have ever seen and had belonged to William Holden, who had recently sold it to an Arabian oil shiek.

Everything about the club was elegant, from the lovely landscaped grounds to the rich decor in the buildings. The meals were gourmet feasts, the breakfast and lunch buffets serving exotic fruits, vegetables and unusual dishes fit for a king and set on a fabulously decorated table. Our "cottage" was more like a town house. A large, comfortable living room separated two bedrooms and baths. The baths were like spas with walk-down steps to the sunken pool (usually called a bath tub.) The toilet was discretely concealed in a private alcove, and the dressing counter was lavish with theatrical lights over the mirror. With glistening black and purple tiles, the whole thing looked like a movie set. Beyond our lanai-style porch, a winding stream flowed past with connecting foot bridges to the rose gardens. Swans swam up and down with regal dignity and egrets pecked around the grass. The peacocks contributed a certain tone of class. They strutted snobbily around, spreading their fantails proudly. I couldn't decide which were more beautiful — the pure white ones or the multi-colored irridescent ones, the color of fire opals.

That night Anita and Walter planned a cocktail party for Sam in their plush quarters. We sat around a comfortable fire in their living room with the rest of our group having drinks and snacks, when suddenly a commotion outside attracted us to the porch. Assembled there with drums thumping was a group of Watusi dancers, who gave us a private performance. The Farrells had arranged for the dancers knowing it would be Sam's birthday.

Another night, at Keekorok Lodge, we caught a "still life" portrait as we left the dining room. On the front lawn grazed a large herd of zebra. It was a serene, peaceful sight, and this time I wasn't nervous walking past them on the way to our cabin.

At Samburu Lodge we were across the river from a thick jungle. At dusk natives hung a carcass in the trees and we watched, by floodlight from the hotel, to see a leopard come and feed on the bait. Crocodiles lolled on the banks of the river, and we were obliged to walk fairly near their hang-out to reach our cabin. We saw several night creatures at close range, particularly a bright blue lizard with a bright red head. He sat still and let us observe him as he checked us out with his bright green eyes. Turtles almost as large as tortoise struggled up from the river to find food on the banks, and a genet cat fled by us into the rushes as we stood on the path. The cat was after turtle — not us, thank goodness.

At Lake Nkwiu Bird Sanctuary we saw many more birds in their natural habitat than elsewhere. The weaver bird and their nests were everywhere, and we even saw a nesting eagle with eaglets (through binoculars.) Although we loved seeing the colorful birds of all sizes and descriptions, we felt more attracted and closer to the animals. Birds were a thing of the moment — in and out of sight in flashes. But the animals lingered long enough to get a better view, without the need for binoculars.

It was a thrilling trip, one to remember forever, and one we would like to repeat. My memories are of unspeakably bad roads everywhere — clouds of dust, and breathing through dust masks; beautiful skies and sunsets; arid and fertile land covered by thousands of animals — a peaceable kingdom on the surface, a vicious fight for life beneath; good food and accommodations with variety and adventure; the wild night in the tent with the "white elephant;" dodging cape buffalo at Ngorongoro Lodge, and the lion pride in the crater; tsetse flies in Tanzania, and the gentle wood carving artist at the Tanzanite Hotel, where we bought some carved statues; the Nairobe Hilton Hotel in the city of Jacaranda and bougainvillia; Treetops, with all the monkeys and the single portrait of the nursing monkey baby in the rocking chair cuddled by its mother; snuggling in the beds under the mosquito nets with the scampering of baboons on the roof; Sam's birthday party with the African dancers at the Safari Club — the peacocks, the food; good friends and good times together — the shopping fun; buying copper and silver bracelets from black arms stretched through our bus windows, hung with dozens to choose from; Mrs. Huntington taking pictures; hippo and baby grazing on our pathway and the zebra herd on the front lawn in the moonlight; terrible elephant destruction.

And hellishly long air flights!

Sveti Stefan, Yugoslavia

Haydn poster, Austria

Schloss Esterhazy, Eisenstadt, Austria

Bergenkirche, Eisenstadt, Austria

[418]

The Gellert Hotel, Budapest, Hungary

Prague, Czechoslovakia

CHAPTER SIXTY-TWO

TEACHING piano to youngsters has brought me much pleasure and many rewards. One great reward was teaching three blind students over the years, beginning with a two-year-old girl of remarkable talent. I learned braille to help them, which enlarged my own understanding of the difficulties a handicapped person struggles to overcome.

Another of my students was born without a right arm. Only eight when she began lessons, she had an ambition to sing when she was old enough to study voice. In the meantime, her mother asked me to give her a foundation in music theory. I was already teaching Lisa, her talented older sister, and agreed to give Susie theory lessons, but I also wanted her to be able to read notes well enough so that later she could accompany herself at the piano as she sang.

It wasn't long before Susie was picking out tunes and gaining agility with her left hand. She began asking for more difficult pieces to play, as she thought one-finger melodies were "babyish." It was difficult to find music for her, but I arranged several pieces and found others written for the left hand, which were decidedly advanced in the repetoire, but I thought she could tackle them in the future. A beginner with small hands and little strength has many problems to overcome. It takes time to develop the maturity and skill to cover the keyboard with arpeggios, big chords and flashy scales. We played many duets for awhile to make her pieces more harmonic, while Susie was challenged and worked hard to reach a technical prowess with her left hand. She was soon maneuvering the entire keyboard, and performing without self-consciousness at class.

Susie as an individual was exceptional. Her beautiful inward self glowed with magnetism; her poise, intelligence and sweet spirit commanded respect and love from everyone she met. She learned early to overcome hurt feelings and embarrassment when others made thoughtless, cruel comments about her handicap, as children and even adults do in ignorance. She matured rapidly, probably because of her sensitivity, quickly learning how to put people at ease by her own tactful replies. She studied with me until she went to Smith College, returning for lessons during the summer. She started singing at age sixteen and continued in college, improving, maturing and receiving high commendations from her teachers. When she left for college, she was working on Ravel's Left Hand Concerto, a monumental challenge in piano masterpieces for any artist to play. Her playing was always musical, with a sensitive, personal touch. She has continued to study on her own.

Along with the rewards, funny flashes come to mind from the years with my students. Julia, age nine, was learning her scales, and I had just explained the scale of A flat, with contains four flats — B,E,A, and D.

Julia built the scale from its pattern of whole and half steps and found the four flats quickly. When I asked her what those four flats spelled, she had no idea. I told her the letters spelled *BEAD*. She nodded, and the lesson continued. The following week I reviewed the scale with her and again asked her what the flats were. "B,E,A, and D," she responded readily. I asked her again, "And what do the letters spell?" She thought and thought as she struggled to remember. Finally, she brightened, her eyes sparkled, and she burst out "Pearl!" in triumph. Julia was a fourth-grader at Orchard School.

I also taught her two brothers and sister. Hall, the youngest was just three when I reluctantly started his lessons, at the insistence of his mother. One day Hall indicated he needed to go to the bathroom. I asked him if he wanted me to help him, but he shook his head and trotted off to the lavatory. A few moments later he emerged, head hanging and a tear on his cheek. "I didn't make it, Mrs. Moxley."

"Never mind," I comforted him. I had him remove his wet undershorts and hung them in the open window to dry in the spring breezes. He continued his lesson unconcerned. A short while later Sam came home and took in the situation at a glance, suggesting he should take out a diaper service for me.

Another little boy always admitted he "for-to-got," whenever I asked him a pertinent question. But the prize belongs to a five-year-old girl, who had just begun lessons and had attended one of my music appreciation classes highlighting some of the great pianists. One day after a lesson when Annie, a very gifted child, was already on her way to their car, her mother told me that one of her friends had asked Annie how she liked her piano lessons. Annie replied with enthusiasm she just loved studying music. The friend then asked what she was learning. "Oh," Annie sparkled, "I'm learning all about famous penises!"

———◆———

Roofmen and carpenters were still hammering away on our porch when we left on another extended trip to Europe. We were enclosing the large terrace on the southwest corner. The screening, plastic storm windows and corrugated plastic roof had seen their day. My many plants were growing so prolifically, it had become nearly impossible to find a place to sit down.

It was July thirtieth, 1982 when we flew to Dubrovnik, Yugoslavia for a week before proceeding to a two-week seminar in Eisenstadt, Austria, after which we would spend ten days in Czechoslovakia and Hungary before returning home September second.

Never having been "behind the iron curtain," we were prepared for an unusual experience, but we found Yugoslavia a beautiful country full of pleasant people and hordes of tourists, far from sinister (as long as one left politics out of the conversation.) Though obviously a poor country, the

[421]

people looked happy and fairly prosperous. Everyone worked — the government saw to that.

The coast of Yugoslavia is the most spectacular, boasting the most perfect beach in all of Europe, coupled with the warmest weather. The beach draws the sun-starved Europeans by the thousands each summer. Dubrovnik, the medieval walled-fortress town, is a drawing card by itself. You could spend many days wandering within the shelter of its rambling walls, exploring the cobbled streets and cul-de-sacs. The old walled city is not merely a resort for tourists or an historical "monument," but an ordinary town with extraordinary character. The week we were there, the city was celebrating a yearly arts festival. Concerts, ballets, Shakespearian theater and visual art exhibits all took place in the ancient walled-in section of the city.

Our hotel was on the top of a cliff outside of Dubrovnik, necessitating a taxi ride to the gateway entrance. (No cars were permitted inside the walls except for delivery trucks and vehicles on official business.) The hotel commanded a magnificent view of the town, the old walled city and the Mediterranean Sea stretching endlessly into the distance.

After three days we rented a car and drove down the coast to the island of Sveti Stefan. (In the stifling heat it was a "Sveti" ride.) Formerly a fishing village, Tito took it over for his private vacation spot during his reign as dictator. After his death the entire island became a resort with the well-designed hotel and cottages covering most of the land. The hotel was superbly run and served gourmet food on the outdoor terrace dining room. Our pretty room was in one of the connecting rows of stone cottages that followed the contours of the rocky island. We overlooked an expansive beach, which was the link to the mainland, almost like a sandy causeway. No cars were allowed on the island, but a large parking lot housed them on the mainland. We were met and driven across the beach causeway to the island by a porter in a golf cart.

If we ever return to Sveti Stefan, we plan to stay longer than one night. It is an enchanting island with narrow stone cobbled streets winding up and down the hills leading to gardens with bubbling fountains, a tennis court, swimming pool, and even an old stone church, now a ruin to explore.

We discovered a dungeon-style bar in a cozy section near the dining room and enjoyed our drinks, while the bartender practiced his English, relating the story of his life in a friendly manner to us, his only customers.

My strongest memory of Sveti Stefan is the bees. Instead of the usual flies during hot months, there were at least four times as many bees, which swarmed over us at breakfast and lunch. By dinner they had mercifully returned to their hives. Sugar bowls and breakfast jams were left on the tables as well as flower centerpieces, which attracted the bees in great numbers. We didn't get stung, but the bees were so persistent it was hard to enjoy the fine meals.

In any case, we loved the resort but left the next day to drive back to Dubrovnik because we had reservations for the all-day ferry trip from Dubrovnik to Split.

The scenery following the coast of Yugoslavia was lovely. The many islands and rocky spits of land formed coves, harboring sailboats by the hundreds. The beaches were literally obliterated by bodies lying cheek-to-jowl on the sand, an unbelievable sight. The weather was very hot, and bathers were out in staggering numbers.

We took a walking tour in Split with a very nice guide. The Dioclecian Palace amazed us, a 1700 year-old Roman fortress with only the under-ground rooms and foundation remaining. As the palace fell into decay, other homes and buildings were built on top, actually covering and protecting the ancient ruin. There were possibly ten acres of rooms in the foundation revealing the kitchen, water pipes and plumbing in the many rooms below street level.

Our Hotel Marjan was on the waterfront. We sat on the balcony of our room watching the sun set and the lights come on in the town and harbor. Ships were continuously passing, lit from stem to stern. After dinner we joined the pleasure-seekers, lovers and loafers along the waterfront, grateful for the fresh breezes after the stifling day. We sat on the square with mobs of people having coffee and slivovitz. When we returned to our hotel, a huge orange moon hung in the sky.

———————◄◉►———————

The next morning we flew to Vienna to join the group attending The Classical Music Seminar in nearby Eisenstadt. Everyone met at the airport arriving on planes from the States or elsewhere in Europe, and we were bused together to Eisenstadt. The two-week seminar, sponsored by the University of Iowa, was celebrating its seventh year in Eisenstadt. All of Austria was celebrating the two-hundred and fiftieth anniversary of Haydn's birth. Franz Josef Haydn was the music director and composer for Prince Esterhazy, whose castle was the headquarters for the concerts, lectures and master classes of the seminar. Posters of Haydn giving information about the special celebration in Eisenstadt were posted in Vienna and throughout Austria. The government had minted coins and commemorative stamps to honor the great composer. There was an outstanding exhibit of artifacts from Haydn's time collected from around the world on display, well over one thousand articles, pictures, man-uscripts, costumes and instruments.

I was most interested in the story behind the focal point of the exhibit—the oil portrait of Haydn, which had been reproduced for the posters. The English artist, John Hoppner, had painted the portrait for the reigning

Queen of England, wife of George III, and, since that time had hung in the queen's private apartments. For the first time Queen Elizabeth II had allowed it to be publicly displayed. I bought one of the posters to hang at home in my "studio" near another portrait by Hoppner, which we have owned for many years.

Haydn had always been my favorite of the classical composers, although I had never really understood why until that summer. I had registered for the seminar as an observer with no intention of performing in a master class. Sam planned to relax or wander around Eisenstadt, while I sat in on the seminar programs. There were many conducted tours and concerts for us to enjoy together.

The seminar far exceeded our expectations. The expertise of the artist-teachers, Paul Badura-Skoda, Jorg Demos and Hans Kann, as well as the superb directorship of the seminar by Dr. Ed Rath, and the music director of the choir and orchestra, Dr. Don Moses, was impressive. Robert Demaree and H.C. Robbins Landon were among the prominent lecturers. The theme of the programs centered on Haydn's life and music, but other works by Schubert, Mozart, Beethoven and Brahms were performed by the choir and orchestra to balance the diet. An opera in concert form was performed in the exquisite hall of Schloss Esterhazy, where acoustics are said to be the most perfect in all of Europe. The opera, Le Pescatrici recently discovered, was the world premier performance under the direction of Dr. Moses.

We expected our accommodations to be in a dormitory or pension of dubious merit, with "the bathroom down the hall." We had requested a private bath when we applied for a reservation (at more than the flat rate, of course,) and because of this, we were given splendid accommodations in a spanking new hotel, opened that spring. Thirteen of us who had requested private baths were given rooms in the new Hotel Burgenland. Our room not only had the bath, but a T.V. and a well-stocked refrigerator of snacks and drinks for our convenience. A large indoor swimming pool was just two steps away from our room on the third floor. A continental breakfast was included in the rate, that excelled any "continental" breakfast we had ever encountered in Europe or anywhere else. A groaning table was lavishly set with great baskets of fresh fruit and bowls of mixed, cut fruit compote; platters of cold meats, sausage and cheese with long, fresh loaves of pumpernickel, rye, black and white breads placed on cutting boards; cereal, jugs of milk and fruit juices; pots of coffee and tea, and even choices of yogurt were offered. After such a tempting variety of food for breakfast, lunch became unnecessary. We felt sorry for the rest of our group, who spoke of their continental fare in the morning. A hard roll and cup of strong coffee was "it" for them.

The dining room on the hotel roof was an expensive, gourmet restaurant, and we had dinner there a few times. On my birthday Sam gave a cocktail party for all staying at The Burgenland and he also asked the Don Moseses and Ed Rath to join us. They stayed at another hotel, which housed the administration, faculty and guest artists of the seminar. The dining room prepared trays of delicious canapes to go with the drinks and set a special table (nicely decorated with a fresh floral centerpiece) in the lounge adjacent to the dining room.

The tours were especially delightful, conducted by a knowledgeable guide, Jack Goodwin. Nearly every day we were taken by bus to various places of interest in the area of Eisenstadt. The tours were designed to interest musicians in particular. A typical day's agenda would feature a lecture or master class all morning, a guided tour in the afternoon and a concert in the evening. Participants in the master classes, choir and orchestra were alloted necessary practice time in the modern conservatory, set in a woodsy area. We, as observers, were able to do anything or everything offered by the seminar, and Sam and I took advantage of every opportunity.

We were taken to Vienna on two separate occasions. One day was spent inspecting the marvelous collection of keyboard instruments at the Hofberg Museum. Hans Kann personally conducted a private tour for our group, before the museum officially opened. We were there for three hours while he played each instrument (kept in excellent working condition and in tune) and even offered to let us "touch" the keyboards to try them if we wished. He demonstrated and explained the difference of each clavier, from the earliest melodian and virginal, to the later clavichords, harpsichords, forte pianos and finally the early to modern pianos. I was in awe of the nine-foot instrument, which had been played by Clara Schumann at her last concert. I ran my fingers over the keyboard where hers had been and felt touched by her presence.

Another "experimental" piano was very unique. I believe the experiment ended with this one, as the first and only piano of its kind. It had a semi-circular keyboard. When seated before it, I had the peculiar sensation of the keyboard wrapping itself around me. It was funny to play because, as I extended my arms to reach the bass and treble extension, my hands sort of "flew away" into space beyond the keys. The intention of the inventor was to relieve the performer from stretching his arms to the far reaches of the bass and treble. The curvature brought all the keys closer to the player, but it would have taken long hours of practice to change the built-in habits of playing normal pianos.

We toured both factories and offices of the Bösendorfer piano-making plants. One factory makes the mechanism of the instrument in a small town outside of Vienna. The pianos are finished in their cases in the Vienna plant. We were treated to lunch in the Vienna office and viewed the many shiny pianos in the showroom. The Kimball Piano Company bought Bösendorfer some years ago, and now the instruments are being sold at premium prices around the world. Kimball's plant is in Jasper, Indiana. They continue to make their own pianos there but have used some of the fine features of the Bösendorfer in their more expensive grands. The superior, hand-made instrument was designed at the outset for Liszt, but for many years, not more than a few were made during a year. With Kimball's expertise in mass production, the Bösendorfer business has made great strides in sales.

We were admitted to the inner shrine of the Albertine Library, where priceless manuscripts were explained by the director, Dr. Gunther Brosche. It was a fascinating day of learning many new things. That evening a concert was given by the seminar choir in the old church, Piaristenkirche Maria Treu in Vienna, followed by a festive gathering at a nearby rathskeller.

One tour I nearly skipped because Sam had elected not to go, became one of the most interesting of all. It was a tour of organs in the churches near and around Eisenstadt. The Domkapellmeister, Professor Harold Dreo, was the gentle, informed man who guided us all day to see and play the historical instruments still used for services in the churches and cathedrals. Harold Dreo was the organist for the large cathedral in town, and we were shown the impressive edifice and the organ loft, where he played for services.

We visited many smaller churches in the villages near Eisenstadt, climbing steep steps to reach their entrances. Churches are always built higher than any other of the surrounding buildings, if possible (in order to be closer to heaven, I suppose.) Although most of the organs, even fifteenth century ones, had been restored and worked by electricity, there were still some with the original bellows mechanism. One of us had to kneel on the floor to pump furiously while Herr Dreo demonstrated its tone and power.

The drive around the countryside and through quaint villages, was as interesting as the churches themselves. We traveled the road in and out of Eisenstadt, which had been the main riding path in Haydn's day. It wound through the woods and "over hill and dale." I could visualize the hunting parties or carriages traversing the same dusty road. We were told Haydn often rode and hunted through these woods.

The organ Haydn played in the Bergkirche was fabulous. It was high in the loft overlooking the sanctuary. Later, we attended high mass when the seminar choir sang Haydn's Harmonienmasse. It was an inspirational experience. I felt Haydn must be aware of the honor paid to him and listened with pleasure and gratitude from his bier close to the sanctuary. We left the church with tears in our eyes and walked to the priest's residence across the street, where a reception was given for us by the Bishop.

It was Corpus Christi Day, an important religious holiday in Austria. There was no church procession through the town, as we had seen years before in Vienna, but the festivity at the party outdid any parade. The Bishop himself poured the wine and welcomed all of us to Eisenstadt with a flowery toast. There were trays of sandwiches on each table, and we sat together in groups enjoying the ambiance and congeniality of our host as he passed among us, speaking to the groups at each table, a bottle of wine in each hand. The wine flowed continuously as he refilled the glasses around the great reception room. We didn't realize how festive we had all become until we finally walked back to our separate hotels. All agreed the party had been a great success. We felt it was quite out of place to get tipsy on Sunday after church, especially in the holy residence, but the high priest himself had encouraged us.

———————————<◉>———·————

One day we were escorted into Hungary. Eisenstadt is only a few miles from the Hungarian border, and in Fertog there is another mansion, which had been the summer residence of the Esterhazys, the Schloss Esterhazâ, built on a large estate much like its counterpart in Eisenstadt.

It was exciting to cross the border after much delay and examination of papers by the police. Each soldier carried both revolver and rifle. Machine guns were stationed at intervals "at the ready." Foreigners did not seem to be all that welcome in Hungary.

Once inside Hungary, after an hour-and-a-half delay, everyone was cordial and friendly. Our guide, Madja, was especially charming and informative. We felt she was not a communist sympathizer. Although she talked freely about the sorry conditions in her country, we were careful not to express our views too freely to her.

The palace of Esterhazâ was nearly empty of the fabulous furnishings it had once held. The Russians had occupied it during the war using it as a hospital. Every stick of furniture, rugs, draperies — even the woodwork and wall paneling — was used for firewood. The severe winters coupled with war rationing created a crisis of cold and near starvation. The Russians stole, or sold the treasures for food and burned the remains. Some valuables had been taken by loyal servants of the Esterhazys before the Russian occupation. They were hidden for safe keeping and returned to the palace after the war. Gradually, the palace is being refurbished with funds from tourist revenues, but the poverty in Hungary has kept the government from allocations for "non-essentials."

Schloss Esterhazy in Eisenstadt is leased by the family to the government for one shilling a year. It is used for such events as our Classical Music Seminar, concerts in the great Haydnsalle, public or private functions such as balls, business and political meetings and so forth. Government offices are also in the building, but apartments on the second

[427]

floor are reserved for the family's use. However, Prince Esterhazy does not dare return to his home in Eisenstadt for fear of being recaptured by the Russians or Hungarians, since Eisenstadt is just a few miles from the Hungarian border. Prince Esterhazy was in residence at Schloss Esterhazâ in Fertog when the Russians occupied Hungary and took over the Schloss. He was captured and imprisoned. Seven years later, staff members from Schloss Esterhazy in Eisenstadt infiltrated into Hungary, broke into the prison and liberated the prince, fleeing to Switzerland, where the prince still remains in sanctuary. Prince Esterhazy, now in his eighties, is the last living member of the family.

The most fabulous day in the entire two weeks was spent at Jorg Demos's home for a master class on his rare keyboard instruments. We left by bus from Eisenstadt at 7:30 and drove all morning though the mountains to the lake district near Salzburg. Demos's summer home lies high on a hill overlooking Lake Altensee in Skammergut. After lunch in a restaurant-chalet, we arrived at his property and spent the afternoon examining, listening and playing the many instruments that filled his home. These rare instruments are but a portion of his collection of over seventy and date from 1705 harpsichords to a 1914 Pleyel piano from France. About twenty instruments were crowded into the living room, with no space for sitting except the straight-backed ballroom chairs lining the wall around the room. He demonstrated each one, playing dextrously and beautifully, and explaining the instrument's mechanism, then invited anyone who wished, to play. Registered participants in his master class took up most of the playing time. I longed to try several of the instruments, particularly one exquisite harpsichord. The keys were made of bone, each one carved with a circle design at the base. The inlay decorating the instrument was delicate, and the instrument itself bore such a personality of grace and distinction I couldn't keep from looking at it. When played it had a mellow, sweet tone to match its appearance.

A tour of the house and grounds revealed two other farm houses, used as dormitories for students, who came in groups from around the world to study with Demos for the summer. At this time there were twenty Japanese living in the houses, crowded into the small rooms, sharing the one piano for practice in the minute living-dining area.

The two farm houses were rather far from the main house. We walked along the fence line in tall, weedy grass to reach them. Cows on the other side of the fence joined us on the parade, wanting to be recognized and petted. It would have been more fun to be close to their wet noses if swarms of flies hadn't found them so attractive also. They swarmed over us as well, making it difficult to see our way through the black clouds.

The entire day was unforgettable. The fascinating house with the gorgeous instruments in its breathtaking setting on the hillside, the lake a

[428]

peaceful picture below. We were all inspired by the excitement and beauty of the day and sang together on the bus as we drove back to Eisenstadt, not at all tired but exhilarated when we arrived at midnight.

The last day was spent in Vienna before our respective flights took us home, or on more travels in Europe. A routine city tour was arranged for those who cared to see the opera house and Schonbrunn Palace, but we spent the day shopping for music and strolling on the wide "walking street" near Hotel Sacher. We had such a memorable time at the seminar we vowed to do it again another year. We were sorry the two weeks had come to an end, but we had more to look forward to.

———·——⟨◉⟩——·———

Julieta and Agustin Salvat had been good friends of ours in Mexico. Agustin, a lawyer, had been the Secretary of Tourism with the Mexcan government, the next most important cabinet post behind Agriculture in Mexico. In 1981 he was appointed to the post of Mexican Ambassador to Czechoslovakia. They had invited us to visit them in Prague at any time, and we accepted their invitation for the week following the seminar in Eisenstadt. The Salvats flew to Vienna to meet us, after spending a few days at the Salzburg Festival. An arrangement had been made for their chauffeur to drive from Prague, pick us up in Vienna and take us all to Prague in their embassy Mercedes. We were thankful we did not have to undergo the usual hassle at the border. The diplomatic passports of the Salvats gave us immediate entry into Czechoslovakia. It was only a three-and-a-half hour drive and a pleasant one.

We stayed at the Salvat's Mexican Embassy home and had a wonderful visit, enjoying everything we did. Their daughter, Diana, was there visiting with her two daughters, and we explored the city of Prague together, seeing the famous sites I had only read about in Marcia Davenport's books. I pondered the difference between the great city her eyes had looked upon and what we saw, the result of the communist takeover. She would have felt even sadder, probably more disillusioned by the comparison than I, having seen Prague in the days before World War II. It was easy to see the crumbling, disintegrating buildings had once been majestic, architectural splendors. Even though Prague is the only major city in Europe undamaged by war in its history, it is a city in a stage of decay. Nothing is done to preserve the beauty of the city or to restore the historical monuments of the past, either because of lack of funds or lack of interest by the Soviets. The Czech people are unhappy, depressed, poor and oppressed by the communists, and show it in their faces, which rarely smile. Commodities are scarce, and people line up for the shops where food and clothes are sold. The luxury stores are in-tourist, meaning only foreign currency is accepted. These shops offer the glamourous items made in Czechoslovakia, such as beautiful cut-crystal glassware, porcelain china, lovely jewelry and handmade linens. Electronic or mechan-

[429]

ical merchandise made in Russia are also for sale quite reasonably.

We dined well at the Salvats and realized "politicos" in this country get the cream off the top. Foreign diplomats are given deferential treatment and have great social prestige. The Salvats lived quietly, not indulging in many of the political-social functions, but they were esteemed by the other diplomats in Prague. They lived in luxury with two chauffeurs, cook, maid and houseman in a beautiful suburb on a street lined with other embassies, the entire section privately policed and guarded at night. The home was filled with antiques, and Julieta had bought a piano for each of four drawing rooms to take home to Mexico, when their term of office expired. The pianos were made in Czechoslovakia and were excellent. They also had a sound movie projector with full screen to show Hollywood-made movies. They both loved living in Prague and were sorry when Agustin was recalled to Mexico after the election of President de la Madrid. Julieta writes that living in Mexico today cannot compare to the gracious existence they enjoyed in Prague.

It was while we were with them that Mexico's peso plummeted, and the government faced near bankruptcy. Agustin was beside himself with worry over his country and his own financial status. Today the future of Mexico is still precarious, with inflation and a national deficit as alarming as ours.

The last day of our visit ended with two unfortunate incidents, which marred our otherwise perfect time with the Salvats. That afternoon their chauffeur was driving us to a concert at the great St. Vitus Cathedral. As he drove through an intersection, we saw a fast-moving car speeding toward us from a side street. The car plowed into the side of our white Mercedes, hitting the right rear door beside Sam's seat. I was in the middle with Julieta on my left. The three of us were jarred almost senseless. Sam was thrown forcefully into the side of the car, hitting his head soundly. Julieta and I had painfully wrenched muscles. Agustin and the chauffeur were in front, not hurt at all, but the car was a mess. We were all badly shaken, and Julieta complained of a swollen, painful knee. Sam did not complain aloud, but he had a bloody knot on the side of his head and felt pain at each breath.

The Salvats took us to the airport with their #2 chauffeur and car, and after we went through security, we were informed of a change of schedule on our flight. Our six-thirty flight had been changed to eleven p.m. The Salvats refused to leave us sitting alone for six hours in the dismal airport; so we had dinner together in the airport dining room, the meal an inedible fiasco. Never have we been served such terrible food. We finally persuaded the Salvats to go home and rest, as they were tired and miserable also, and we sat the remaining hours like zombies until our flight was called.

———••—◄◉►—••———

Sam suffered through the night with the pain in his side, and I decided he must see a doctor about his injury. We were at the stately old Gellert Hotel, luckily, and learned from the concierge there was a clinic in the basement. We were amazed to discover not only a long hallway opening into about a dozen examining rooms, but many patients, obviously not hotel patrons, waiting to be seen. We sat for ages waiting to be called, but it never seemed to be our turn. After an hour or so, an attractive young woman entered the door of an office across from us, and, shortly, appeared in a white coat beckoning us to enter. The lady doctor examined Sam competently and gave him an order for X-rays at the general hospital.

After an endless wait for a taxi, we returned to the Gellert and the doctor's office, who confirmed our suspicion that Sam's ribs were broken. Five broken ones showed up in the X-ray. The doctor wrote a prescription for the pain and was very kind and helpful. We were relieved Sam's injury was not more serious. There was no charge for her service, nor the X-rays, and it cost only a few pennies for the prescription at the pharmacy. Medical service is totally free in Hungary. I was becoming more positive that I might have a cracked collarbone, as I had constant pain, but I didn't bother to consult the doctor.

Besides the clinic in the basement of the Gellert, there was an immense pool, which looked like a Roman bath house. There is much emphasis on spas and thermal baths in Hungary. The Gellert was equipped with all these facilities. It was a huge, old-fashioned hotel with all the elegance of the 1920's. The pool had marble pillars, four on each side, reaching two stories high to the roof. Made of glass, the roof could be opened completely in nice weather, and people could sunbathe on the elegant balconies above the pool. At the far end was a huge marble fountain with "Niagara Falls" cascading into the pool. Potted palms and stained glass windows completed the vintage decor. Unlike most luxury hotels and clubs, with facilities only available to guests or members, the entire set-up seemed to be a free public health service with massage rooms, therapy equipment and thermal baths. An open entrance at street level permitted anyone to enter, use the pool, clinic and other services, as they liked. The basement buzzed with activity, mostly filled with people who were obviously poor and underprivileged. They used dressing gowns supplied by the hotel and walked to and from the pool and therapy rooms to the doctors' offices. There was even a post office in the basement.

Budapest seemed to be a much happier city than Prague, more prosperous and enterprising. There were many shops selling colorful, Hungarian crafts, besides the in-tourist ones to choose from, and the restaurants were good. We enjoyed the gypsy music and entertainment and the wonderful goulash served with rough red wine. If it had not been for our automobile accident, we would have done much more sightseeing, but

[431]

long bus trips were out of the question for Sam's painful ribs. We rested a good deal in our comfortable room overlooking the Danube, walked a few blocks to shop for lovely embroidered blouses and Herend china, and took a three-hour boat trip on the Danube. A short bus tour showed us the beauty and antiquity of the city.

After five weeks of near-perfect weather and experiences, it was finally time to leave for home. As always, we were reluctant to have our adventures come to an end but were anxious to be home again with our family and friends.

CHAPTER SIXTY-THREE

A FTER Dad died on September fifth, 1980, Mother valiantly tried to live a normal life, coping with her grief as well as she could. We tried to keep her interested and busy, encouraging her to attend the symphony, opera and theater, which she loved, and to accept invitations to social functions. But, as the years passed, it became increasingly difficult and more of an effort for her to leave home, where she sat for hours brooding over the past years of her married life.

She presented two magnificent concert grand Steinway pianos to the Indianapolis Symphony as a memorial to Dad — a very appropriate gift, since he was the first president of the Symphony Board in 1936. Dad had transformed the amateur orchestra into a professional group, which ranked among the top symphony orchestras in the country. The Paratore brothers, Anthony and Joseph, an excellent two-piano team dedicated the pianos at the opening concert of the 1982 season, on October fifteenth and sixteenth. After the exciting performances, the brothers autographed both pianos at a reception for Mother backstage.

Later that year, Mother made headlines in the papers and on television news. The media dubbed her the "Angel of Mercy," because she wished to remain anonymous. When they discovered who had rescued a team of trained oxen from the slaughter house, the news broke with redoubled force. We were as surprised as anyone to discover Mother was the mysterious "angel." But when we first heard the story on T.V., I remember remarking to Sam with a grin, "It sounds just like Mother." Opposite is a reprint of a news article concerning the "rescue."

[433]

'Angel' in Rolls Royce
rescues Jericho

By ANNE WILLETTE

An "angel of mercy" who drives a Rolls Royce is saving doomed animals in Indianapolis.

In her latest good deed, she found a home for Jericho, the wayward pig. He had overstayed his welcome at the Indianapolis Humane Society, 7929 Michigan Road, and was headed for market.

A week earlier, she paid $2,000 to save a trained oxen team from becoming oxburgers.

After a story about Jericho appeared in The Indianapolis Star Wednesday, the woman "just showed up" at the Humane Society and offered to donate the pig to Stonycreek Farm near Noblesville, according to Cindy Porteous, a society spokesman.

THE HELPFUL woman asked to remain anonymous.

She gave the society $20 for the care of Jericho, loaded him into her Roll Royce and headed for Stonycreek, a historic farm.

"It was a sight, seeing the pig come out of the Rolls Royce," said Stonycreek owner Loren E. Schmierer.

To this angel, treating animals like royalty has been a way of life.

"I used to pick up all the strays that followed me home from school. I'd put them in the attic in my parent's home, and in the middle of the night my mother would have to get up and see what was making all the noise," she said.

AT ONE TIME, she said, she owned more than 90 "beautiful show horses." Now she has nearly 100 show poodles, which her trainer keeps for her at Mobile, Ala.

Schmierer calls her "a very kind lady," and is honoring her at an open house at Stonycreek July 25. She will formally donate the trained oxen team of Bob and Sam to the farm and pose with them for pictures.

But no names, please. This angel of mercy insists on anonymity.

(Star_illustration)

Mother topped this story herself a few days later when she rescued Jericho, a pig, that was to receive the same fate as Bob and Tom. Tony, her houseman, drove Mother to the Humane Society's headquarters in her Rolls Royce. They put Jericho in the Rolls and transported him to Stonycreek Farm, where they left him to join the oxen team. The news story was printed under a hilarious cartoon of a pig in top hat riding in the Rolls Royce. Mother thought the story as funny as everyone else and laughed at herself with great amusement. But she was very serious in her love of all animals. I remember her saying many times when I was a little girl, "The more I see of some people, the better I like horses."

We gave a large reception for Mother on her ninetieth birthday, December third, including many of her friends and members of our family from Muncie, as well as those from Indianapolis. She had such a good time seeing everyone, her spirits were revived, and she declared she was ready to "live to one hundred." She looked so pretty in a pink chiffon cocktail dress decorated with crystal beads bought for the occasion. It was the dress she wished to wear for her funeral.

Mother's love of music and her animals kept her interest alive for awhile, and she continued to sing with a strong, full voice, still fresh and youthful, even to the day she died, on March fourteenth, 1985, when, at age ninety-four, she slipped away from us.

My father's love of music brought the two of them together in the first place, paired as lovers in *Madame Butterfly*. Their mutual interests were shared with much love and pleasure throughout their marriage. Father's love of his fellow man was greater, however, than his love for "all God's creatures," which was Mother's passion. He tolerated the poodles that swarmed under his feet, sometimes tripping him, but would have prefered a quieter household, without the frantic barks that pierced the air from time to time. He touchingly expressed his love for friends and family in the following poem, which I discovered among the memorabilia of cherished memories in Mother's desk.

> I would rather have one little smile
> from the faces of my friends,
> Than to have the choicest flowers
> when my stay on earth must end.
>
> I would rather have a "Hello, Bill"
> and a smile that I can see
> Than all the Holiday Greetings
> that are placed under the Tree.
>
> So let's drink a toast to '64
> and see the old year through
> And hope the years to come
> will find our dreams come true.

[435]

I can remember Dad saying almost every day of his life, "Is everybody happy?" He hated contentions, arguments and sour faces, loving harmony and happiness, pleasing others and wanting love in return. His exuberance infected everyone, and nothing pleased him more than having friends and family around. He hated being alone and was impatient to be doing and seeing new things, meeting old and new friends, socializing and traveling. His love of writing was inherited from his mother, who wrote a great deal of poetry. My greatest gift from Dad was the book "Recollections of Lucina Ball," which he presented to me the first Christmas after my marriage to Ed. It came as a complete surprise and caused a flood of tears, knowing how much he must have loved me to write such a book about me and my growing up years with the family. My book has become a sequel to his, written forty-five years later, and with further recollections from my life as it has unfolded since 1940.

Mother's death seems to have brought an end to an era of another day, which can never be recaptured. The life style of that era seems simple now, in retrospect. We created our own entertainment and pastimes without outside pressures and the barrage of today's "media." The general trend in America began its down grade with Franklin D. Roosevelt's New Deal policies and, over the fifty-year span, the quality of life style has continued to deteriorate. Many things have been altered besides government intervention in our lives. Wars have embittered and disillusioned us and created the fear of a future holocaust. The concept of morality, as I understood it, is today old-fashioned, now that people must "do their own thing" or "find out who they are." I am such a conservative person I could not bring myself to include intimate details of my sex life in my book, such as almost every book contains today. I am offended with salacious sex, foul language and degenerate "music" with screaming "stars" squirming in front of the T.V. camera. So I have dubbed myself a "Square Ball," bouncing through life at all sorts of angles, "rolling with the punches" and trying to make each day count for something.

I am completing the end of my story just a few months after Mother's death, wishing I could write a proper eulogy to my parents, who so greatly enriched my life with their love and support. They taught me to have high ideals and gave me a wealth of benefits, both tangible and intangible. As I reflect on all the goodness life has showered on me, I feel I have been given more than my share of luck and happiness. I can only hope the end of my life will be as comfortable and full as my first sixty-seven years.

I laughingly tell people I was "drug" back to Indiana from Mexico by Sam. A part of me was unwilling to leave the happy life there, but another part looked forward to the challenge and the old familiar pattern of life at home. However, I had always said I never would want to live in Indianapolis, feeling New York the only stimulating place to be. "The old stamping ground" of home territory seemed dull by comparison.

[436]

I have long since recovered from my insatiable desire to live in New York. Soon after moving to Indianapolis, Sam and I went there, he on business, and I to immerse myself in the delights of the city and to see my good friends again. While we were taxiing in from the airport, I was suddenly struck by a feeling of hostility in the attitudes of the people. I watched them scurrying along the streets, intently bent on their errands, while traffic jammed, scuttled and ducked impatiently in and out of lanes. Our driver muttered and grumbled throughout the journey, rolling down his window in frustration to curse at yet another driver. "Git outa de way!" he screamed, shouting epithets at each and every unfortunate person near us. The rudeness was appalling after living two years in the polite society of Mexico. Had New York changed so much, or had I changed? Perhaps it was a little of both. I didn't feel at home here any more. All I wanted to do was leave the hectic, uncomfortable, dirty city as soon as possible. I felt sad and disillusioned to be in a place I had loved with a passion but now was totally foreign to me. I was glad to get back to Indianapolis where life went at a more normal pace with the advantage of a more comfortable life style.

I have often made promises to myself that were eventually broken. I had thought from childhood that the last person I would ever marry (next to a minister) would be a doctor, and the only place I *never* wanted to see again in my life, after my first glimpse of it in 1938, was Mexico. But these reverse decisions were great peaks of happiness in my life. After living in Indianapolis thirty-five years, the longest period I have lived anywhere, I now feel it has been a perfect place for me.

We became increasingly concerned for Leona as time went on and she showed more signs of aging, weakness and inability to cope with simple, daily chores. It was not until she had slipped to the floor one night, unable to get up, and was forced to spend the night there, that she realied it was finally time to have someone with her. From then on nurses aides were in attendance around the clock. Three years later, at ninety-seven, she had failed to the extent of being bedfast following a stroke on Christmas Day and spent more and more of each day sleeping life away. She had a valiant will and determination not to give up without a fight, but it was an agony of sadness that continued for Polly and Sam.

Judy and Ann seem happy with their lives, and I am happy for them. Ann, married to Michael Lach and living in Boulder, Colorado, finally is happy and productive. Her creative art has been her outstanding talent. She does beautiful work in many medias. Judy has not remarried since her divorce, but has found a rich, full life in Indianapolis. I give her my grateful thanks for editing this book for me and for being a person I could always depend and rely on. I love both girls deeply and also consider them my dearest friends and confidantes.

[437]

My four grandchildren, beautiful girls and boys, are becoming young adults, and I pray they will be able to avoid the strong temptations to follow the wrong path in today's relaxed society. I fervently hope I could say I have instilled the strong values and religious faith in my children and grandchildren my parents and Nana gave to me. They live in a generation as remote from mine as mine was remote from my parents. Changes in social behavior and way of life constantly fluctuate with historic events, scientific inventions and time. We can't help but be different from our forefathers, but basic values and strength of character can remain the same.

How blessed I have been to have had two such wonderful husbands as Ed and Sam in my life. I don't know whether it was luck or good sense that led me to choose them. I have learned that life with a partner is always give and take. Understanding, forgiveness, patience and unselfishness by both partners are the basis for growing love and contentment. I only had Ed for a tiny portion of my life, yet the five years we had together are as a solid gold coin in a bucket of silver. The life I have had with Sam is a bucket full of gold.

As The Years Go By

Mother and Dad in the 1950's

Mother and Dad in the 1960's

Mother and Dad in 1979 — attending the opening of the symphony season

The family in Muncie: Back Row, L. to R.: Edmund Ball and wife, Virginia; Janice Ball Fisher and husband, John; Rosemary Ball Bracken and husband, Alexander; Margaret Ball Petty; William Ball. Front Row: L. to R.: Adelia Ball Morris; Elisabeth Ball; Doris Fredericks, Agnes Medsker Ball

Anthony and Joseph Paratore sign the two concert grand Steinways given to the
Indianapolis Symphony Orchestra by Mother in memory of Dad, 1982

Signatures on sounding board of piano.

Mother's ninetieth birthday—
December third, 1982   [441]

Sam at his desk at Haag's in the 1950's

Lucina and Sam, 1984

Lucina in the 1950's

Julie and Janet Ball, flower girls in Ann's wedding, 1963

Bill and Jeanne Peck Ball in the 1950's

Julie and Janet Ball

Janet, Julie, Jeanne, Chip and John Ball

Bill Ball, 1984

Judy Growing Up

Tudor Hall graduation picture

Judy, age 2, 1943

Eileen Poston's dance recital 1954 — Judy and Ann

[445]

Marriage of Judy and William H. Cummings, Jr., January 3, 1963

Bill, Judy and Breck at Culver for a visit

[446]   *Judy, 1983*

Breck and Scott Growing Up

Breck and Scott ages two and five

Breck and Scott ages four and seven

Breck and Scott 1978

Breck

Scott

[448]

Ann Growing Up

Judy, Lucina and Ann at one month, 1943

[449]

Eileen Poston's dance recital, 1953

Tudor Hall graduation picture, 1961

Ann, 1944

Aunt Mark Eckerson's portrait of Ann, 1947

[450]

Ann wearing my wedding dress

Ann and Jeffrey Hay Strohm,
August 24, 1963

Centenary Junior College graduation
picture, 1963

[451]

Ann marries Michael Lach, November 19, 1983

Mike and Ann

Ann Eckerson-Lach

Tracey and Bryan Growing Up

Ann and Tracey at two-and-a-half months, August 18, 1964

Ann and Tracey at one year

Tracey, age two

The Strohm family

Bryan and Tracey, ages four and six

Bryan and Tracey, ages eight and ten

Tracey at sixteen

Tracey and Jeff at her Dramatic Club debut

*Tracey and Bryan with their step-sisters, Tiffany and Tania Lach,
November 18, 1983*

Postscript

A FTER sending this book to the printer, I received a box of family photographs and a scrap-book from my Aunt Margaret Fitzgibbon's estate. Margie died in April, 1986. Leafing through her scrap-book I found this page of prose written by Nana in 1944 when she knew she was dying of cancer. I felt moved to include it in my book at the very last moment. Nana's expression of her feelings reveals and parallels my own thoughts so clearly I find it a proper conclusion to my story.

This was my house, this house of gray
For half a century I lived here,
On this corner.
This house has sheltered much over the years,
My husband, my five children, myself,
And all my thoughts.
Fifty years of hopes, fears, despairs
Were sheltered beneath that roof.
There I worked,
There I bore my children,
There I went with my husband as a young woman
And there I lived my life.
There is my furniture, that I lived with,
There are the things that I made with my hands.
There is my yard, and my flowers.
                    Goodbye!
This was my street that I lived on
And walked down nearly every day.
These are the trees that shaded me.
These houses are my neighbors',
This is where my Mother lived, and my Father,
Across the way is the home of my sister,
This is where the doctor lived
Who brought my children into the world.
Here is the courthouse
I remember it as a little girl
With the old horse trough in front of it.
                    Goodbye!
This was the main street of the town.
It has changed in fifty years.
Over there I bought the material for my wedding dress.
The store is gone now.
There is the building
Where my husband had his office.
There he set up in business as a young man.
How proud I was of him.

[457]

There is the old opera house,
They have made it into a movie now.
I heard Adelina Patti sing there once.
This old hotel has stood on this corner
For over fifty years.
There we celebrated the golden wedding anniversary
Of my Father and my Mother.
                                        Goodbye!
These are my children gathered here
And my grandchildren
And my great-grandchildren.
These are my friends, and my neighbors.
These are the people with whom I lived
and loved.
These are all the things I loved.
Oh, that I didn't have to say
                                        Goodbye!

Appendix

To The Editor of The News:

I have sent the following letter to the offices of the presidents of several colleges in answer to one I received from the president of my own college, Sarah Lawrence, in Bronxville, New York, which supported and joined the National Student Strike:

"I feel compelled to add my one small voice to the clamor over this long siege of students versus alma mater. I have always been under the impression that colleges and universities were for the purpose of educating our children academically.

"These children were sent to college for this purpose (and most generally at a substantial financial sacrifice) by parents expecting their offspring to return from these insitutions as responsible citizens, fitted for a career of their choice, and advanced intellectually and culturally—not to be aided and abetted by radical faculty members to indulge in revolutionary tactics and treasonable behavior against our country.

"If the war in Vietnam is the basis of the student revolt, there are several questions which enter our minds, and I think each one of us should try to concern himself with an answer.

"Is there no need in this world for an agency to deter aggression of one nation or group of people from taking over by force another nation or people? Is there any international agency, such as the U.N. or the League of Nations, or any other organization which has been able to accomplish this?

"If international agencies fail for generation after generation, should the leading powers shun the undesired mantle of responsibility falling on their shoulders by default?

"If it is proper for this nation to turn its back on the invasions of South Vietnam, Laos, and Cambodia by a North Vietnam backed by China and Russia, then should not this nation be consistent by refusing to support Berlin against a take-over by East Germany, backed by Russia, and to refuse support when a group of Arab nations, backed by Russia, choose to settle permanently the Jewish problem by eliminating Israel?

"Everyone wants peace, but could we really enjoy it if we buy it for ourselves at a price of freedom of others? Is that to be our future idealism? Did some element of our similar thinking in the past encourage Hitler and Mussolini in their belief that their aggression would succeed?

Has faculty leadership in our universities instilled such a sense of guilt in our youth that the future ambition of our country will be

to become number two, with our backs turned on the desires for freedom and self-determination in the many smaller nations that will face aggression in the future?

"How can the administrations be so intimidated that they can allow terrorism, violence and anarchy on campus? Why are not the participants in violence expelled? They are not there for an education, so why should the colleges tolerate such action?

"My personal belief is that this is a concerted subversive effort to undermine our youth, infiltrate treasonable thinking, and generally weaken the foundation upon which this country was built, so that we will be fair game for the real force which is just around the corner waiting for us to degenerate enough to take us by storm.

"It is no wonder that the youth of our country is disgusted with our generation. We have bungled national and world affairs for many years. Witness the great disillusionment of the first meeting of the U.N. in San Francisco after World War II. The handwriting was on the wall from that very day when Molotov swaggered off the scene, the victor of the first round.

"I say that if the young people are to have any respect for us, their government, their leadership, then we must lead them with firm hands down the right paths, and renew a patriotism for the greatest nation on the earth. Without America this world might just as well succumb to its own pollution, and it would well desrive its fate."

LUCINA B. MOXLEY

Carmel

[459]